D1084294

Franz Baermann Steiner

SELECTED WRITINGS

Volume I

Methodology and History in Anthropology

General Editor: David Parkin, Director of the Institute of Social and Cultural Anthropology, University of Oxford

FRANZ BAERMANN STEINER

Selected Writings

Edited and with an Introduction
by Jeremy Adler and Richard Fardon

Volume I

Taboo, Truth, and Religion

With a Memoir by Mary Douglas

Berghahn Books
New York • Oxford

First published in 1999 by

Berghahn Books

Editorial Offices:
55 John Street, 3rd Floor, New York, NY 10038 USA
3, NewTec Place, Magdalen Road, Oxford OX4 1RE, UK

Library of Congress Cataloging-in-Publication Data
Steiner, Franz Baermann, 1909–1952.
    [Selections. 1999]
    Selected writings / Franz Baermann Steiner : edited by Jeremy Adler and
Richard Fardon.
        p.   cm. -- (Methodology and history in anthropology : v. 2)
    Includes bibliographical references and index.
    Contents: v. 1. Taboo, truth, and religion / with a memoir by Mary Douglas.
    ISBN 1-57181-711-5 (alk. paper). -- ISBN 1-57181-712-3 (alk. paper)
    1. Taboo. 2. Religion. 3. Ethnology. I. Adler, Jeremy D. II. Fardon, Richard.
III. Title. IV. Series.
GN471.4.S622 1999   99-15631
306--dc21   CIP

British Library Cataloguing in Publication Data
A catalogue record for this book is available from the British Library.

Printed in the United States on acid-free paper.

CONTENTS

LIST OF ILLUSTRATIONS

CONTENTS OF VOLUME II

ACKNOWLEDGEMENTS

It is possible to appreciate Aristotle's sociological thought much better now than during the last few centuries; and this is very significant, not only for the stage reached in the development of sociological reasoning but generally for our cultural situation.

Franz Steiner on Aristotle's sociology

In the conviction that today's intellectual climate also is a more auspicious moment for their appreciation, we have collected Franz Steiner's more important anthropological writings in two volumes. Steiner would have recognised with approval the origins of many of the changes in our sociological reasoning and cultural situation that have occurred in the fifty years since he settled in Great Britain and set about transforming himself into an English-speaking anthropologist, though we can presume he would have expressed his inimitable doubts about others. It is a conducive moment, therefore, to consider his ideas together and to contextualize them in two essays on his biography and his intellectual projects. We are fully aware that what we have to say cannot be definitive, but we trust that it may hold surprises even for those familiar with Franz Steiner's published works.

That we are able to do this is thanks, in the first instance, to those without whom Steiner's anthropological writings would not have been been preserved in a usable fashion: H.G. Adler, as Steiner's literary executor, preserved Steiner's papers and devoted himself tirelessly to the promotion of his *Nachlaß*. Steiner's close friend Dr Esther Frank typed up an invaluable three-volumed selection of his aphorisms for Steiner which we have used with profit. Laura Bohannan and Paul Bohannan each prepared two essays and one book of Steiner's for publication. Sadly, one of the books never appeared. Other than introducing uniformity into the styles of referencing and bibliography, in Volume I we have entirely relied upon Laura Bohannan's editorship of *Taboo* and 'Enslavement and the early Hebrew Lineage System', and have incorporated her edition of 'Chagga Truth' into our new text of that paper, and in Volume II we have relied entirely on Paul Bohannan's editorship of 'Notes on Comparative Economics', 'Towards a Classification of Labour', and we are also indebted to his unpublished edition of *A Prolegomena to a Comparative Study of the Forms of Slavery.*We are grateful to the Bohannans both for permission to reprint their work and for their staunch encouragement of our editorial project. We also wish to record our debt to Alfons Fleischli, whose doctoral dissertation provides an invaluable starting-point for the study of Steiner's life and works; he kindly made his correspondence available to us, and we are pleased to record our debt to his biographical chapters on Steiner.

We have been overwhelmed by the personal response from friends and colleagues of Steiner's Oxford period. Of his three surviving colleagues at the Institute: Mary Douglas's enthusiasm sustained our conviction that a re-edition of Steiner's anthropological writings was intellectually important; we are grateful also for her eager contribution of a memoir in Volume I; M.N. Srinivas graciously consented to provide a memoir to introduce Volume II; and the late Louis Dumont wrote us a moving private letter. Several other of Steiner's contemporaries at Oxford or in London have been kind enough to respond to written or personal enquiries, sometimes at great length: Paul Baxter, David Brokensha, Kenelm Burridge, Anand Chandavarkar, Ian Cunnison, Sir Raymond Firth, Ioan Lewis, John Middleton, Rodney Needham, William Newell, Julian Pitt-Rivers, and David Pocock.

Iris Murdoch, one of the few readers familiar with his private writings, profoundly encouraged us in our aim to revive interest in the writings of Franz Steiner, and particularly championed the plan to publish his aphorisms. Thanks to her generosity and that of her husband, John Bayley, we are able to quote extracts from Miss Murdoch's private journal on Steiner written in 1952-53, which have kindly been made available to us by Dame Iris's official biographer, Peter Conradi. Elias Canetti responded to our request to write a memoir on Steiner, published elsewhere, which has proved invaluable. Johanna Canetti kindly provided us with copies of Steiner's letters to her father, Sybille Miller-Aichholz generously transcribed for us Steiner's letters to her, and the late David Wright kindly lent us Steiner's letters to him. Michael Hamburger has been unfailing in his support of Steiner, both through his translations and his own writings. Mary Donovan thoughtfully shared her personal memories with us, and Franz's cousin, Lise Seligmann, kindly wrote and talked to us about Franz Steiner, and has taken a constant interest in the publication of his works.

Franz Baermann Steiner's *Nachlaß* has been housed at the Schiller Nationalmuseum, Deutsches Literaturarchiv, Marbach, since November 1997. We are grateful to Herr Jochen Meyer and Dr Ingrid Belke for making these papers available to us.

The wide-ranging nature of Steiner's prodigious scholarship would have overcome our flagging attempts to follow his footsteps to an even greater degree without the help of: David Arnold – Professor of South Asian History at SOAS; Professor Yehuda Bacon – Bezalel Art School, Jerusalem, for help with a reference on Hugo Bergman; Christian Bartolf – Director of the Gandhi-Informations-Zentrum in Berlin; Matthew Bell – Goethe scholar and historian of eighteenth-century German anthropology at King's College London; D.C.K. Glass, also at King's College London – German scholar and bibliographer extraordinary; Professor Sir Ernst Gombrich – formerly of the Warburg Institute, University of London; Linda Greenlick – Chief Librarian of the Jewish Chronicle; Michael Knibb – Samuel Davidson Professor of Old Testament Studies, King's College London; Jeremy Lawrence – Professor of Spanish, University of Manchester; Mike Morris – Librarian of the Institute of Social and Cultural Anthropology of Oxford University; Robert Pynsent – Professor of Czech Language and Literature at the School of Slavonic and East European Studies, who kindly helped remove some of the worst errors from a draft of our Introduction to Volume I; David Riches – of the University of St. Andrews as an ethnographer of the Arctic and sub-Arctic; J.W. Rogerson – emeritus Professor of Theology at the University of Sheffield who gave us his views on Steiner's 'Hebrew Lineage' article; Gabor Schabert – freelance scholar and linguist who provided us with an evaluation of Steiner's unpublished first dissertation, on which we have relied for our assessment; Erhard Schüttepelz – scholar of Elias Canetti who filled some interesting bibliographical gaps and kept us up-to-date with current developments in Germany; Chris Thornhill – scholar of German social and political theory, King's College London, for whose views on Steiner's Simmel lectures and German social science we are grateful; Zdeněk Vašiček – historian of archeology, political scientist, and expert on all things Czech and Slovak, who commented in detail on our Introductions to Volumes I and II; Bernard Wasserstein – President of the Oxford Centre for Hebrew and Jewish Studies, who read the sections in our Introductions concerned with Steiner's Zionism and Steiner's relevant texts; Shamoon Zamir – scholar of English and American literature at King's College London, who helped us with ethnopoetics. Professor David Parkin, formerly of SOAS and now Professor of Social Anthropology at the University of Oxford, first saw the link between our interests, brought us together, and helped us through the sources at Oxford. Chris Rojek grasped the point of our project quickly and supported it consistently. Marion Berghahn put us in her debt by taking the risk of allowing full rein to our ambitions for a two-volume edition. This has enabled us to include both the published papers we had originally intended to edit and selections from the large body of unpublished or hitherto untranslated material, including aphorisms and poems, which we believe are essential to a full grasp of Steiner's work. Needless to say, we alone are responsible for the remaining errors.

Michael Mack's doctoral research at the University of Cambridge will relate Franz Steiner's work to that of Steiner's friend Elias Canetti. We are grateful to Michael for his sincere support of this project and for permission to make use of his draft translation of 'On the Process of Civilisation'. Nicolas Ziegler, doctoral student at King's College London, who is writing a thesis on Steiner's poetry, has been a constant support, too; he kindly made copies of many of Steiner's letters and unpublished manuscripts for us, and also made available two unpublished research papers, which we cite. We look forward keenly to reading their completed accounts of Steiner's work.

A word about our editorial principles may be in order. In editing Steiner's writings, we advanced from a decision to re-edit *Taboo* into preparing a one-volumed collection of Steiner's published papers, but this also expanded the more we became familiar with Steiner's ideas and the more we began to recognise the interdependence of his different productions, including minor writings and fugitive texts. Whereas the Bohannans edited some of Steiner's major writings as 'papers', almost half a century later, now that the period in which he wrote has itself assumed historical interest, we were forced to come to terms with his newspaper articles, private writings, and the character of some 'papers' as 'lectures' delivered to an audience at Oxford. His views are firmly embedded into his time, not just intellectually, but politically. This can be seen in the different possible approaches to Steiner's classic paper on 'Chagga Truth'. Laura Bohannan singled out the lecture's central intellectual achievement for editing, which implicitly puts Steiner's work into the context of contemporary philosophy. In printing the full version, without, we hope, risking the impact of its points about 'truth', we include the contextual opening, which contains a polemic on the German view of society: Steiner's anthropological ideas take on a new focus against the background of Zionism, Nazism, and the Shoah. This simple fact has also dictated our inclusion of personal and more occasional writings.

As to the texts. We began by making exact transcriptions, with emendations in square brackets, conjectures, footnotes, and so on of Steiner's unpublished writings. It soon became clear that such an exact rendition would divert attention from what Steiner said. We have therefore adopted the method used by Laura Bohannan and Paul

Bohannan in their editions and silently emended inconsistencies, un-English word order, and so on, keeping editorial comment to a minimum. Wherever necessary and possible, we have supplied missing references and bibliographies in the currently accepted format. Full reference to our sources and to the previous publication of Steiner's works can be found in the footnotes and in the select bibliography of Steiner's writings at the end of each volume.

In rendering extracts from Steiner's *Conquests*, Jeremy Adler has been helped by Franz Wurm, who checked the translations against the originals, and made many suggestions that have been gratefully adopted. The aim has been to reproduce Steiner's idiosyncracies to the maximum extent compatible with English usage. In translating Steiner's German prose, we have taken a different route. *Orientpolitik* is written in an exceedingly clipped style, and Steiner never prepared his 'Letter to Georg Rapp' for the press or fulfilled his plan of revising the text of his *Essays and Discoveries*. Indeed, the extant text reveals occasional omissions and infelicities. The style, cut off from the German mainstream, is sometimes idiosyncratic. Occasionally we have silently emended the remarks, and have in all the prose writings aimed to make an idiomatic English version, in the belief that fluent English, such as Steiner wrote so well himself, will do more for the reception of his ideas at the current stage of research than an apparatus, square brackets, explanations, and the other devices at an editor's disposal. The remarks aim at immediacy, and this is the effect we have tried to reproduce. We trust that in the process the ideas are rendered accurately.

For permission to republish 'Enslavement and the Early Hebrew Lineage System: An Explanation of Genesis 47: 29-31, 48: 1-16', which first appeared in 1954 in *Man* 54 (article no. 102): 73-75, we are grateful to the Royal Anthropological Institute; to republish 'Chagga Truth', which first appeared in 1954 in *Africa* 24 (4): 36-49, we are grateful to Professor Last, Editor of *Africa*, the Journal of the International African Institute; to republish 'Notes on Comparative Economics', which first appeared in 1954 in *The British Journal of Sociology* 5.2: 118-29, we are grateful to Routledge and *The British Journal of Sociology*; to republish 'Towards a Classification of Labour', which first appeared in 1957 in *Sociologus* NS 7,2: 112-39, we are grateful to the Editor, Professor Georg Elwig of the Institut für Ethnologie, Freie Universität, Berlin, and the publishers, Duncker & Humblot; and to republish 'The Steps Swings Away' and 'The Heart', which first appeared in 1994 in *Comparative Criticism* 16: 157-60, we are grateful to Elinor Shaffer and the Press Syndicate of the Cambridge University Press. For permission to reproduce photographs from their collections, we are grateful to the Deutsches Literaturarchiv, Marbach am Neckar, and the Marie-Louise von Motesiczky Charitable Trust, London.

We are grateful to our Colleges for granting us periods of sabbatical leave in the academic year 1997-98 which has enabled us to complete our research and editing. Grants from the Research Committees of the School of Humanities, King's College London, and the School of Oriental and African Studies (both of the University of London) allowed us to engage the services of Carol Tully and Lisa Rowland as research assistants and of Christel Ahmad and Mary Warren, without whose help we could not have brought this project to completion. David Yeandle and Rita Pannen's keyboard wizardry have ensured that our intentions took the correct electronic format. A special word of thanks goes to our departmental colleagues. Eva Adler and Catherine Davies have both been a constant support.

We learned more than even we expected from the privilege of editing and thinking about Franz Baermann Steiner's writings and formed a friendship in the process. As a general rule, Richard Fardon initially edited the previously unpublished works in English and Jeremy Adler those in German. However, with the exception of the translations of Steiner's *Conquests*, we each revised and commented upon the other's work. In this respect, as in the Introductions, our efforts have been fully collaborative.

J.A. and R.F.
University of London 1999

A NOTE ON QUOTATIONS

All quotations in F.B.S.'s works have been standardised and checked wherever possible. His sources are listed in the bibliographies attached to each article. Printed sources used in the Editors' introductions are given at the end of each volume. A list of F.B.S.'s cited unpublished writings, letters to F.B.S., and Ms writings about F.B.S., are also included, and individual items referred to in the Introductions may be sourced in this list. Quotations from letters and verbal communications to the Editors by F.B.S.'s friends and colleagues are signified by 'PC' (= personal communication). A list of other such sources is contained in the bibliography.

Fig. 1. *Franz Steiner and his sister Suse, Prague, ca. 1920*

Fig. 2. *A street scene, by Franz Steiner, Jerusalem, 1930 or 1931*

Fig. 3.   A camel train, by Franz Steiner, Palestine, 1930 or 1931

Fig. 4.   Portrait of Suse Steiner, Prague, 1932

Fig. 5.   Franz Steiner after his return from Jerusalem, Prague, 1932

Fig. 6.   Franz Steiner, Joseph Marcus and H.G. Adler, Prague, 1935

Fig. 7.   Franz Steiner, ca. 1935

*Fig. 8.   Heinrich and Marta Steiner, Františkovy Lázně,
Czechoslovakia, July 1938*

Fig. 9.   *The Steiner home, with Franz's ethnic collection, Prague, 1939*

Fig. 10.   *The Steiner home, Prague, 1939*

Fig. 11.   Christopher Cookson with his dog, by Franz Steiner, Oxford, 1940s

Fig. 12.   Franz Steiner, London, 1938

Fig. 13.   *Franz Steiner, Oxford, 1948*

Fig. 14.   *'Conversation in the Library' (Franz Steiner and Elias Canetti),*
by Marie-Louise von Motesiczky, London, 1950

Fig. 15. Bullfight, by Franz Steiner, Andalucia, 1952

Fig. 16. Franz Steiner and Iris Murdoch, Trafalgar Square, Autumn 1952

PART I: INTRODUCTIONS

FRANZ STEINER. A MEMOIR

Mary Douglas

I remember Franz Steiner very well, but until I started to think about writing this note I had not realised how much I owe to him. After the war I went back to Oxford in 1946 to study anthropology in the first year of Evans-Pritchard's tenure as Professor and Director of the Anthropology Institute. Steiner was there already, registered as a student, struggling to obtain a D.Phil., but something of an anomaly, since he was a better qualified scholar than any of our teachers. He had been in Oxford since 1938 as a refugee, and was a student of Radcliffe-Brown's. His fellow students naturally held him in some awe. It was disconcerting to have as a fellow student a scholar conversant in so many languages, ancient and modern, and so erudite in philosophy, ancient history and German ethnology. Steiner had a quiet voice and unassuming manner, kindly, patient, though his wit could be lethal and he sometimes seethed with suppressed irritation. He never gave us the sense that he was too big for our little pond.

All the same, he was a somewhat isolated figure. Aside from the fact that there was no one in the group who could share his literary or philosophical background, his overwhelming personal losses set him apart. He never spoke about his family, and I only heard in private about their deaths at Nazi hands, in hushed voices, from E.-P. and Meyer Fortes. The aura of tragedy casts a ring around its victim. Ill health also set him apart. This is not to say that he was unapproachable. Perhaps the main surprise in getting to know someone with this heavy background was to find an observer of English culture with a strong sense of whimsy. The idiosyncrasies of the British class structure amused him endlessly. He had been befriended and taken into the home of an elderly gentleman in North Oxford; on his birthday the housekeeper wanted to give him a little present, but fearing it would be presumptuous to sign it as coming from herself she hit on the device of signing the birthday wishes in the name of the pet dog. He thought this was charming and inordinately funny, while we were too familiar with the dilemma to be so amused (see Figure 11).

The site of the Institute was a large Victorian family house in South Parks Road, Tylor's old house. It was easy to make friends as staff and students tended to spend a lot of time there, having coffee, talking, lending and borrowing books. On Fridays everyone came to the afternoon seminar and went on afterwards to drink together in the King's Arms. Our teachers were Evans-Pritchard, Meyer Fortes, and later, John Peristiany. Fellow students were of different nationalities. Srinivas from India, Issa from Egypt, Bill Newell from New Zealand, Paul Howell, Adam Curle and me, the English students, that made six of us, plus Franz Steiner from Czechoslovakia. When in 1947 Max Gluckman, director of the Rhodes-Livingstone Institute joined, we could not fail to know that we were small fry into whose midst a very big fish had swum. He was accompanied by John Barnes and Clyde Mitchell coming fresh from their fieldwork in Central Africa. Others quickly expanded our group, John Middleton from Uganda, Emrys Peters to write up his fieldwork among the Bedouin, Godrey Lienhardt from the Sudan, Ian Cunnison from the Lulua in the Congo, Paul and Laura Bohannan from Nigeria, and later Julian Pitt-Rivers doing fieldwork in Spain, Kenelm Burridge, Rodney Needham, Jean Buxton, Eleanor McHatton, Paul Stirling. I fear my memory is incomplete and that I have left out other figures soon to become famous in anthropology.

Franz Steiner was unobtrusively present, a charter member, as it were, of this mixed assembly, and he came with us to the King's Arms after the Friday evening seminar. That was where I heard him complain when the barmaid offered us something to eat: 'Why should I be exposed to ham sandwiches when I come for a drink?' This remark started me off on thinking about food taboos, pollution and taboos in general.[1] Srinivas as a Brahmin was also rejecting ham sandwiches for the sake of religious laws against eating meat, and I too, as Catholics did at that time, abstained from meat on Fridays.

Drinking together on this basis meant that the discussions about our work were regular and intimate, so that inevitably ideas became common property. For me this is an important point as I need to explain to myself why the strong influence that Steiner exerted on Oxford anthropology was almost anonymous. Why did he receive so little published recognition from those who were there in his lifetime? One reason was that he was not seeking renown amongst British anthropologists. The esteem of his friends in London mattered much more to him. He told me that nobody in Oxford had a clue about the kind of person he was perceived to be in London where the obscure student of anthropology became the esteemed poet and scholar. There were other reasons, his shyness, the way his own commitments fitted in so smoothly with E.-P.'s intellectual project, his early death, and something about how their shared interests ran counter to the prevailing culture.

I am not sure that he made special friends with any of the anthropology students apart from the two Bohannans, Paul and Laura. They came very close to him as friends in his life, and after his death worked devotedly as his editors. It is not difficult to guess what drew them together. As Americans they were not afflicted by this British reserve which doubly distances the object of tragedy and possessor of learning, so it would have been easier for them to break through his shyness. Second, unlike most of us, they were anthropologists before they came to England, they knew American cultural anthropology and German ethnology, so there was a common background. Furthermore, they also had to respond to the strangeness of English culture. Risking a guess, they may also have shared an interest in ballroom dancing which I discovered in Steiner, to my great surprise, in 1948 when we went to Brussels for the International Congress of Anthropological and Ethnological Sciences. I certainly did not expect the great scholar to skip evening meetings so as to go to a dance hall. Above all, the Bohannans had this joyous wit which complemented Steiner's quaint, acerbic humour. Great narrators, both, with a fund of quips and funny stories, quick in repartee, spontaneous hilarity – every department of anthropology needs members like them. When once I twitted them for their American pronunciation of 'institute', they exclaimed that it must be correct. To prove that the word really rhymes with 'root' they sang us the mid-western ditty of which I only remember the chorus:

> Rootity toot, rootity toot,
> We are the girls of the Institute.
> We don't smoke and we don't chew,
> And we don't go with boys that do!

Point made. I now try always to conform to their pronunciation.

Of course everyone knew about the loss of Steiner's mammoth thesis on 'Servile Institutions', which he was still patiently reconstituting. Anyone of us talking to him about our own research would be always astonished to find how far the topic of enslavement reached and how many regions of the globe he had studied for it. There wasn't any one else's thesis to which he could not contribute information. Economics was obviously included, but less obviously, also marriage, because he needed to define the difference world-wide between a free wife and a slave concubine. Research on slavery led to systematic discernment of lack of freedom for women in general, married or not, and consequently to an interest in inheritance and succession, the fate of children of irregular unions, and so on. He was before his time, he would have been very much at ease, perhaps even a hero, when feminism swept the board in the sixties.

I myself started on a master's thesis on 'Bridewealth in Africa' which involved reading about restrictions on choice of marriage partners, a topic about which he knew a lot. We talked about the rules which recommended a man to marry one of the set of women classified as his granddaughters. When I commiserated with the girls, he interjected, 'But how very nice for the grandfather!' As this was typical of his quizzical, lighthearted style in conversation, a great surprise lay in wait for those who came to his 'Lectures on Tabu'. As anyone will recall who was present at those lectures, attended by staff as well as students, the erudition was not veiled nor the load of learning noticeably lightened by the witticisms lavishly scattered throughout.

Rereading those lectures gives me a shock of recognition. Why did I not acknowledge his influence more fully? I did say straight away that *Purity and Danger* (1966) was conceived and planned according to his teaching, but much of *Natural Symbols* (1970), and many of the things I have written subsequently on risk are without specific acknowledgement. Much of what I have written on the Pentateuch more recently sounds to me now like quotations from *Taboo* (1956). Of these personal debts, more below. I was not the only one who took what he wrote so much for granted that I forgot that he wrote it first, thinking it was part of the mainstream of social anthropology. But I honestly think that his presence, catalysed with that of Godfrey Lienhardt, E.-P., and Srinivas, enlivened by the Bohannans, was what made Oxford Social Anthropology so different in mood and scope from the anthropology of London or Cambridge, or Manchester, at the time and after.

Between Evans-Pritchard and Steiner an unexpected sympathy was discovered. I mentioned above an unexpected convergence of deeply held views: Evans-Pritchard on the one hand, with the fieldworker's sturdy no-nonsense attitude, committed to explaining abstruse ideas in simple language, open to Wittgenstein's programme to demystify philosophy; on the other, Steiner, familiar with the parallel intention of the phenomenologists to describe things as they appear, conversant with the radically critical philosophical movements of Germany between the wars and after. Both were interested in the place of religion in anthropology, and both lined up against the current rationalist consensus. In the history of the subject they agreed on whom they disagreed with. They were both interested in religious belief, both against idealism, both against materialism and rationalism. They agreed with each other that religion was to be given a place in its own right, not to be treated as an emanation of something else. We might picture them talking to each other over coffee or beer, each increasingly less sure as to whether what the one was saying was original or something that the other had been saying for a long time. For example, E.-P. was credited with the idea that an anthropologist without a personal religious commitment would be at a disadvantage trying to understand the religion of another people. I am not sure whether he actually said it, but it was used as an exam question, (in London, I think, expecting the answer, 'No'). But was it E.-P.'s idea or Steiner's? Compare Steiner's criticism of Margaret Mead's interpretation of taboo:

> I think a misunderstanding is at work here, one due to a limitation which Dr Mead would no doubt call cultural, but which to my mind is a limitation in the field of religious experience. Such a lack of experience does not, of course, completely invalidate the statements of the inexperienced. Nevertheless one is inclined to make reservations of the kind one would make when asked to read a treatise on sexual psychology composed by a eunuch, though of course sexual phenomena can be observed by all, and the observations can be analysed by the intelligent.... (1956a: 146; p. 213 below)

In *Nuer Religion* (1956a) E.-P. certainly criticised the intellectualist ideas of religion that are presented by sages and theologians. He tried to demonstrate how religion could be studied through the everyday practices of the believers. Though it could be said that his three books on the Nuer made the demonstration, as a general teaching the lesson remained unarticulated. His language of denunciation was restrained compared with Steiner's vitriolic attacks on rationalist smugness and theological intolerance, and roundly derided explanations of difference of belief which invoked evolution from an irrational past. Diatribes tend to get dated quickly. In the book, *Taboo*, the sarcastic attacks he made on the muddled mixture of scientism, sanctimonious theology, and nineteenth-century complacency in Bible scholarship, are still logically correct, and perhaps it had to be done that way, but the points he laboriously scored are no longer so interesting. A sustained posture of attack on Victorian culture is dull now that the outposts are unmanned. Looking back, neither book shifted the current of thought or made more than a small local blip. Who outside of anthropology now knows about the Sudanese Nuer? Steiner's book on Polynesian taboo has been more influential, though too learned to be popular. Rationalists had already given up the old evolutionary theory about the development of human culture from darkness to present enlightenment, so no one was hurt by shafts accusing them of being narrow-minded Victorians.

The convergence of intellectual sympathies partly explains how it was that Steiner's work came to be taken for granted by so many who knew it. That many others never got to know it is partly because it was published after his death. His ideal of scholarship slowed him down. E.-P. wrote in his preface to *Taboo* that Steiner could never bring himself to 'publish anything that was not based upon a critical analysis of every source, in whatever language; and he had published almost nothing on anthropological subjects before his death' (1956a:11-12). We should not be surprised, then, that Steiner's contribution has been not just underestimated but totally omitted in recent histories of social anthropology (Kuper 1983; Stocking 1995; Goody 1995). If these authors had taken account of his influence they could have focused less on the superficial academic feuding that has interested them so much, and attended more to the substance of what was going on in anthropology in the period after 1946. For in those days there was less diversity among social anthropologists than now, but they were more deeply divided by major differences of opinion as to priorities, method, and goals, and this division gave a sting to the normal academic rivalries.

Part of the problem was that neither E.-P. nor Steiner had a formula or method to teach students who were not members of that privileged face-to-face community. The concluding chapter of *Nuer Religion* falls into incoherence, dissolving the argument into the form of mysticism that declares reality to be inexpressible in words. Evans-Pritchard had gone to great lengths to keep the word 'God' in his account of Nuer religion, involving himself in elaborate qualifications for which he also used the theological terms which the Christian fathers invented for addressing the same problems. Godfrey Lienhardt later (1961) evaded these problems by shifting to a slightly more neutral terminology: he used the word 'Divinity' instead of 'God'. Steiner went more boldly along the neutralising road. He wanted to have foreign religions analysed in terms of the active principles or powers in the universe. He did not see that the word God was necessary at all. This could have been a bold step towards doing without the concept of religion altogether. I am not sure that anything would have been gained by dropping both 'God' and 'religion' out of the terminology, but in my view that would be the only consistent course if they so much wanted to relieve the analysis of religion of the historical burden of prejudice. Under this influence I used the word cosmology in *Natural Symbols* (another unacknowledged debt), and found it very much more flexible and accurate than 'religion'.

Leaving out Steiner from the history of anthropology means leaving out the discussions of meaning that were being eagerly pursued in the common room and in the King's Arms as well as in tutorials. It is true that since Malinowski the correct translation of words was a central place concern in social anthropology. But Steiner was concerned with different issues, the meaning of truth and the origin of meaning. 'Chagga Truth' (1954) explains how specific rituals endow a spoken phrase with validity, how an oath dispels ambiguity and fixes the volatile meanings of evidence, and how a contract can be entered and enforced. But for the framing and formalising of stated intentions, there would be no meaning and social life would be impossible. In those days philosophers were trying to face those issues, indeed they came out of the then current critique of Kant, but they could only see them as problems of individual perception and action. If Tom Schelling's (1960) and David Lewis's (1969) work on the role of conventions and Bernard Williams's search for the foundations of logical necessity in the requirements of social life (1993) had been available they would have been hailed with delight. In 1961 Godfrey Lienhardt took this as one of the central themes of his great book on Dinka religion. He would have known Steiner's essay on the framing of truth and intention when he wrote about the words spoken by the Dinka officiant before a peace-making sacrifice. In a rite to end violence and bloodshed, was it not untruthful for the Spear Master to deny that there had been any quarrelling? Much later Ernest Gellner (1969) made a brilliant development of the theme of 'Chagga Truth' when he described the Berber use of the collective oath to establish a contested political fact. Neither Gellner nor Lienhardt quoted Steiner, not because the particular teaching had been forgotten, but that everyone had learnt it and used it. It was part of a stream of ideas received from *L'Année sociologique* about the nature of commitment, of which Georges Davy's *La Foi jurée* was the most famous example. Incidentally, I remember Davy himself coming to Oxford around this time and giving a lecture at the Institute.

These analyses turned old-fashioned problems about individual beliefs in magic into questions about social institutions. Questions about what is true lead to questions about identity and existence. What kind of ritual can turn a cucumber into a sacrificial ox (Evans-Pritchard 1956b)? As for the truth in genealogy, simplistic ideas were rocked by Laura Bohannan's account (1952) of the Tiv habit of blending generations and transforming brothers into sons and fathers. By the time Jean Buxton (1973) was describing how a black cock had to be turned into a white cock, or a red cow into a black cow, for a particular Mandari sacrifice the idea that correct rituals have the power to transform existences had become familiar. General epistemological problems about logic and meaning, and psychological questions about belief, dissolved into questions about the active principles or powers in the particular universe of the people under study.

The roots of this research go back a long way. It was the natural development of E.-P.'s 1937 study of witchcraft among the Azande, and part of E.-P.'s personal project to prove Lévy-Bruhl and Malinowski wrong. Both these great anthropologists had a mentalist theory to explain the peculiarity of primitive beliefs, particularly beliefs in magic. First of all Lévy-Bruhl (1922) proposed that primitives had a prelogical mentality, later he amended it slightly to say that the affective qualities of their individual experience would outweigh their powers of reasoning. Malinowski, who in the main part of his work was scrupulous to deny a basic difference between modern and Trobriand mentality, when it came to magic proposed an interesting psychologistic explanation based on perception of uncertainty and danger (1935; 1948). In fact his 'uncertainty explanation' of why there was more magic for risky deep sea fishing than for safer lagoon fishing is not unlike theories that are proposed nowadays about risk perception. But E.-P. had said long ago in his Cairo lectures (1933a; 1933b) that the whole issue of magic should be shifted away from individual mind sets to the different kinds of world that are constructed by each society. The words I have just used are an anachronism: though the idea was in the air he would not have expressed the idea of social construction in those terms. This is not the place to give a fuller account of E.-P.'s thought, and I only mention it to show the congruence between the interests of these two different anthropologists, and how far in the past the fuse had been laid. The last point to make about Steiner's near invisibility to the historians of anthropology is that what he was saying did not make history, it was too countercultural.

Steiner was very clear that meanings come out of social life and it is a waste of time to look for them anywhere else. Evans-Pritchard would have been uncomfortable with a position that smacked of social determinism, and though Steiner's formulation was not deterministic, to have followed him on this issue would have been a decisive break with the historians of *mentalités*. Purely psychological explanations would be discredited, the nascent cognitive sciences would have had to be fitted out with a set of sociological tools. A new era would have really been inaugurated. He was saying it throughout *Taboo*, denouncing the scholarly habit of separating culture from society:

> You can see what this writer is doing. In the first place he drags into a problem confused enough as it is the all too familiar dichotomy of structure or social organisation on the one hand, and on the other belief or culture or psychology... (1956: 19; p. 109, below)

Meanings are generated in social life; society has to be studied as part of the system of beliefs. Asking why the system of taboo developed in the particular circumstances of Polynesian society, he said: 'All these are really sociological questions' (1956: 87; p. 165, below). I must say this more emphatically or historians of anthropology will continue to miss the kind of revolution in anthropological thought that *Taboo* inaugurated. Steiner had poured scorn on anthropologists who explained by invoking universal principles of the mind or a universal gamut of emotions. If Steiner had had more of a following, Leach's attempt (1976) to make a general theory of anomaly would have been seen to be absurd because it rested on cognitive principles without regard to social classifications. My own essay, *Purity and Danger*, which derived from *Taboo*, was essentially a sociological approach to the question of belief. It attempted to link cognition systematically to social concerns by focusing on processes of classification. I admit it was often expressed ambiguously, and I suppose that the ambiguity allowed it to be received (always generously) as an essay on human cognition in general. If Steiner had had more influence beyond Oxford there would surely have been some feedback and discussion in sociological terms, but this part of his message was not received.

Taboo was based on lectures, and the lecturer did not himself put them into the form of a book. The published version edited by Laura Bohannan is faithful to what we heard him deliver in person. If he had written a book based upon them, I wonder if Claude Lévi-Strauss would have read it, and whether it would have made a difference to the conception of his book, *Totemism* (1963). Certainly in all his writing on structuralism Lévi-Strauss has shown a sociological concern; the classifications of the universe that he analyses have their counterpart in marriage customs, understanding the myths depends on knowing about the division of labour between sexes and young and old, about horticulture and hunting. But there is still room for a more overtly sociological treatment in the structural study of myth. If Steiner had lived long enough, he might have written a marvellous commentary on that mythological corpus. The topics were complementary. One anthropologist was a great poet, the other transformed literature. It is not fanciful to imagine a scintillating conversation on classification between the author of *Totemism* and the author of *Taboo*.

It is tempting to say that Steiner was before his time; he was working in a transitional period, which is why he had to spend so much energy laying ghosts. He seems to have been about to sociologise all the big, old questions by the rediscovery of context. His technique was constantly to re-embody beliefs into social life. He brought philosophers' favourite questions about truth and value down to earth by incorporating them into questions about social mechanisms. He was making us ready for a new era, but what happened next was structuralism, which effectively swept away the old landmarks of social anthropology.

I get another shock of recognition when I read Steiner's pages on danger:

Here it might be said that all situations of danger, not merely those created by taboo-breaking, are socially or culturally defined, and that it is precisely this relation between the defined danger and the restrictive pattern which we should study in each case. For until taboos are involved, a danger is not defined and cannot be coped with by institutionalised behaviour. ... To face danger is another power. Indeed, the older meaning of the English word danger is 'power', 'jurisdiction', 'dominion', 'the power to dispose of or to harm'. ... It is the job of the psychologist to study the emotions of fear in terms of the human mind, to conjecture the situations in which these fears are allayed, and to relate these situations to the conditioning of the individuals concerned. But to study how danger is localised in social institutions, and what social pressure is needed in order to regulate abstentions so that the danger can remain localised, is to approach the problem sociologically. (1956: 146, 147; p. 213, 214, below)[2]

This was written for the 1950s, but it was uncannily prescient for the anthropologist trying to think about technological dangers in the 1970s and 1980s (Douglas and Wildavsky 1982; Douglas 1986).

I have also to acknowledge Steiner's influence for my study of the Pentateuch, and particularly for biblical ideas about defilement, (another offshoot from *Taboo*). Several of my own attempts to write on contagion, secular (1992) and religious (1996), were consciously derived from my student days, and so unconsciously from him. I wish I had reread *Taboo* in time to have quoted direct from his discussion of negative and positive transmissions of power, blessings, and contagions (1956: 61-67; pp. 142-47, below). I believe that his chiding of the nineteenth-century scholars for their biased inconsistency has had an effect. They disapproved of beliefs in defilement as unacceptably primitive, while they approved of transmission of sacred power through blessings, while never troubling to work out why one was 'the lowest form of superstition', and the other was modern and a good. Chapters 4 to 7 of *Taboo* are specifically about defilement in the Bible. Steiner was fighting the legacy of evolutionary ideas in Robertson Smith and Frazer. However, though I notice that Frazer's ideas about purity are now widely discredited, Robertson Smith still reigns in most scholarly works on biblical purity.[3] Steiner says of defilement as of taboo that it is a demarcation device. It does not make sense when studied apart from the whole pattern of classifications and powers in use. I find it liberating to be given secular as well religious examples of how it works. When I tried to find my own way through the contemporary writing on impurity in Numbers and Leviticus I had forgotten how well he had prepared it.

I didn't know, until the editors of this volume told me, that I also owe Steiner a debt in respect of economic anthropology. I knew that he had worked extensively on the division of labour, as part of his research into servile institutions. But I did not know that he had written about ranked, distinct economic spheres. This is something of immense potential interest to sociologists. I only knew of it from a splendid account of the Tiv economy by Paul Bohannan (1959). Among the Tiv the social ranking was based on age, and on renown in war or success in trade. Each separate rank was distinguished by exchanges of specific valuables between its members. Bohannan called it a system of restricted currencies. Without first gaining access to a particular social sphere no one would be able to acquire the objects necessary to behave in it as a full member exchanging with the others. Gaining access was like getting rationing coupons or a licence (Douglas 1958 and 1967). I found there were many accounts of this system of economically backed stratification in the literature, working the opposite way from money. With money, social barriers often melt away; but conversely money can make barriers (Douglas and Isherwood 1979; Zelizer 1994). There are potentially important implications for economies with big structural holes in the networks of exchange. For example, houses in modern society can become very similar to a restricted currency. If the price of a house is so high that only existing house-owners could be in the housing market, an exclusionary situation would lead to rigid stratification, with possibly dire social effects.

Recognising Steiner's influence in recalling these restricted currencies to the notice of anthropologists one suspects that he was unobtrusively giving power to the argument between 'substantive economics' and 'formal economics' in the 1950s and 1960s. The argument was mainly about whether in moneyless economies the anthropologist could make much use of textbook economics based on money prices and rates of monetary exchange, and whether an economy based on ceremonial gift exchange could be analysed in terms of market supply and demand. Now the debate has virtually closed down because of the advances made by economic anthropologists of both persuasions in finding imaginative ways of studying their field. In this achievement the two massive volumes edited by George Dalton were a storehouse of information and ideas (1967; 1971).

Looking back on all this, it strikes me that I am now one of the oldest living members of the group of students and teachers at the Institute of Social Anthropology in the last eight years of Franz Steiner's life. I suspect that I am also one of the people who owe him the most. I won't dispute that claim with either of the Bohannans, but I can just say that I am very grateful for the opportunity the editors of this volume have given me to think back to those privileged days. If I can name two radical teachings I got from Steiner which held all the rest together, one was the courage to challenge existing scholarly classifications, to bypass established traditions in order to assemble contexts more intelligibly. The other was to remember that ideas do not act as independent agents but are always made and set in circulation by individuals.

NOTES

1. See reference in Introduction to *Purity and Danger* (1966) and my article on 'Pollution' in the *Encyclopaedia of the Social Sciences* (1968).
2. The importance of the concept of 'power' in Steiner's work suggests that he influenced Lienhardt in his use of the word 'powers' for spiritual beings in his account of Dinka religion.
3. An exception is P. J. Jenson who makes good use of Steiner's *Taboo* in his book on Leviticus, *Graded Holiness, a Key to the Priestly conception of the World* (1992).

BIBLIOGRAPHY

Bohannan, L., 1952 'A Genealogical Charter', *Africa*, 22, (4): 301-15.

Bohannan, P. J., 1959 'The impact of money on an African subsistence economy', *Journal of Economic History*, 19, (4): 491-503.

Buxton, J., 1973 *Religion and Healing in Mandari*. Oxford, Clarendon,.

Dalton, G. ed., 1967 *Tribal and Peasant Economies, Readings in Economic Anthropology*. American Museum Sourcebooks in Anthropology, New York: The Natural History Press.

―――― ed., 1971 *Economic Development and Social Change. The Modernisation of Village Communities*. American Museum Sourcebooks in Anthropology, New York, The Natural History Press.

Douglas, M., 1958 'Raffia Cloth Distribution in the Lele Economy', *Africa*, 28: 109-22; reprinted Dalton, ed., *Tribal and Peasant Economies*.

―――, 1966 *Purity and Danger. An Analysis of Concepts of Pollution and Taboo*. London: R.K.P.

―――, 1967 'Primitive Rationing', in R. Firth, ed., *Themes in Economic Anthropology*, Association of Social Anthropologists, Mongraph 6, London: Tavistock.

―――, 1968 'Pollution', *Encyclopaedia of the Social Sciences*. London: Macmillan.

―――, 1970 *Natural Symbols. Explorations in Cosmology*. London: Barrie and Rockliff.

―――, 1986 *Risk Acceptability According to the Social Sciences*. London: Routledge.

―――, 1992 *Risk and Blame: Essays in Cultural Theory*. London: Routledge.

―――, 1996 'Sacred Contagion' in *Reading Leviticus: Responses to Mary Douglas*. ed. by John Sawyer, Sheffield: Sheffield Academic Press, pp. 86-105.

Douglas, M., and Isherwood, B. C., 1979 *The World of Goods. Towards an Anthropology of Consumption*. London: Basic Books.

Douglas, M. and Wildavsky, A., 1982 *Risk and Culture*. Berkeley: University Press of California.

Evans-Pritchard, E., 1933a 'The Intellectualist (English) Interpretation of Magic'. Cairo, extr. *Bulletin of the Faculty of Arts*, vol. 1, pt. 2.

―――, 1933b 'Lévy-Bruhl's Theory of Primitive Mentality', Cairo, extr. *Bulletin of the Faculty of Arts*, vol. 2, pt. 1.

―――, 1937 *Witchcraft, Oracles and Magic among the Azande*. Oxford: Clarendon.

―――, 1956a *Nuer Religion*. Oxford: Clarendon.

―――, 1956b 'Preface' to Franz Steiner, *Taboo*. London: Cohen and West, pp. 11-13.

Gellner, E., 1969 *Saints of the Atlas*. London: Weidenfeld and Nicholson.

Goody, J. 1995 *The Expansive Moment. The Rise of Social Anthropology in Britain and Africa 1918-1970*. Cambridge: C. U. P.

Jenson, P. J., 1992 *Graded Holiness, a Key to the Priestly Conception of the World*. Sheffield: Sheffield Academic Press.

Kuper, A., 1983 *Anthropologists and Anthropology. The British School, 1922-72.* rev. edn London: Routledge.

Leach, E. R., 1976 *Culture and Communication. The Logic by which Symbols are Connected.* Cambridge: C. U. P.

Lévi-Strauss, C., 1963 *Totemism.* trans. R. Needham, Boston: Beacon Press.

Lévy-Bruhl, L., 1922 *La Mentalité primitive.* Paris: Alcan.

Lewis, D. K., 1969 *Convention, a Philosophical Study.* Cambridge, MA.: Harvard University Press.

Lienhardt, R. G., 1961 *Divinity and Experience.* Oxford, Clarendon.

Malinowski, B., 1935 *Coral Gardens and their Magic.* 2 vols, London, Routledge.

———, 1948 *Magic, Science and Religion.* Glencoe, Ill.: Beacon Press.

Schelling, T. C., 1960 *The Strategy of Conflict.* Cambridge, MA.: Harvard University Press.

Steiner, F. B., 1956 *Taboo.* London: Cohen and West.

Stocking, G., 1995 *After Tylor.* Madison, University of Wisconsin Press.

Williams, B., 1993 *Shame and Necessity.* Berkeley: University of California Press.

Zelizer, V. A., 1994 *The Social Meaning of Money.* New York: Basic Books.

AN ORIENTAL IN THE WEST:
THE LIFE OF
FRANZ BAERMANN STEINER

Jeremy Adler and Richard Fardon

> *My created heart says so with every beat:*
> *Stay on the border ...*
>
> *Conquests*, V, 'The Lonely Man'

Introductory

Franz Baermann Steiner occupies a unique place in modern social and cultural anthropology. The fact that his uniqueness was recognised by only a handful of influential contemporaries is attributable to his early death which occurred – cruelly – just when he had embarked upon his most mature and innovative writings. Working at the confluence of many of the significant theories and methodologies of the twentieth century, in the early post-war years – and especially in the all-too-brief period he enjoyed as a Lecturer in Social Anthropology at the University of Oxford from 1950-52 – he had begun to select among these various currents. At the time of his death, he was developing an unprecedented synthesis in mid-century anthropological thought. Broadly speaking, Steiner's thinking stakes out a territory between German post-Enlightenment philosophy, modern linguistic thought, Marxism, Central European ethnology, German sociology, British social anthropology, and early structuralism. He deploys these resources with a scholarly passion for truth – which for Steiner is never far removed from its Biblical source – allied to an overriding concern for the right to self-determination of non-Western peoples, among whom he includes his own Jewish people. In their equal concern for geopolitics and detailed local ethnography, his writings foreshadow trends in anthropology that were to become apparent only as the twentieth century wore on. In their deep aversion to the imposition of Western values on non-Western peoples, his writings relentlessly expose biases brought by Western reporters to their texts. His work may, indeed, be read as entirely critical, which is how Evans-Pritchard presented Steiner's lectures on *Taboo* on their posthumous publication. But Steiner's early deconstruction of Western presuppositions in fact clears the ground for a fundamental defence of the scholarly, political and religious values he held dear.

The present volumes are designed to encourage a re-evaluation of Franz Baermann Steiner's work by presenting his ideas in their most complete form to date. Our Introductions set the development of Steiner's ideas in a biographical context, recognising Steiner's affinity with various intellectual schools, and point towards a synthesis of the ideas that he was beginning to wrest from his massive and extraordinarily wide-ranging scholarship in those two-and-a-half years that he was a lecturer in the Institute of Social Anthropology at Oxford. To appreciate the numerous tensions this synthesis sought to contain, the reader needs to know something about the complexity of Franz Baermann Steiner: poet, aphorist, thinker, ethnologist, anthropological and philosophical theorist, Zionist, political activist, friend and mentor.

Born in Prague in the final years of the Austro-Hungarian Empire, the young Steiner fully partook in the intellectual ferment that characterised the early part of the twentieth century, just as he was to witness at first hand some of its greatest political cataclysms. Political and intellectual engagement were two of the opposite if ultimately complementary facets of his life's work. In the 1930s he went through an early Marxist phase and subsequently studied at the Hebrew University in Palestine. His early Marxism was thereby tempered with political Zionism, and both these theories were to leave their trace on his anthropology. After completing his degree in linguistics at Prague, he went on to train in the Central European tradition of cultural anthropology at the University of Vienna, where he had the opportunity to study with some of the major exponents of the 'culture circles' school which then dominated German-speaking ethnology, and was to exercise considerable influence in the United States. At this stage in his career he specialised in Arctic ethnology. Then, in the mid-to-late 1930s, he came to England, largely to study with Malinowski at the London School of Economics. However, he gravitated towards Oxford, where he became a student of A.R. Radcliffe-Brown and, later, of E.E. Evans-Pritchard. At first he continued to concentrate on material culture, but reached a turning-point in his work around the year 1942. This was perhaps his period of deepest isolation. It was at this time that he started fully to internalise the persecution that his people were experiencing at Nazi hands, and a sense of this suffering appears to have transmuted his thinking. Yet great as the changes clearly were that took place around this time, it is hard to pin them down precisely. His scholarly focus, according to the prevailing mood in England, switched from the Arctic towards Africa, and from ethnology to the study of social institutions. And it was to the institution of slavery, a subject selected as a penance for his people's suffering, that Steiner now devoted the best years of his life. Many of his deepest thoughts can be traced to this study. He also brought to this area a profound interest in religion, values, and epistemology. The project was phenomenally wide in conception and involved Steiner in the comparative study of practically every known society – from Europe to North America, Africa, India, and the Far East. Although only a fraction of this learning materialised in his writing, it provided a sociological grounding for all his other work. A project on this scale was doomed from the start. Doomed also in its attempt to combine continental comparative method with British particularism. For even in its more specialised British garb, the habitual mode of his thought remained continental in its syncretism. This was to prove one of the many rewarding tensions in Steiner's writing, the division between universal comparative aspirations and local, particular realities.

From Evans-Pritchard himself to Mary Douglas, colleagues valued Steiner for his learning which, in Godfrey Lienhardt's phrase, made Steiner 'an intellectual's intellectual'. Thanks to his voracious reading – Professor Sir Ernst Gombrich always imagined Steiner as a veritable 'bookworm', practically eating his way through the stock at the British Museum (PC) – Steiner developed into a polymath. And his implicit but ever-present sense of universality informs the bewildering variety of projects he eventually worked on. From slavery, he was led to comparative economics, taboo, and the theory of truth. In the early post-war years at Oxford, working beside Meyer Fortes, Godfrey Lienhardt, Mary Douglas, Paul and Laura Bohannan, Louis Dumont, and M.N. Srinivas, Steiner emerged as a central intellect in that small group of Oxford anthropologists which Stefan Collini has called 'the power-base from which the science of social structure could be developed as the defining core of the discipline of social anthropology' (1996: 5). However, in a metonym for his fate, a celebrated picture of the members of the Institute of Social Anthropology at Oxford taken in 1949 (Stocking, [1995] 1996: 428) does not include Steiner. The handwritten caption – itself omitted by Stocking – describes him as 'missing'. To some extent, because of his early death this has been his fate in the historiography of modern British anthropology. He has gone 'missing' and gains scarcely a mention in such standard texts as Kuper's *Anthropology and Anthropologists* (1973) and Stocking's *After Tylor* ([1995] 1996). Yet had he lived longer, had he undertaken his projected field trip to Tanganyika, and had he remained an academic, Steiner would presumably have remained at the centre of the anthropological stage, and would have retired only in 1974, four years after Evans-Pritchard. There would be no need to write him back into the picture. He would have written himself into our consciousness by his own endeavours. Like his closest friends at Oxford including Godfrey Lienhardt, Mary Douglas, and Iris Murdoch he would inevitably have achieved visible recognition, at the very least from the anthropological community, but possibly – as was his undoubted ambition – among the wider reading public. Even so, there is enough in his extant writings to suggest that his impact on modern anthropology and anthropologists had already been substantial and, had he lived longer and developed the ideas burgeoning in the texts collected in these volumes, that he would have exercised substantial influence on anthropological debates in the second half of the twentieth century. This is a bold claim, which the present volumes will seek to substantiate.

To some extent, Steiner's outsider status was endemic to other practitioners of the discipline. Like Malinowski, Firth, Schapera, and the other 'foreigners' who Leach has observed were 'mainly responsible for the high prestige that was attributed to "British" anthropology in the 1950s and 1960s' (1984: 11), Steiner 'assimilated himself into the life style and conventions of Oxbridge academics' but remained 'highly ambivalent' towards his 'adopted milieu'. Yet Steiner was perhaps even more detached from the 'British' school than some of these others. While fully occupied at Oxford, Steiner was also busy on at least three other, quite separate fronts. He was at work on his poetry, which would in itself have sufficed for a life's work. He was active politically as a Zionist. And he was engaged in wide-ranging discussions with another exile writer, the anthropological outsider and his own close friend, the future Nobel laureate, Elias Canetti. As a consequence of this complex arc, Steiner's writing is marked by some very disparate cultural traces. In Marxism and Zionism, it is touched by some of the twentieth century's most virulent ideologies; yet, like Canetti and Wittgenstein, he was also shaped by the anti-ideological streak in the century's thought, exemplified by Karl Kraus and his cultural critique. This brings to Steiner's other work, his aphorisms and the brief essays he wrote in German – as distinct from the anthropology, which he drafted and wrote exclusively in English from as early as 1938 – a wholly different character, closer to the ambit of Walter Benjamin, Theodor Adorno, and the Frankfurt School than to Radcliffe-Brown or Evans-Pritchard. However, there is no evidence that he knew Benjamin's work, though he may have been acquainted with Adorno's writing, but he appears to have reached his convergences with them by starting from similar premises and facing a similar situation. This fragmentary and aphoristic but major part of

Steiner's output is largely unpublished, even in the original German, despite the best efforts of Adorno and others. Its existence none the less informs the English writings and adds further, enriching complexity to Steiner's work.

To grasp Steiner in the round, it therefore needs to be remembered that at the same time as he was working and writing in English, using scholarly method, logic, and argument, which are conventions inimical to the aphoristic mode, Steiner was privately writing a religiously grounded cultural critique in German. This led him into a very different territory from that known to his Oxford colleagues. An area bordered by books like *Masse und Macht* (1960; *Crowds and Power* 1962), on which Canetti was working at that time, and Adorno and Horkheimer's contemporaneous *Dialektik der Aufklärung* (1944; *Dialectic of Enlightenment* 1972). Yet whereas these latter have long since in differing degrees established themselves in the arena of modern critical debate and from there entered the wider scholarly sphere, Steiner's contribution, though known to both Canetti and Adorno, still awaits belated discovery. Only when one juxtaposes Steiner's two styles of production, the English scholarship with the Central European aphorisms, does the full picture of his thought begin to emerge. In the present *Selected Writings*, we have therefore chosen to open with his most public and best known English work, his lectures on *Taboo*, which have established themselves as a key text in their field, and to follow this with the related articles on religion and truth. We introduce these with the first full biography of Steiner to appear in English. The Introduction to this, the first volume of *Selected Writings*, aims to provide the necesssary biographical and intellectual background for a new reading of Steiner's work. The task continues in the second volume. There we present other texts by Steiner which saw their way into print, together with many others which are published here for the first time. The selection includes writings published as articles prior to and contemporaneous with *Taboo*, political writings early and late, a section from his unpublished D.Phil. dissertation, hitherto unpublished lectures, a significant number of aphorisms, and a selection from a major cycle of poems. Whilst the body of work collected does not aspire to completeness, we feel confident that it represents Steiner fairly, and is substantial enough to provide the broad basis for a revaluation. The notable lacunae are the papers in Arctic ethnology, which are of more specialist interest, and the dissertation on slavery in its entirety. Our edition of Steiner's *Selected Writings* thus aims: to initiate a discussion of Steiner's role in developing the post-war Oxford contribution to modern social anthropology, to indicate just how powerful we believe his contribution to have been, and to encourage both the specialist and a wider audience to gain an insight into Steiner's thought in all its variety and complexity.

Beginnings:
The Prague German-Jewish Community

There is a childhood, in pieces, sweetened by the cool sun.
Three meagre firs in the garden of a limping suburb.
Chimney-stacks over the quarrelsome lust of blinded windows ...

Conquests, II, 'Memories'

Franz Steiner was born in the Prague suburb of Karlín (Karolinental) –
at that time still a separate town – on 12 October 1909. In later years –
following the old Jewish custom – he adopted the forename of his paternal grandfather, and called himself Franz Baermann Steiner. Among
his childhood acquaintances in Karlín was the young H.G. Adler,
Steiner's junior by a year, and the two boys became lifelong friends, sharing as they grew up mutual interests in biology, poetry and the social sciences (J. Adler 1996: 126). They belonged to a small circle of talented
children living a stone's throw from one another. From childhood to
adolescence, these youngsters stimulated each other's development and
remained staunchly loyal to one another throughout the historical
vicissitudes that overwhelmed them. They included Franz's cousins, Lise
Gross, who later emigrated to Australia, and her sister Lotte, who married the physicist Záboj Harvalík, with whom she went to the United
States. Another cousin was Gerta Weißbach, the wife of the philosopher Joseph Marcus, who later befriended Wittgenstein's companion,
Paul Engelmann, in Jerusalem. These precocious children were born
into that small, hot-house community, the German-Jewish minority in
Prague from which Kafka had also come just a few years earlier, and
which contributed so significantly to Central European culture in the
first half of the twentieth century. If perhaps not quite comparable to
Wittgenstein's Vienna (Janik and Toulmin 1973), Kafka's Prague was
certainly one of the most intellectually lively of Central Europe's cities,
and Steiner's circle seemed set to enrich Prague's varied if fragile culture. Commenting on the city's character in later life, Steiner summed
up some of Prague's paradoxes: 'A town of narrow aspirations and terrifying historicity. Avignon and Königsberg in one. Or Toledo and Bres-
lau.' Steiner was perhaps the first to make the now common comparison
between Prague and Dublin, major provincial centres which produced
two of the century's major writers, Kafka and Joyce:

> Modern German literature is unthinkable without the Prague literary cir-
> cles. After all, the greatest poet and the greatest prose writer that German
> literature has produced in the first half of this century come from Prague:
> Rilke and Kafka. And the smaller figures clustered around them in manifold
> combinations, explaining and to a modest extent determining the appear-
> ance of the greater ones. The dominant position of Prague in this literary

epoch has never been denied – because nobody had the courage to state the fact. But it is true none the less. There is only one parallel in the history of literature: the position of Dublin. Dublin was also a contemporary provincial capital and the centre of an oppressed country. In its relations to London, as in other things, Dublin recalls Prague. Here too there was a long-prepared flowering which lasted only two decades and which is sharply distinct from the literary decay evident in English literature itself. Joyce, an exile like Rilke; Kafka as lonely as Synge and as local as Yeats .... (Steiner 1988: 57)

In the century of the outsider, the periphery became the centre – not least in the case of the Jewish migrants who moved from the Bohemian villages and small towns to Prague (Kieval 1988: 10). As we will see, reflections on circles, colonialism, marginality, and repression colour much of Steiner's thought. Just as it is common to locate the origin of Kafka's sense of alienation in his experience as a Prague German Jew, cut off both from his heritage in the past and the cultural centres of the present, it is helpful to view Steiner's later life in terms of origins that are broadly similar to Kafka's. After the Second World War, he himself implicitly drew the comparison in his poem 'Kafka in England', which grafts his thoughts about the exile's isolation after Belsen onto an image of Kafka's mysterious genius (see Volume II, p. 81). Steiner, following Kafka, turned his origins into his work by reflecting them, and so it will be helpful to review them in some detail.

Around the time of Steiner's childhood, Prague was celebrated by many writers and poets in the quasi-mythical terms that have since become a byword in the phrase *Praga magica* (Ripellino 1994). Prague German writers emphasised the fantastic, the bizarre, and the ghostly as central to their experience of the town. In this spirit, the Prague writer Paul Kornfeld called Prague a 'metaphysical madhouse' (Serke 1987: 284). Less wittily but no less evocatively, in his article on 'German Writers from Prague' published in the journal *Wir* (We) in 1906, Oskar Wiener, commenting on the destruction of the old Jewish quarters and the rebuilding of the city, described the town as follows:

> Prague, that unspeakably beautiful but dissolute castle on the Vltava! Old Prague is dying but a new, sober Prague is emerging from massive stones among the rubble. The place we loved which provided a homeland for all our dreams must die. We wander like disinherited spirits among the streets and mourn .... (H.G. Adler 1976: 79)

In 1919, introducing his anthology *Deutsche Dichter aus Prag* (German Poets from Prague), Wiener represented Prague once again in these terms, calling it 'this city of eccentrics and fantastics, this restless heart of Central Europe ...' (Wiener 1919: 5). From Bismarck – so it has been said, though the source seems somewhat allusive – to André

Breton, the centrality of this apparently marginal city has been recognised from viewpoints as different as the military and the cultural (Serke 1987: 38 and 377), and at several times during Steiner's own lifetime, it had cause to be seen as lying at the heart of Europe. The perception lends centrality to Steiner's own experience, too.

At the end of the First World War, Prague became the capital of the vibrant new Czechoslovak Republic, under its cultured president, T.G. Masaryk (Hoensch 1987: 416-20). The proclamation of the republic marked the end of the Austro-Hungarian Empire and symbolised a new European order. The economic and industrial strength of the new country – in the late nineteenth century it grew into Austria-Hungary's leading industrial region (Polišenský 1991: 100) and in 1918 it possessed three-fifths of its industrial capacity (Sayer 1998: 163) – placed Czechoslovakia among the most advanced European states. The economic rise was accompanied by an equally significant cultural development (Demetz 1998: 348-53; 394f.). Indeed, political modernisation and cultural modernism were interconnected thanks to Masaryk's policy of shaping a forward-looking polity by encouraging an aesthetic revival (Sayer 1998:155f.), beginning with the renovation of the Prague Castle by a contemporary architect: many telling stylistic details (like the obelisk before St. Vitus's Cathedral) add a distinctly modern but discrete elegance to the ancient centre of Bohemian power. By virtue of their closeness to Masaryk, many Czech intellectuals, like the brothers Čapek, were to play a leading role in this young country. The arts flourished. Czechs like the composer Janáček and the novelist Hašek made international reputations. They were not isolated figures. Following the cultural surge of the late nineteenth century, all the arts continued to enjoy an extraordinary boom to an extent which has yet to be fully appreciated outside Czechoslovakia. Poetry, prose, drama, theatre, cabaret, music, painting, sculpture, photography, film, architecture, book-making, and graphic design all produced major achievements. German-language culture likewise enjoyed a brief efflorescence that brought forth a host of significant writers in the generations just before Steiner and in his own age-group. Max Brod and others have analysed the writing of 'the Prague school' (1966; Hoffmann 1997), and Jürgen Serke's generous reassessment of Prague German literature treats almost fifty German-speaking writers from Bohemia, including Steiner himself (Serke 1987: 300-313). This was a coffee-house culture. A German contemporary of Steiner's, Hermann Kesten, observed the scene, which may evoke nostalgia in us, with a more scornful eye: 'The entire Prague School of writers is telephonically connected with God himself, they're all coffee-house artists fitted out with mystical symbols of the world. Most of the objects of their desires also sit in the coffee-houses ...' (Serke 1987: 377). It requires little effort to imagine the young Steiner in this context. The common perception of Prague as being somehow central to Europe was, accordingly, very much a fact of life in his day, both culturally and politically. But this was a doomed world. After the Republic's first ten peaceful years, stability was undermined (Polišenský 1991: 100), there were frequent political troubles and economic problems (see e.g., Sayer 1998: 164), and the imbalance between Czech and German aspirations, inbuilt into the new country from the start by Masaryk's unwise marginalisation of the German language, are said to have contributed to its collapse, although in fact the collapse is less attributable to Czechoslovakia's supposed weaknesses than to its neighbours' lack of principle. When the Nazis rose to power in 1933, Prague became a brief haven for many German nationals, including Bertolt Brecht and Heinrich Mann (*Drehscheibe Prag* 1989), but their arrival heralded the end of an era; the Sudeten Germans in the Bohemian Lands – a group quite distinct from the Prague German Jews, which had developed its own national identity via its opposition to the new Republic (Hoensch 1987: 423) – desired incorporation into a Reich which was eager for Czechoslovakia's territory and industrial power; after Czechoslovakia had existed independently for less than twenty years, it was broken up in 1938.

The kind of idealisation often associated with the perception of Prague as a magical city, as in the quoted passage from Oskar Wiener, clearly does not stand up to scrutiny. The contemporary American scholar Peter Demetz, who was born and bred in Prague, has often stressed Prague's other, darker, violent side, a face of the city which was also to become Steiner's Prague. Demetz is at pains to point out that the different groups which dominated Prague's cultural, social, and political landscape – namely the Germans, the Czechs, and the Jews – did not live harmoniously, but competitively, both in practical day-to-day matters and at a deeper, structural level, as is evident even in their choice of professions and dwelling places in the city (1982: 278). Demetz also stresses the massive failures in Prague history; a comparative account would need to contextualise these events on a broader European canvas in which comparable violence was the norm at similar intervals: 'Behind the ideal of a Golden Prague hide the people's uprisings, the pogroms, the riots, the demonstrations, the arson attacks, the fights and plunderings of 1844, 1848, 1863, 1897, 1904, 1905, 1920, 1921 ...' (Demetz 1982: 278). The atrocities go back beyond the expatriation of all Protestants after the Battle of the White Mountain in 1620, extend into the eighteenth century, and down to our own time, with the genocide perpetrated on Bohemian territory from 1940 to 1945, and the subsequent forcible expatriation of all Germans in 1945 to 1946 – these last two actions effectively robbing the city of two key groups, Germans and Jews, which formed the Prague Steiner knew. The consequences of the Munich Agreement, which determined the shape of the next fifty years in Europe, spelled the end of the Republic and, doing so, also decided Steiner's fate. On 14-15 March 1939 Bohemia and Moravia were turned into a 'Protectorate'. When Britain sold out Czechoslovakia to Hitler in a vain bid for peace, the betrayal strengthened Hitler's hold over Europe, and prepared the end of the world into which Steiner had been born. Yet notwithstanding his own experience of these terrors, Demetz is also keen to point out the moments at which 'multi-ethnicity' and the ideal of a polyglot 'Bohemian community' in a peaceful homeland promoted by Bernard Bolzano (Demetz 1997: 275) proved to some small degree successful in Prague. Whilst not subscribing to the idealisation of 'Golden Prague', he yet finds much to cherish. For Demetz, the Prague that Steiner inhabited was an essentially liberal community:

> There were many moments when Prague societies lived with each other, or at least next to each other, and the names of those who attempted to guide different people to tolerance and sympathy with each other deserve new respect today, whether they are famous or known only to the happy few. I am thinking of the philosopher Bernard Bolzano, of President T.G. Masaryk, his disciple Emanuel Rádl, and the German ministers who served Masaryk's republic loyally in the shared government of 1926-38. I also think of Kafka's onetime friend Milena Jesenská .... (Demetz 1997: xiif.)

Many of these conflicting forces apparent in Prague (and the interpretation of Prague) make themselves felt in Steiner's thought: the city's dominant sense of its multi-ethnic identity, so many of its writers' predeliction for myth and fantasy, but also the ideal of liberal humanism which Demetz himself represents and that formed such a strong element in Steiner's own upbringing.

The picture is further enriched by Steiner's Judaism. Some comment on the German-speaking Jewish community in Prague is in order since it is to this social group that a central tension in Steiner's thought, which runs between Western and non-Western values, can be traced. At the turn of the century, it has been claimed that Jews made up as much as 8 percent of the entire Bohemian population (Haumann 1990: 159). This seems unlikely although, even without allowing for under-registration of Jews, the proportion of Jews in Prague in the late nineteenth century did approach such a figure. The distinctive German Jewish community in Prague shared and shaped its city's history in its own peculiar way, both by its perennial difference from its surrounds and by its considerable size. However, because identity had political implications, some caution in interpreting official figures for the ethnic breakdown of Prague's population is necessary. Fewer citizens registered as Jews (rather than Germans or Czechs) under the Monarchy, while under the Republic more German-speakers elected to register as Czechs (H.G. Adler 1976: 69; Rybár 1991b: 77). In 1880, the Prague population was thought to comprise 228,000 Czechs and 42,000 Germans; of these two groups over 20,500 were Jews. By 1921, when Steiner was twelve, largely thanks to migration from the smaller towns and the countryside, the Jewish population reached between 27,000 and 31,500, depending on the figures chosen, albeit both sets were presumably boosted in part by increased registrations. Although their numbers continued to grow, Jews subsequently declined as a proportion of Prague's population thanks to burgeoning Czech numbers: in 1930, when Steiner was twenty-one, the Czech population had risen steeply to 806,000, German-speakers apparently remained at their 1880 level, but the Jewish population had grown steadily to reach 30,000-35,000 including the inner suburbs (Kieval 1988: 14). Thus, the Jewish community of Prague grew numerically by at least half over a fifty year period but declined proportionally by the same factor. Though they endured expulsions, persecution, harassment, and pogroms, Prague's Jews entered the early years of the new Republic as a comparatively large if vulnerable social group, situated awkwardly between an ancient faith, Rabbinic law, religious rituals, and Hebrew and Yiddish on the one hand, and modernisation, assimilation, civil state, modern *Kultur,* and the Czech and German languages, on the other. Kafka graphically defined the conflicting worlds that a Jewish writer in Prague felt compelled to bridge. He describes the 'terrible inner situation' of his generation, noting that most of the Jews who began to write in German 'wanted to break away from Judaism, usually with the unclear agreement of their elders ...; their hind legs still glued to the Judaism of their fathers while their front legs found nothing to stand on. The resulting despair was their inspiration' (Kafka 1958: 337). These oppositions also proved an inspiration for Steiner. In his mature thought, he learned to generalise the local tensions between the Jewish, Czech and German peoples into the tools for an intellectual analysis of modernity and, on a political level, into geopolitical principles.

Today the Jewish world from which Steiner came has vanished. As we wander through Prague's old Jewish quarter we can perhaps imagine the bustling life that must once have filled its streets and the half a dozen synagogues which survive. The striking Old-New Synagogue, the oldest synagogue in Europe, with its ascetic front bears mute witness to seven centuries of Jewish history. In the old Jewish cemetery the sunken tombstones loom before us like petrified ghosts. We may try to rediscover the past in the Prague Jewish Museum, where a belated piety pays homage to ritual – as if somehow a value could be attached to Torah rolls outside their use, and in the absence of the people to whom they actually belonged. Perhaps we will also exercise our imagination and recall figures like the great sixteenth-century Rabbi Löw (Yehuda Liwa ben Bezalel) and the legends that surround his name. When he bravely confronted the Emperor Rudolph II on Charles Bridge, the faeces hurled at him in abuse turned to flowers. Most famously, we may recall the story of the clay Golem the Rabbi is said to have created, which formed an active part of the popular imagination in Steiner's time – and does again today. Gustav Meyrink's celebrated novel, *Der Golem,* appeared in 1915 when Steiner was six years old and was turned into a successful film with Paul Wegener in the lead in 1920. In the last year of his life, Steiner – still connecting with this world – bought a copy of the original edition. In the Prague of his day, clearly one could still witness a living Jewish community that had its roots in the middle ages, and observe the immediate contiguity of ancient Jewish legend and secular modernity. That is no longer possible. Today even the aura that the ancient places and legends once exuded seems to have dispersed. The destruction of European Jewry also destroyed the relations between contemporary Prague and the Jewish past. As a scholar in England, Steiner bore conscious witness to this destruction. His mature scholarship, we shall see, derived in part from his need to respond to the convulsions which destroyed his people. In rescuing the values that their world enshrined he returned to the cultural streams that had sustained them, but which had been poisoned in his homeland.

According to legend, Prague was built with stones removed from the Second Temple after its destruction by the Romans in AD 70. As to the facts, Jews are attested in Bohemia as early as the tenth century, and were given their earliest privileges in Moravia in 1254 (Rybár 1991a: 26). Their history in Bohemia and Moravia is one of repeated persecutions, not least during the Enlightenment, which also saw the beginnings of Jewish emancipation, and this tension between repression and self-determination is often reflected in Steiner's aphorisms. The Jewish population in the Prague Ghetto reached its greatest extent in the early eighteenth century with around 12,000 inhabitants, who worked both inside and outwith the Ghetto (Rybár 1991b: 53ff.). However, the Enlightenment was slow to affect Prague Jews; after the Prussian occupation of Prague in 1744, the Jews were accused of collaborating with the enemy, and the Ghetto was plundered; subsequently, Empress Maria Theresa issued an imperial edict expelling them from the city, and they left in 1745. As a concession, they were permitted to remain 'within two hours' of Prague. They were readmitted in August 1748, not least thanks to the intercession of the local merchants (Rybár 1991b: 57). When Maria Theresa's son Joseph II came to the throne in 1780, he initiated a period of reform. The overdue political improvements which he introduced in Austria-Hungary, such as the abolition of serfdom, also heralded the start of Jewish emancipation in Bohemia and Moravia. The Tolerance Patent of 1781 (Kieval 1988: 5), and the so-called System Patent of 1791, introduced limited religious freedom for Jews, who were tolerated as a minority, albeit without full civil rights. Discriminatory legislation still shackled them, like the limitation on marriage which permitted only eldest sons to found a family; this grim practice was not abolished until 1847. However, Jews were freed from wearing their degrading yellow badge – reintroduced as a yellow star by the Nazis 150 years later – and were granted their first civil liberties, such as the permission to attend public schools and matriculate at the university. They were also increasingly permitted to reside outside the Ghetto walls. The economic reforms initiated in the Josephine period also played a major part in shaping the future life of Prague. It was now that the factories were founded in the city, such as those for printed cloth, which a century later were to give families like the Steiners and the Adlers their livelihood. The Enlightenment also introduced important internal changes to Jewish belief, and it needs to be stressed that the Jewish community in the Josephine period and after was by no means homogenous. Three different strands of belief now offered themselves to Prague Jews (Demetz 1997: 281f.), and Steiner was heir to each: firstly, traditional orthodoxy; secondly the Frankist path, a mystical way that followed the Kabbalist false Messiah, Sabbatai Ṣevi; and thirdly the direction proposed by Moses Mendelssohn, the Enlightenment thinker who inaugurated Jewish emancipation. Although Steiner was initially cut off from each of these lines, his own, reinvented Judaism oscillates between Rabbinic Law, kabbalism, and rationalism.

Mendelssohnian Enlightenment and the various Josephine changes created the political, legal, religious and social preconditions for the process of assimilation which now set in during the nineteenth century, and eventually released an unprecedented wealth of talent – scholarly, scientific and artistic not to mention enterpreneurial skills – into the gradually modernising yet declining world of Austria-Hungary. A watershed came in 1848, when the proclamation of the first Austrian basic law introduced equality; in 1852, Jews were allowed to leave the Ghetto; and they subsequently achieved full citizenship rights in 1867 (Haumann 1990: 159). However, because at first the Jews tended to adopt German and not Czech as their language, their assimilation into the local community met with resistance; this was aggravated by the fact that the upper-class Prague Jews were disproportionately involved in the rapid modernisation which was turning Bohemia into the most advanced region in the Monarchy: traditional anti-Jewish opinion was exacerbated by a class struggle (Haumann 1990: 159). The problem was further complicated by the fact that just as the Jews were entering the civic arena, the Czechs themselves were asserting their identity against the German speakers in Bohemia and Moravia, and were setting out on their own path towards self-determination. Enlightenment emancipation – contrary to the Enlightenment's optimistic expectations – entailed a conflict between contemporaneously emancipating groups. This paradox was never fully resolved, as Steiner himself was to recognise more astutely than most. The late nineteenth century witnessed numerous assaults on the Jews, culminating in the notorious case of an alleged ritual murder – the Hilsner affair (Kieval 1988: 73-74, 79) – in 1899. An economic and cultural divide opened between the more successful, German-speaking Jews and their poorer brethren, who opted for the Czech language. This resulted in a dilemma. The former, even when tolerated by German-speakers, were often opposed by the Czechs, while the latter generally remained unacceptable to both other groups. This division contributed to a serious loss of shared Jewish identity. Out of this, two new options emerged, both of which also shaped Steiner. On the one hand, Czech social democracy preached toleration; and on the other, Martin Buber's ideas took root among the Prague Zionists, emphasising dialogue, mediation, and spiritual renewal.

Steiner was deeply influenced by these patterns. His paternal family came from Tachov in Western Bohemia. His mother's family was from Prague. His father fought in the First World War and never fully recovered from his experiences, which included fighting on the notorious Italian Isonzo front. When Franz was three years old, his sister Suse was born, by all accounts a talented but difficult child. In a series of photographs of Suse in her teens, taken by the Czech avant-garde photographer František Drtikol, she appears as an attractive, thoughtful, wilful girl. Steiner doted on her. When she succumbed to an infection and suddenly died in 1932, he was heartbroken. Her death was the first of the many blows which were to give his life an ultimately tragic pattern. He regularly spoke about Suse to his closest friends, even late in life, and a large number of photographs of her survive in his estate. Shortly after Steiner's own, equally sudden death, Iris Murdoch poignantly recalled Suse in her diary: '20th anniversary of Franz's sister. Agony!' (Ms 1952-53: 3).

Steiner's family spoke German at home, although they could also speak Czech, and were fully assimilated to the bourgeois milieu typical of Prague Jewry. His parents did not practise Judaism, but Franz received a religious education at school, and so also came into contact with Jewish ritual and with the world of the synagogue. By trade, his father was a small businessman. In the mid-1920s he bought a shop at the centre of Prague selling waxed cloth, leather goods, and linoleum. Later he moved to Dlouhá ulice, and from Autumn 1934 the family lived on the top floor of the Sušický Palais. This provided them with a relatively solid financial foundation, enough to pay for Franz to travel, to enjoy a university education and to begin academic life as a freelance scholar. It was only in exile that Steiner began to suffer hardship. As to his views, his father tended to atheism. Politically, he was a social democrat. By all accounts he and his wife were an educated, well-read, and humane couple. In later life his father became an ideal figure for Steiner. Writing to Paul Bruell in 1947 he praises his father's 'strict logic and boundless shyness' (Fleischli 1970: 9). His finest, most moving poem, 'Prayer in the Garden', which is written as a meditation on the destruction of European Jewry, commem- orates the birthday of Steiner's father, and remembers the man as 'the noblest earthly presence ever shown to me' (Steiner 1992: 83).

Steiner's liberal family background enabled him to develop those interests that were to shape his career at a relatively early stage in his life. His childhood passion for reading never left him. In his autobio- graphical poem, *Eroberungen* (*Conquests*, see Volume II, pp. 249-66, below), reading is one of the earliest memories he recalls:

> On either side of an open book
> The hours of the day fell away.
>
> (*Conquests*, II, 'Memories', l.14f.)

Among the books that the young Steiner devoured, travel writing had a prominent place, including works by Nansen and Sven Hedin, and it is presumably to this early childhood interest that the first stir- rings of his anthropological interests can be traced. In the *Conquests* he recalls Robinson Crusoe, a figure who was to accompany Steiner throughout his life and provide him with a point of reference in his personal mythology. In *Conquests*, he singles out Robinson Crusoe's experience of solitude, his merging with his new environment, and what Steiner takes to be the growth of Crusoe's 'piety':

> He had a lot to tell:
> How, many years ago, he had been hurled
> By black storms onto a land he feared
> That then became his own.
> How he grew together with the wilderness.
> 'That feathered tree, for example,
> Is a proven friend.
> We both love the raging monkey in the branches.'
> And he sighed, the sufferer:
> 'I did not sail in vain.
> You make me pious.'
>
> (*Conquests*, II, 'Memories', l.18ff.)

Steiner does not offer an exact reproduction of *Robinson Crusoe* but transforms the story as a living myth. The youthful fascination with dis- tant places and vegetation recorded here prefigures the later Steiner's botanical and anthropological concerns. His emphasis on Robinson Crusoe's piety foreshadows the subsequent closeness between Steiner's religious thought and his scholarship. Indeed, Defoe's novel sets out a leading idea in Steiner's work. Steiner's mature relativisation of Western ideas in his aphorisms and anthropology is indebted to views expressed in literary accounts of non-Western civilisations. Thus, in the chapter entitled 'I see the Shore Spread with Bones', Crusoe reflects on the barbarism of the cannibals and withholds condemnation of their non-Christian behaviour when he asks himself:

> What authority or call I had to pretend to be judge and executioner upon these men as criminals, whom Heaven had thought fit for so many ages to suffer unpunished to go on, and to be, as it were, the executioners of His judgements one upon another. ...
>
> When I had considered this a little, it followed necessarily that I was certainly in the wrong in it; that these people were not murderers in the sense that I had before condemned them in my thoughts; any more than those Christians were murderers, who often put to death the prisoners taken in battle; or more frequently, upon many occasions, put whole troops of men to the sword, without giving quarter, though they may threw down their arms and submit. (Defoe [1719] 1994: 168f.)

The 'piety' that Steiner's poem finds exemplified in Defoe's narrative is no simple Christian faith – for that could be learned at home. What Crusoe has brought back from the 'wilderness' – and presumably what Steiner began to learn from Defoe in childhood – is a respect for values that lie beyond his own experience: the cannibals have no Christian values; their actions must be judged according to a different framework. Besides recognising the validity inherent in native lore, Defoe affords the intellectual correlative a hearing: namely that Christian values may look different from the cannibal's viewpoint. It is impossible to overlook the irony with which Defoe presents the virtuous Christians who 'often put to death in battle' and 'give no quarter' even though their opponents 'may threw [sic] down their arms and submit'. Defoe's contrasting of native with Christian virtue is one of the ultimate lessons that his hero brings back from the island. This attitude, as will be seen shortly, subsequently entered Steiner's anthropological writing, notably *Taboo*, in his own characteristic technique: the reciprocal subordination of opposite values. In Steiner's *Taboo*, just as native ideas are analysed in a Western critique, Western ideas undergo an implicit critique in the light of native practice. There are various possible sources for this technique, which Steiner will have encountered at different points in his career. Views similar to those which Steiner will have met in *Robinson Crusoe* also figure in another favourite of his, *Moby Dick*. Steiner's copy of *Moby Dick*, which bears his signature and the date 1941, has many reading marks, among them one against the penultimate paragraph of Chapter X, 'A Bosom Friend'. The marked passage contains the following rumination:

I was a good Christian: born and bred in the bosom of the infallible Presbyterian church. How then could I unite with this wild idolator in worshipping his piece of wood? But what is worship? Thought I ... And what is the will of God? Now, Queequeg is my fellow man. And what do I wish that this Queequeg would do to me? Why, unite with me in my particular Presbyterian form of worship. Consequently, I must then unite with him in his; ergo, I must turn idolator. So I kindled the shavings; helped prop up the innocent little idol. (Melville ([1851] 1938: 73)

The importance Steiner attached to *Moby Dick* can perhaps be seen from his lending his own copy to Mary Douglas after the War. Like Defoe, Melville recognises the comparability of Christian and idolatrous practices. Steiner's earliest reading, including *Robinson Crusoe*, reinforced by later books, clearly provided his mature work with a significant axis, even though it was to take quite some time for his religious views to emerge, and the technique of reciprocal subordination to develop into a highly effective intellectual tool. Before that came about, science and Marxism provided his world with its chief spiritual content.

Another formative experience of Steiner's childhood was his fascination with biology. Botany, zoology and entomology became lifelong interests. In the *Conquests*, he recalls his botanising as follows:

Wandering breathless along the scorched edge of the field:
The green butterfly-net fluttering above his head.
And every butterfly carried on its outstretched wings
Coloured marks, the warm eyes of life.

(*Conquests*, II, 'Memories', l.43ff.)

The childish delight at the chase, so charmingly evoked in these lines, was backed up by a growing scientific interest. His biographer Alfons Fleischli notes that Steiner spent his summer holidays studying caterpillars, butterflies, moths, beetles, and other insects. In botany, he was particularly interested in mosses and lichens (Fleischli 1970: 11). Biology was eventually to become Steiner's preferred subject of study at the university, but his poor eyesight prevented him from using a microscope, and forced him to look elsewhere when deciding on a career.

In 1920, Steiner entered the German State Gymnasium in Štepánská Street in the centre of Prague. It had earlier been attended by such well-known writers as Max Brod and Franz Werfel. In 1925 the school merged with the German State Gymnasium in Jindřiška Street. Attending the same class was Wolf Salus, son of the well-known Prague German poet Hugo Salus. Franz and Wolf Salus became firm friends. Hugo Salus had been a friend and mentor of Rilke, and an influence on Rilke's early poetry, and one senses that through his early friendship with Wolf Salus, himself an aspiring poet (Brod 1966: 71-3), Steiner was beginning to gain entry to the literary world which was subsequently such an important part of his life. However, literature did not immediately play a role in Steiner's life at school. In the early 1920s, he joined a group of *Wandervögel* – the popular German youth movement, broadly comparable to Baden Powell's Boy Scouts, though lacking the formal organisation of the international scouting movement. The particular brand of ideas that Steiner now embraced is described by H.G. Adler in his unpublished 'Letter to Dr Rabin'. (Chaim Rabin, a linguist and a Zionist of great learning, was a colleague of Steiner's in Oxford, and after Steiner's death, by which time Rabin had accepted a post at the Hebrew University in Jerusalem, H.G. Adler took the opportunity of an enquiry by Rabin to write a long biographical assessment of his friend.) Commenting on Steiner's adoption of the *Wandervögel's* youthful ideals, Adler writes:

> He took the ideals very seriously and developed them according to his own ideas and took them to an extreme. A 'Natural Life' was what he wanted. He combined the opportunities that the hiking and summer camps gave him with his own scientific interests and so became a quite idiosyncratic member of the group. His social and socialist enthusiasms, which he carefully guarded from sentimentality, decided his life and his future. He even went so far as to reject all industrial products. He wanted to make his own equipment out of natural produce and almost went over to giving up paper and writing entirely on the bark taken from birch trees. (H.G. Adler Ms 1953: 3r.)

Steiner's love of country walking and hiking dates to this period and continued into his time in England. Poems like 'Dream of Loch Lomond' (Steiner 1992: 5) reflect his love of the countryside, and his English colleagues knew Steiner from this side, too. Ian Cunnison first met him when rambling in the Lake District and their conversation then convinced Cunnison to study anthropology at Oxford (Cunnison: PC). However, the ideals that Steiner developed as a *Pfadfinder* could not find fulfilment within the movement itself, and he left it in 1926 and joined the *Roter Studentenbund* (Red Student Union). He later joined another left-wing organisation, though it is not clear which. It may have been the *Kommunistische Jugend* (Communist Youth Organisation), or it may have been the Communist Party itself. Years later in a letter to the editor and critic Rudolf Hartung, Steiner recalled the period of his political activity 'when I ran from meeting to meeting and knew Marx and Trotsky by heart' (Fleischli 1970: 14). In his 'Letter to Dr Rabin', H.G. Adler analyses the various facets of Steiner's thinking and behaviour in his late teens. First, he notes Steiner's idealism, which corresponded largely to Bukharin's thought. His lead ideas included social justice, free love, the abolition of money, and common ownership of all property. Secondly, Adler notes how Steiner now turned to older people, including workers, foreigners, and other outsiders ('fantastics'). Thirdly, he confirms Steiner's intensive study of Marxism, in which he displayed his characteristic thoroughness. As he later made it his business to read everything written on his research interests, he now read his way through all the major Marxist classics and many minor works, too. He read Marx himself, the pre-Marxist thinkers, as well as Lenin and Trotsky. His reading opened up a perspective on sociology, and developed the interest in distant peoples that had originated in his earlier reading of travel literature. Among the cultures and subjects that fascinated him were China and the Chinese Civil War, on which he began a study which has since been lost, as well as Mexico, India, colonialism, and the problems faced by Blacks (H.G. Adler Ms 1953: 3v.). Although his Marxist phase only lasted about two years, the experience proved decisive. His future sense of political action and social justice would go hand-in-hand with sympathy for politically oppressed peoples and minorities. His interest in Marx himself also continued. He planned to give a major lecture series on Marx at Oxford, but was dissuaded by Evans-Pritchard, who instead suggested the subject of *Taboo*. More generally, it was the encounter with Marxism which opened a window on the social sciences for Steiner, and so eventually led him to study social anthropology. However, Steiner cut his links with all Marxist organisations in 1930. According to a letter Steiner wrote to Hartung, the event is recorded in a poem, which he composed in March 1930, and originally entitled 'Turning back in the spring'. Here, Steiner asks 'Why did I argue with people' and longs to 'forget' himself in the forest. Typically, the decision to break with his political past was taken during the course of several hikes in the Bohemian woods (Fleischli 1970: 13).

The turn Steiner's thought now took was towards mysticism in both its Western and Eastern varieties, an interest which actually appears to have begun during Steiner's Marxist phase. He read the seventeenth-century poet Angelus Silesius and the German mystical writer Jacob Böhme. The latter interest is remarkable, though perhaps more understandable in the light of Martin Buber's choice of Böhme (along with Nicolas of Cusa) as the subject of his dissertation (Schmidt 1991: 39–44). Steiner's lifelong passion for Eastern religions was kindled by his reading of the *Bhagavad Gita* – his boyhood copy of the book survives in his literary estate today, inscribed in an ornate hand with his signature and the date 'Prag Januar 1927'. The volume is handbound in leather – almost certainly by H.G. Adler's father, the bookbinder Emil Adler – and is finely tooled in gold, with marbled end-papers of red, yellow, and blue on a purple ground. The Introduction was removed before binding, as is also indicated on the contents page. The edition is in the standard and highly popular Diederich's series, the attractively yellow-bound *Religiöse Stimmen der Völker*, but Steiner's new binding lends the volume the overwhelming impression of a precious book, redesigned according to the seventeen-year-old's somewhat mystical taste, and cherished as a sacred object. Over ten years later at Oxford, the *Gita* was still Steiner's favourite book (Frank Ms 1964). Steiner also encountered Chinese religious texts in the same series. His copy of Kung Futse is dated 'IX 1928', and his heavily annotated copy of Lao Tse 'Prag XII 1928'. We can safely assume that Steiner's Marxist phase, which on his own account ended in 1930, overlapped with his early interest in world religions. In later life also, political and religious themes were to coexist in Steiner's thinking. The specific interest in Eastern religions, however, took its most concrete form not in Steiner's scholarship, but in the religious syncretism evident in the autobiographical *Conquests*, where Buddhist, Taoist, Jewish, and Muslim ideas are combined (J. Adler 1994a: 151ff.).

The later 1920s also mark the beginnings of Steiner's literary interests. Fleischli notes that among his favourite authors were E.T.A. Hoffmann, several of whose books still survive in his library from those years, and the Russian novelists, notably Dostoyevsky, who enjoyed immense popularity at that time. The young Steiner also explored the poetry of Rilke, who became a lifelong favourite, and the German Jewish mystical poet Alfred Mombert, who had a major influence on his early poetry. He also appears to have discovered Kafka at an early stage: his well-worn, pencil-marked copy of the first edition of *Das Schloß* (The Castle), published in 1926, is inscribed 'Prag Januar 1927' – the same date as his *Gita*. Given that Steiner's early literary tastes – with the possible exception of Mombert – exerted a lifelong hold over his imagination, we may ascribe to them a considerable formative effect. The later poet and anthropologist will have met several mature interests in his adolescent favourites: Hoffmann, Mombert, and the mature Rilke share a common fascination with myth as a fruitful mode for re-casting modern values; Adalbert Stifter, the nineteenth-century Austrian prose-writer who celebrates the *Böhmerwald* region where the young Steiner spent his summers as a *Pfadfinder*, displays a scientifically exact eye for the linkage between specific landscapes and local people; this is allied to a morality both biblical in its austerity and humanist in its generosity; whilst Dostoyevsky and Kafka exhibit the incisive dual focus which connects a guilt-ridden inner world to a corrupt political scene. These diverse strands seem to have merged in Steiner's thinking as late as 1942-45 when his poetry and anthropology took a decisive new turn.

Looking back over the experiences of Steiner's early Prague years H.G. Adler summarises his character and indicates how fully the future anthropologist and poet had developed even before he embarked on his studies. His summary indicates a complex, multi-faceted figure, whose personality encompassed the contradictory extremes of scientific analysis and religious mysticism, theology and sensuality:

To the natural sciences he owed his precision, his love of detail, his reliability and self-control in his own work and writing, as well as the cool critique of his own achievements and those of others; to Marxism, which he first extended and then gave up as completely untenable, he owed his sense of social, historical and philosophical connexions within a universal mathesis, which he saw before him in his mind's eye though he never developed it systematically – his deep mistrust of systems preserved him from that; he also owed to it his interest in people and human relations and in practically all peoples of the world; he did not wish to evaluate different peoples or play them off against one another, but to understand and explain them in their own uniqueness; finally he owed to Marxism the unprejudiced freedom with which he carefully confronted both natural peoples and the high cultures of the East and the West as an observer; and to mysticism and religion he owed his personal relationship to all phenomena, his imaginative penetration and overview of them, the actual essence of his art, which even when he was not treating religious themes he always understood as a religious act. The more mature Franz became, the more these elements interpenetrated and their interplay can be seen in his most successful achievements. He also tried to nourish his relationships with women from the same roots, but many unhappy circumstances and an often overpowering sensuality largely prevented him from doing so. (H.G. Adler Ms 1953: 6v.)

Some characteristics of Steiner's later anthropological writings – such as his scientific exactness – are apparent here; others – like his mysticism – only become clear in his poetry and aphorisms. The idea that Steiner possessed an inexpressible, *'universal mathesis'* which unified these contradictions, a hidden core at the centre of his strivings, is both an immensely suggestive construct for grasping his work, and a tantalising, ultimately unspecifiable idea. We will return to this concept of a 'universal mathesis' later in our discussion.

Student Days in Prague and Jerusalem

In magnificent nights
I spoke to the palms about my girl.
Sure, they will forget me. but i,
How can i escape their scraggy song?
My dreams will leave me,
And go back to Jerusalem.
'Farewell to Jerusalem' (Steiner 2000)

After completing his schooling at the Gymnasium in June 1928 with his *Matura*, Steiner enrolled as an examinable student at the German University of Prague in the Autumn of 1928. Somewhat to the surprise of his friends, who expected him to study ethnology as his main subject, he specialised in comparative philology with special reference to Semitic languages. His choice of philology may have been prompted partly by his growing interest in Ancient Greek during his last year at school (H.G. Adler Ms 1953: 4v.), and partly because there was no Chair in Sociology in the German University at Prague at that time (Fleischli 1970: 14); there was only a single Professor of Ethnology, Professor Paudler, who had very few students. Indology, another subject in which Steiner was interested initially, soon receded for academic purposes, while ethnology became increasingly important to him. He studied it as a minor subject with Paudler (with special reference to Eastern Europe, Asia Minor, Siberia and the Arctic), and also studied *Völkerpsychologie* as had Malinowski in Leipzig two decades earlier (Thornton with Skalník 1993: 14). Simultaneously he took courses in Siberian ethnology and in Turkish studies as an external student at the Czech-language Charles University of Prague (with Professor Jan Rypka, a specialist in Greek, Turkish and Persian philology). Among the languages he studied more or less assiduously apart from Classical and Modern Arabic were Hebrew, Turkish, Armenian, Persian, the Malayan languages, English, French and Russian. In later life at Oxford, though some of these dropped away, he was still acquainted with an extraordinary variety of languages: aside from the classical ones – which in his case meant Hebrew, Greek, and Latin – he knew German, English, French, Spanish, Italian, and Czech; he spoke Yiddish well; he had different degrees of competence in six other Slavonic languages, including Russian; he continued to speak colloquial Arabic, he gained a reading competence in Scandinavian languages and Dutch, and – to judge by his notebooks – he was teaching himself to read Chinese. Thoughts on etymology, comparative philology, and linguistics form an integral part of his scholarship and, as we shall shortly have occasion to note, appear to have formed a point of departure for his thinking on specific topics.

In 1930-31 Steiner interrupted his studies in Prague and spent a year at the Hebrew University of Jerusalem in Palestine, where he studied modern Arabic in the School of Oriental Studies. The idea of a Hebrew University in Palestine went back to the origins of the Zionist movement, having been discussed at the first Zionist Congress in 1897 and endorsed by Zionist conferences in Vienna and Minsk in 1902 (Gilbert 1998: 8). By 1914 money had been raised to buy a site on Mount Scopus 'overlooking the Dome of the Rock and the Dead Sea' (Gilbert 1998: 29). The University was eventually founded in 1918 and officially opened on Mount Scopus in 1925. For a young German-speaking Jewish scholar, studying in Jerusalem must have made good sense as an academic decision. Steiner also used the opportunity of the trip to pay a brief visit to Egypt and a more extensive one to Greece and Cyprus. In Jerusalem, after staying briefly with an Arab family, he was allegedly forced to move out by the British authorities (H.G. Adler Ms 1953: 5) and then stayed with the Jewish philosopher Shmuel Hugo Bergman, a schoolfriend of Franz Kafka, and a lifelong supporter of Buber. Bergman himself does not appear to have taken Steiner seriously as an intellectual at this time. In a letter to Alfons Fleischli of 1967, he commented: 'For me, Franz in those days was a charming young student, full of good humour, but I had no idea of his later significance' (Fleischli 1970: 15). Bergman's son Michael, however, formed a more positive picture – and his account explains why the older man found little to commend in his young guest. Writing in English to Fleischli, Michael Bergman remembers: 'He made upon me a very profound impression .... He did not, however, pursue his studies very actively. He believed that like a person afloat on the ocean, one should let life direct one without coercing life into a predetermined direction' (1970: 15). Bergman's influence on Steiner was long-standing. Steiner maintained contact with him, mainly via a correspondence with Bergman's wife Martha, until the end of his life. After the Second World War, Bergman himself wrote Steiner a highly appreciative letter on his poem 'Gebet im Garten' (Prayer in the Garden) and invited Steiner to return to the Hebrew University as a guest lecturer to speak on British social anthropology – a visit that never came about, presumably for lack of funding (Bergman Ms 1952). By that date, at least, the older man must have formed a better opinion of his former guest. As to Bergman's effect on Steiner, we can well imagine that the philosopher, who had published on both physics and theology, was a good friend of Albert Einstein, and had been an intimate of Steiner's most admired author, Franz Kafka, could have exerted a considerable fascination on the young student. At the Bergman home, Steiner could have seen for himself one of the the earliest examples of Kafka's handwriting (Wagenbach 1958: 50; Bergman 1969: 7), and listened to the conversation of a man who had debated philosophical, political and Zionist ideas with Kafka since their schooldays (Wagenbach 1958: 60-63; 107), and whose own thinking since his Prague days had developed aspects of Buber's thought. Bergman, before he migrated to Palestine, had been one of the central figures in the development of Prague Zionism (Kieval 1988: 99-103; 113-116). His importance for Steiner may well have manifested itself in his developing attitude to Judaism in the particular form of Zionism to which Steiner now felt drawn. If Steiner's later Jewish inwardness ultimately recalls Buber's call for a spiritual revival (Friedmann 1988: 130), his synthesis of Oriental religions in his poetry also follows Bergman, 'the great syncretist among his colleagues in Jerusalem' (Kluback 1988: 134). At Bergman's house in Jersualem, the young Steiner may also have come into contact with Bergman's plans concerning cooperation between

Indians and Jews (Bergman 1985: 292) and will have encountered the thinking of Brit Shalom, which met in Bergman's home. According to Bergman's diary, around the time when Steiner may have been staying, Brit Shalom meetings took place there on 25 October and 2 November 1930 (Bergman 1985: 316 and 319). Those present included Gershom Scholem and J.L. Magnes. Brit Shalom's proposals for rapprochement between Jews and Arabs are subsequently reflected in Steiner's own earliest publication, 'Orientpolitik' (Volume II, pp. 107-11, below). An 'Appendix' on Brit Shalom which appeared in the *Jüdische Rundschau* for 8 July 1927 explains its policy:

> The organisation begins from the premiss that the future of Palestine and the creation of a national homeland [for the Jews] can only be achieved on the basis of harmonious collaboration between Jews and Arabs. To this belongs – to start with quite non-political matters – getting to know each other and a friendly, non-aggressive attitude. The belief in the necessity of understanding and cooperation has to take root among both peoples. Brit Shalom regards propagating this view as one of its main tasks. ... (Bergman 1985: 229)

Steiner's first steps as a political writer follow the line here taken by Bergman and his influential friends. Besides a political orientation, Bergman may also have offered the young Steiner a new focus for his scholarship. Importantly, Bergman offered an ideal of comparative study. In an essay written for the silver jubilee of the Hebrew University, he stresses the pivotal role of Judaism as the spiritual centre of the University's activities, but pleads for comparative religion to be established there, too:

> Is not a Jewish university that fails to study the fundamentals of Comparative Religion something in the nature of a contradiction in terms? We do not teach the fundamentals of religion in general: we do not give give our students the opportunity to become acquainted with the great religions of the world, and to contrast our own Judaism with the other great religions – those of India, Christianity and Islam. An Institute of Religious Studies, composed of several Chairs, is for us an essential need .... (Bergman 1952: 176)

It is perhaps not going too far to see in this model of Judaism – a Judaic spiritual centre surrounded by the comparative study of world religions – the same pattern that Steiner employed in his mature thinking. Steiner's poetry and private writings similarly revolve around Judaism, but *Conquests*, his aphorisms, and especially his scholarship afford an equal moral place for non-Jewish religions as part of his wider intellectual scheme. One may imagine the effect of Bergman's teachings in the light of Kieval's description of Bergman's former Jewish circle in Prague, the Bar Kochbar group:

[Bar Kochbar] interpreted cultural Zionism to mean that [an] upheaval was to transform assimilated Jews into national Jews [by means of] a personal, spiritual revolt. It was to take place within the consciousness of the individual, stripping one, as it were, of one's assimilationist personality and rendering one for the first time culturally active and creative. (Kieval 1988: 106)

The more immediately obvious impact that the visit to Palestine had on Steiner was, then, on his self-understanding as a Jew, and on the development of his Zionism. According to Fleischli, the Jerusalem experience led Steiner to regard himself as 'an Oriental born in the West' (1970: 15). The view of the Jews as Orientals was (of course) a common one, enshrined in both the popular and the sociological thought of Steiner's day. In a letter to her sister of 13 May 1939, the great Jewish poetess Gertrud Kolmar, who perished in Auschwitz, observed when considering where she might escape that she was a *verhinderte Asiatin* (a hindered Asiatic) (1970: 25); and for the economic historian Werner Sombart, the Oriental character of the Jews was axiomatic (1911: 340ff.). Steiner's own Orientalism was quite distinct from such accounts of a homogeneous Jewish 'race' based on supposedly immutable biological continuities that derived either from the Jews' origins in the East or from Buber's different notion of Jewish 'blood' (Friedman 1988:134). The former type of Orientalism entailed recognising fixed biological and behavioural characteristics which survived in assimilation. Whilst accepting the historical origins of the Jewish people, Steiner's own belief had nothing to do with biological 'race', and is perhaps closer to the more conceptual side of Buber's belief in the Jews as Orientals. However, unlike the early Buber, Steiner's positive acceptance of Jewish identity depended on embracing religious orthodoxy and, with Bergman, the Hebrew language (Friedmann 1988: 261). Steiner distanced himself from essential features of Buber's philosophy, too, as in the following scathing remark directed against Buber's 'I and Thou':

> God does not reveal himself in dialogue. He communicates with man. This gives rise to two misunderstandings.
> 1. The belief that God is human.
> 2. The belief that the human monologue is a dialogue.
> Revelation cannot be answered. (1988: 86f.)

Steiner tried progressively to dissociate himself from 'Western' views and urged Jews to identify with their Oriental character and to seek solidarity with other Orientals. The various tensions intrinsic in this progression are examined in our Introduction to Volume II (pp. 16-28, below); however, *in nuce* they are early variations on problems that will later be addressed by (and to) post-colonial critics located (either physically or intellectually) in the West and its traditions. Steiner's 'Orientpolitik' (1936), although written after his Marxist phase, draws upon linked ideas of modernisation, agricultural innovation and education close to the heart of many Jewish settlers in Palestine before statehood. He seeks common cause with Muslim Arab modernisers. By the time of his essay 'On the Process of Civilisation' of 1944 and the 'Letter to Mr Gandhi' of 1946, Steiner's views on a shared Oriental identity – now opposed to the modernising 'process of civilisation' in the West – have hardened, at least on an ideal (quasi mythological) level. Like the early Buber, he links Jewish and Indian religions, albeit without Buber's sense of competition (Friedman 1988: 135f.). However, unresolved tensions remain. Although Steiner was sympathetic to a wide range of religious expression, one searches in vain in his writings for positive appreciation of two such traditions, between which he seems to find similarities: Protestantism (especially in its German form) and Islam (particularly in its more fundamental forms). Given his own ethnicity and religion, the pairing is strongly motivated. As Steiner's Oriental solidarity is expressed less in a modernising context, so Muslim Arabs seem to disappear from his analysis. And, despite his expressed antipathy to Western individualism, his own analytic tools (the logic, science and rationality he stresses) were transmitted to him via a context which is the same as that within which Western ideas of individual rights, freedom of expression and conscience (*and* their antitheses) were developed. All this lay in the future. H.G. Adler sums up the immediate effect of Steiner's year in Palestine as follows:

> He returned from Jerusalem a changed and a happy man. ... Franz now emphasised his Jewishness, but it took some time before he could accommodate his new thoughts and feelings to his actual nature. ... At first the contradictions between his origins and his previous views and his newly-gained spirituality were apparent. This occasionally manifested itself in illogical behaviour and intolerance towards others. But gradually he managed to achieve a highly individual synthesis of his own private nature and received religion. He favoured a strictly traditional understanding of Judaism, disliked liberal tendencies, or at least found them dubious, although in practice he hardly kept to Jewish laws except in occasional sallies, when he observed individual ordinances. However, he never glossed this over, but felt it to be a weakness. He considered it beyond his power to resolve the matter. He never attended Synagogue regularly, and only began to see the value of attending during his Oxford days (from 1939). In his later years he recited the daily prayers (more in his heart than aloud) and uttered many blessings. He always considered his Jewish education to be inadequate, although he acquired considerable knowledge during repeated bouts of study. (H.G. Adler Ms 1953: 5v-6r)

To contextualise this phase of Steiner's development historically, it may be seen in the light of the Zionist cultural renewal promoted by

Ahad Ha-Am and developed by Buber, which had such a strong following among Prague Jews, though Steiner's orthodoxy and political Zionism distanced him from this group, bringing him closer to scholars like his revered model, Gershom Scholem. The experience of Palestine also had a decided effect on Steiner's scholarly development. As Fleischli observes, he was prompted to find a new theoretical basis for his scholarship that would not simply impose Western categories and understandings on the East. However, before this insight could bear fruit, Steiner had to embark on a second period as a student, this time as an ethnologist.

In 1935 Steiner completed his studies in Prague with a short, and, we are advised, not very distinguished thesis (Schabert: PC), on word-formation in Arabic, entitled *Studien zur arabischen Wurzelgeschichte* (Studies on the History of Arabic Roots). The viva became the occasion for one of the earliest of the many stories Steiner liked to tell about himself. It involves his apparent ignorance of the Russian island of Sakhalin, which lies to the north of Japan; this nineteenth-century penal colony was well known at the time, not least as the subject of a monograph by Chekhov, and was an obvious viva topic given Steiner's interest in Siberian ethnology, but his chronic exam fever made him forget the name entirely. H.G. Adler reports:

> The chief examiner was Grohmann, the expert in Ethiopian studies, whom Franz did not like very much. He put him off so much that Slotty, the kindly Professor of General Philology and Indo-European, who was the co-examiner, had to calm him down. He offered Steiner a cigarette in the middle of the viva with the words: 'Here you are, Steiner, have a smoke, then everything will go alright.' Everything went well for a while, but then it was the turn of the ethnologist, Paudler, of whom Franz was particularly fond, to examine him. He was a touching and slightly confused fellow who was even more frightened of the exam than Franz himself. Paudler wanted to know something about Sakhalin, but Franz said nothing. ... Then Paudler very nervously said: 'Tell me something about the fauna. You must know something about the animals on Sakhalin.' Franz remained silent. Almost pleading, Paudler asked: 'So do tell us, Mr Steiner, what animals live on Sakhalin?' At last Franz made his reply: 'Camels!' Paudler reached for his head and called out in horror: 'Sakhalin and the camels!' After many extraordinary somersaults, the viva came to a successful conclusion. (H.G. Adler Ms 1953: 5r)

The Steiner of these early Prague years already appears to have divided his life into distinct segments: academic, Zionist, literary, and sexual. His habit of living in mutually exclusive circles, which became more accentuated in his later years, makes it difficult for the biographer to reconstruct his life – especially with regard to his lovers, the identities of several of whom survive only as unidentifiable snapshots among his papers. The trait of seeking to balance seemingly incompatible ideas, apparent in the intellectual sphere of his life, translated socially into 'an oppressive lack of coordination between apparently disparate social provinces' (H.G. Adler Ms 1953: 7r.ff). This abiding adolescent feature seems to have predisposed Steiner towards theories of a highly formal stripe: 'culture circles' ethnology, which seeks to account for the co-presence of associated cultural elements that differ in origin, and Simmelian formal sociology, which seeks to explain why the same individual may behave so differently in the various 'social provinces' of his life. As we shall see, he seeks to resolve these issues in *Conquests* (see Volume II, pp. 249-66 below).

According to H.G. Adler's testimony (little other documentation survives) we know that Steiner enjoyed an active social life in Prague, building up a large circle of friends and the beginnings of a reputation as a poet in the city's somewhat fading establishment as well as among the younger artists. In the view of Zdenek Vašiček (PC), whereas Jewish intellectuals in Prague until 1914 to 1918 tended to adopt German as their cultural *ambiente*, after the First World War and with the foundation of Czechoslovakia, a greater number of Jews followed a cultural trend inaugurated in the later nineteenth century (Kieval 1988: 19; 27ff.) and assimilated more into the Czech context, with the result that the groups to which Steiner turned tended to be smaller and more marginal than the equivalent circles of German-speaking Jews before the War. This might explain the rather mixed groupings Steiner became involved with, though it must be said that in Prague, the rearguard was inextricably entangled with the avant-garde, as can be seen in the tensions between Kafka's conservative prose style and his innovative themes, or in the writings of Paul Leppin – according to Max Brod, the central figure in the German literary scene in Prague in the half-generation before Kafka (Brod 1966: 67). Thus, Leppin's novel *Severins Gang in die Finsternis* (Severin's Path into Darkness, 1914) disconcertingly mixes neo-Romantic, decadent imagery with eroticism, pornography, symbolism, dreams, astute psychology and vividly observed details in an almost surrealist, kaleidoscopic manner, anticipating Breton and Hrabal. This heady cocktail exaggeratedly reflects the world that fashioned Steiner's interests.

Steiner's first steps as a Prague writer anticipate the pattern of his later progress in England as an anthropologist. In both contexts, he gravitated towards the leading figures of his day, without fully capitalising on his recognition by becoming a public figure. In Prague, he entered the leading artistic circles and made friends with several colourful figures, including some of the best-known men of letters. He had long enjoyed links with the establishment through his schoolfriend Wolf Salus, whose father, Hugo, was a grand old man of Prague German letters, a poet whose skilful verse – published in a dozen volumes between 1898 and 1924 – exudes a melancholic lyricism. Hugo Salus, as Max Brod records, was a central figure among the Prague writers who first came into prominence two generations before Kafka and Brod (Brod 1966: 67). Steiner also met Max Brod himself, Kafka's friend and perhaps the central figure of his own generation, as well as the celebrated Prague Expressionist poet Franz Werfel, albeit Steiner distanced himself from Werfel and others, despising what he regarded as their shallow pretensions. In his own generation, apart from Salus's son, Steiner also had contact with the son of Kafka's friend and correspondent, the poet Oskar Baum, and Paul Leppin Jr. More surprisingly, perhaps, he made friends with Paul Leppin senior, author of both the aforementioned *Severins Gang in die Finsternis* and the suitably shocking satanic novel on the constrictions imposed by Christianity, *Daniel Jesus* (1905). Though Leppin's own days of dancing in drag on bar-tops (Hoffmann 1982: 18) were ending in syphilitic decay, his work enjoyed a revival in the mid-1930s, and Steiner always retained a high opinion of him. In tales like *Das Gespenst der Judenstadt* (The Ghost of the Jewish Town), Leppin's stylistic mastery and subtle evocations of old Prague rise above the rather crass eroticism: in just a few pages, via the tale of the sexually insatiable Johanna from the brothel beside the Synagogue, Leppin vividly evokes the end of the Ghetto and the downfall of old Prague (see Demetz 1982: 33-39). Steiner's career began with readings from his poetry at Fritz Baum's bookshop, and he was a co-founder of the literary circle *Freie Gruppe Prag* (The Prague Free Group), which gave a public poetry reading on 6 December 1929 that was reviewed in the Prague German newspapers, *Prager Presse* and *Prager Tagblatt*. The latter records that the high-point of the evening was a *Moritat* (cabaret song) by Franz Steiner, 'Das Lied von Bettys Strumpf' (The Song of Betty's Stocking), to which Gerta Freund danced most expressively with 'passion' and 'wonderful gestures' (Atze 1998: 13f.)

Noted young sculptors such as Mary Duras (Plichta 1961) and Bernard Reder (Baur 1961) also belonged to Steiner's circle. He became friends with the mystical art deco painter and photographer, František Drtikol, who taught Franz photography and took a series of hitherto unrecognised photographs of Steiner's sister, Suse, and probably Franz himself (Figs 4-5), the former clearly made at the same sitting as several others preserved among Steiner's papers (Fárová 1986: 42). Drtikol was a charismatic personality whose artistic blend of modernism, eroticism and syncretic mysticism cast a spell on young Czechs and Germans alike. In Drtikol, the young Steiner will have met a successful artist who renounced his career as a photographer to pursue his insights into the mystical light of the world – a path illuminated by both Christian and Buddhist imagery. The mystic tendency dominated the work of the Czech poet and prose-writer Emanuel Lešetický [Lešehrad] whose dramatic poem *Planety* from the volume *Most nad světem* (1932) Steiner translated into German as *Die Planeten* and published in 1935. The Czech title page calls the work a 'symphonic triptych' and the collophon refers to it as a 'mystical oratorium'. Lešehrad, the Czech translator of Alfred Mombert (a German Jewish poet who exercised a profound influence on both Steiner and H.G. Adler), was also a noted occultist and wrote a history of secret societies in Bohemia. The action of Lešehrad's symbolic drama of the planets takes place in the 'terrestial sphere' and involves a dialogue between Earth, Night, the Spirit of Dead Humans, and so on. Spiritualism and pathos are the hallmarks of this verse. In Steiner's hands the language possesses a stern nobility (occasionally echoing Goethe's *Faust*) in which the future poet can be recognised. The book was brought out by a noted publisher, Orbis, and the cover was done by a leading avant-garde designer, Jindřich Štyrský (see Primus 1990). Meanwhile, Steiner himself gave another poetry reading in 1933, this time together with his friend, the later scholar and critic, Heinz Politzer (Atze 1998: 17). On this occasion, he read the first act of his play on Ramon Lull – to which we will return (Volume II, pp. 88-89, below) – a work which has not survived, but the theme of which becomes understandable within the mystical Prague context. Altogether, Steiner's friendships, readings, and publications indicate that had it not been for the gathering political dangers, Steiner's career as a young Prague poet seemed assured.

First Ethnological Studies in Vienna and London. Fieldwork in Sub-Carpathian Ruthenia

> *Even to retain a little*
> *Of wandering journeys, countries,*
> *Over which the perfect sun*
> *Rises through fiery planes ...*
>
> Conquests, IV, 'To retain a little'

After completing his studies in Prague, Steiner involuntarily became a 'wanderer'. In order to acquire a more thorough ethnological training than could be obtained at home, and following a pattern of movement typical for Prague Germans, in the autumn of 1935 he went to Vienna to study at the Ethnological Institute, specialising in Siberian ethnology – and it was in Arctic ethnology that he subsequently made his first academic publications (Steiner 1939a, 1941). India and the Arctic were perhaps the regions closest to his heart as a scholar. The former retained its hold chiefly on his religious sensibility and inclined him towards many of his friendships in England. The latter continued to appear in the form of Arctic or sub-Arctic examples in mature writings, e.g. 'On the Process of Civilisation' (Volume II, below). He went to Vienna to study with some of the leading German-speaking ethnologists of the day: attending lectures and classes with Koppers, Father Schmidt and Heine-Geldern. Less typically, perhaps, and indicative of his quickly developing anthropological know-how, just over a year later he moved on via Paris to London to attend Malinowski's seminars at the LSE, and work in the Library of the British Museum, arriving in England in late autumn 1936. He remained until July 1937 and then returned briefly to Prague (Fleischli 1970: 20); after a short holiday at home, he made his first and only field trip, spending a few weeks studying the Gypsies in Sub-Carpathian Ruthenia. Back in Prague, he held his first series of ethnological lectures – an 'Einführung in die Kunstgeschichte der Naturvölker' (Introduction to the History of Art of Primitive Peoples) – in autumn 1937 (Ms 1937a). At about this time, he also wrote his first ethnological study, an introduction to ethnology for young people (Ms 1937b). He stayed at home until the beginning of 1938, when he left again for England. By now, he was beginning to establish himself as a young scholar, and wrote a paper on 'Dog Sacrifices and Parturition Confession, Their Relations to North-Eurasian Beliefs in Reincarnation' which he presented at the Second International Congress of Anthropological and Ethnological Sciences in Copenhagen, 1-6 August 1938 (Ms 1938; 1939b). What should have been a hopeful trip for the aspiring young academic at the threshold of his career was, however, fraught with difficulties, being overshadowed by Munich and the growing threat of a war which Steiner already regarded as inevitable. A Czechoslovak national when he set sail for Copenhagen, he risked being barred from re-entry to the United Kingdom, and had a foretaste of the entrapment that so many of his people, among them his own friends and family, were to suffer. In the event, his return to Britain proved unproblematic, but he never saw Prague, his home, or his parents again. Nor did he ever again have a single, identifiable home. He had entered England as a student, but remained a refugee, unable to emigrate to the United States (where he had an uncle) and tragically incapable of helping his family in Bohemia, who were shortly to be ensnared in the greater tragedy of their nation.

In Vienna he had made friends with Paul Bruell, like Steiner an aspiring poet, to whom he addressed some of his most informative autobiographical letters; Bruell has also preserved some of the earliest extant versions of Steiner's poetry. It was in Vienna, too, that Steiner first met Canetti, who lived there. H.G. Adler had invited Canetti to hold a reading in Prague in 1937 – Steiner was in London at the time – and suggested to him that he should meet Steiner on the latter's return to Vienna (Canetti 1985: 341; Atze 1998: 24-27). This was the beginning of a friendship that became Steiner's chief inspiration during his English period, when Steiner and Canetti developed an intense, mutually productive relationship which lasted – with one long interruption – from Canetti's arrival in England in 1939 until Steiner's death in 1952. The surviving letters between Canetti and Steiner indicate a passionate, occasionally strained and always vibrant friendship based on the two men's profound mutual respect of each other's artistic talent and scholarship. We have unfortunately found no documentary evidence of their meetings in Vienna. However, we may imagine Steiner in Vienna soaking up the cultural atmosphere, possibly attending such major events as Karl Kraus's last public reading with Paul Bruell, as well as making major advances in his ethnological work. Bruell reports that the Viennese period was for Franz a 'happy and carefree time', and paints the following picture of his friend, clearly recognisable as a younger, less stricken predecessor of the figure recalled later by Iris Murdoch who, unaware of Bruell's letter, was to echo his sentiments many years later:

> He was young, lively and full of good humour, full of learning, full of literature and poetry, all together and all at once, and he coped with the difficulties and hardships of student life with ease. He studied assiduously, bought old and valuable books whenever he could ... and was writing a novel which was partly serious, partly satirical .... (after Fleischli 1970: 18)

Bruell also reports on Steiner's literary interests in the Viennese days. Hoffmann was still a special favourite. The *Gita* is again mentioned. But this list has widened out to include the Presocratics, Marcus Aurelius, Proust, and Musil; a notable shift can be seen in his interest in English literature, including Thackeray, and – a passion he was to share with Canetti – Blake, whose poetry Steiner now began to translate (Fleischli 1970: 18).

H.G. Adler summarises the motivation which drew him to study in Vienna and which soon after led him to England, and gives the earliest account we have of Steiner's method. In Vienna and London:

> He wanted to acquire the necessary education and support to enable him to do fieldwork and prepare for an academic career. Franz owed both institutions a great deal, even if the direction he later took had little in common with them, and was closer to the Oxford School and the work of a few individual Americans: a careful comparativistic ethnology, based on painstaking research in the field of study itself, which seeks to understand and explain neither by means of an *a priori* social theory nor by deriving its subject matter from a particular civilisation or social group. The social theories and the psychology with which Western society past and present seeks to understand itself and other civilisations could not serve as the ... basis for a science of this kind; it would have to be given up. Franz, who in a sense considered himself to be a by no means willing guest in the West-

ern world, and therefore regarded it extremely critically, had little difficulty
in adopting an unprejudiced attitude. In his reflections, he saw the Orient,
and any other culture which he studied, in the mirror of the West, which
was not an ideal for him ..., but a technical tool; and even that was to be
used carefully and with critical reflection. (H.G. Adler Ms 1953: 9v)

This is the earliest appreciation we have of a method which is not
employed explicitly in Steiner's writing before the wartime aphorisms
and does not surface fully in his anthropological work before the Oxford
lectures: put at its simplest, the epistemology entails a critical balancing
of Eastern and Western ideas. If, as Steiner contended in 'Chagga Truth'
(pp. 244-50, below), all regimes of truth are relative to forms of life,
then the status of exotic or non-Western beliefs depends upon the ana-
lyst's commitment to (or distance from) that form of life. For his part,
Steiner was complexly – sometimes almost contradictorily – committed
at least to two forms of life: the academic community and the collective
ideal of Oriental life. As a result, he weighed the standards of truth relative to each of these life-forms in a single balance. The epistemological
imperative to interpret each life-form was inseparable from the ethical
commitment to enact what the resultant insight entailed. Hence his
epistemology was always consequential politically. Like theorists of a
much later generation, Steiner saw clearly that the will to knowledge of,
and the will to power over, other societies were inseparable from the
Western form of life. Western preconceptions were unable to reconcile
common humanity with the recognition of essential difference: what
was different must be eradicated or expelled (see Volume II, pp. 23-26,
54-55, below). Therefore any positive ethical commitment to non-Western life-forms entailed some degree of antagonism towards Western
beliefs: whilst for example accepting analytic tools from Aristotle, Simmel, or Weber, Steiner vehemently opposes the kind of superstructures
which e.g., post-Kantian idealism, erected on such logical bases (Steiner
1966: 124f.). If H.G. Adler is right to locate the early crystallisation of
this epistemology in the Jerusalem and Viennese years, this has several
important implications. Genetically, it confirms our assumptions about
the literary antecedents of the method in texts like *Robinson Crusoe* and
its experiential basis in Steiner's turn to Zionism. Furthermore it points
to a long, slow evolution in Steiner's thinking, from the moment of
insight in Palestine around 1930 to the moment of execution in England between 1942-52. In terms of his output, we can note how Steiner
only gradually achieved a shift from a private, aphoristic expression of
his method to its application in the Oxford lectures, although to the end
of his life crucial fissures remained between the different forms of his
written expression. All this lends further credence to the sense that
Steiner intuited an unstatable centripetal *mathesis* around which his

work revolved – an idea we encounter again in Iris Murdoch's literary transmutation of Canetti and Steiner in *Message to the Planet*.

But let us return to the early years. It is time to consider Steiner's ethnological background.

His later anthropological writings frequently distinguish two sorts of ethnographic data which, he emphasises, need not be coextensive: 'cultural elements' and 'social institutions'. The phrase 'social institutions' is clearly at home in British social anthropology; the concern for 'cultural elements' has roots in Steiner's Central European training in ethnology, philology and linguistics or, more generally, in the Central European tradition of *Völkerkunde* which was echoed only crudely in the British diffusionism anathematised by functionalists for its excesses. As Adam Kuper explains in expressly schematic terms:

> There was ... by the early twentieth century an accepted distinction between a broadly geographical approach, which was concerned with migration, cultural diffusion and the classification of peoples and objects, and what was generally called the sociological approach, which dealt with social institutions. ... The ethnologists inclined towards diffusionism. Cultures were patchworks of traits, borrowed from others, the superior traits moving outwards from a centre like the ripples made by a stone thrown into a pond – to echo a favourite analogy of diffusionist writers. (1996: 2-3)

Kuper is concerned with the British scene, but his distinctions make a useful introduction to German-language ethnology. Although they may seem diverse nowadays to an English-speaking reader, the combination of studies Steiner pursued as a student – philology, Semitic languages, ethnology, *Völkerpsychologie* – were historically related in the development of German anthropology. The traditional, text-critical approaches of German philology developed into German anthropology through the intermediate discipline of *Psychologie* understood, as Steiner translates it in his curriculum vitae of 1939, as a type of social psychology. 'To [German] Greek scholars, *Psychologie* literally signified the study of *Geist*, the great iconic concept of German romanticism' (Whitman 1984: 218).

German anthropology developed from roots in the Enlightenment which set it apart from Anglo-Saxon developments. These schools parted ways around 1800 (Bell 1994: 17f.): the amorphous field of Enlightenment anthropology stabilised in the nineteenth century as two distinct disciplines, Germanic philosophical anthropology and the Franco-Anglo-American discipline of empirical ethnology; whereas the latter considered eighteenth-century preoccupations to be unscientific, the former regarded them as foundational, and rejoiced in extending the cultural heritage of philosophy from Leibniz to Hegel. Within this tradition, therefore, articulate thinkers from Lichtenberg and Herder down to Nietzsche, whose work crosses the boundaries between philosophical anthropology and social criticism, could directly affect the development of writers like Steiner and Canetti. Central to the German anthropological tradition was Herder's definition of the *Volksgeist* inherited by Humboldt (Bunzl 1996: 20-2); Humboldt as philologist and anthropologist could hold in balance both the future German and Anglo-American concerns by treating classical philology as the study of the supreme expressions of the human *Geist* embodied in ancient Greek culture; at the same time, he developed his own nascent field of comparative lingusitics, which he defined as the study of the relative expressions of the universal *Geist* within each specific *Volksgeist*. Language, thought, action, and culture were conjoined in the specific *Weltansicht* (world-view) of each *Volk*. Importantly, Humboldt extended his research beyond Western Europe to include not only Chinese (Humboldt [1836] 1848: 329-35), but also the languages of the North-American Indians (1848: 323-39), thus opening up quite radical cultural diversities for research.

In Whitman's account, Bastian appears as the pivotal figure who annexed the legacy of the nexus between philology and *Psychologie* but without the strategic interests of a classical scholar (Whitman 1984: 226; Bunzl 1996: 43). In Bastian's hands the discipline of ethnology was transferred to the natural sciences. 'Only because he lacked their loyalties [to classical civilisations] was he willing to look indiscriminately for genius in jungles and deserts. No philologist could have accomplished the productive introduction of philological understanding of the rise and nature of culture into the study of primitive man' (Whitman 1984: 226). In his account of an overlapping period and set of personalities, James Ryding concurs in the judgement that for all the continuities between Bastian's project and German historicism, it is to the natural scientific aspects of Bastian's work that we should look to explain its institutional success (1975: 13). The competing claims of history and science were at the very foundation of the German-language project of ethnology.

We know from his diary entries at the time of attending Malinowski and Radcliffe-Brown's seminars that Steiner was acquainting himself with the English-language reception of German scholars. In London, he records having read Alfred Haddon's brief *History of Anthropology* (Diary II Ms 1936-37: fol.7v), which attributes to Bastian a major role in 'the recognition of the importance of psychology in ethnology' (Haddon 1934: 64) and, in Oxford, Robert Lowie's then recently published *The History of Ethnological Theory* (1937). Steiner – like his teacher Heine-Geldern (1964: 410) – approved of Lowie's chapter on 'Bastian' (Diary IV Ms 1939a: 20r). This is an amused and judicious account that, whilst recognising the faults in Bastian's prolix, turgid style, pays tribute to his importance in promoting the 'gospel of saving vanishing data' (1937: 37) and his significance as a 'forerunner' of later developments in ethnology (1937: 38).

Bastian's Humboldtian belief in the 'psychic unity' of mankind was expressed in his emphasis on the independent development of cultures. The later German ethnology we know Steiner to have studied, and which is reflected in his early writings, was concerned with disputes surrounding the ramifications of the contrary, diffusionist, position that asserted the essential uninventiveness of man. Steiner's library contained several studies in this mode: among them Friedrich Ratzel's *Völkerkunde* (3 volumes, 1885, 1886, 1888) and its successor, Georg Buschan's edited *Illustrierte Völkerkunde* (in the three-volumed edition of 1922; Book List Ms 1952: 1). While also accepting the principle of 'psychic unity', Ratzel 'reverses Bastian's principle that resemblances are merely evidence of a common mentality. The uninventive human beings that were constantly migrating hither and yon simply transported what they had picked up as their cultural inventory' (Lowie 1937: 123). According to Heine-Geldern, Ratzel was responsible for ending three decades of stagnation in German ethnology (1964: 411).

It is clear that, from his earliest training, Steiner was immersed in debates concerning the problems of comparison and historical reconstruction, as well as the philosophical foundations of the different positions adopted. A small pamphlet which survives in his *Nachlaß* contains several reading marks, of the kind which we know from other works in his library suggest fairly detailed study. This text is a pamphlet by Julius Lips, *Einleitung in die vergleichende Völkerkunde* (Introduction to Comparative Folkways; Leipzig n.d.), which Steiner inscribed 'IX 1934'; aged twenty-five, he was studying in Prague for his D.Phil., and had yet to make the transition to ethnography. Lips's pamphlet may provide a guide to the way he became familiar with the prevalent ideas and methods at an early stage of his interest in anthropology. It is noticeable, at all events, that Steiner's first completed writings in anthropology contribute to the very debate about ethnographic problems in the *Kulturgeschichte* tradition which Lips describes.

Lips's exposition is highly critical of evolutionism, a purely speculative approach hardly worthy of the name 'method'. He is scathing about the 'construction' of a history of mankind that leads from 'primitive' to more developed cultures using a *völkerpsychologische Konstruktion* (Lips: 9) to flesh out the evidence of material culture. Such evolutionism relies on a theory of 'elementary ideas' shared by Tylor and Bastian but with precedents in Voltaire and Humboldt. According to Humboldt's theory of the essential identity of the human spirit, similar cultural products appear under similar conditions in different geographical locations because they 'are invented and must be continually reinvented independently of one another' (Lips: 10). The theory of 'elementary ideas' can thus be used to add an entirely speculative evolutionary narrative to the relations between a series of individual cultures. It is an approach that Steiner, like Lips and indeed like post-Malinowskian British anthropology, consistently rejects.

As the antithesis of this, Lips presents Ratzel's 'migration theory' which presupposes that every artefact is invented only once and then migrates from one culture to another. It is necessary to study the complete migrations of cultural artefacts before conclusions can be reached about their development. Such migrations may be identified by studying the particular features of an object that are not essential to its nature and function. The task of ethnology is to study such 'trickling through' of cultural artefacts, which need not imply human migration. This is easier in neighbouring cultures than where similar artefacts appear in physically distant regions such as Melanesia, Africa and South America. The task is to translate 'spatial simultaneity into temporal succession', an approach shared with what in Britain became known as diffusionist theory and was portrayed, in the early twentieth century, as the antithesis of Malinowski's functionalism which emphasised rather the integrity of different cultures.

The approach reflected in Steiner's anthropology of 1937 to 1938 broadly derives from what Lips describes as the *kulturhistorische Methode* proposed by Leo Frobenius, in which migration theory was extended by the notion of 'culture circles' (*Kulturkreise*). As Steiner underlined in his copy, 'Frobenius proposed linking not just individual artefacts, or *elements*, but entire cultural *complexes*.' However, Frobenius himself did not develop this technique, and the extension of the culture circles method was left to Ankermann and Graebner, the latter defending the method in *Die Methode der Ethnologie* (1911). In order to move from the examination of individual artefacts to the delineation of 'areas of homogeneous culture' two criteria are proposed, as Steiner also underlined in his copy, 'the formal criterion and the quantitative criterion. The former consists in determining the similarities of two objects, which do not necessarily arise out of the essence of that object or the materials used for making it.' The quantitative criterion means that similarities should not be judged by isolated examples, but whole groups of them, i.e., not just animal fells, but bows, masks, clothes, and the shapes of drums and houses. This collection of items is known as a 'complex'. Widely spaced appearances of the same culture complex may derive from distant historical relations. But such relations must be demonstrable by the principle of continuity.

> If we consider the individual cultural regions which are spread across the whole earth with all their mixtures, contacts, overlays and overlappings, quite distinct cultural elements can be observed, which always reappear at

quite different places across the earth with quite specific different cultural elements having the same connexion. The totality of the same cultural complexes across the the whole earth we call a culture circle. (Lips: 12)

The heterogeneous elements found in a culture circle are not linked by their inner nature but by purely external, historical facts. And it is the non-functional character of their association which holds out the possibility of deriving a history from their distribution.

This theory of culture circles was influential in American cultural anthropology, especially in its application to indigenous North American cultures (see Harris 1968: 388-90 for reception by Lowie and Kluckhohn). Moreover, reference to 'cultural elements' in the review of Murdock published at the end of Steiner's life suggests that he did not abandon his earlier professional formation but brought it into a productive relation with a sociological insight that matured in Oxford. However, for Steiner the systematic properties of the social phenomenon were to be found at the societal rather than cultural level of analysis. Thus, while sharing some of the sources of American cultural anthropology, and alert to issues of language and material culture more central to that tradition than to most mid-century British anthropology, Steiner cannot be described as a cultural holist. What most strikingly remains of his continental training – apart from his continued interest in linguistic context – is Steiner's commitment to comparison, and his sensitivity to the difficulties of comparison. Moreover, the basic imagery of his comparison was not that common in British comparative anthropology, fundamentally of a coincidence between the boundaries of cultures and societies, but rather of a disjunction between the distribution of social and cultural phenomena. Thus, he never argued himself into the problem of explaining how inter-comprehensibility was ever possible at all for the inhabitants of different bounded cultures that were self-sufficient in their generation of meanings.

Steiner's earliest application of *kulturhistorische Einordnung* can be appreciated from his 1938 lecture on 'Dog-Sacrifice ...', which is preserved in typescript and – with a slightly different emphasis – as an abstract. He identifies a cultural complex in various north-Eurasian subarctic societies which has the following features: there is belief in reincarnation and newborn children are named according to this belief; oracles are used to assist in naming children; women in labour declaim the name of their child's genitor and thus ease birth; dog sacrifice is made; a dog guards the underworld; and dogs may be conceived as guides for the souls which await reincarnation in an underworld which is presided over by a female deity. These features are connected by the need to identify which of the souls of the dead has been reincarnated. In this reincarnation complex, the role of shamans at birth – mentioned only in the lecture abstract – is less important than it is in cultures from which the reincarnation complex is absent. Here, Steiner seems to be emphasising, contrary to extreme diffusionism, that local culture complexes may vary because they are integrated by social practices.

Two other brief but scholarly articles of the same period are highly specialist contributions to disputes over the origins and distribution of items of material culture. A 1939 article on the Yakut *xayik* (usually kayak in English) is devoted to the critique of superficial readings of the distribution of skin boats among both Yakut and Inuit. Looking at historical and linguistic evidence, as well as that of material culture, Steiner concluded that Yakut skin boats, if they ever existed, were probably introduced from the south-west and that, if *xayik* meant anything at all for Yakut, it probably referred to European boats. A 1941 article on the *ulu*, or semilunar knife, written on the basis of research in the Pitt-Rivers Museum in Oxford, is a studious illustrated account of specimens in East and South-East Asian, American, Polar and sub-Arctic regions. Somewhat noncommittally Steiner argues, using the familiar terminology of disputes in Central European culture history, that the widely distributed forms had 'ultimate historical connexions' but in the present state of knowledge 'we must, however, treat the coinciding similarities of derived forms as phenomena of independent convergence' (1941: 12). In terms of specific content, there is remarkably little in common between these ethnological writings, of the late 1930s and early 1940s, and the social anthropological writings of his final Oxford period. However, their residue is an ease of thinking in broad comparative terms, and a methodological skill in handling sources on a large scale, that contrast markedly with the initiation via intensive field work that had become the hallmark of professionalised social anthropology.

Having considered how one line of Steiner's work remained constant from his first encounter with the 'culture circles' theory in Prague in 1934 down to his scholarly publications in 1941, it is time to consider his one and only field trip of Summer 1937. For beside the constancy which embeds varieties of 'culture circles' theory into his most important writing, his thinking is replete with unexplained fractures. Steiner's work is defined by loss. Loss of loved ones, most painfully. But no less catastrophically for his scholarship, the associated loss of records, notes, drafts, materials. The student of Steiner repeatedly runs up against empty spaces, memory holes, where we would expect records, documentation, and extensive debate. The first case is his field trip, for which not even the notebooks have survived. The second, of course, is the original version of his thesis, about which we will have more to say shortly. Almost all that survives in terms of documentation about that only field trip is a brief, largely factual article in the *Central*

European Observer, some photographs, a fine poem called 'Ruthenian Village' (Volume II, pp. 14-15, below), and the plans for a poem in the *Conquests* intended to deal with the trip – a poem which, tellingly, remained unwritten. Whereas Steiner's great contemporaries are defined in terms of their fieldwork – Malinowski among the Trobriand Islanders, Evans-Pritchard among the Azande and Nuer – Steiner, whilst theoretically wedded to fieldwork, was perhaps the only one among his Oxford colleagues whose output is not tied to the field; although, if he had had his way after the war, we would have been able to list 'Steiner among the Pygmies'. Malinowski, trapped in Australia by the outbreak of war, skilfully exploited the opportunity to explore Melanesia, but Steiner remained stuck in England, making use of his anthropological training to reflect at great length on England, the English – even the English weather (Volume II, p. 88 below).

Why did Steiner go to Sub-Carpathian Ruthenia? What were his research goals? What actually was his subject? Was he following Malinowski, who had holidayed in the Tatra Mountains while studying in Cracow and encountered shepherds whom he later described as 'semi-savage Carpathian mountaineers' (Thornton with Skalník 1993: 11)? Did he mean to study Ruthenians or Gypsies, or both, or was his unit of study bounded geographically? Ruthenia was part of Steiner's native Czechoslovakia, and may have afforded a relatively accessible site for a first field trip.

According to a curriculum vitae he prepared in 1949, Steiner was planning to practise Malinowskian research methods in the field, and it may also have fitted in to his plans for other, more popular works, such as the Prague lectures. Among the ethnological books Steiner purchased in 1934, we find two photo-essays in the popular series *Schaubücher*: Heinz Perckhammer's *Von China und Chinesen* (On China and the Chinese, 1930), and Ewald Banse's *Frauen des Morgenlandes* (Women of the East, 1929). In these books, high quality photographs (including erotica masked as ethnology) are accompanied by a brief introductory essay. Perhaps the Carpathian trip might have led to a study of this kind. Certainly, the thirty-odd pictures that survive among Steiner's papers include some excellent portraits.

Ruthenia, which was the 'least developed' area of the Austro-Hungarian Empire, had become part of Czechoslovakia in 1918, and was one of the poorest areas in the new country. Its official name was that which Steiner uses in the title of his article, Sub-Carpathian Russia (Krejčí and Machonin 1996: 37f.). Steiner's published article is a drily factual account of Gypsies living in this eastern part of the Czechslovak Republic as a small minority amidst a Ruthenian majority. Its appearance in the cosmopolitan Prague English-language newspaper *The Central European Observer* published by Orbis – the same house that had brought out Steiner's first book (p. 45, above) – from 1933 to 1938 is indicative of Steiner's intellectual and political context. The paper's dates tell the story of its line. It took a left-of-centre stance towards the rising Nazi threat, and orientated itself towards England and America politically, emphasising democratic values. Apart from international relations, it examined minorities at home, cautiously distancing itself from Sudeten politics, abjuring the politics of the old Empire, and stressing the harmonious integration of ethnic minorities. Steiner's piece thus falls into the same general frame with respect to Czechoslovakia as does his first published essay, 'Orientpolitik', within the context of pre-war Palestine: modernisation, education, and peaceful coexistence are the common themes.

The Ruthenians, or little Russians, constituted the fifth largest ethnic group in the Republic (after Czechs, Germans, Slovaks, and Hungarians), and lived in an area that had previously been – as Steiner tells us – a neglected frontier of the former Hungarian economic system. The gypsy population of Sub-Carpathian Ruthenia was minute – here Steiner follows the dubious 1930 population census in putting their numbers at under fifteen hundred – and differed from the majority of more than thirty thousand Gypsies in the remainder of eastern Czechoslovakia which had formed a more central part of the Hungarian economic system prior to 1918. In studying the gypsies of Sub-Carpathian Ruthenia, Steiner was turning eastwards in several senses: the most easterly part of Czechoslovakia, the region which had previously belonged to the northeastern corner of the Hungarian Kingdom and, in the Romanies, people whose Eastern origins were traced from India. Moreover, like the Prague of his upbringing, and the Jerusalem of his coming into adulthood, Sub-Carpathian Ruthenia was politically and ethnically complex. Its languages included Russian, Ukrainian, Czech and Magyar (Krejčí and Machonin 1996: 38) as well as Romany and Yiddish.

There might be some trace of 'culture circles' thinking in the way that Steiner situates the gypsies in opening. However, there are equally plausible resonances of his period of reading the marxist classics. The Gypsies of south and southeast Europe, he tells us, retained occupational specialisms from their days of settlement in India: coppersmithing and tinkery (skills complementary to communities based on agriculture), and musicianship (in demand in a 'feudal system of rural life or with an orientally influenced form of amusements and amusement establishments in town'). This analysis might apply to Slovakia, but Ruthenia was a different case: a marginal area of forestry, pastoralism and self-sufficient peasants which was unfavourable to the spread of Gypsies. Gypsy settlements were correspondingly limited to the larger towns in the plains, with the single exception of Rachov, the largest of the mountain settlements.

Using the same 1930 census figures, Steiner notes that of the (presumably 1,442) people who returned themselves as Gypsies: 142 claimed to follow a 'free calling' (most as musicians), 314 were agricultural workers, 171 metalworkers, 216 nonagricultural labourers, and 37 beggars (a total of 880). Steiner's further figures from the 'social angle' come to a total of 1,399, making it difficult to square this figure with either the preceding or with the supposed gypsy population of Carpathian Russia. Leaving aside these obscurities, some conclusions – albeit not wholly explicit – seem to follow. The number of people practising the 'traditional' gypsy callings of metalworking and musicianship is matched by the number working in agriculture, and exceeded by the number working as labourers in all spheres. Few Gypsies are beggars. Thus, the Gypsies are an example of a culturally and ethnically distinct category of people, living apart from the host community, and relating to it through the market – to which they supply labour, commodities and cultural services. As an Oriental people, living among Westerners, and relating to them through the marketplace, the Gypsies could not but evoke for Steiner the situation of the Jews. Perhaps Steiner also saw analogies between the Jews as exiles from Israel, and the Gypsies as travellers from India? The record is too slender to do more than guess, although below (and in our Introduction to Volume II) we shall add evidence from the poetic and photographic refractions of Steiner's Ruthenian experience.

The second, and longer, half of this brief paper suggests an explicit agenda concerned with education. Although most Gypsies spoke Romany, their language competences otherwise differed: some speaking Magyar, others Slovak or Ukrainian. Steiner then goes on to outline both how schooling exclusively for Gypsies evolved as a result of the difficulties that gypsy children experienced at Slovak schools, and how these gypsy schools had sought to cater for the special cultural and educational needs of their charges, as well as combating the social problems to which they were prone. In short, and in so far as its brevity supports a detailed reading, the single, published scholarly paper deriving from Steiner's fieldwork seems to point in the same direction as his almost contemporary opinion expressed in the essay on 'Orientpolitik' (1936). 'Serious cultural problems such as the question of emancipation are not broached, and it is impossible to speak of a planwise cultural policy in that respect'; nevertheless Steiner suggests that the educational initiatives taken in respect of gypsy schooling are important. Like 'Orientpolitik' this brief essay seems to be the work of a man committed to the preservation of cultural differences and cultural identity, but within an overall context of co-modernising and simultaneously enfranchising populations. This optimistic vision was not to survive the later 1930s.

The Impact of the First English Years

Don't speak of the war, but don't conceal it.
Let others squander and catalogue
All the infamous deeds and the vulgar conspiracy
Which preceded it,
Let them mint their comfortable outrage in fashionable toys,
Lamentably studious
Let their flourishes adorn
The great lamenting faces of the peoples …
                                              Conquests, X, 'The Wheels'

Steiner's life curve displays a constant string of new beginnings, at first mostly positive, but later the falls in the graph are thrust ever deeper by loss, and a new rise finally became impossible. His first studies in Prague were followed by a reorientation in Jerusalem and a fresh start in Vienna. After Vienna came London. And – as he had now lost his homeland – Oxford, where he became a refugee and began another thesis. But as if that new beginning were not hard enough, he lost his thesis and all his notes and had to start yet again. Meanwhile, the presumed loss of his parents during the war was followed by the certain news of their death. His health suffered a reversal so extreme that not even the completion of his thesis and the final success, an appointment to an Oxford post, could save him. Friends who knew him from such different perspectives as Mary Douglas and H.G. Adler knew that his life was marked by tragedy. The biographers can hardly demur. The reading is supported by Steiner's iconography, in which we discern a relentless shift from the self-confident and cheerful youth to an increasingly tormented, suffering man, who aged far beyond his forty years, though – from the accounts we have – we know that the carefree, fun-loving, life-affirming satyr was ever able to break through the mask of tragedy. This is how his friend the poet David Wright recalls him in his poem 'Franz Steiner Remembered':

Franz, barely forty, an old man already:
His face had a scorched look. It is my fancy
Those burnings – books, then bodies, the nightmare
Of middle Europe, unimagined here –
Withered the skin of the survivor,
Always unlucky Franz, man without family
In exile from his language, living on.
                                              (Wright 1990: 10)

Steiner did not like England much when he arrived and maintained an ambivalent, love-hate relationship with it afterwards, when he had

come to know, admire, and love many of its ways. To Bruell he wrote
on 9 November 1936:

> It is cold and lonely here. Where are the happy days when all I lacked was
> a woman. And how expensive everything is – oh dear! I make a big detour
> around all the bookshops. (Fleischli 1970:19)

Steiner's view of English scholarship was similarly disparaging.
Writing to H.G. Adler in Prague on 19 March 1939, he lambasts his
host nation:

> The English are so backward in the human sciences (*Geisteswissenschaften*)
> that it makes one shudder. If they didn't have the emigrés, many subjects
> would not be taught. ... At the British Museum they don't even have an
> expert on Armenian, they can't even catalogue the relevant publications
> properly .... (Fleischli 1970: 22)

The discrepancy between Vienna and London clearly displeased
him in every way. He concluded that he had only two alternatives:
'America or linoleum', i.e., emigration or the family business (Fleischli
1970: 20). Yet both his parents' idea that he apply for a Rockefeller in
Spring 1937, and his plans to emigrate to the United States in 1938,
came to nothing. He was constitutionally incapable of dealing with
authorities (H.G. Adler Ms 1953: 12f.). Writing to his friend and editor
Rudolf Hartung after the war, he observed:

> I would not have been able to cope with a difficult situation under the Nazis
> and was far too awkward to manage a planned flight or emigration. (Fleis-
> chli 1970: 21)

His finances and his feelings began to suffer as the Nazi persecutions took effect. It became increasingly difficult for his parents to support him when restrictions on sending currency abroad were imposed
in mid-March 1939. His father advised him to get a teaching job and,
when he did not, read his by now thirty-year-old son the riot act:

> You will have to break the habit of getting enthusiastic about something for
> a few weeks and then having no further interest in it. ... You can't go on like
> that any more. I'm no longer young enough or healthy enough to afford
> superfluous expenses. ... (Fleischli 1970: 20)

Was the universality of the mature Steiner built upon the way-
wardness of his younger self? Or did his father misunderstand him?
Whichever the case, the deepening which his character underwent
stood in direct proportion to the suffering he was now forced to wit-

ness. Not just the persecutions were hard; society's moral collapse was too. In May 1939 Steiner's father wrote:

> The horror of the time is the way in which people fail. All their worst characteristics multiply, so that the neighbour on whom you were counting suddenly disappears or just walks over you. Everyone thinks only of themselves. (Fleischli 1970: 21)

As the wall of censorship descended, ominous remarks reached him from his parents like 'nothing has changed here' and 'all is well as always'. The final, shattering message from his mother came in a letter of 24 April 1940:

> There is nothing to write about us. What I most like to do is dream. I imagine what I will do when you come home, how I will clean everything for your arrival. As I say: dreams ... (Fleischli 1970: 21)

As Fleischli notes, Steiner's mother will have known that this was just a dream. Less than a year earlier, SS-Obersturmbannführer Adolf Eichmann had set up the *Zentralamt* in Prague, and the gradually increasing harassment of the Jews and the restrictions on their everyday life had begun; emigration became fraught with difficulties, and Jews were excluded from public institutions like schools, swimming pools and particular streets in Prague in what was to prove the prelude to their physical extinction, the Final Solution (H.G. Adler 1960: 3-15). Although Steiner was fortunate to find safety, he took upon himself the sufferings of his people and turned his life towards them, bending beneath the burden, until it broke him.

Two traditional alternatives faced Steiner: marriage or further study. He became somewhat implausibly engaged to a New Zealander, Kae Faeron Hobhouse, but the relationship broke up. The other alternative, continued study, was made possible by a chance meeting. As an intellectual refugee, Steiner was invited to visit Oxford around Christmas 1938, where he met the retired Classicist and Fellow of Magdalen College, Christopher Cookson. This time, Steiner fell on his feet. Cookson had previously been Secretary of the College's Tutorial Board (i.e., Senior Tutor) when the German Expressionist poet Ernst Stadler attended Oxford as a Rhodes Scholar; but whereas Stadler never hit it off with Cookson, Steiner did (Sheppard 1994: 7, 12). Cookson – a man in his late seventies – invited Steiner to visit him for a few days after Christmas and he stayed for ten years, until Cookson's death in 1948. A pen portrait of Cookson suggests the basis of an affinity between the old man and his continental guest: like Steiner, Cookson hid 'the kindliest of hearts' beneath a 'sarcastic tongue' (Sheppard 1994: 7). Steiner was looked after by Cookson's housekeeper, and Cookson supplemented his modest funds – he received grants from the Czechoslovak government in exile to support his studies during the war; none the less, Steiner gave an even more impoverished impression than necessary as he refused to save, spent extravagantly on books and nothing at all on clothes. Cookson was a senior figure in the College who had wielded great influence in his day, an influence he was presumably still able to command as it was through Cookson that Steiner gained admittance to Magdalen and through him that he won an entrée to Oxford as a young anthropologist (Frank Ms 1964: 3). Cookson also gave Steiner an invaluable insight into English life. Mary Douglas relates how Steiner told her of the subterfuge that Cookson's housekeeper employed to give the old man a Christmas present. Since this would have been inappropriate in one of her class, she presented the gift on behalf of his dog instead. This, as Mary Douglas recalls, gave rise to interesting reflections on class, Christmas-giving, and animals (pp. 3-4, above). Altogether, the meeting with Cookson could hardly have come at a more opportune moment, and assured that after Malinowski, Steiner would meet the other two major figures in British anthropology of the day.

The early London and Oxford years are a period of transition in Steiner's work. We see him still applying the lessons of his Viennese studies in continental comparative method until about 1941; at the same time, we see him beginning to absorb a new set of concepts emanating from Durkheim and from his British teachers. To form some idea of the subjects Steiner worked on now, one can examine the materials in his *Nachlaß*.[1] This still requires systematic evaluation, and what we offer here is a first foray into a series of unfinished projects. The notes are particularly tantalising because of Steiner's working method. His approach was to initiate a vast reading programme, designed to encompass everything in the field; to make, often long, excerpts from the sources, where relevant supplementing them with maps and his own, technically accomplished, drawings; and then to store the materials systematically in envelopes and folders. What makes his findings so hard to evaluate is that Steiner made no notes on his hypotheses or conclusions, but whenever necessary wrote up the results at great speed – as he eventually did with the final version of his Oxford dissertation.

At first he marked the folders in German, later in English. One large group of materials, from which his Copenhagen lecture must have come, concerns 'The Reincarnation Complex in the Northern Hemisphere'. The regions and topics covered are: 'General; Outside Northern

1. As Steiner's papers have yet to be catalogued, we refer to them according to the archive box numbers (S24, S25, etc.) in which they are currently housed in the Deutsches Literaturarchiv (=DLA), Schiller Nationalmuseum, Marbach am Neckar. We indicate some of Steiner's folders by colour.

Hemisphere; Finno-Ugrian; Samoyed; NE Asia; isolated tribes; Sin. Turks, Yak. (Mongols) Tangus; Eskimo; American Indians; North American Indians' (beige folder in S28). There is also a vast amount of data collected separately on Shamanism. A related 'cultural complex', partly researched in the British Museum, includes 'Funerary Boards and their relation to the Megalith Culture' (orange folder in S21). Among the Oxford work on material culture, there is a major collection on arrow studies (the title in English now), and another on 'European Outrigger & Catamarans' including a map 'Distribution of double-bladed paddle' (blue folder). This project was probably influenced by Heine-Geldern, to whom Steiner left the material in a wartime will. The wealth of materials indicates a major study at an advanced stage of work. A world map included here shows the distribution areas of catamarans encircled and numbered, and what are possibly routes of diffusion indicated by arrows. There is also a European map covering the distribution of dugouts, catamarans, and compound catamarans. Other artefacts studied include: 'Wooden horses', 'Funerary Decorations', 'Milk Churns' (in S16) and 'Cradles and Child-Carriers' (green folders in S29).

His unwritten project for a sociology of the elephant is documented only by a similar collection, 'Diffusion, Taming and Worship of Elephants' (green folder in S21). After the war, this theme surfaced as a poem, 'Capturing Elephants' (see p. 86, below) – anthropology and poetry truly underwent a symbiosis in Steiner's work. All the independent studies of this transitional period can be understood within the context of 'culture circles' ethnology. Although they show evidence of research in London and Oxford, there is no sign of influence from Malinowski or Radcliffe-Brown. However, from the notebooks, we do know that at the same time as developing the Viennese method, Steiner was opening up to a new world of theoretical concepts.

The names of Malinowski, Radcliffe-Brown and Evans-Pritchard have become iconic for the major currents in early modern British anthropology. Steiner came into contact with all three. Treating them as icons of the discipline is, admittedly, in part a convenient, if sometimes intellectually lazy, device; and in part, it also recognises the propensity of those three figures to personalise their differences. Given the smallness of the British anthropological establishment of the inter-war years, many practitioners of the discipline knew all three well, and – despite their misgivings – found themselves designated the followers of one or another. Sir Raymond Firth, describing himself as a Malinowskian in very qualified terms, noted how this trend has tended to 'iron out nuances of theoretical statement' (1975: 5). He also describes the complicity of the personalities involved in what amounted to self-stylisation:

Evans-Pritchard, for instance, was a great polariser, defining his views, first
in reaction against Malinowski and then against Radcliffe-Brown, and
using a skilful reductionism against the standpoint of each to state his own
more trenchantly. (1975: 8)

We can imagine Steiner negotiating these relationships as he made
his way into British anthropological circles. He may well have been
drawn to England by Malinowski's reputation, and it was through
Malinowski (a quarter century his senior) that he had his initiation
into British anthropology at the famous seminar Malinowski had
established over a decade before, in 1924. A comment on the Trobriand Islanders, presumably mediated by Steiner, appears in H.G.
Adler's pre-war writings; and among Steiner's early purchases in London, we find preserved a copy of Raymond Firth's monograph with a
Preface by Malinowski, *We, The Tikopia*, bought – in an extravagant
moment when Steiner could not manage his 'detour' around the book-
shops – in 1936, the publication year. Yet Steiner was not one of those
immediately impressed by the hurly burly of Malinowski's seminar. As
he writes in his German diary on 21 February 1937:

> 2 o'clock. At a Malinowski seminar. Lasted 3 hours. Malinowski gave an
> introduction to what he understands by 'Anthropology'. The usual 'mate-
> rialist', 'evolutionist' rubbish, presented as if it were infallible. In atten-
> dance: Negroes, Chinese etc. ('With the participation of the objects of
> enquiry themselves.') I will visit the seminar regularly. Not because of the
> ethnology, but to learn English and meet people. (Diary II Ms 1936-37: 7v)

Whether Steiner recognised but repudiated Malinowski's irony – or
simply missed it – is unclear; but from the outset he numbers himself
(the Oriental) among the 'objects of enquiry' 'in attendance'. Hilda
Kuper's evocation of the same seminar only a few years earlier makes
clear that it was a highly theatrical event (see also Goody 1995: 33-
35, and 36-37 for the substance of the seminar):

> Evans-Pritchard was brilliant, really brilliant – as was Malinowski; they
> sparked off each other, and the sparks flew. Fortes, Nadel, and Hofstra ... sat
> close together, and Malinowsi labelled them 'the Mandarins' – and treated
> them abominably. He provoked and insulted them; it was at times quite extra-
> ordinary, but it was stimulating, and he did it deliberately. He was a master
> swordsman, and could make his thrusts dangerously sharp. (1984: 197-98)

Nothing could have been more remote from Steiner's own cautious,
questioning and self-effacing style of scholarship. His aphorism on 'Conrad and Malinowski' (Volume II, pp. 239-40, below) describes Malinowski as an anachronism – a man purveying a naively uncritical

eighteenth-century rationalism. Malinowksi's desire that societies possess a *telos* strikes Steiner as tragicomically akin to Conrad's 'wish-nation' of staunchly individualist English adventurers. None the less, that same critical aphorism records Steiner's debt to Malinowski: Steiner describes himself as Malinowski's 'student'. According to Esther Frank – a close friend in Steiner's Oxford years, unconnected to the anthropological world – Steiner continued to value Malinowski as a teacher (Frank Ms 1964: 3). For Steiner, the term 'teacher' possessed talmudic dignity, and loyalty to a teacher – notwithstanding any conflicts that might arise – was a paramount virtue. And, in many respects, these two men belonging to adjacent generations of the old Austro-Hungarian Empire possessed similarities – from their multilingualism to their debt to Ernst Mach and a shared poor eyesight. Traces of Malinowski's influence can still be detected at various points in Steiner's mature work, from the style of his poetic *Variations* which recalls the verse forms Malinowski used for translating Trobriand magic to Steiner's ultimately misconceived aspiration to encyclopaedic monumentality in his Oxford dissertation.

The invitation to visit Cookson at Oxford at the end of 1938 could hardly have come at a more opportune moment for Steiner's anthropological development; for one thing, Malinowski could not provide Steiner with any assistance or instruction as he was to spend the war years in the United States; and for another, the invitation gave Steiner the opportunity to study with Radcliffe-Brown, who – having been appointed to the Oxford Chair in Anthropology in 1937 – was in those days replacing Malinowski as 'the head of the profession' in England (Kuper 1996: 46). According to Esther Frank, Steiner genuinely liked Radcliffe-Brown (Frank Ms 1964: 3), and he for his part appears to have remained a loyal supporter of Steiner's. We know from an inscription that on his return to Oxford after the war Radcliffe-Brown gave Steiner his own copy of Simmel's *Soziologie* – perhaps as a gift on his retirement from the Oxford Chair – dedicating it 'To Dr F.B. Steiner from A.R. Radcliffe-Brown 1946', a nice gesture towards someone who formally remained his doctoral student. The gift had considerable symbolic value. Simmel was the only German sociologist mentioned respectfully in Radcliffe-Brown's lectures (Srinivas 1973: 140); whose affiliation otherwise to the *Année sociologique* school was established at least as early as his 1910 Cambridge lectures (Stocking 1984a). Converging views on Simmel, who was to become a subject for Steiner's Oxford lectures, will undoubtedly have linked teacher and pupil. Other convergences will have included a shared interest in things Chinese. Steiner's surviving notebooks give evidence of his attendance at Radcliffe-Brown's classes, and his diary for 20-30 April 1939 records that he is 'beginning to get used to Radcliffe-Brown's seminar' (Diary IV Ms 1939a: fol. 20r). In the *Nachlaß* we find much evidence of his attendance in the notes on 'RB lectures'. A Spiral

Notebook is labelled 'RB Sem 2'. This contains an early indication of Steiner's discovery of the French School via Radcliffe-Brown: 'Durkheim (*La division de trav. soc.*) .... Solidarity 1. mechanical 2. organic .... Division of labour is in every case a union of labour. Union of labour: organic solidarity'. This is followed by 'Sem RB 3', on 'differences between castes and classes in India (4 classes)' – just five lines of notes – and the next 'RB Sem' on 'polarity of joking relationship and avoidance' – accorded a total of one line by Steiner! Another spiral notebook labelled 'Anthrop' includes comments on 'Cultural setting', and lecture jottings which appear to record Fortes, with remarks like 'Western Sudan. French literature. Not reliable'. It is indicative of Steiner's work at this stage that a reference to 'E.-P. Witchcraft. Azande' is followed by more culture circles material – some notes on '*Sloven. Doppelboot*'. As he moves from culture circles to social structuralism, major new preoccupations begin to enter Steiner's horizon. The terminology in his notes now includes joking relationships, totemic avoidance, kinship and segmentation. If Steiner came to Britain to study functionalism, he quickly took another line. In this light, one suspects that the growing separation between Malinowski and Radcliffe-Brown (Kuper 1996), as well as Evans-Pritchard's uncordial detestation of Malinowski, posed Steiner few problems of intellectual loyalty (Burton 1992: 32-34). The deterioration in relations between Radcliffe-Brown and Evans-Pritchard may have been more problematic.

It has been seen that, like Evans-Pritchard, Steiner could on occasion be generous to Malinowski, e.g., in *Taboo* when describing Malinowski's essay in C.K. Ogden and I.A. Richards's *The Meaning of Meaning* (1923) as brilliant (see p. 119, below). In this essay Malinowski's notion 'the context of situation' anticipated the concept of 'language games' formulated by Wittgenstein and shared by both Evans-Pritchard (Douglas 1980: 36-38; Gellner 1998: 145-56) and Steiner. Malinowski's studies of the Trobriand Islanders created a crucial if generally ignored link between the philological method of Central European ethnology and the modern British school by their emphasis on the importance of the anthropologist's acquiring and studying native languages. His description of the 'context of situation' is a pale reflexion of Humboldt's notion of the 'worldview' tied to language, which manifests in stronger form in Whorf's hypothesis. Steiner remains faithful to this linguistic line throughout his career, combining the nineteenth-century style of pursuing etymologies at the start of his thesis on slavery as in the 'Tabu' lectures, but combining this with a more contemporary analytic approach. At some point between the 1930s and the end of the war, he seems to have envisaged implementing the Humboldtian project with some precision, as emerges in two letters from Joseph Marcus preserved in Steiner's estate: 'What has happened to your thoughts about "syntax – language character – ethnological character". How far have you got?' (26 December 1945). And then again: 'What about your examination of the relation between the structure of language and a people?' (29 March 1946).

On Radcliffe-Brown's advice, Steiner registered for a research degree at Oxford in the Michaelmas – i.e., first – term of the academic year 1939-40. The subject was 'A Comparative Study of the Forms of Slavery' (1949). The reason for his choice was twofold and signals the curious – indeed unique – convergence that now took place between his fate as a Jew in exile and British social anthropology. This meeting of cultures defines his mature work. On the one hand, the subject offered itself to him at the deepest level of his religious experience; he called it a 'duty' and a 'sacrifice' for the fate of the Jewish people (Fleischli 1970: 24): he took it upon himself to redefine in sociological terms the suffering of the Jews that had determined their lives from the day when Joseph – Steiner's favourite biblical character – was sold into slavery, down to his family's current suffering in Bohemia; and, on the other, the shift in focus to a social *institution* marks the turn from Central European ethnology to the more British method of his mature phase (Volume II, below). And yet, when we come to evaluate the change, Steiner's loss of the materials for the first version of his thesis confronts us with a problem: we face the second major memory hole in his career. When we attempt to define exactly how and when his major turn took place and – most importantly – how Steiner's own views actually crystallised in his encounter with Radcliffe-Brown, we simply lack the evidence. Later, Steiner was to complain that Radcliffe-Brown had misguidedly directed him to concentrate on legal systems in relation to slavery, which resulted in his losing himself in law studies (Frank Ms 1964: 2), but master and pupil seem to have remained on good terms. In Steiner's later period, although he expresses profound intellectual disagreements with Radcliffe-Brown when lecturing both on 'Tabu' and on Simmel, Steiner – typically – still honours him as his 'teacher'. Like Malinowski, Radcliffe-Brown remained for him a mentor, an intellectual point of departure, a man whose ideas were to be considered seriously and who had posed what on Steiner's terms were real problems to do with topics like totemism and taboo and concepts like structural form and value.

To recapitulate. In the light of Steiner's earlier ethnological work, it seems fair to associate Radcliffe-Brown with his turn towards a more sociological grasp of institutions. Radcliffe-Brown's emphasis on the difference between historical and sociological method in anthropology (Kuper 1996: 45f.) will have fallen on fertile soil in Steiner's case, since the latter was little disposed to history as a discipline. Radcliffe-Brown's detestation of evolutionism will similarly have appealed to the pupil who first mocked this view in his 'Ethnology for Young People' (Ms 1937b), and his emphasis on analogies with methods employed in the natural sciences, especially biology and zoology, may have struck a chord in the young continental who began life as a botanist (Kuper 1996: 47). Likewise, Radcliffe-Brown's emphasis on comparison (Kuper 1996: 51) will have provided Steiner with a natural extension of his earlier work. His geographical interests were also forced into new directions: as he complained to a friend, his fascination with Arctic ethnology (and India, too) met with no interest in England; essential Russian periodicals were impossible to find, and so he had to follow the prevailing trend, as he writes in his curriculum vitae of 1949, and study the ethnography of Africa (the region crucial to structural functional theorists). However, this was not all loss: for just as Malinowski's functionalism helped Steiner transcend the limitations of Viennese ethnology, so Radcliffe-Brown's structural functionalism enabled him to proceed beyond Malinowski, eventually to Simmel's formal sociology. And, in his turn Radcliffe-Brown would give way to Evans-Pritchard as a reference figure. Steiner's encounter with Radcliffe-Brown was therefore decisive.

Indeed, after acclimatising to Radcliffe-Brown's seminar, and with a rapidity which belied his awkwardness, Steiner made quick headway in networking among the Oxford school. His German diary for 10 May 1939 records:

> Met Evans-Pritchard. Has the best head [*bedeutendster Kopf*] among the English ethnologists. Really top class. Going to Yale in the Autumn as a Visiting Professor. His lectures on 'The Theory of Magic' are very good. To have a friend like that! (Diary IV Ms 1939a: 22r)

A day later, meeting the patron of both Malinowski and Evans-Pritchard, he notes:

> Meeting with Prof Seligman. A very fine chap [*Ein sehr feiner Kerl*]. Will support my request for a post with Radcliffe-Brown. (23r)

Although the outbreak of war changed the Oxford scene, it does not appear to have impeded Steiner's advancement. Despite the vast comparative scope he appears to have made rapid progress with his thesis. On 6 January 1942, Radcliffe-Brown wrote him a highly positive reference to support his grant from the Czechoslovak government in exile, and optimistically anticipates an imminent conclusion:

> Dr Steiner's book on Slavery should be completed in the autumn of this year. I hope to get it published by the Oxford University Press. ... It is an excellent piece of work and will make an important contribution to the scientific study of human society which we in England call social anthropology. (Radcliffe-Brown: Ms 1942)

Even allowing for the window-dressing required in references (and that R.-B. wrote on the point of leaving Steiner under the supervision of 'Professor Daryll Forde who is to act as my deputy'), it is hard to imagine that Radcliffe-Brown could have supported Steiner with such confident warmth if from their conversations he did not have a fair idea what the thesis would contain. However, Steiner had not yet actually begun writing up (Frank Ms 1964: 1). In Spring 1942 fate intervened. Steiner regularly travelled between Oxford (where he worked at the Bodleian) and London (where he spent his days in the British Museum Reading Room). On a journey commuting between the two cities, the heavy suitcase containing his entire collection of material for the D.Phil. was lost, and he was handed a similar case containing the possessions, so he told H.G. Adler, of a luckless nurse. Writing much later to his friend Paul Bruell on 13 April 1947, Steiner was able to describe the loss with wry humour:

> for years I collected material for a highly interesting, innovative sociology of slavery taking various points into consideration. I worked on West African forfeit-slavery and Malayan parallels, I spent months exploring the caste systems and principles of bondage in India, I found a clever theory for manumission under Aztec law. ... So the work grew so extensive that it almost filled a whole suitcase. And the suitcase was so heavy, that the man who stole it from the guarded baggage carriage must have believed that it was filled with jewelry or at least with sardines. (Fleischli 1970: 24)

Srinivas records another version of the tale (see Volume II, pp. 4-5, below), current at the Institute of Social Anthropology at Oxford in the late 1940s. These variants testify to Steiner's relish in telling stories about himself, each appropriate to the recipient, but we do not feel that they cast substantial doubt on the actual loss: the Institute got to hear a version which recalls Lawrence's celebrated loss of *The Seven Pillars of Wisdom*. H.G. Adler – ever concerned about Steiner's health – is regaled with the version in which Steiner is given a nurse's possessions in exchange for his work, whilst the Viennese friend in exile in New York is treated to different translations of post-war value in the references to 'jewelry' or 'sardines'. In each instance, Steiner has simply transformed the personal value of the lost article into the equivalent value that would best be appreciated by the listener.

As to the fact of the loss, its occurrence is evidenced by Steiner's correspondence about it with the Great Western Railway which survives in his *Nachlaß*. On 23 May 1942 a 'further' but unsuccessful 'investigation' was announced and on 24 August of that year solicitors acting on Steiner's behalf acknowledged receipt of £50 from the Railway in compensation for the lost baggage, terms that they describe as 'favourable'. By the time of writing his account to Bruell, Steiner had in some ways distanced himself from the disaster, but he was devastated, and the loss – he was not yet to know that it occurred in the same year that his parents fell victim to the Nazis – became for him and his friends a defining moment. David Wright remembers this scholarly bereavement in his elegy on Steiner:

> The notes and MS lost at Paddington
> With all the labour to be done again,
> (And done it was.) Always unlucky Franz ....
>
> (Wright 1990: 10)

Esther Frank confirms that the loss of his suitcase 'with almost all his material' was 'a mighty shock', from which 'he never recovered' (Frank Ms 1964: 1f). Like the works of the victims for whom it was meant as a penance, his thesis became another of what Robert Neumann poignantly called the war's 'silent books' (Wiemann 1998: 127).

It is difficult to fully trace the progress Steiner made in the first English years because of the loss of the materials for his thesis and the lack of a recorded dialogue with other Oxford anthropologists during the war. It needs to be stressed that besides his isolation as a refugee, he was also isolated because of the absence of other colleagues. There was no chance to collaborate further with Radcliffe-Brown, who was away from Oxford in São Paulo (Brazil) for the academic years 1942-43 and 1943-44 on what Stocking calls a 'cultural mission for the British Council' (though one wonders what such a 'cultural mission' might have entailed in the middle of the war; Stocking [1995] 1996: 427). We have found no evidence for close collaboration with Daryll Forde during this period. Lecture schedules suggest that Radcliffe-Brown did not resume lecturing until Hilary (i.e., the second) term in the academic year 1944-45. There was no opportunity for contact with Evans-Pritchard either, since E.-P., who had been employed at Oxford as a Research Lecturer in African Sociology since 1935, upon the outbreak of war cancelled his plans to take up a Chair at Yale, and immediately joined the Welsh Guards. He did not return to Oxford until Radcliffe-Brown's enforced retirement on grounds of age from the Oxford Chair in 1946. In 1946, according to Daryll Forde's letter of 15 May 1950, Steiner began work for the International African Institute on Radcliffe-Brown's recommendation. We know that Steiner's grant from the Czechoslovak government in exile was no longer paid towards the end of the war (Fleischli 1970: 24); presumably, on returning from Brazil, Radcliffe-Brown found Steiner unable to continue his research for want of funding. The International African Institute with Colonial Office money employed Steiner to work on two interrelated projects involving translation, research, and writing. According to Forde's letter of 5 November 1948, Steiner was given the commission as 'a research worker capable of supplementing

Paulitschke' and 'making a concurrent analysis of the Somali, Danakil and Galla peoples for the *Ethnographic Survey*', but the work dragged on – as Forde laments in several letters – and remained unfinished until 1950, as Forde noted on 5 May that year. Philipp Paulitschke wrote a number of books on this area in the last two decades of the nineteenth century, including *Ethnographie Nordostafrikas* (two volumes bound as one, 1893). Steiner was supposed to revise a draft translation of this volume by a Miss Cory. Additionally, Steiner was engaged to contribute to the International African Institute's *Ethnographic Survey of Africa's* coverage of *North-Eastern Africa*. We know that Steiner had been hard at work on bibliographical research because on 7 August 1946 Christopher Cookson wrote him a reference to Sir Hubert Sams at Cambridge:

> ... the bearer of this, Dr Franz Steiner, has been living with me for the last seven years. He is a very learned anthropologist and is a candidate for the D.Phil. degree, he is also for this term employed by the Colonial Office to bring up to date some papers about Somaliland.
>
> He has exhausted all the material for his subject in the British Museum and in the Bodley and other Oxford Libraries and is now anxious to get admission to ... books in your University library ....

Although Steiner never completed either the volumes or the revision of the Paulitschke translation, we know from Ioan Lewis who inherited it, that Steiner's bibliography was 'splendid'. Lewis was supervised by Steiner at Oxford and recalls that Steiner 'felt guilty' about not completing the book (Lewis: PC), which does not appear to have advanced much beyond the initial stages. This became something of a joke at Oxford, and Mary Douglas recalls that if Steiner's colleagues at the Institute wanted to play a practical joke on him, they would announce that Daryll Forde was 'just round the corner', and Franz Steiner would scurry out of sight (MS 1994: 3). The Paulitschke volume was among Steiner's anthropological books when he died and, like the rest of this library, following his last will, was donated to the Library of the Hebrew University in Jerusalem (Book List Ms 1952: 25).

The volumes in the area that Steiner was engaged to research did eventually begin to appear in 1955: *North-Eastern Africa* Part I, I.M. Lewis's *Peoples of the Horn of Africa: Somali, Afar and Saho;* Part II, G.W.B. Huntingford's *The Galla of Ethiopia, The Kingdoms of Kafa and Janjero.* In the foreword to Part I, Daryll Forde writes 'The author [i.e., Lewis] wishes to acknowledge a specific debt to the late Dr. R.B. [*sic*] Steiner under whose supervision he carried out his first Somali studies'. The wrong initials – was R.B. a motivated error linking Steiner with the man who had recommended him? – were corrected in the 1964 reprint. In Part II, the author acknowledges the use of an unpublished version of Paulitschke's

Ethnographie Nordostafrikas prepared by Miss Cory. Steiner's own efforts bore some slight fruit in his articles published on 'Amharic Language', 'Danakil', 'Galla' and 'Somalis' in *Chambers Encyclopaedia* (1950a-d). Though the years between 1942 (when Steiner lost his thesis and Radcliffe-Brown left Oxford) and 1946 (by which time Radcliffe-Brown's return had been followed by Evans-Pritchard's elevation to the Oxford Chair) were crucial to Steiner's development, they were not wholly centred on the Institute. The best evidence that we have of Steiner's developing anthropological views in these years is contained in a paper written in 1944, 'How to Define Superstition?' (pp. 223-29, below). This confirms his turn away from 'culture circles' ethnology of the 1930s and early 1940s. Steiner's presentation had four parts, only the first three stages of which can be reconstructed fully from his notes. His account began – as would the thesis on slavery and the lectures on 'Tabu' – with an examination of the etymology and uses of the term that concerned him (via a mixture of nineteenth-century philology and twentieth-century ordinary language philosophy). Steiner noted both that the term 'superstition' had changed its sense, and that it filled a gap between the practices of the observer and observed. Yet anthropologists (observers par excellence of such gaps) abjured the term. Next he distinguished two senses of belief; as faith or trust in particular authorities, and as an alternative reality (citing Old Testament Judaism and Buddhism as contrasted examples). Without using the terms 'great' and 'little' traditions, Steiner then contrasted belief and superstition at different institutional levels of Catholicism and Judaism, basically to demonstrate that things counted as one or the other depending upon the social context which was treated as relevant.

The next, and most crucial, section is clearly related to Steiner's analysis in the contemporary German-language extended aphorism, 'On the Process of Civilisation' – a work whose key position in Steiner's oeuvre we elaborate upon in our Introduction to Volume II. Briefly, in his lecture on 'Supersitition', Steiner distinguishes two extreme types of religion. In one type the relation between the whole society and the universe is preeminent. Dangers are thought to lie outside society and must be contained there (but not at the cost of becoming too involved with whatever it is that makes those very forces so dangerous). Rituals are designed to put the whole society right with the universe; social concerns coordinate with cosmic concerns. At the other extreme are religions in which the individual soul is preeminent, and the wellbeing of society depends on dealing with dangers that lie within, especially the right behaviour of individuals. However, the more important this notion of spiritual welfare, the more unknowably diffuse becomes the nature of the soul which is crucial to it. The first type of religion seeks to perfect society by addressing its cosmic pattern; the second seeks to perfect society by perfecting the individuals who comprise that society. It is the second, we learn from 'On the Process of Civilisation', which is typical of Western individualism and implicated in its consequences. The examples Steiner gave to illustrate his thesis are noted cryptically and might be reconstructed with intensive research. But even without going so far, the importance of this large fragment of a lecture in tracing his intellectual trajectory is considerable. Any vestiges of 'culture circles' thinking are extremely minor; but his earlier training remains important in the philological and philosphical stance he adopts when, as it were, 'shaping up' to an idea he means to tackle. However, the backbone of his theoretical apparatus now derives from the 'Oxford School' which he actually cites by name. The insistence on social context would certainly have gained Radcliffe-Brown's approval. But there are also influences that derive neither from Viennese ethnology nor British social anthropology: we catch references in the text to Weber on charisma and to Gershom Scholem's term the Jewish 'masses' (1944: 302); he cites Wittgenstein by name and invokes the theory of relativity generally. Most important, there are clear intimations of Steiner's developing theory of the relations between social formations and regimes of danger – the constellation of ideas that was to allow a cathexis between his political and anthropological thought.

Ironically, when Steiner invoked the 'Oxford School' in his lecture on superstitition in 1944, he almost was that school. Yet it is clear that with this paper and his contemporaneous essay 'On the Process of Civilisation', Steiner's work had reached a turning-point and henceforth displays a new intellectual maturity. It seems unlikely that he was assiduously recuperating his dissertation between 1942 and 1946. Esther Frank's comments on his problems of concentration probably relate to this period:

> Attempt to reconstitute his material. He lost himself in his sources, could never limit himself. He was hard-working in his way. But he dissipated his energies, suddenly started to write poetry .... (Frank: Ms 1964: 2)

H.G. Adler's testimony after 1947 (corroborated by Evans-Pritchard 1956b: 11) is that Steiner completed writing up his D.Phil. at great speed, culminating in several months' work in 1949, this being Steiner's normal working method (H.G. Adler Ms 1953: 10v). Although Steiner complained that his work suffered since some sources for the first version were destroyed by bombs, there are references and ideas in the later work could not have been available to him in 1942. Franz Baermann Steiner emerged from the war years a thinker transformed.

The Exile

The lonely man is the guardian of home, the guardian of time.

Conquests, V, 'The lonely man'

As a refugee, Steiner belonged to the large group of European academics who found a new home in Britain in the twentieth century and impacted upon academic life. Perry Anderson has argued that twentieth-century British scholarship, notably the social sciences and the humanities, were decisively influenced by such immigrants. His examples include philosophy (Ludwig Wittgenstein), history (Lewis Namier), social theory (Karl Popper), political theory (Isaiah Berlin), psychology (Hans Eysenck), psychoanalysis (Melanie Klein) as well as anthropology (Bronislaw Malinowski):

> The wave of emigrants who came to England in this century were by and large fleeing the permanent instability of their own societies – that is, their proneness to violent, fundamental change. England [i.e., the United Kingdom] epitomised the opposite of all this: tradition, continuity, and orderly empire. Its culture was consonant with its special history. A process of natural selection occurred, in which those intellectuals with an elective affinity to English modes of thought and political outlook gravitated here. (Anderson 1968: 17)

However, as Gerhard Hirschfeld points out in an essay which corrects some of Anderson's assumptions, in spite of the English academic community's spontaneous expressions of solidarity towards Hitler's victims, the immigrants in the 1930s fleeing central Europe had extreme difficulty in finding academic employment in the U.K. Britain proved intellectually to be a more hostile environment than the United States (Hirschfeld 1996: 61). For example, as Hirschfeld remarks, Adorno spent almost four years as an 'honorary guest' Research Student at Merton College, Oxford, before removing to Princeton in 1938, and Karl Popper, having first spent almost seven years in New Zealand, only advanced to a Readership at the LSE in 1946 (1996: 61). The different organisation of British academic life, the different school systems, and the deep-rooted differences in social structure, political culture, and cultural life all posed severe problems for the immigrant community. Typical of these differences was the reaction of a headmaster at a Yorkshire grammar school on being faced with a job application from the historian Hans Liebeschütz, who enquired: 'Has he any experience of coaching Cricket or Rugby Football ... ?' (Hirschfeld 1996: 62). This cultural divide was also the reason that Steiner, already possessed of a Prague D.Phil., was obliged to begin work on a second doctorate at Oxford. The long wait for an academic appointment until that degree was completed was not unusual among the scholars who shared Steiner's fate. Yet if integration into British life proved difficult (the poem 'Kafka in England' testifies to this; Volume II, p. 81, below), Steiner shared the benefits of acculturation with many of his fellow exiles. As Marion Berghahn has pointed out, it was not uncommon for German Jewish scholars of a theoretical disposition to acquire more concrete, pragmatic methods from the host community (Berghahn [1984] 1988: 81), and to some extent, this was also Steiner's case. Nor was he cut off from human contact. Although he does not appear to have belonged to any of the better known exile literary clubs, he was a member of the Association of Jewish Refugees (Berghahn [1984] 1988: 150-72), and belonged to other organisations, too.

Moving regularly between Oxford and London from 1939 to 1945, Steiner built up a complex life that was to provide the basis for his mature achievement after the war, both as poet and as anthropologist. Although more research is needed on his Oxford friendships, the impression we have is not that of a recluse but of a man who entered fully into social life, availing himself of all the possibilities for contact and intellectual stimulus available. If he was lonely, this was the loneliness of the solitary, cut off from home, family, and long-standing friends and the spiritual nourishment which all these would bring. He moved in very different circles. There was a circle of Jews and Zionists at Oxford among whom one should mention his close friend and supporter, Esther Frank, whom he met in 1939; keeping up his political activities in this group, in 1943 he became a founder member of the Oxford Branch of Poale Zion – the Jewish Socialist Labour Party (affiliated to the British Labour Party); there were other German-speaking exiles, like Eva Erdély, with whom he could share his literary interests; there were various student circles in which Steiner appears to have been active: for example, in 1941 he was the Czech representative on the Committee of the International Students' Club; in 1942 he addressed the Oxford University Slavonic Club on 'Karamazin: The Russian Discovery of England'; on 6 May 1943, he addressed the Oxford University Russian Club on 'The Carpathians' – other speakers that term included C.M. Bowra, Lord David Cecil, and Eugen Wellesz; on 1 November that year he addressed the German Literature Society on 'Rilkes Weg zur Beschwörung' (Rilke's Path to Conjuration); and in the same year, on 10 June, he was advertised as addressing the Graduate Society on 'How to Define Superstition?', albeit the typescript of the paper is dated 1944. If some talks, like that on the Carpathians, enabled him to go over old ground, the majority provided him with an opportunity to develop fundamental insights in his thinking; away from the university, there was the circle of Indian, Malayan, Chinese, and Arab friends whom Steiner met and went dancing with at the Student Movement House in London (Canetti 1995: 207); there were the more private Indian friends among whom Steiner could relax, proudly addressing them with the words 'we Orientals' (Chandavarkar 1994: 15); there were meetings and walking trips in the Lake District and Scotland with his cousin Lise Seligmann and her husband, on one of which the three of them spent the night together in the open, huddled under a single winter coat (L. Seligmann: PC); there was a circle of young emigré writers which included the poet and future publisher of the Liverpool poets, Georg Rapp; and there was a connected circle of English poets, notably Steiner's friend David Wright, whom he met not later than 1942, and through whom he contacted the legendary Tambimuttu – or 'Tambi-what's-'is-name' as Steiner jokingly says in a letter to Edward Wright, playing on the abbreviation by which Tambi was usually known: this led to Steiner's debut in Tambimuttu's celebrated *Poetry London* (1944), an appearance rewarded with recognition by Stephen Spender (1944) and plans for a volume which, however, came to nothing. All the while, we must imagine him in his truest home in those years – in the world of books – writing new poems, revising old ones, correcting endless drafts for his closest friends to read and admire, and losing himself in libraries, whether at Christopher Cookson's house 'eating his way through a wall of books' (Fleischli 1970: 22), or at the Bodleian or at the British Museum. It was in this period that he acquired his knowledge of English literature, encompassing all the major poets – Donne, Milton, Blake, Wordsworth, Keats, Hopkins, Eliot were special favourites – as well as a host of more minor figures, such as Gray, Collins, or even Shenstone. He was particularly fond of lesser known writers like Christopher Smart, John Clare, and Richard Jeffries. And at night from early in 1941 onwards – according to a letter of Cookson's dated 11 January 1941 – he will also have been assisting the Oxford Air Raid Wardens as a Watcher. Steiner's war, then, was a time of intense intellectual and cultural activity.

Apart from his meeting with Radcliffe-Brown, the renewed encounter that probably had the major impact on Steiner's work during these years was his friendship with Elias Canetti. A fortnight after reaching England in 1939, Canetti contacted Steiner, and they began a close collaboration that – with one severe interruption – was to last until Steiner's death in 1952. Until recently, Steiner was awarded only a walk-on part in Canetti's biography as a source for the anthropology in *Crowds and Power* (Barnouw 1979: 47), but when we were beginning our work on locating Steiner (J. Adler 1994a: 141), Canetti wrote a memoir on him, published after his death (Canetti 1995: 205-209), and this at last provides more insight into Canetti's relation to Steiner. Since then, the relationship has been presented in the Marbach exhibition *Ortlose Botschaft* (Placeless Message; Atze 1998: 29-48).

Because of Steiner's early death and Canetti's rise to fame, insofar as the friendship has been noted at all, Steiner has come to stand somewhat in the shadow of his famous friend, and there is a need, as Iris Murdoch stressed 'to set things right between Franz and Canetti' (PC). This problem is exaggerated by Canetti scholarship, which tends to see him in isolation, without reference to some of his closest friends. Although in literary matters Steiner regarded Canetti – who was some years older and had already published his first novel – as his senior, intellectually the two men were equals, and in matters anthropological, to which Canetti now turned (1966: 7), the literary relationship was reversed. With this in mind, two interesting parallels can be noted. First, just as Steiner took it upon himself to write on 'slavery' as a sacrifice in 1939, at the outbreak of war Canetti abjured all creative writing and devoted himself exclusively to his studies on *Crowds and Power*. This sacrifice indicates a link between the projects, which are in some ways complementary, notwithstanding the methodological gulf that separates the professional anthropologist from the student of crowd phenomena. Interestingly, the two also began writing-up at about about the same time, in 1948-49. The second parallel developed around 1942. Early in that year, to create a counterweight to the pressure of work on *Crowds and Power*, Canetti began to write his aphorisms, first collected as *Aufzeichnungen 1942-1948* (1966: 7f.). Steiner started work on a similar project at about the same time, the aphorisms which, following the renaissance tradition of such collections as Ben Jonson's *Timber or Discoveries*, he called *Feststellungen und Versuche* (Essays and Discoveries), only a small selection of which has been published (Steiner 1988; 1995; J. Adler 1994b: 283-85). Hitherto, it has been accepted that Steiner began writing his aphorisms in Summer 1943 at Canetti's prompting, a view confirmed by Canetti himself and other friends (Fleischli 1970: 58; 116). However, against this, one needs to place Esther Frank's account, which includes more circumstantial evidence:

> It was about 1942 that Franz began to recount aperçus and so on about literary criticism (Kafka, Rilke), and sociology as well. He just said the things freely in conversation. Whole theories. I thought it was a pity that he told these things to someone who might forget them. I suggested that he write them down. At first he was reluctant: everyone knew what he had to say, it was self-evident. I pressed him more and more and one day I bought him a black notebook. He was angry that I was pressing him and went away in annoyance. After a few days he came back and had already written something down. At first they were clumsy, longer pieces. I soon copied the things out. Then he got used to it. Later he enjoyed writing many of them. He had so many ideas himself. Before my departure Canetti told me that Franz had 'stolen' many things from him, especially on the division of labour. I say: Franz had so many ideas that he had no need to borrow any. Canetti: during the war there was a temporary break. (Frank Ms 1964: 9)

In the somewhat incestuous world of exile, Canetti was clearly jealous of his ideas and had an interest in demonstrating both his independence from Steiner and the latter's intellectual dependence on him. Their disagreement seems to have affected even their friends, as both H.G. Adler and Iris Murdoch comment on it. The former observed that Steiner and Canetti often noted down their ideas after a conversation and subsequently each accused the other of having appropriated his ideas (PC). In her journal, writing some months after Steiner's death, Iris Murdoch explains that the argument was in fact prompted by one of Canetti's lady friends, who mischievously reported to him that Steiner had represented Canetti's ideas as his own. Murdoch records the scene about a decade later on 4 February 1953, basing herself on Canetti's account given to her on the previous day:

> I saw C. yesterday in London. I left the first notebook of my novel with him (small & dry as a walnut, it seemed). C. told me at length the story of his quarrel with Franz. The scene in the garden, when Friedl accused F. of stealing C's ideas. ... C. and F. then quarrelled violently about the 'stolen' ideas. F., at last – now I suppose I have lost your friendship. (How every vista into F.'s past is one of pain.) After that, C. was brutal to Friedl, and punished her by not seeing her for a fortnight. ('She had to write twenty letters') But he didn't see F. for two years. He says he now thinks F. was a bit in love with Friedl, & wanted to impress her by showing her how ideas of C's were to be found everywhere in literature. The scene was vivid to me, the hot garden, Friedl very desirable ('She is a summer person') and full of her triumph over the two men both of whom were wanting her. (Murdoch Ms 1952-53: fol.4f.)

Murdoch's vivid journal entry wonderfully evokes the mixture of sexual and intellectual jealousies which seems to have coloured relations between Steiner and Canetti, though the accuracy of Canetti's account – which conveniently exculpates both the quarrelling males whilst finding a female culprit – may be open to question. More research will be needed in both Canetti's and Steiner's papers to resolve the issue. In the light of Steiner's other work, such as the study on labour (see Volume II, below), his ideas on labour cited by Frank as the cause of the problem seems a curious topic for them to have disagreed about, especially since there are a number of aphorisms in which Steiner is much more obviously reflecting Canetti's concerns, e.g., in thoughts on death and power (J. Adler 1995a: 229-230), whilst elsewhere it is demonstrable that Canetti explores more typical concepts of Steiner's: Canetti's treatment of the 'slave' as 'isolated' in *Crowds and Power* (Canetti 1960: 440f.) recalls Steiner's definition of slavery as the exclusion from kinship relations; and Canetti's much-quoted definition of the poet in 'Der Beruf des Dichters' (The Writer's Profession) as 'Hüter der Verwandlung' (The Guardian of Transformation'; 1978: 262) rehearses Steiner's own stronger and much earlier formulation that the poet is 'the only guardian of the myths of every people' (Steiner 1964: 125); this idea of intellectual stewardship goes to the heart of Steiner's thinking around 1942, as when in the *Conquests* he calls 'the lonely man' 'the guardian of time': whereas Canetti's terminology ties the idea of poetic stewardship to his concept of 'transformation', Steiner's notion is embedded sociologically, in that particular roles (the poet, the *homo religiosus*) perform specific functions. Yet even here there is convergence. Both Steiner and Canetti are thinking in a context of *danger behaviour*: Canetti emphasises the dangers wrought by modernity (1978: 258f.) against which the poet as transformer should act; whilst elsewhere Steiner, in 'Superstition' and 'On the Process of Civilisation' (Volume II, pp. 123-28, below), locates modern danger in a related manner, and himself as a poet sets out to counter danger by acting as a 'guardian of metamorphoses' in his *Variations* – a cycle of poems which 'transforms' into modern verse the ethnic folk songs of several peoples, selected because they took no active part in the war (Steiner 1999). Both Canetti and Steiner positively reactivate Shelley's idea of poets as 'the unacknowledged legislators of the world'. What makes the dialogue between them so fascinating is not the issue of priorities, but the extraordinary convergence of related but different standpoints; to juxtapose their writings is to recognise a seminal wartime debate, endlessly stimulating in its implications for the area that links poetry, theology, sociology, and anthropology. As regards Steiner's development, discovery of the aphoristic form was crucial. For one thing, it enabled him to tap into a German tradition of aphoristic writing which, originating with Lichtenberg, combined elements of the Baconian scientific aphorism with the French moral maxim, that made it highly suitable for anthropological thought; indeed the inversion of values that typifies Steiner's mature work is inscribed in the very genre he now alighted on, as is exemplified in Lichtenberg's scathing remark: 'The American who first discovered Columbus made a ghastly discovery' (Lichtenberg 1968-92: II 166). From Lichtenberg to Novalis, Nietzsche, Kraus, Wittgenstein, and Adorno, the German aphorism has enjoyed a privileged place as a countercultural tool, occupying a territory between social critique, anthropological discovery, and philosophical analysis. The *form* of the aphorism cannot be uncoupled from the method, and the method from the meaning. Devices like Lichtenberg's perspectival reversals – employed in the Columbus aphorism (see also 1968-92 I: 301, 756) or Novalis's use of the *ars combinatoria* (Neubauer 1978) – provide stylish aphoristic techniques for effecting surprising connections between apparently remote topics. For Steiner, the form provided the crucial bridge from the divided genres of his 1930s writing (poetry, politics, ethnology) to the critical anthropology of his mature Oxford phase which, to some extent, synthesised aspects of all these.

Canetti had privileged access to Steiner's thoughts, and recognised clearly what we would today call the *deconstructive* tenor of his method. He notes that the *question* was one of Steiner's two main 'constants', his 'question' being posed 'so moderately that it did not require the certainty of an answer. You had to know your way around his thought a little to see that he was only concerned with colossal answers. These are so rare that a reasonable person doesn't even expect them' (Canetti 1995: 204). Deconstructive questioning informs Steiner's aphorisms. It was to become a mainstay of his anthropology, and is one of the features that he singles out in his appraisal of Simmel. We can see it at work in the following piece which, characteristically, hovers between poetry, religion, philosophy and social satire. The piece shows Steiner in his most mature and witty manner, deploying a genre he perfected – the dialogic aphorism:

> What becomes of a presentiment?
> It becomes certainty.
> And if it was wrong?
> It still becomes certainty.
> And if nothing occurs that the presentiment predicted, and nothing is true that it assumed?
> It still becomes certainty. (Steiner 1988: 12)

Read in one way, this aphorism is satirical: it mocks the posturings of self-assertive belief which, all evidence to the contrary, is grounded in nothing more than a hunch, a presentiment, or an intuition – that auratic sensation which German untranslatably calls *Ahnung*. The dialogic form of Steiner's statement reflects on itself and demonstrates the gulf that separates question and answer: the gap between the query and its response is non-negotiable. An answer may respond to a question, but does not end the questioning. Indeed, the answer notwithstanding, the question itself remains valid. Questions are a form of statement *sui generis*, temporally antecedent to their answers, but logically equal or even superior in value: whilst the answer remains unique, the anterior question entails a multiple, and is capable of generating innumerable other answers which have not been given. Steiner shows that the formal symmetry of question-and-answer and the pseudo-symmetry which values the answer more than the question both belie a more fundamental logical and semantic asymmetry, by which the question retains the force of a determining subject whereas the answer can only be a contingent predicate. Hence the continued existence of even a weak question can gnaw away inexorably at the strongest answer. Read within a social context, this aphorism works as a satire on the false belief in certainties; read within a philosophical context, it provides an early example of deconstruction; yet treated in a religious framework, it could be read – against our exegesis hitherto – as a justification of faith. What does this mean? Steiner has adapted the Talmudic questioning method perfected by the Rabbis into a modern intellectual device, operating in a mythical mode. This requires some elaboration. Myth was central to Steiner's thought. Canetti recognised that he 'was free in myth' and adds: 'He was the only person I knew with whom I could talk about myths.' Given the central role of myth in *Crowds and Power* this is a revealing claim:

> It was not only that he knew many myths ... he did not touch them, did not interpret them, did not order them according to scholarly principles, he left them alone. They never became a means to an end for him. For him, too, they were the greatest and most precious things which humanity had produced. We could talk together about myths for days on end, each of us discovered new ones which we presented to the other, and these myths had always been the essential feature in a particular human group, they had always counted and had a decisive effect. ... They were myths ... according to which people had arranged their lives. ... The trust between us was grounded on our respect for myths. (Canetti 1995: 205)

In his acceptance of myth, Steiner entered into a highly active German debate which has no exact equivalent in Anglo-Saxon philosophy. A central issue here, harking back to the first moment of German Romanticism, is the character of modernity. From Friedrich Schlegel, Novalis, and Hoffmann to Nietzsche and Buber, writers and thinkers in the German tradition have emphasised the significance of myth as a way of moving beyond Enlightenment rationalism and as a means to create a new spiritual centre. A key text in this line, of which Steiner owned the first edition, is the so-called *Ältestes Systemprogramm des Deutschen Idealismus* (Oldest System-Programme of German Idealism), a two-page fragment in Hegel's hand reflecting the ideas of Schelling and Hölderlin (Jamme and Schneider 1984; Anon 1988). The central idea here is for a 'mythology of reason', i.e., an intellectual mode that goes beyond both myth and reason by creating a new synthesis of the rational and the non-rational. Significantly, it was after editing this text that Franz Rosenzweig turned his attention from German philosophy to Jewish religion; for him, the possession of a living national myth was a distinguishing feature of the Jewish nation. The earliest figure in Steiner's ambit who accentuated myth and reinterpreted it in a manner which anticipates his own methodology was the philosopher Erich Unger, who presided over a philosophical circle in Berlin between about 1925 and 1931 and like Steiner spent the war years at Oxford. Steiner knew Unger, and at least two of Steiner's friends – Joseph Marcus and

H.G. Adler – belonged to his Berlin circle. Unger's first major work, *Wirklichkeit Mythos Erkenntnis* (Reality Myth Epistemology, 1930), provides a critique of major theories of myth (Durkheim, Lévy-Bruhl, Spengler, Cassirer, Freud), and – echoing the 'Oldest System-Programme' – defines myth as the true paradigm of philosophical understanding (pp.188ff.). But it is in his essay on *Mythos und Wirklichkeit* (Myth and Reality [1928] 1992) that Unger presents in purest form the methodology that Steiner was to make his own. Unger claims that the study of myth occupies a special place among the sciences:

> In myth the scholar for the first time faces an object of investigation *equal in value* (*ebenbürtig*) to himself and his entire world: neither an extrapersonal natural world nor an individual human spirit – but a *human being itself, and as a totality*, a cultural world with an *alien* structure, confronts the observer in myth, who together with his own world also represents *the human being as a totality* – our own culture with its *known* structure. Everywhere else the researcher is the conduit for the world's enquiry into *subordinate* things. But in the case of myth one world is enquiring into another (*equality* develops between the enquirer and his object), and here the extremely curious thing happens that the world into which we are enquiring *asks back*: that is to say, working back, the mythic world casts doubt upon our own – the firm outlines, the apparently eternal contours of our own reality are made uncertain and shatter: *our sense of reality*, the final ground which remains untouched by all other objects which we research into, *is attacked.* (Unger [1928] 1992: 90; emphases original)

What Unger regards as specific to research on myths themselves Steiner generalises into an anthropological method for examining societies that live according to myth, whereby the particular object of enquiry – e.g., native danger behaviour – 'works back' by casting doubt on the value-system of the anthropologist's own world. In a reflection dating to early 1943 which belongs in the context of the unwritten eleventh poem of his *Conquests*, 'At the time of the Flood', Steiner elaborates his view on the conflict between myth and philosophy, lodging his critique at the post-Kantian moment, in the intellectual niche occupied by the 'Oldest System-Programme'. He attacks idealism, which for him originates in a 'fear of the mythic world picture', and pours scorn on philosophical *ersatz*-mythologies; these latter are 'individualistic' whereas the true myths which the poet engages with are 'collective' (Steiner 1964: 124f.). In focusing on the post-Kantian moment, Steiner's trajectory daringly recoups the philosophical line that reaches back to Schelling, Hölderlin, Hegel and 'The Oldest System-Programme', and unpicks their idealism from the new mythic project they inaugurated; in place of their Western *individualism*, he envisages a sociologically grounded 'forgotten' Oriental *collectivism*; and in the place of philosophical nonbelief, he envisages a poetically supported, socially integrated faith (p.124f.): this is precisely the place that he most fruitfully connects with Hölderlin, with whom he identifies as another 'wanderer' in the *Conquests* (Steiner 1964: 114f.). Yet, crucially, linking him to all the authors of the 'System-Programme' is the focus on the poet as the pivotal figure in generating myth: 'Poesy will become ... what she was at the start – the teacher of mankind'; 'we need a new mythology ... a mythology of *reason*' (Jamme and Schneider 1984:13). We can recognise, in what Steiner extracts from this text and the debate with Canetti, a dynamic vortex in Steiner's thinking in the darkest years of the war, which is only glimpsed in the lecture on 'Superstition'; while Oxford anthropology was in a wartime slumber, and he was beginning to gather material for the second version of his thesis, his intellectual development made an enormous leap forward, as his poetry, aphorisms, and anthropological thinking converged in a personal vortex that mirrored the European maelstrom into which the rest of the world was being hurled. This also goes some way to explaining the convergence of his critique of the Enlightenment in his aphorisms and the major essay, 'On the Process of Civilisation' (1944; Volume II, below), with that of the Frankfurt School. At the same time that Steiner was developing his attack on idealism in wartime Oxford and criticising fundamental Enlightenment concepts such as that of a universally common humanity, Adorno and Horkheimer were developing their convergent assault in *Dialectic of Enlightenment* (1944): parallels include such strong similarities as the focus on myth, culture, power, materialism, anti-Semitism, the anti-rational aphoristic form, and even the fact that both Steiner and Adorno's work had a theological ground. After the war, Adorno himself remarked on the similarity apropos of Steiner's reading of Kafka. For Steiner, implicitly arguing against Scholem's reading of him as a mystic, Kafka was a 'mythical thinker', and he demonstrates his view by analysing Kafka's mythic procedures (J. Adler 1992a: 153); on reading Steiner's aphorisms on Kafka, Adorno was struck by the deep similarity between his own Kafka interpretation and Steiner's. Writing to H.G. Adler in January 1954, he comments on Steiner's posthumously published work:

> The impression that I had of it was quite extraordinary. First because of his writing itself, which has a quality that one very rarely finds ... and then for an even more important reason to me: his Kafka interpretations appear to coincide with my own thinking in an almost disconcerting way – in contrast to almost everything else that was ever written about Kafka. ... My concept of Kafka's antinomistic theology coincides right down to the very core with Steiner's thesis ... and the mythical god of which I speak is nothing other than the gnostic demiurge mentioned by Steiner. (Adorno quoted by Hermann-Röttgen 1988: 132)

In the same letter, Adorno explains that he would offer his services in the project of publishing Steiner's work were he not already fully occupied – as is now well documented, but could hardly have been known at that time – in securing the publication of Walter Benjamin's writings: 'Of course everything must be done to ensure that Steiner's work is published' (1988: 132). That Adorno could be taken at his word in these matters can be seen from his assistance in assuring the publication of H.G. Adler's *Theresienstadt* book (Atze 1998: 138). He promised Adler to write to Scholem about the matter, and did so in the strongest terms in a letter to Scholem dated January 1954 (Adorno 1992: 178). However, Scholem pointed out that Steiner's work was unavailable to him in Israel, and added pointedly: 'You are probably not completely clear about the degree of almost complete estrangement between everything that happens' in Israel and Germany (Scholem in Adorno 1992: 179). One of the defining moments of modern German-Jewish intellectual engagement failed to occur: at the very point that the paths of Walter Benjamin and Franz Steiner crossed during their post-war publication history, instead of promoting a fruitful dialogue between their surviving friends, the non-meeting meant that – in all innocence – the plans to publish the former choked those to bring out the latter. Ironically, Steiner the Jewish thinker was a closed book to Scholem just because his work had appeared in Germany, and Steiner's thought was excluded from its place in a dialogue with scholars who shared the interests of the Frankfurt School. This omission rehearsed another that had taken place before the war.

Although Steiner and Adorno must have arrived at their views on Kafka independently, Adorno wonders whether Steiner knew any of his work, and the answer is possibly 'yes'; in a diary entry of 2 January 1937 Steiner records having had 'an important meeting about an article' with the editor of the *Zeitschrift für Sozialforschung*, who was just over for ten days from New York (Diary II Ms 1936-37: 2v). Nothing appears to have come of this, but had Steiner written his piece, he might have entered the ambit of the Frankfurt School and enjoyed a very different career. Even so, the convergence between one aspect of Steiner's work and a central motif in Adorno – subsequently recapitulated in the dialogue between Adorno and Canetti – does help to locate Steiner's place on the intellectual map of the mid-twentieth century. According to Habermas, the root point at which we argue Steiner and Adorno meet, i.e., the post-Kantian 'Oldest System-Programme', is in fact the defining moment of postmodernity (1985: 85f.); if Habermas is right, this would help explain the strong contiguity, yet complete independence, between Steiner's thinking and Derrida's deconstruction, Said's Orientalism, post-historicism – and Habermas's own notion of the public sphere.

The central event of the war years was also the one which finally
determined Steiner's thought, as indeed it changed his life and ultimately hastened his death. The atavistic renewal of the ancient
pogroms that are the inheritance of his people struck him with its full
force. He responded by internalising the persecutions. To a greater
extent than anyone else whom we are aware of who did not himself
experience the Camps, Steiner spiritually assumed responsibility for
the pain that his fellows were forced to suffer physically. The centre
which his thought now found lay in the equation between suffering
and value. He explains this in his 'Letter to Georg Rapp' of 1943 (see
Volume II, below):

> If we seriously consider whatever could be called 'value', it must be this:
> everything that contributes to the alleviation of suffering, everything
> which gives us the strength to overcome suffering, everything which can
> make suffering cease.
>
> A life without suffering is valueless. A world without suffering is value-
> less. What the religions of mankind have to offer – and when I say religions,
> I mean religions, not myths, not mystical absorption, not rituals, but the
> symbolic systems which result from all of these and are accepted as reli-
> gion, which is binding – what the religions of mankind have to offer, then,
> is in the end nothing other than the ground upon which, and the language
> in which, people can communicate about the possibility of ending their
> various sufferings and our own, common age of suffering.

The experience of suffering, as Steiner reflected on it in the years
1942 to 1944, came to form a new centre for his work as poet, thinker,
and anthropologist; in our view, it provided a new ground for his poetry
as religious activity; it located his thought on society within the core of
human experience; and it gave the necessary impetus to the turn in his
anthropology from the ethnological description of cultural tools
towards a politicised grasp of beliefs, values, practices, and institutions.

Steiner's internalisation of the Shoah did not end with the war. If
anything, it deepened after 1945, when the knowledge of his parents'
death in Treblinka become a certainty, the first pictures from the
camps were published, and he resumed contact with his oldest friend,
H.G. Adler. When the latter returned alive from the Camps in 1945
and emigrated to England in February 1947, Steiner and Canetti
heard at first hand the experiences of a man who had been in
Auschwitz. The old triumvirate that had never before lived in close
proximity was briefly restored, and to the dual project inaugurated by
Canetti and Steiner on power and slavery came a third, Adler's *Theresienstadt* monograph. The closeness between these projects can be seen
from the fact that after surving the initial shock of his internment in
Theresienstadt, Adler adopted a form of anthropological method as a

survival strategy. Having found unexpected strength in his decision to write a detailed study of the camp, if he survived, he developed what he calls 'the will to know and bear the whole truth':

> This will had to mature and I had to look around for an example, which I found in the fieldwork of the anthropologists. I always had to tell myself: you have to judge the life in this society as coldly and be as free from prejudice as a scholar who wishes to research an almost unknown tribe .... (H.G. Adler 1998: 116)

At the time when Franz Steiner was applying his anthropological method to a comparative study of slavery as a 'penance', his best friend adopted Malinowski's field work technique in order to study that self-same slavery at first hand. We infer that Adler owed his introduction to this method from Steiner, and that the similarities between Malinowski's encyclopaedic studies of the Trobriand islanders and Adler's own monumental depiction of a single camp in his *Theresienstadt* monograph derive from this mediation. From this we may perhaps also infer that Steiner was more deeply impressed by Malinowksi in the years 1936 to 1938 than his diaries or published statements admit – an inference further supported by Steiner's removal to London in the first place. Whether Adler's arrival in London in 1947 impacted on Steiner's anthropology it is hard to say, although it clearly affected aspects of his thought just as, conversely, the renewal of friendship led to Adler's reflecting on Steiner's view of slavery in his own work (H.G. Adler 1960: 638). It is perhaps not coincidental that Steiner's dread-filled poem, 'Capturing Elephants', which dates from 1947 – not 1942 (*pace* Steiner 1992) – transfers a central insight of Adler's *Theresienstadt* monograph to the animal kingdom:

Capturing Elephants

The tame beasts threatened silently,
Heads lowered against the grey-black sea
That milled within the palisade,
Trumpeted, snorted.

But when the wild ones, wholly overcome
By hungry days and a tightened world,
Found no more strength, gripped by ancient terror,
The tame ones were admitted.

With trunk and tusk the tame attacked.
Merciless the well-fed hatred thrust
Against the jungle smell, the distant kind:
Punished with relish.

So they slaughter their own, petty wildness
Scar by scar in their brothers' bodies,
But the bleeding beasts, almost broken into tameness,
Did not complain.

(After Steiner 1992: 30f.)

The poem compresses several strands of Steiner's concerns: its subject is all that came of his pre-war project to write a sociology of the elephant; it may recall Orwell's celebrated colonial allegory 'Shooting an Elephant', first published in 1936 and republished in 1940 (Orwell 1970); and it may also embody the tragic insight that under the pressure of the Nazi terror, Jews were forced into complicity with their oppressors' crimes (H.G. Adler 1960).

The Oxford Anthropologist

The sun's leave-taking is slow,
Still slower his going down.
When the sun is down, the bat streaks
And there's nothing more.

'Variations on a Song of the Papago Indians' (Steiner 1992: 59)

The rebirth of the Institute of Social Anthropology after the war must have encouraged Steiner to develop his thinking on anthropology which had been maturing over the last few years. Lecture schedules suggest Radcliffe-Brown resumed teaching at Oxford in Hilary (second) term of the 1945-46 academic year and was joined in Trinity (third) term 1946 by Meyer Fortes. There followed a procession of students returning from the armed services, civil service or prisoner-of-war-camps – Jack Goody, David Brokensha and Louis Dumont had been PoWs – and these were all anxious to make good their lost years. Evans-Pritchard began his lectures, having taken up the chair, in January 1946. Max Gluckman joined Fortes and Evans-Pritchard for the academic years 1947-48 and 1948-49, so that the post-war professors of Social Anthropology at Oxford, Cambridge and Manchester were briefly an Oxford triumvirate. Godfrey Lienhardt and M.N. Srinivas make first appearances as lecturers in the schedules for 1948-49 (Evans-Pritchard, however, dates Lienhardt's permanent appointment to 1949 (1970: 105)), while J.G. Peristiany joined the Institute from U.C.L. in 1949-50 on the departure of Gluckman to Manchester.

It was Peristiany who acted as external examiner for Steiner's dissertation during Trinity term 1949; Evans-Pritchard being the internal examiner. Although he had by then retired, Steiner's doctoral registration continued to be in Radcliffe-Brown's name. Apparently,

Steiner consented to examination only because he was bound to supplicate ten years after his first registration, and his time was up at the end of 1948-49. In Trinity term 1948-49 Franz Steiner, by then in his fortieth year, was 'given leave to supplicate' having satisfied his examiners, that his thesis 'A Comparative Study of the Forms of Slavery' should be awarded a D.Phil., and the degree was formally awarded in July 1950. On Fortes's departure for the Cambridge chair, Evans-Pritchard was able to appoint Dr Franz Steiner to a lectureship from 1950-51 – the year in which Mary Tew (Douglas) also joined his staff. It seemed that at long last, Franz Steiner's years in the wilderness had come to an end, but nothing in his life was to prove so simple.

For a period just after the second European war as – in common with Steiner – he preferred to call it, there can be few grounds on which to dispute Evans-Pritchard's belief that Oxford was 'the best, and best-known, postgraduate school in the world' (1970: 106). This was particularly true of Steiner's time, when Oxford – with a staff of varied backgrounds and singular talents – seems virtually to have become a clearing house (both for personnel and ideas) for much of the post-war establishment in the discipline of social anthropology. During 1951-52, Steiner's last full academic year at Oxford, John Barnes, Emrys Peters, Laura Bohannan, Paul Bohannan, Godfrey Lienhardt and Paul Stirling completed their doctorates. Additionally, Paul Baxter, John Beattie, Audrey Butt, Jack Goody, John Middleton, Rodney Needham, Julian Pitt-Rivers, and David Pocock are listed as students engaged in field work that same year. Among the anthropologists, apart from Evans-Pritchard himself, Steiner's particularly close friends appear to have been Laura and Paul Bohannan, Godfrey Lienhardt, M.N. Srinivas, and Mary Tew (Douglas). There is evidence of Steiner's advice to several of these on a variety of topics. Long letters from the field written by both Laura and Paul Bohannan and by Mary Douglas survive among his papers. Apart from the personal affection they evince, they are also evidence of Steiner's ability to advise on subjects as diverse as warfare and markets (among the Tiv where the Bohannans were working) and classification of the natural world (among Douglas's Lele). From his unpublished calendar entries, we can see that Steiner appears to have thoroughly discussed Lienhardt's dissertation on the Dinka before its submission, which lends further support to Mary Douglas's belief (1975: 128) that Lienhardt's views in *Divinity and Experience* (1961) show the mark of Steiner's thought. When Srinivas left Oxford in 1951, his replacement Louis Dumont also became a friend. Thus it was that on completion of his doctorate Steiner found himself a valued member of what, to slightly later arrivals, seemed an Oxford inner circle (Paul Baxter: PC and David Pocock: PC). The stage seemed set for Steiner to play a leading part in the development of social anthropology at Oxford.

Steiner, however, was a sick man. He suffered a fainting fit in 1946 and was diagnosed as suffering from a nervous breakdown (Fleischli 1970: 25); in 1948 he suffered chest pains and was found to have hypertension. Then, in 1949, he was hospitalised with a heart attack. Later ones followed, and such life-threatening events occasioned some typical Steiner tales. Laura Bohannan records how Steiner told her that he lay immobile in hospital, just able to take out his watch, and, using the second-hand to time his spasms, restored his heart to its normal rhythm (PC). In 1949, having no kin of his own, Steiner had nominated Meyer Fortes as his next of kin, as we know from the incident described by Julian Pitt-Rivers, who became Steiner's doctoral student and close friend on Meyer Fortes's departure:

> Despite the fact that his heart was weak [Steiner] was determined to do field work and was preparing to do it in Africa among the pygmies. As he explained to me: 'All my life I have been a little man, I want to know what it feels like, just for once, to be a big man.' Alas! he was never to know. He had already had an attack of heart failure which landed him in the Radcliffe Hospital for a few weeks. In fact his heart beat fainter and fainter and the authorities of the Hospital had secretly given him up for lost and told the truth only to his official next of kin. ... Franz gave me an account of how Meyer saved his life: while he lay there, expiring, Meyer, informed of his unlikely survival and knowing his religious faith, started to recite to him appropriate words of Judaic script. To hear this old atheist spouting holy text which he did not believe in to an apparently dying man appeared to Franz idiotic hypocrisy and made him so angry that his heart took strength from his fury and started to beat at twice the pace – and he was saved! (Pitt-Rivers Ms 1997: 38)

An uncanny echo of this story can be found in the writing, some forty years later, of one of his closest friends, the novelist and philosopher Iris Murdoch, whom Steiner met in 1951. After years of ultimately unsatisfactory relations with a series of more or less suitable partners, it seemed to Steiner that he had now found a woman whom he could marry, a possibility also entertained by Iris Murdoch's husband, John Bayley, in his recent memoir (Bayley 1998: 54). A poem Steiner wrote for Iris Murdoch on her birthday celebrates their fragile love:

> I give you this wine-glass,
> Drink from it, drink from me.
> Preserve the beautiful balance
> And don't break either of us.
>
> (Summers 1988: 20)

The poem gains a tragic poignancy in view of the custom of breaking a wine-glass at Jewish weddings to bring good luck.

Having read 'Greats' (ancient history, classics and philosophy) at Oxford, Iris Murdoch was able both to share many of Steiner's intellectual interests and meet his emotional needs. Ten years his junior, she had spent the early war years as a civil servant in the Treasury before joining the United Nations Relief and Rehabilitation Administration in Belgium and then Austria between 1944-46 (Conradi 1989: 11). As Peter Conradi relates, this period both brought Murdoch into contact with existentialism and saw her witness a 'total breakdown of human society'.

> What excited her about [existentialism] was the primary place it gave to the consideration and depiction of *experience*, a subject then absent from Anglo-Saxon philosophy, and its willingness to tackle problems of value and morality. (Conradi 1989: 11)

In 1948, Iris Murdoch became a fellow of St Anne's College, Oxford. As her journal records, she first met Franz Steiner briefly in 1941 but their friendship only began in the summer of 1951. The tragically brief refractions of Steiner's personality in Iris Murdoch's journal sketch out one of the richest, most insightful portraits we have of the man. The picture is remarkable not least for the many sides of Steiner's personality that Murdoch records: his family, his closest friends, his faith, his anthropology, his interest in the Orient, and his poetry all find a sympathetic home in her understanding of him. At their first recorded meeting on 3 March 1952, her notes on their conversation rehearse his ideas on time, which reflect ideas we know from *Conquests* (Volume II, pp. 249-66, below), as well as his ideas on the untranslatability of cultural experience and on 'value'; on 22 October, she records his views on God: 'On Saturday I talked of religion with F. He said, in answer to my asking if he believed in God, that he *loved* God. In him, it seemed no affectation'; and on 26 December – after Steiner's death – she recalls reading Rilke with him: 'I told F. that asking him to read Rilke with me was like asking Baudelaire to read Rimbaud' (Murdoch Ms 1952-3: fol.1ff). Clearly, Iris Murdoch will not only have been able to satisfy Steiner's intellectual and emotional needs, but, most significantly, will have been able to bring him that recognition as a poet which he so desperately craved to achieve through the publication of his selected verse, *In Babylons Nischen* (In the Niches of Babylon).

Murdoch's close friendship with both Elias Canetti and Franz Steiner helps explain Conradi's sense that 'it is no accident that the plot of her novels ... often concerns the disruption of a court of settled, rooted English *Grands Bourgeois* by displaced persons and refugees' (1989: 12). Elsewhere he wonders, 'Is it impertinent to find something owed to Franz Steiner in the gentle, scholarly and dying Peter Saward' of Murdoch's early novel *The Flight from the Enchanter* (1956) whose book-crammed study and patterns of taxing work are affectionately and meticulously described (Murdoch 1956, chapter 3; Conradi 1997: xx). Like Saward, Steiner lost a beloved younger sister in her teens; and like Saward also, the knowledge of his impending death has made him 'strangely gay' (1956: 23), an adjective Iris Murdoch was later to use of Steiner. The novel employs Murdoch's characteristic redistributive justice in depicting elements of the three Central European Jews (Canetti appears in Misha Fox; Steiner in Peter Saward; and H.G. Adler is partly refracted in John Rainborough) and in the processes mixes in other characteristics, some of them derived from English sources; in pursuing this creative alchemy, she affectionately transfers Adler's height and full head of hair to the short and balding Steiner. It is noticeable that Murdoch adopts Steiner's term 'Oriental' to describe both Misha Fox and Peter Saward – the characters who recall Canetti and Steiner – in the novel. Murdoch's friendship with Steiner, common knowledge among their friends, did not become public until 1988, when she spoke to Sue Summers:

> Franz was certainly one of Hitler's victims. But, though so terribly sad and wounded, he was one of the wittiest, merriest, sweetest people I ever met, with a remarkable capacity for enjoyment. He was gentle and good and full of spirit and imagination. (Summers 1988: 20)

In her later years, Iris Murdoch returned intellectually to some of her earliest concerns, too. One of her last novels, published when she was seventy in 1989, seems to revisit the likely preoccupations of the days when she, Steiner and Canetti were younger friends attempting to make sense of the senseless destruction that overshadowed their lives. *The Message to the Planet* tells the story of Alfred Ludens's pursuit of Marcus Vallar, in the conviction that he is capable of realising a philosophical project of the greatest significance to humankind. Both scholars are Jewish, and their concerns exist in the light of the attempt to annihilate European Jewry. Moreover, the plot of the book opens, in a scene with plausible relation to Steiner's own tale of his rescue from near death, when Marcus Vallar apparently raises from the dead, or from near death, the Irish poet Patrick Fenman. No easy identification between Murdoch's fictional characters and friends can be suggested, however the interests of real friends do appear once again to have been distributed around her characters who, in different ways, seek to give meaning to their lives through intellectual activity, direct experience, artistic expression or emotional fulfilment. Aspects of Steiner's complex personality may be refracted through these concerns: in the course of the novel Ludens is forced to recognise Vallar's inability to commit his experience of suffering to paper in a philosophical tract. As the psychiatrist Marzillian – a character who possibly recalls the psychiatrist Paul Senft, a friend of Steiner's at Oxford who later collaborated with R. D. Laing and Michel Foucault – explains:

> Great pain, the pain of others taken on in the imagination, may seem like a punishment, but then where there is a punishment there is a crime. This can be one of the dialectical games which is played by the soul, it can be a very destructive game, it can be a source of energy for good or bad. It concerns too the mystery of how the suffering of expiation can be transformed into the suffering of redemption. (Murdoch 1989: 499)

The acceptance of suffering, as Steiner explained in his 'Letter to Georg Rapp' (Volume II, pp. 115-22, below), was central to his experience of exile and loss. It also provides the nub of his 'Gebet im Garten' (Prayer in the Garden), which is also the central theme of Murdoch's novel. The poem's speaker addresses his dead parents and recalls 'The sufferings you went through':

> My light and grief are that you were.
> What you have been in me was horribly perverted,
> Darkness more than grief extinguishing I must bear
> Because from you, so pale already and so frail,
> The monster's clutches could not be averted.
> For your sake I recover from your death,
> And now this darkness, now this light
> And other light:
> At the time of my ripeness
> Together merged into my inwardness.
> Witnesses, witnesses,
> Join me in what I speak, be near me now.
> Let me speak truthfully. ...
> On pain I stand and firmly plant my feet,
> It is my rock, a rock I did not form.
>
> (Steiner 1992: 83, 85)

Steiner's poem, using a meditative form that he had developed from his reading of T.S. Eliot and had first employed in his own *Conquests*, locates the mystical centre of his work in a union with his destroyed people. His meditations on himself as a mere 'part' of this 'whole' – 'One part alone has survived' (1992: 79, 82) – provide an uncanny spiritual correlative to the fragmentary character of his life's work: if perfectionism prevented him completing the *Conquests* and dictated that even the completed portion of his dissertation remained fragmentary, on a spiritual level this accorded with his religious self-understanding, by which he recognised himself and his experiences as a mere fragment of a greater whole. Franz Steiner's failure – or unwillingness – to bring his ideas to a final synthesis seems principled as well as explicable by his early death. Whatever the comforts of insidership (Steiner finally became a British citizen in 1950), friendship and love during his final years – according to Evans-Pritchard he was 'at least happier and more secure' (1956b: 11) – these existed against a background of the suffering of his people and family that Steiner experienced simultaneously with bodily suffering and the certainty he was near death. Regardless, he set himself to work unrelentingly, writing in whole or part at least six lecture series on very different subjects. Simply listing them gives an impression of his range and the intensity of his work in his final years.

The details we print are those advertised in Lecture Lists of the Faculty of Anthropology and Geography as published in the Oxford University Gazette. We have supplemented details contained in these sources with what we can infer from Steiner's papers in Marbach. We have also consulted another source: in the Library of the Institute of Social and Cultural Anthropology at the Oxford University is a volume indexed as 'Franz Steiner, Lectures and Papers at Oxford 1949-52, bound typescript' which contains copies of Steiner's Lectures on 'Theories of Tabu' and 'The Division and Organisation of Labour', as well as Steiner's versions of the papers published posthumously as 'Notes on Comparative Economics' and 'Chagga Truth'. There must be a very strong presumption that these scripts are typed fair copies of his own notes made for, and subsequently edited for publication by Laura and Paul Bohannan. In Steiner's *Nachlaß* there is additionally a lecture on 'Aristotle's Sociology' given to the Oxford Classical society that may also have formed an early part of a series of introductions to anthropological thinkers delivered during this period.

Steiner's lectures are as follows:
1. *Theories of Taboo*, twelve lectures first given during the Michaelmas and Hilary terms 1950-51 and repeated during Hilary and Trinity 1951-52. (See pp. 103–219, below.)
2. *The Division and Organisation of Labour*, eight lectures. Seven of these survive in Steiner's note form, and an eighth as an excerpt of his dissertation (1949a: 88-104). First delivered during Hilary term 1950-51 and repeated during Michaelmas terms 1951-52 and 1952-53. (See Volume II, pp. 174-190, below.)
3. *The Study of Kinship*, delivered together with Evans-Pritchard and Lienhardt during Hilary 1950-51 and with 'others' during the same term 1951-52. Notes for two lectures survive in the *Nachlaß*. (See Volume II, pp. 197-201, below.)
4. *Some Forms of Servile Symbiosis*, delivered during Trinity term 1950-51. According to Paul Bohannan's note (in Part III of his unpublished abridgement of Steiner's doctoral dissertation), this series was based on Steiner's recently completed dissertation.

5. *Social Anthropology and Language/Language and Society*, a seminar run fortnightly under slightly different titles with J.G. Peristiany during Michaelmas 1950-51 and with Louis Dumont during Hilary 1951-52. A brief position paper on this subject exists in the *Nachlaß* and probably derives from this series (see Volume II, pp. 193-96, below).

6. *Some Problems in Simmel*, a scheduled series of four lectures during Michaelmas 1952-53, three of which survive in the *Nachlaß* (see Volume II, pp. 208-26, below).

Even this was not the sum of Steiner's anthropological endeavours: while completing his dissertation in 1948 he had delivered to the International Congress of Anthropological and Ethnological Sciences in Brussels the paper published posthumously as 'Enslavement and the Early Hebrew Lineage System'; in 1949 he gave a paper at Oxford 'On Gutmann's *Das Recht der Dschagga* (both reprinted below, pp. 230-34, 235-50); and at the time of his death he apparently had in mind three books: a revision of his dissertation, a book on economics (a fragment of which survives as Steiner 1954b) and a book on Aristotle – some indications of which survive as a lecture and a thesis chapter. Allowing that there were connexions among elements of his projects, the sheer range, let alone quantity, of work involved for a man as seriously ill as Steiner is staggering. Indeed, Steiner was sufficiently disabled to have difficulty reaching the first floor lecture room of the building in which he taught so that a chair was placed on the half-landing for him to rest and catch his breath, from which he liked to speak to students (Paul Baxter: PC).

His enormous investment of energy in his anthropological writings notwithstanding, Franz Steiner still found the time to continue writing his aphorisms and to develop his poetry, which now entered its major phase. He willed himself to work day and night in an almost superhuman way, observing – tragically – in an aphorism that he is 'burning too slowly' (1988: 13). The wartime project of the *Conquests* lay abandoned. Exactly why Steiner left this central work unfinished is not clear. However it is apparent that his aesthetic changed, moving on from the meditative cycle represented by *Conquests* to the short, more concrete 'exemplary poems' of his last period. He now wrote some of his best pieces, such as 'Kafka in England', which mixes irony with pathos and mysticism in a brilliant display of artistry (Volume II, p. 81, below), and 'Leda' in which he re-examines a classical artistic theme in terms of his ideas on danger, purity, and pollution (J. Adler 1994a: 144f.); interestingly, too, this poem – which comes to terms with others on the same theme by Spenser, Rilke, and Yeats – not only embeds the Leda story into an ethnically conceived context that recalls his field-trip to the Carpathians, it takes a sociological

view of Leda by presenting her within the family unit. We believe that
Steiner's poetry, as it became increasingly imbued with anthropological
insights, reached new heights of expression in the years 1945-7. However, the tragedy that touched Steiner's family life also affected his life as
a poet. Although he was the much admired intellectual centre of a group
of exile poets in London (see J. Adler 1995b; Ritchie 1998: 270-71)
which included Erich Fried among their number, and although he also
began to register an impressive series of magazine publications in Germany, the collection of poems that he set his heart on, *In Babylons Nischen*
(In the Niches of Babylon), never got beyond proof stage. Whereas the
publishers, Willi Weismann Verlag in Munich, produced a new edition of
Canetti's *Die Blendung* (*Auto-da-fé*), financial problems prevented the
scheduled appearance of Steiner's volume. In the publisher's catalogue
for 1949 it is announced on the same page as Canetti's novel as containing 'among the purest poems in the German language'. Only a handful of
proof copies bearing the date 1950 on the title page survive, two of them
bound in red cloth at Iris Murdoch's expense. What he perceived as the
outward failure of his verse together with the energy he devoted to
anthropology led to a decline in literary output in his last years, though
he continued to write an astonishing number of aphorisms.

Neither his work, misfortune nor sickness made Steiner inaccessible
to students. Evans-Pritchard – who wrote of him as 'a teacher of rare
ability ... beloved both by students and colleagues' (1956b: 11; 1981:
196), and elsewhere that 'he was greatly loved and respected by all his
colleagues and students at Oxford' (1952: 181) – had a particularly
soft spot for Steiner. For instance, while his own student Paul Baxter
undertook fieldwork, Evans-Pritchard transferred his registration so
that Franz Steiner could get the supervision fee without his health
being put under any extra burden (Paul Baxter: PC). And, when Steiner
needed to be hospitalised, apparently it was Evans-Pritchard who paid
for him to have a private room (Ian Cunnison: PC). On Steiner's side,
however, as Anand Chandavarkar recalls, the affection was also tempered by a 'sadness' at what he took to be E.-P.'s typically British
'unthinking Arabophilia and phil-Islamism'; in a conversation in
Steiner's presence, Evans-Pritchard dismissed Zionism with the words 'I
have nothing against Jews or Judaism but I have always regarded Palestine as an Arab country' (Chandavarkar Ms 1996: 1). Steiner's attrac-
tion to his Oxford contemporaries had various sources: he was the very
figure of the middle-European Jewish intellectual. E.-P. characterised
him to Rodney Needham as 'the most scholarly' of them all (Rodney
Needham: PC). Slight, short-sighted, described on one occasion by Ian
Cunnison as 'slightly distrait, slightly disorganised, slightly unshaven'
(PC), he was the source of numerous anecdotes, some told by himself
(such as his being raised from the dead by Meyer Fortes), others told

about him. Godfrey Lienhardt, in his obituary of Evans-Pritchard, tells that Evans-Pritchard 'thought it a duty to adorn a tale before handing it on ... I believed for years on his authority that Franz Steiner had been in such straits when he first came to Britain as a refugee that he had been forced to earn a living as a table-tennis player in Scotland, and I thought I should not recall those humiliating days in the life of an *intellectual of intellectuals* by referring to them in Franz's company' (1974: 300, emphasis added). Anyone familiar with British (male) middle-class humour will recognise this as a piece of familiarly, affectionate leg-pulling. Another tale, recorded by Laura Bohannan, concerns her viva, at which Steiner was an examiner. She was seated opposite Steiner, Daryll Forde, and the third examiner; when Forde asked her a question of which Steiner took a dim view, he would wiggle his ear, making it difficult for her to keep a straight face and look at her examiners (Laura Bohannan: PC). Yet if Steiner enjoyed acceptance and esteem at Oxford, and even friendships with his Oxford colleagues, writing to his central European friends, he stressed his loneliness. To his friend Isabella von Miller-Aichholz, he wrote on 11 February 1951:

> There is only work here. If I otherwise meet with people, they fall into another one of those endless conversations about the war. It's usually just waffle. People only want to be calmed down and comforted. Unfortunately, I can't do that. I prefer not to go into company at all. No, I can't give anyone the feeling of calm and protection, nobody can do that any more.

The social and cultural gulf that had separated Steiner from his British colleagues before and during the war was now compounded by the existential division brought about by his knowledge of the extent to which the Second World War had changed the world – a lesson, it seems, only belatedly acquired in England. The failure of his volume of selected poems, *In Babylons Nischen*, to see the light of day – negotiations dragged on interminably and the book was finally aborted at proof stage in 1950 – only heightened his sense of isolation. Loneliness is also a theme of Steiner's letter of 4 November 1951 to the editor of the projected volume, Rudolf Hartung, who had by now become Steiner's friend; there, Steiner paints a characteristically ironic picture of his multicultural allegiances:

> And here I sit night after night with a picture of Buddha, a Jewish prayer book, a few English thrillers, a few unpublished poems and a bundle of work. And at the same time there are shining lands, loveable peoples, people who cheer me up and share their vitality with me ... (Fleischli: 1970: 36)

Even towards the end, something of Steiner's naïve childhood love of distant lands and exotic peoples seems to have sustained him in spirit, contrasting with his Oxford exile. At this time, around 1950, he practically gave up poetry, and started a new career as an artist. Writing to Canetti on 14 August 1952, he comments: 'Drawing gives me a lot of pleasure. I have also used coloured pastels. Human groups interest me most of all.' But there was a deeper reason for his sense of isolation. Writing to Canetti on Institute notepaper on 2 December 1951, he stressed his inner loneliness: 'Nothing has changed in Oxford. I still live in enforced, degrading solitude. You will have noticed how inaccessible I am in conversations about important matters, how inattentive I am, how I always direct the conversation to my personal problems.' The point at issue is his inability to form a lasting attachment. One lady who seriously wished to marry Steiner around this time, the eminently suitable but over-motherly Zionist friend, Esther Frank, he rejected (Canetti: PC), whereas the young belle on whom he had just set his heart turned him down; as Steiner says in the same letter to Canetti: '... and so I've lost everything once again ...'. Here was the inner void that the recent and growing attachment to Iris Murdoch was, as we have noted, on the point of filling out with new hope.

In the final years of his life Steiner was able twice to visit Spain, in the hope of seeing the cities where Jewish intellectuals of the Spanish Middle-Ages had lived before their expulsion (Pitt-Rivers: PC). Spanish culture had already had a major impact on his poetry – his 'Gebet im Garten' (Prayer in the Garden) of 1947, in being dedicated to the memory of his father, recalls Manrique's *Coplas por la muerte de su padre.* Julian Pitt-Rivers, who became his doctoral student when Fortes left to Cambridge, was pioneering the social anthropology of the Mediterranean at this time. In 1951 Steiner took his first holiday in Galicia (northern Spain) to escape the heat, and experienced Spain as a release from English life. As he wrote to Isabella von Miller-Aichholz – when he was in Cangas de Morrazo on 5 August 1951:

> Only a few days have passed since I landed, but a long time seems to have passed, I've seen so much and am reeling with enthusiasm. ... The fourteen years in England have just fallen away like a sickness or an old skin; and people say: you are young, Usted joven! Enjoy yourself! And to tell the truth I still haven't touched a drop of water, and danced through the night until 4.00 a.m. without the slightest problem ....

Everything enchanted Steiner in Spain: the landscape, the architecture, the language, the manners, and the women. To Hartung he wrote that he made more friends in Spain in ten weeks than in fourteen years in England (Fleischli 1970: 36). His enthused, long letters from Spain – full of vivid perceptions and details about his own private life – present a happy, carefree Steiner, though not a Steiner who has renounced his own fundamental interests in civilisation or his sympathies with the oppressed. Writing to Isabella on 2 September 1951 he observes:

And now to Oviedo: What a sad land is Asturias! The wild mountain land-scapes, the poor inhabitants of the mountain villages, the poverty and oppression. It is a conquered land that is still held down by every means at the disposal of power. The Moroccan troops are still here, whom the Fascist agitators had to bring across from North Africa, in order – as they say now – to defend Christian culture. However, these defenders of Christianity have to make do with the ordinary local brothels, and are no longer offered every woman in the defeated villages ....

Steiner's second trip the following year was to Andalusia where he visited Cadiz before being met by Pitt-Rivers and visiting his research site in Grazalema. Steiner himself lived for some time in the red-light district, and Pitt-Rivers reports that it was thanks to discussions with Steiner that he was able to analyse why the sons of prostitutes, literally *hijos de putas*, so often became priests, thus rendering their own paternity irrelevant at the same moment as they became 'Fathers' (Pitt-Rivers Ms 1997: 40). He returned from this holiday on 8 October 1952, arriving in Oxford the following day. Iris Murdoch met him from the train, and his journals record the shame he felt when she carried his suitcase upstairs.

The journal Steiner began after his return from Spain records his developing relationship with Irish Murdoch in tragically intimate detail. On 18 October, he writes:

> The lights of Oxford. Saw them with love, probably for the first time in fifteen years. And Iris was at the station, dressed in trousers and a grey duffle-jacket, serious and smiling, sweet and lovely, holding a little bunch of gentians in her hand for me. (MS 1952a: 1)

The intellectual and emotional closeness which united Franz and Iris appears, *inter alia*, from the way he reads poetry with her, and from a metaphor for their relationship, which speaks of them 'opening and closing each other like the pages of a book' – 'it almost feels like being married' (MS 1952a: 9). Their humour, likewise, emerges:

> How Iris is endlessly surprised about me, as if I were the sole example of a species, a little dog with feathers, or a bird with six legs instead of wings. I probably am, but I never thought of such a creature as loveable before now. (MS 1952a: 12)

The entire relationship is fraught with pain. Knowing Steiner's anger when a young friend contemplated marriage with a Christian (Vol. II, pp. 121f., below), we are left to imagine the tensions which the religious Jew experienced in his liaison with the young Oxford philosopher, whom his contemporaries regarded as 'quite a catch' (Mary Douglas: PC); for all the sometimes grotesque circumstantial details in their physical relationships which Steiner commits to paper, when it comes to religion, he remains silent, as if circumventing a spiritual taboo, instead dwelling on the pain caused by his sick heart, and the danger to which this exposes him, or on the embarrassment (and, later, tenderness) which he feels when his lover must assume the role of nurse. Their first night together, 25 October, is fully analysed:

> What torture! Did two people who love each other so much and who were so experienced ever fear each other more than we do? Her marvellous passion evaporated, her coldness infected me. In the end, I was afraid that this was happening because she had decided to surrender just to comfort me, and her feelings would not obey her. Then I talked myself out of this desperate view, and in the end it happened. But I was too fearful because of my heart, neither of us could manage to be really spontaneous, and we disappointed each other. (MS 1952a: 18)

Steiner then 'showed her Walther von der Vogelweide's poem "Under der Linden"', that charming medieval poem of innocently consummated love. With an irony that brings out another parallel to his great Prague model, the same journal entry also notes the forthcoming appearance of Kafka's *Letters to Milena*: 'I'm a little afraid of this Milena who reminds me too much of my problem at the moment' (MS 1952a: 19). Having not yet seen the correspondence, which he bought some days later, Steiner is presumably thinking of Kafka's entanglement with a non-Jew – a rare intimation of his own, unarticulated guilt. Eventually, on 10 November, after a happy evening with Iris, the diary cites Faust's last, ominously contented words, *Verweile doch* ... (MS 1952a: 57). The sense of doom culminates in the final entry, that for 18 November: 'Paul Eluard, that noble poet is also now dead ...' (MS 1952a: 76).

According to Iris Murdoch's diaries, apart from visits to friends, he was preoccupied with writing his lectures on Simmel. Among his younger Oxford colleagues, Simmel may have been becoming a vogue. He was read in German by Laura Bohannan, and in the Preface to the second edition of the monograph based on his doctorate Pitt-Rivers notes that the book which became his 'Bible' in the field was Kurt Wolff's 1950 edition of the *Sociology of Georg Simmel* (1971: xvi). Steiner and Louis Dumont were almost neighbours in Oxford and they, together with Dumont's wife and Iris Murdoch, spent the evening of 26 November together (Dumont: PC). During the past year, Steiner had lamented to friends about his relations with Iris Murdoch: 'Now at last I have found the woman I wish to marry, she does not wish to marry me.' On that fateful night, according to Canetti, Iris Murdoch did agree to marry him (PC) – the proposal is recorded in the final pages of Murdoch's *The Flight from the Enchanter* in which Rosa, a recognisable projection of aspects of Iris, proposes to Peter Saward:

She knelt before him and her black hair fell about her almost to the ground. She put a hand on his arm.

'Peter,' she said, 'what would you think of the idea of marrying me?' He looked at her calmly and a little sadly. 'You can imagine, my darling,' he said, 'how much it moves me to hear you say this, but you don't really want it. Ah, if only you did! But you don't.' (Murdoch 1956: 315)

With a typical reversal, Murdoch has transformed her blonde hair into black locks, but the characteristic posture on the floor, recorded in both their journals and in Steiner's photographs of his young lover, lends the episode a ring of authenticity. In the novel, Peter Saward distracts himself with photographs of a city we recognise as Prague. In reality, Steiner died that night. He was buried on 28 November 1952 in the Jewish burial ground at Oxford.

I remember his funeral – the weather was bleak and cold: in my memory there is even some snow on the ground. But the only *person* that I remember there was Iris Murdoch standing somewhat apart from the rest and near the grave, dressed unconventionally for a funeral in those days, that is to say in her usual day-to-day clothes, and looking utterly desolate. (Pocock: PC)

An acquaintance of Iris Murdoch's at the time reports how she regretted not having 'the consolation of widowhood' (Donovan: PC). At the time of his death, Steiner was revising a poem, 'Über dem Tod'. Iris Murdoch's journal records how Franz impressed upon her that the definite article in the title was in the dative (*dem*) and not the accusative (*den*), so making the poem not 'On Death' but 'Above Death'.

A nurse who had looked after Steiner earlier at Freelands Hospital provides the following epitaph in a letter of 20 June 1953:

The other patients in his ward called him the Professor. They were all working-class men, except for one young coxcomb aged about fifteen. F.B. was simply marvellous with them. When he was better he used to get up for a few hours each day, and I nearly wept to see him shuffling about in his bedroom slippers doing little services for the other men. They thought the world of him and always spoke of him with great affection – 'a real gentleman', said one of them (an ex-bus driver) and coming from him it couldn't have been higher praise.

When I was on night duty we often used to have little talks. Going round, I would see him, propped high in bed, sitting quietly and peacefully in the darkness, not clattering round and ringing bells to disturb the long silence, as the other patients did. And when he was asleep, I used to stand and think – 'there lies a frail body, but he has the spirit of an eagle.' I shall always remember him as an example of great courage and a proof that a person can remain whole or integrated in spite of so much. And people don't believe in miracles! (Diana Buchannan Ms 1953)

Many of his colleagues and students have subsequently recorded their intellectual indebtedness to Franz Steiner. Mary Douglas attended Steiner's 'Tabu' lectures (p. 6, above) and acknowledges inspiration for *Purity and Danger* in the ideas on classification and danger he first expressed publicly in these lectures (1964, 1966); subsequently, she has said that Steiner 'invented' the concept of 'purity' that she used (Douglas Ms 1994: 2). The debt to *Taboo* was noticed by two fellow Oxonians: Rodney Needham in his *Times Literary Supplement* review of her book (anon. 1967: 131), and T.O. Beidelman in a review for *Anthropos* (1966: 907). Via Paul Bohannan, Steiner's ideas directly impacted on the 'substantivist' school of economic anthropology which sought institutional grounds to make comparisons between market and non-market economies. The application of his interests in classification, values and social organisation pioneered an analysis of institutions of slavery that was later to become one of the major contributions of anthropology to historical scholarship. Godfrey Lienhardt's phenomenological study, *Divinity and Experience among the Dinka*, was directly influenced by his discussions with Steiner and by Steiner's paper on 'Chagga Truth'. The three general accounts of social anthropology written by Oxford-trained scholars in the first half of the 1960s each drew upon his writings, and did so in different ways: Lienhardt draws on Steiner for a discussion of values (1964: 88, 90); Beattie in the context of exchange (1964: 199-200); Paul Bohannan during a review of forms of inequality (1963: 166). Steiner's direct and acknowledged influence on his friends and contemporaries is demonstrable; however, as significant to a retrospective appreciation of his ideas are the concerns developed to a greater and lesser extent during his lifetime which seem, looking back a half-century, to foreshadow later anthropological concerns. Just to itemise these for the present: we find in Steiner anticipations of later debates linking the politics and epistemology of anthropology, the relation between ethnography and comparative anthropology, and the cross-cultural study of the institutionalisation of regimes of value. We shall discuss these in the second part of our Introduction in Volume II.

PART II: TABOO

CHAPTER I

THE DISCOVERY OF TABOO[1]

When I came to the Institute of Anthropology at Oxford in 1938, as a student of Professor A.R. Radcliffe-Brown's, we were told that social anthropology and comparative sociology were the same thing. Nothing seemed more reasonable than such an equation. Comparative sociology referred to a body of theories and concepts concerning the nature of the social life of human beings. These theories and concepts had been developed, so we then thought, through the study of records and observations of various societies, chiefly the simpler societies. Simplicity seemed to enhance observability; the emphasis was on observation and on variety. In this emphasis lay the difference between comparative sociology and the common variety, sociology pure and simple, the much ill-used offspring of philosophy.

Social anthropology was an empirical pursuit. It was represented by field monographs, written chiefly by contemporary British students. Field techniques were much discussed; they were supposed to lead to great discoveries, but they themselves were the chief inventions of the time. Field techniques were still 'problems' – so much so that Malinowski remained unchallenged when he confused general rules concerning the comparative relevance of field data with theories of society.

Comparative sociologists consistently made use of the ethnographers' work, but they no longer used these records – as once Tylor, Frazer, Westermarck had done – to extract bits of evidence which could then be strung together by the theorist. Men like Durkheim, whose school represented comparative sociology, took over whole vistas of foreign societies; their extracts were on a lavish scale. In those days it seemed as though field data had to undergo two scrutinies, that of the collector and that of the theorist, and the second could not dispense with the first. It was for the theorists to argue out the definite evaluation – the meaning for our knowledge of human society as a whole – attributable to the exotic vistas they selected. Without this expert evaluation the collector's work would have been wasted. The two were seen as stages of one process.

But even fifteen years ago when Radcliffe-Brown spoke of 'social anthropology or comparative sociology' ([1940a] 1952: 189), the equation had become rather misleading, for an important change was taking place. Today, when we take the results of this change for granted, the equation is no longer misleading; it is meaningless. This great change consisted in a shift of expert activities; experts began to go into the field; contributions to comparative sociology became fewer and fewer, and definitely less significant. No comparative study of any importance has been published in this country during the last twenty years. Indeed, the last important contribution made on a broad comparative basis was Radcliffe-Brown's theory of kinship, now most important equipment for the field worker.

In his last statement on comparative sociology Radcliffe-Brown says that social anthropology 'must combine with the intensive study of single societies (i.e., of the structural systems observable in particular communities) the systematic comparison of many societies (or structural systems of different types). The use of comparison is indispensable' ([1940a] 1952: 194). Comparison, mark you, of whole societies, of whole structures, and not of attitudes, systems of values, cultural idioms or institutions. It sounds extremely plausible; it is, in fact, very desirable. But Radcliffe-Brown himself has compared only institutions, those of kinship. 'Whole structures' – this implies at the present stage of research such a wealth of detail, such a complexity of abstractions, that comparison becomes an impossibility. Radcliffe-Brown cannot give an example of such an ambitious comparative study, for there is none. We do not even find it in books like *African Political Systems*, for the systems outlined and analysed in them are not actually compared.

Radcliffe-Brown was simply restating the old claim of comparative sociology in a kind of unconscious anachronism, as though the great change, which he more than anybody else helped to bring about, had not taken place. Actually the two have, on the whole, drifted so far apart that it would be fair to give them new labels, to retain the expression 'comparative sociology' for the one, but to call the other 'analytical and descriptive sociology'. Such a distinction would be fair but its usefulness doubtful because of the scarcity and unimportance of comparative work. I am not referring to American culturology. The dichotomy is, nevertheless, there. Furthermore, the relation of the two kinds of study in the past, and the eclipse of the one in the present, have had results which we must take into account in dealing with a subject like taboo, in which we must be aware of what we mean by comparative studies and by terminological categories.

The first consequence has been the general watering down of the comparative method. In Radcliffe-Brown's usage of the word, 'comparison' means two quite different things. One means postulating a general notion, a kind of 'ideal type' like a joking relationship. This ideal type is defined in an abstract manner, and cases are then selected to illustrate the concept. These instances ought to be as dissimilar as possible, marginal cases just covered by the definition. Then a set of statements is made about the ideal type, and their validity is tested with reference to the comparative material, that is, to the marginal cases. The other meaning of comparative study applies to the study of a variety of social phenomena, the similarities as well as the differences of which must be accounted for. These uniformities and divergencies are set forth in statements which are produced in the course of the comparison and which are not the results of observation or other direct methods of apprehension (1931: 11-14, 22-26). It need not be stressed how different the two processes of comparison are, how different their aims. The very fact that such ambiguities and methodological errors caused no serious confusion shows how unimportant this kind of research had become.

Another result of the relation between comparative and analytic studies, and one which is of even greater interest in this context, concerns terminology. We are still working with the broad concepts and categories which were developed in the comparative period. But we now use them for the close scrutiny to which the expert, when in the field, subjects his own data. In this use the categories are found unsatisfactory. They are then redefined, and by this process they become so narrow as to lose all significance outside the individual analytical study to which they were tailored.

Totemism is a case in point. The general category 'Totemism' – which had been widely and elaborately defined in order to cover as many types as possible – proved too clumsy as soon as we tried to speak of totemism in terms of particular societies. What we too often fail to realise is that what we define as 'totemism of M' or 'totemism of N society' is not a category like 'Totemism' in its old comparative use; 'totemism of M or N society' is an analytical concept necessary to the understanding of M or N society. The broad significance which 'Totemism' had as a comparative category has evaporated. This significance was twofold: it bore the import of an assumed stage in human evolution; it also demarcated totemism as a solid block of 'otherness', which it remained even after thinking in terms of stages had been abandoned by the earnest. Was it not the purpose of anthropology to explain this 'otherness'?

But the question remains: How can we, for our purposes today, use terms developed for such different purposes? And if we strip our vocabulary of these significant terms of the comparative period, what are we going to put in their place, not only as labels for pigeon-holes, but also as expressions indicating the direction of our interest? We do retain them and, sooner or later, each of us in his own way makes the unpleasant discovery that he is talking in two different languages at the same time and, like all bilinguals, finds translation almost impossible. This kind of difficulty appears again and again in our literature. Let me quote just one example, selected at random. R.J.B. Moore begins his article, 'Bwanga among the Bemba', with this statement:

> The conception of *bwanga* among the Bemba of Northern Rhodesia is very similar to that recorded ... among the Ila and the Lamba. In collecting material I have, however, followed a slightly different method. The traditional method of studying this subject has been in the main categories of 'Magic', 'Taboo', 'Omen', and so on. While this has proved useful in collecting together many facts under their appropriate heads it has resulted in taking, as it were, a cross-section through native thought. The native does not think in these categories, he observes an object and knows certain facts about it: whether it is edible, fierce, or dangerous, whether if found in a certain way it constitutes an evil omen. The arrangement of my material, therefore, has been according to this latter method, i.e., taking one object at a time and recording as much about it as possible. ... The traditional method is equivalent to reading the columns *vertically;* the method here adopted reads them *horizontally.* To change the metaphor, social organisation and beliefs have been compared to a pattern worked in cloth; the pattern can only be there while the warp and woof remain intact, and without the interweaving of both the whole would be unintelligible. The major classifications of *bwanga*, taboo, etc., are comparable to the warp and are unintelligible until we have also examined the woof, which is composed of the individual objects. (1940: 211)

You can see what this writer is doing.[2] In the first place he drags into a problem confused enough as it is the all too familiar dichotomy of structure or social organisation on the one hand, and on the other belief or culture or psychology. We can cut out this confusion to start with. There remains, secondly, the incongruity between what the writer regards as broad categories and what he calls the way the native thinks; what the native thinks cannot be satisfactorily summarised under the categories. The writer then projects this difficulty, which certainly has no existence except as a terminological problem, into social reality. The two incompatibles become, as it were, social forces which cooperate in weaving the fabric of social life. One is represented as the general, universal, categorical, the other as the particular, individual. The writer thinks of the *observable* attitudes of individuals and of particular situations against the background of sociological categories.

But the divisions in the vertical column of Moore's diagram – 'Folklore' (by which he means mythological associations), 'uses as *fishimba*' (that is, an object's magico-medical properties), 'Taboos', 'Omens' –

are not sociological categories. His horizontal divisions, containing what appears to him individual and particular, are headed: rabbit, python, tortoise, owl, chameleon, antbear. Now, taking the owl, under the heading 'Folklore' we find a quite different statement from that under 'Taboo' or 'Omen'. Are we to be surprised at this? The author wants to be sure we understand that for the native all these various statements are only aspects of the same thing, the owl. What else could they be? Surely this was never in doubt. The differences, however, inevitably result from the varied social contexts of the diverse situations in which antbears or owls are relevant. But the writer was clearly trying to make quite another point: he wanted the vertical categories ('Folklore', etc.) to have a pragmatic significance. As they have none, he looked for some other classification which seemed to him to contain more social reality – though social reality is not to be found, by the way, in the owl itself.

This example could be paralleled by others. I give this one only to illustrate my thesis: that the meaning of words appearing in the terminologies of comparative and of analytic sociology have drifted apart without our noticing it. Such a discussion is a necessary preliminary to consideration of any of these broad categories, the most important of which are, perhaps, 'Magic' and 'Taboo' – the latter being our particular concern.

This book will fall into two parts, the first serving as a necessary background to, and basis of evaluation for, the second. In the first three chapters I shall start by outlining the initial usage of the word 'taboo' in ethnographic literature; this is necessary if we are to have a background for the early stages of the concept and theories of taboo. I shall at the same time briefly sketch the sociological contexts of the usages referred to under taboo, since many of the arguments and criticisms of the theory of taboo concern either its Polynesian meaning or the difficulties inherent in using a word with particular ethnographic associations as one of the broad comparative categories that we have just discussed. In the second and longer part I shall review diverse theories perpetrated in the name of taboo, and then try to find a basis for a general criticism of these theories.

Definitions of Taboo

A warning is necessary at the very outset that several quite different things have been and still are being discussed under the heading 'Taboo'. Taboo is concerned (1) with all the social mechanisms of obedience which have ritual significance; (2) with specific and restrictive behaviour in dangerous situations. One might say that taboo deals with the sociology of danger itself, for it is also concerned (3) with the protection of individuals who are in danger, and (4) with the protection of society from those endangered – and therefore dangerous – persons. As I suggest tentatively later, taboo is an element of all those situations in which attitudes to values are expressed in terms of danger behaviour. Now we cannot see all this in terms of a single problem, whether we solve it or leave it unsolved. There is no sociological-situational unity in the attitudes and customs under discussion; a psychological unity is equally absent. Frazer himself testifies to this when, in the famous volume on *Taboo* in *The Golden Bough*, he lists, among the many other interesting and curious things in his chapter on 'Knots and Rings', the following items: (1) instances in which priests, or worshippers of a female deity, or pilgrims, or pregnant women must not wear rings or knots – taboos if ever there were any; (2) instances in which people have to loosen knots, women have to let their hair flow free, garments are unbuttoned, cattle stalls are thrown open, in order to help and hasten a woman's delivery – certainly magical practices; and (3) instances in which a lock is locked or a knot tied into a cord and these things flung into water in order to prevent a marriage taking place – magical practices again, but of a quite different kind which do not belong to the magical observances of daily life and which cannot be fostered by respectable social institutions: black magic, in fact (Frazer 1911: 293-317).

Now it is very easy to see, even easier perhaps today than in Frazer's time, that these instances belong together. There is a psychological unity implicit in the meaning of knots and rings; therefore Sir James grouped them together in one of his chapters. But no variation in this basic meaning (which I warn readers not to regard as a nonsociological element) can account for knots becoming the object of a taboo observance in the one case and the means, in other cases, of magical practices.

We are thus in the position of having to deal, under 'Taboo', with a number of diverse social mechanisms expressed in forms which, from the psychological standpoint, stretch beyond this one category. This dual diversity is one reason for the many attempts to narrow the definition of taboo, as a comparative category.

Margaret Mead, to quote only one of many, opens her article 'Tabu' in the *Encyclopaedia of the Social Sciences* with a warning that such an effort must be made:

> Tabu may be defined as a negative sanction, a prohibition whose infringement results in an automatic penalty without human or superhuman mediation. The word was introduced into English from Polynesia, and special Polynesian usages have coloured the interpretation of the institution. If the term is going to be employed effectively in comparative discussions, it must be stripped of those accidents of interpretation and be restricted to

describe prohibitions against participation in any situation of such inherent danger that the very act of participation will recoil upon the violator of the tabu ... (1937: 502)

These are severe restrictions indeed. And one cannot expect much success from such an attempt; the world accepts an extension of meaning much more readily than it allows any loss of connotation.

Captain Cook and the South Sea Islands

Before we consider the technical definitions of taboo, let us consider its introduction into European languages. As every dictionary will tell you, the word was first used by Captain Cook in his description of his third voyage round the world. In an important passage he says of the islanders of Atui, one of the Sandwich group:

> The people of Atooi ... resemble those of Otaheite [Tahiti] in the slovenly state of their religious places, and in offering vegetables and animals to their gods. The *taboo* also prevails in Atooi, in its full extent, and seemingly with much more rigour than even at Tongataboo. For the people here always asked, with great eagerness and signs of fear to offend, whether any particular thing, which they desired to see, or we were unwilling to shew, was *taboo*, or, as they pronounced the word, *tafoo*? The *maia, raa,* or forbidden articles of the Society Islands, though, doubtless, the same thing, did not seem to be so strictly observed by them, except with respect to the dead, about whom we thought them more superstitious than any of the others were. (1784, III, ii: 249)

And, in connection with human sacrifice in Tahiti, we are told:

> The solemnity itself is called *Poore Eree,* or Chief's Prayer; and the victim, who is offered up, *Tataa-taboo,* or consecrated man. This is the only instance where we have heard the word *taboo* used at this island, where it seems to have the same mysterious significance as at Tonga; though it is there applied to all cases where things are not to be touched. But at Otaheite, the word *raa* serves the same purpose, and is full as extensive in its meaning. (1784, III, ii: 40)

By the way, Cook's phrase 'mysterious significance' has been the cause of discussion and of some misunderstanding. It does *not* mean, as Marett seems to have believed, 'of magico-religious significance' (1921: 181). Cook only meant that the precise meaning of the word was a mystery to him. Cook, one can see, treated taboo as something already rather familiar in this account of his third journey. It is, indeed, a curious fact that taboo in word and custom should not have been previously observed. No Dutchman, no Spaniard had taken notice of these strange things – or, at least, none had mentioned them. But perhaps they would not have seemed as remarkable to a Spaniard as to a northern Protestant. And, as for the Dutch, their contacts with the natives were of the briefest; there are hardly any accounts of travel so disappointing to the ethnologist as those of the Dutch navigators.[3]

We must, however, remember that Cook was the first European with what one might call a general knowledge of the Polynesian area, and he was interested in those features which, like taboo, were held in common by various Polynesian cultures. Observations which could not have become meaningful during the short periods of stay on each island were brought sharply into focus by the comparisons which forced themselves on Cook. We must also remember that taboo was *not* a word conspicuous in its use. On reading later travellers, one receives the impression that they heard the word frequently and publicly, as one hears the word 'bachshîsh' when coming to a Levantine town. Cook's logbook from his first journey bears witness that taboo was more often seen than heard. For instance, he notes of the Tahitians:

> It is not common for any two to eat together, the better sort hardly ever; and the women never upon any account eat with the men, but always by themselves. What can be the reason of so unusual a custom, 'tis hard to say, especially as they are a people, in every other instance, fond of Society, and much so of their Women. They were often Asked the reason, but they never gave no other Answer, but that they did it because it was right, and Express'd much dislike at the Custom of Men and Women Eating together of the same Victuals. We have often used all the intreatys we were Masters of to invite the Women to partake of our Victuals at our Tables, but there never was an instance of one of them doing it publick, but they would Often goe five or six together into the Servants apartments, and there eat very heartily of whatever they could find, nor were they in the least disturbed if any of us came in while they were dining; and it hath sometimes hapned that when a woman was alone in our company she would eat with us, but always took care that her own people should not know what she had donn, so that whatever may be the reasons for this custom, it certainly affects their outward manners more than their Principle. (1793, I: 91)

This distinction between principle and outward manners is an instance pointing towards the possible religious conditioning of Cook, which I just mentioned. It also shows that he had not yet heard of taboo. He then goes on to remark on another fairly general feature of Polynesia, the *more* or *mare*:

> The *Mories*, which we at first thought were burying places, were wholly built for Places of worship, and for the Performing of religious ceremonies in .... Their *Mories*, as well as the Tombs of the Dead, they seem to hold

sacred, and the women never enter the former, whatever they may do to the latter. (1793, I: 101)

Here Captain Wharton, Cook's editor, adds a footnote: 'Cook did not apparently learn anything in this voyage of the human sacrifices offered in the Morais, such as before war ...' And, we may add, neither did he come across the word 'taboo'. In this passage Cook does use the word 'sacred', but he had not noticed that one and the same word was used by the natives about the food restrictions of women and the sacredness of places of sacrifice.

Let us return to Cook's last voyage – after his tragic death the journal was faithfully continued by his successor, King – and to what was written of taboo once the word had been noticed. In reference to clearing a space for an observatory, we are told:

> We fixed on a field of sweet potatoes adjoining to the *Morai*, which was readily granted to us; and the priests, to prevent the intrusion of the natives, immediately consecrated the place, by fixing their wands round the wall, by which it was enclosed. This sort of religious interdiction they call *taboo*; a word we heard often repeated, during our stay amongst these islanders, and found to be of very powerful and extensive operation. A more particular explanation of it will be given ... under the article of religion; at present it is only necessary to observe that it procured us even more privacy than we desired. No canoes ever presumed to land near us; the natives sat on the wall, but none offered to come within the tabooed space, till he had obtained our permission. But though the men, at our request, would come across the fields with provisions, yet not all our endeavours could prevail on the women to approach us. Presents were tried, but without effect ... we were invariably answered, that the Eatoa and Terreeboo (which was the name of their king) would kill them. This circumstance afforded no small matter of amusement to our friends on board, where the crowds of people, and particularly of women, that continued to flock thither, obliged them almost every hour to clear the vessel, in order to have room to do the necessary duties of the ship. On these occasions, two or three hundred women were made to jump into the water at once, where they continued swimming and playing about, till they could again procure admittance. (1784, III, iii: 10-11)

We have already noted one European element given to the word taboo: 'mysterious significance'. Here, for the first time, as the bewilderment of the European gives way to amusement, we can see the addition of another connotation, which taboo was long to retain: the senseless and funny. Why should women, with a notable lack of restraint, crowd the decks and splash in the water, always displaying, as Bougainville was to remark a few years later, *des formes celestes*, and then be so careful about something like eating, from the European view a much less intimate activity? It was funny. With this passage that superior and slightly irritated indulgence which some people have for others who cannot think clearly begins to creep into accounts of taboo. These food prohibitions puzzled King greatly. He remarks again:

> It must, however, be observed that they fall very short of the other islanders, in that best test of civilisation, the respect paid to the women. Here they are not only deprived of the privilege of eating with the men, but the best sorts of food are *tabooed*, or forbidden them. They are not allowed to eat pork, turtle, several kinds of fish, and some species of the plantains; and we were told that a poor girl got a terrible beating, for having eaten, on board our ship, one of these interdicted articles. (1784, III, iii: 130)

The islanders who tried to beat some respect for the laws and customs of her people into that foolish girl appear to have been quite unaware of Margaret Mead's definition of taboo, according to which the culprit should have found only 'automatic penalty without human or superhuman mediation'.

King also observed the function of the taboo complex in explaining social stratification and creating social distance:

> The people of these islands are manifestly divided into three classes. The first are the *Erees* or Chiefs of each district; one of whom is superior to the rest, and is called at Owhyhee *Eree-taboo*, and *Eree-moee*. By the first of these words they express his absolute authority; and by the latter, that all are obliged to prostrate themselves (or put themselves to sleep, as the word signifies) in his presence. (1784, III, iii: 153)

King did not share Cook's great diffidence in tackling the meaning of this word of 'mysterious significance'. He thought he owed his readers an explanation:

> Having promised the reader ... an explanation of what was meant by the word *taboo*, I shall, in this place, lay before him the particular instances that fell under our observation of its application and effects. On our inquiring into the reasons of the interdiction of all intercourse between us and the natives, the day preceding the arrival of Tereeboo [their paramount chief], we were told that the bay was *tabooed*. The same restriction took place, at our request, the day we interred the bones of Captain Cook. In these two instances the natives paid the most implicit and scrupulous obedience; but whether on any religious principle, or merely in deference to the civil authority of their chiefs, I cannot determine. When the ground near our observatories, and the place where our masts lay, were *tabooed*, by sticking small wands round them, this operated in a manner not less efficacious. But though this mode of consecration was performed by the priests only, yet still, as the men ventured to come within the space when invited

by us, it should seem that they were under no religious apprehensions; and that their obedience was limited to our refusal only. The women could by no means be induced to come near us; but this was probably on account of the *Morai* adjoining; which they are prohibited, at all times, and in all the islands of those seas, from approaching.

Mention hath been already made, that women are always *tabooed*, or forbidden to eat certain kinds of meats. We also frequently saw several at their meals, who had the meat put into their mouths by others; and on our asking the reason of this singularity were told that they were *tabooed*, or forbidden, to feed themselves. This prohibition, we understood, was always laid on them after they had assisted at any funeral, or touched a dead body, and also on other occasions. It is necessary to observe that, on these occasions, they apply the word *taboo* indifferently both to persons and things. Thus they say the natives were *tabooed*, or the bay was *tabooed*, and so of the rest. This word is also used to express anything sacred, or eminent, or devoted. Thus the king of Owhyhee was called *Eree-taboo;* a human victim *tangata taboo;* and in the same manner, among the Friendly Islanders, Tonga, the island where the king resides, is named *Tonga-taboo.* (1784, III, iii: 163-64)

I have quoted these extracts in full, because they are the classic passages from which the word 'taboo' became known to Europeans. It soon became the property of the educated, particularly in Britain where Cook was widely read: he was, after all, the last of the great navigators, the last person to sail round the globe in the grand manner *and* discover new and inhabited land; his writings showed him to be a man of genius and his death was an event of the mythical order.

The *New English Dictionary* shows in what contexts and how rapidly the word came into use. It cites from 1791 'a plain declaration that the topick of France is *tabooed* or forbidden ground to Mr Burke'. In 1822 Southey wrote: 'He has tabooed ham, vinegar, red-herrings, and all fruits.' Sir Walter Scott wrote in his diary for 24 October 1826: 'The conversation is seldom excellent among official people. So many topics are what Otahaitians call *Taboo.*' In the same year, Mary Russell Mitford wrote, in *Our Village, Sketches of Rural Character and Scenery 1824-32*, a sketch 'A Touchy Lady': 'The mention of her neighbours is evidently taboo, since ... she is in a state of affront with nine-tenths of them.' (*NED* IX, Pt 2: 12-13).

Few people today think of taboo as an exotic word. During the last few months I have asked a number of people whether they can remember the occasion on which they first heard it. Younger people brought up in Western and Central Europe said that they had come across it just as one comes across any other word for the first time: hearing it in common talk, reading it in newspapers, and so on. For them it is one of the established words of the language, one which has no greater need of a pedigree in order to be meaningful than words like 'Pegasus', 'democracy' or 'birth control'. Many middle-aged people, both of English and continental extraction, however, first heard taboo as part of the Freudian vocabulary. A group of people of my age and older have shared with me the pleasure of coming across it first in one of those imaginative adventure stories in mid-nineteenth century geographical magazines. And one young woman told me that she first heard the word in a 'scripture class', when a foolish schoolmistress tried to explain features of the Pentateuch by saying, 'It was a taboo, you know.'

In conclusion, I want to mention briefly a few navigators who are of interest in this context. Bougainville, who sailed the South Seas between 1766 and 1769, did not include the word 'taboo' in his *Vocabulaire de l'île Taiti* – not even in the augmented second edition which had been collated with Cook's much smaller dictionaries. Even the great La Pérouse, who when angry with the natives cursed not them but Rousseau – a man with a real flair for ethnology who noticed the affinities of the Malay and the Polynesian languages and advanced the theory that some Polynesian populations derived from Malay colonists – even he did not go beyond Cook's and King's account. He sailed in 1785, fifteen years after Cook, and used Cook's vocabularies in his intercourse with the natives. From Cook he knew the word 'taboo' and apparently used it with success to ward off the islanders when they inconvenienced his ship (La Pérouse 1797, II: 195-202, 271 and 435).

Vancouver did not add to our ethnographic knowledge of taboo, but the two Russo-German expeditions were rather remarkable. The first was that of Adam Johann Ritter von Krusenstern who commanded the *Nadjezhda* and *Neva* and sailed in 1802 with Captain Lisiansky and the naturalist, von Langsdorff; the result was three independent accounts. It is the variations in these three accounts of taboo at Nukuhiva that interest us here; von Langsdorff, according to Lehmann the most reliable ethnographer among them, gives a twenty-one point list of taboo customs, which he knew was incomplete and which also shows that he appreciated the mixed social and religious character of taboo; he translated the word as 'forbidden' (von Langsdorff 1812, I: 114, 124, 158). Krusenstern, who did not go so deeply into the social structure of Nukuhiva, stressed the religious implications of taboo (1812, I:227). Lisiansky spoke of taboo as 'a sacred prohibition' (1814: 104, 118, 169). Taboo had become a legitimate problem. Otto von Kotzebue, commanding the *Rurik* in 1821, mentioned the difficulties of taboo as a matter of course. Again European amusement was registered, though of a slightly heavier kind; the notables of the Sandwich Islands were asked to dinner on board ship, but as the pig meat had not been consecrated at the *Mare* not only this meat but all other viands that had been cooked over the same fire were taboo and had to be eaten by the hosts. 'There sat my guests in their droll costume, and were fasting spectators of an European dinner, till they were induced, at last, on my repeated solicitation, to partake of some biscuits, cheese, and fruit; wine and brandy did not seem to be taboo [why should they be?] for they diligently emptied their glasses' (von Kotzebue 1821, I: 330-31).

Kotzebue, on his first and less spectacular journey (1817), was accompanied by de Freycinet, who wrote the best account we have of taboo from the first half of the nineteenth century. Indeed, his volumes are one of the most important sources for South Seas ethnology. He translates taboo, and it must be accepted, as *prohibé ou défendu*, and he describes the custom of taboo as an *institution à la fois civile et religieuse* (1839: 597).

1836 saw the sailing of the South Seas expedition to end all expeditions: Lieutenant Wilkes with six ships, two painters, five naturalists, and so on – the biggest and best of all South Seas expeditions. True to character, the expedition produced not a book but a library, which was little read (1854, 5 vols).

NOTES

1. *Taboo* was edited for publication by Laura Bohannan after Franz Baermann Steiner's death, and published with an 'Introduction' by E.E. Evans-Pritchard as *Taboo* (London: 1956 Cohen and West; New York: Philosophical Library; Harmondsworth: 1967 Pelican Anthropology Library). Steiner's own typed copies of the lectures (Lectures A-L), with handwritten corrections, survive in his *Nachlaß* in the Schiller Nationalmuseum, Deutsches Literaturarchiv, Marbach am Neckar. A typed fair copy, presumably prepared in connexion with Laura Bohannan's edition, is contained in a volume in the library of the Institute of Social and Cultural Anthropology of the University of Oxford. (*Franz Baermann Steiner, Lectures and Papers Oxford 1949-52*) Steiner's twelve 'Lectures on Tabu' were given in two terms (Lectures A-H, I-L) Michaelmas and Hilary 1950-51, and in Hilary and Trinity 1951-52. We print the text as edited by Laura Bohannan. She made stylistic and presentational changes to the text, added examples Steiner quoted in his lectures, and supplied the footnotes and the academic apparatus. *Taboo* was published in Japanese in 1970, translated by Inoue Kenko, Tokyo: Serikashobo.
2. See p.212 (Moore 1940) for the diagram described below.
3. For example, Roggewein in 1772 mistook Samoan leaves and tattooing for clothing of silk with fringes. (Turner 1884: 89). A convenient account of Pacific travellers is given by Lehmann (1930: 5-54). (L.B.)

CHAPTER II

TABOO IN POLYNESIA (1)

The last chapter was a short introduction to the history of taboo in our literature. I mentioned that the term first came to the attention of Europeans in the course of their exploration of the Polynesian archipelago in the last quarter of the eighteenth and first part of the nineteenth centuries. The passages I quoted from these explorers should have indicated the impression made on the eighteenth-century observer by these Polynesian customs. And much of most theories of taboo still refers to Polynesian taboo customs or compares the Polynesian type with others. Therefore we need as background a brief description of the working of Polynesian taboo.

I want to start with taboo as a word, that is, as a linguistic problem and also as a problem of meaning. One way of beginning – certainly in the nineteenth century – would be to ask: What did the word *tabu* originally mean? What is its etymology? Many answers have been given. Indeed, the word had been so extensively discussed by ethnologists that it became unfashionable to take for granted that it was a Polynesian word; Sanskrit and Indonesian languages were searched for etymologies. But as in all this very learned literature one can find no attempt to show why the word could not be Polynesian,[1] we may safely consider it to be so.

From the various attempts to supply a Polynesian etymology for *tabu* I shall select only two for mention. Both typify the kind of reasoning involved, and the second one may actually be true. The more ingenious, though the less convincing, is: *ta*, to beat, and *pu*, conch. Why? Because chiefs' proclamations were heralded by conch-blowing and drum-beating, and these proclamations were quite often taboos (Handy 1927: 318, *n*.32; also Kern 1886: 174-75)! The more popular etymology is that *tabu* means 'marked off'. The most convincing exposition of this theory is put forward by Edward Shortland, who derives the word from *ta*, to mark, and *pu*, an adverb of intensity: 'The compound word *tapu*, therefore, means no more than "marked thoroughly" and only came to signify sacred or prohibited in a secondary sense; because sacred things and places were commonly marked in a peculiar manner in order that everyone might know that they were sacred' (1854: 81). This etymology appears in Frazer's article on taboo, but he made no use of it in *The Golden Bough* (1875: 15; 1911). My feeling is that he was prompted not so much by a suspicion of Shortland's etymology as by a dislike of all etymologies in discussions of that kind. However, we who live so long after and have learned our lesson, namely, that a word's derivation does not prove a thing one way or the other and often gives no clue to the meaning of the word, can reconsider Shortland's explanation.

I am inclined to agree with Shortland, not because of the intrinsic merit of his etymology, which I am not qualified to judge, but because I have noticed parallel developments in Polynesian languages. The words derived from a root *sa* or *ha* (interchangeable) – 'to breath, to shout' – are a case in point:

MAORI: *haha*, to warn off by shouting; cf. *ha*, to breathe.

SAMOAN: *sa*, forbidden, prohibited (formerly much used as sacred, holy); *sasa*, a sign, a portent.

TAHITIAN: *ha*, a prayer or incantation formerly used for the healing of a person poisoned by eating certain fishes, or of a person who was choked by eating fish bones.

TONGAN: *faha*, a madman, a fool; *fahafaha*, to go shouting as one foolish.

MANGAREVAN: *ha*, prohibited, sacred; *e ha tupapaku*, food sacred to the dead. (Tregear 1891: 40)

Let us now turn from what *tabu* might originally have meant to its meaning and various forms in Polynesian languages. For this I have used two books: Tregear's *Maori-Polynesian Comparative Dictionary* and Lehmann's *Tabusitten*, which has an appendix containing the taboo words not only of Polynesian but of all Oceanic languages. Both sources have disadvantages. Tregear's extremely useful work is no substitute for a modern and truly comparative dictionary of the Polynesian languages. It is a very scholarly, though old-fashioned, Maori dictionary which gives under every Maori root words derived from similar stems in other Polynesian languages. While it thus avoids leaving us with the highly differentiated and often atypical Maori as a point of reference, it does not attempt a reconstruction of early Polynesian roots and their meanings. Lehmann gives us a very useful list, conscientiously compiled, but he treats words as a historical ethnologist would treat culture items.

The most common form of the word is *tapu*. That is the Maori, Tahitian, Marquesan, Rarotongan, Mangarevan and Paumotan pronunciation, which in some cases sounds more like *tafu*. The Hawaiian

form is *kapu,* the Tongan *tabu.* Forms like *tambu* and *tampu* are not
unknown, particularly in the mixed linguistic area or in the Polynesian
periphery. The word is used extensively outside Polynesia proper. Thus
in Fiji *tabu* means unlawful, sacred, and superlatively good; in Mala-
gassy, *tabaka,* profaned, polluted (Tregear 1891: 472-73; Lehmann
1930: 301-12). The *New English Dictionary* remarks: 'The accentua-
tion *taboó,* and the use of the word as substantive and verb, are English;
in all the native languages the word is stressed on the first syllable, and
is used only as an adjective, the substantive and verb being expressed
by derivative words and phrases.'

Up to this point my report is straightforward, and I only wish I could
continue, as so many have done, with the following words: 'A brief
glance at any compilation of the forms and meanings of this word in
the various Polynesian languages shows that in all of them the word
has two main meanings from which the others derive, and these
meanings are: prohibited and sacred.' The comparison of these data,
however, suggests something rather different to me, namely: (1) that
the same kind of people have compiled all these dictionaries, assessing
the meaning of words in European terms, and (2) that, with few exceptions, there are no Polynesian words meaning approximately what the
word 'holy' means in contemporary usage without concomitantly
meaning 'forbidden'. The distinction between prohibition and sacredness cannot be expressed in Polynesian terms. Modern European languages on the other hand lack a word with the Polynesian range of
meaning; hence Europeans discovered that taboo means both prohibition *and* sacredness. Once this distinction has been discovered, it can be
conveyed within the Polynesian cultural idiom by the citation of examples in which only one of the two European translations would be
appropriate. I have no wish to labour this point, but I do want to stress
a difficulty all too seldom realised. It is for this reason that it is so hard
to accept uncritically the vocabulary-list classifications of meanings
on which so much of the interpretation of taboo has been based.
Tregear's definition of the Maori *tapu* is an example: 'Under restriction,
prohibited. Used in two senses: (1) sacred, holy, hedged with religious
sanctity; (2) to be defiled, as a common person who touches some chief
or *tapued* property; entering a prohibited dwelling; handling a corpse
or human bones...' and so forth (1891: 472).

This sort of classification almost suggests that there was in Polynesian life a time in which, or a group of objects and situations in relation to which, the notion of prohibition was employed while the
society did not yet know, or related to a different group of objects and
situations, the notion of sacredness. This is not so. Taboo is a single,
not an 'undifferentiated', concept. The distinction between prohibition
and sacredness is artificially introduced by us and has no bearing on

the concept we are discussing. It is one of those cases Malinowski mentioned in his brilliant essay on 'Meaning in Primitive Languages', in which no abstract classification of meanings can provide a clue: the meaning must be found in the situation, in the manifold simultaneous overlapping and divergent usages of the word (1948: 238 ff.).

Before we go on to the meaning of impurity in taboo, I should like to mention the exceptions I alluded to before: when, according to dictionary evidence, taboo means only 'sacred' and not 'prohibited'. As translations of *tapu* Tregear gives for the island of Fotuna 'sacred', and for the island of Aniwan, 'sacred, hallowed' (1891: 473). There they are, but I think one is entitled to be suspicious of such cases, since they are not accompanied by any examples of non-Christian, non-translatory use, for the word taboo was widely used by missionaries in the translation of the Bible: in the Lord's Prayer for 'hallowed', 'sacred', and as an adjective for words like Sabbath. On the other hand, Tregear's second point is plausible: that the notion of impurity is derived from that of prohibition (or, as one should rather say, prohibition *and* sacredness). A mere glance into Polynesian dictionaries reaffirms this statement, for while there is no use of a word – with, as I said, a few exceptions – which connotes sacredness without implying prohibition, there are many words meaning dirty, filthy, not nice, putrid, impure, defiled, etc. Thus it was possible to convey a notion of an object's unfitness for consumption, or unsatisfactory surface or state of preservation, without any reference to sacredness and prohibition. Only some of the notions of impurity were connected with taboo notions: a state of affairs we might describe diagrammatically like this:

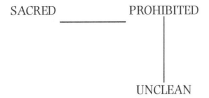

This peculiar constellation of meaning made the nineteenth-century ethnologists think of parallels: the Hebrew *qadosh* and the Latin *sacer* suggested themselves. Here, however, I prefer to stress the uniqueness of this semantic configuration, in which that which causes ritual impurity goes under the same name as all the contexts implying awe, obedience, abstention, or keeping of distance. One has only to think of Indian caste society, the society in which the concept of pollution is paramount, to see how inapplicable the Polynesian range of taboo would be there: it would mean using the same word for

Brahman and pariah, for the sacred cow, and human faeces. The Polynesian concept is so surprising because it seems to lack the polarity which we associate not only with sacredness but with *every* highly charged notion.

Even those who agree that the meaning of impurity in the Polynesian word taboo is peculiar are inclined to regard its double meaning of sacred and forbidden as something universal. Such an opinion cannot be justified while one speaks in terms of meanings and words. True, the Semitic languages have a comparable peculiarity and, to some extent, the Latin *sacer* as well. But such a correlation is not a general feature of human life and speech. In Galla, for example, where the word for prohibition and interdiction is *hirmi*, the word for holy, sacred, soul, is *ayana*, and there is no inherent association of the holy and the prohibited in the language (Tutschek 1845: 8, 199; cf. da Thiene 1939).

Unfortunately, the idea has been spread through ethnographic literature that the Polynesian word *noa* is the opposite of *tabu*, that is, opposite in terms of polarity. Actually the implication is only one of mutual exclusiveness. This is an important point for the understanding of taboo; I shall have several occasions to refer to it, and I want to give the dictionary meanings of *noa* as background. In Maori the word means: 'made common; not under *tapu* or under other restriction; of small account; at random, without object; just, merely'. It has similar meanings in the other Polynesian languages: Samoan, 'of no account; without cause'; Tahitian, 'common in opposition to sacred'; Hawaiian, 'to be released from the restriction of a *kapu* or other restraint, the lower or degraded class of people'; Tongan, 'random, trivial, undesigned, dumb, dumbness'; Paumotan, 'single, simple, spontaneous' (Tregear 1891: 268-69). *Noa* means, in fact, the unspecific, unspecified, the unlimited, free and common. It means, 'not tied to specific ends', whether we are thinking of sheer idleness or of those ties and ends in terms of ritual or civil law. *Noa* means a sphere of life where no taboo obtains and, *ipso facto*, cannot be an opposite of taboo.

Social and Political Aspects of Mana and Taboo

I shall now give a brief sketch of some former Polynesian taboo customs. They were so manifold that every author who had to deal with them attempted some kind of classification, if only to help him marshal his facts. I shall quote Lehmann's divisions, not because I think them particularly relevant, but to indicate the breadth of taboo. His main division is tripartite: (i) 'sociologically conditioned taboos', as he calls them; (ii) taboos of individual parts of the body and of special bodily conditions; and (iii) religious taboos. He lists six points under sociologically conditioned taboos: (1) taboos connected with persons holding high office, subdivided into (a) the power of high officials to give commands and declare taboos, (b) taboos resulting from the sanctity of chiefs, (c) taboos connected with priesthood, and (d) taboos of rank and status; (2) taboos for women (here Lehmann describes the segregation of the sexes); (3) taboos in economic activities and crafts; (4) war-time taboos; (5) the taboo sign as a legal symbol (of a claim and of appropriation); and (6) the custom of *tapa-tabu.* The second main division includes: (1) head and dorsal taboos; (2) taboos of special bodily conditions (such as the temporary ritual impurity of women in connection with childbed and menses); (3) taboos connected with illness and death. The third main group, that of religious taboos, has no subdivisions; it is a very small group, since Lehmann lists under other headings taboos connected with priesthood.

As mere enumeration this sort of classification is extremely helpful. I shall try to show the kind of thing it does *not* tell us about taboo by grouping together a number of taboo customs usually kept under separate headings. It is in studying this group of customs that we come across the purely Polynesian features of taboo, that we see the true connection of *mana* and taboo, and that the politico-ritual meaning of both becomes obvious.

A few words must first be said about Polynesian political organisation.[2] A very prominent feature seems to have been the splitting up of paramount political authority. Some authority was always exercised by – I hesitate to say delegated to – members of the chief's family. This shedding of functions could result from the ruling person's normal life course; he would become older, more and more dignified, more like his father, more powerful and paternal, and he would leave more and more things to be done by those whom he regarded as his children while holding those children in an increasingly firm grasp. It could also result from the purely political career of a man who advanced from the position of a subordinate to that of the paramount chief, creating alliances which he exploited, or subjecting other chiefs. For the Polynesians there was no fundamental distinction between the various processes of increasing power. They regarded the growth of power as a natural thing, so much so that, unless told otherwise, they assumed power to be the greater the longer it had been exercised. The mere passing of time was thus a power factor, both the time an individual had held office and the time a long row of ancestors had held office before him. The importance of an office increased from generation to generation, for power, if not checked by superior power, grows incessantly. Conquest of territory and subjugation of other chiefs was a short cut in this power development.

Now power in its growth constantly begets subsidiary power by the shedding of functions. The subsidiary functions which were divided in the fashion I have mentioned were very clearly defined; the power which was retained had no such clear definition. It did not need it, for the chief aspect under which people were permanently aware of the nature of this personal and official power was the ritual one; this the Polynesians called *mana*. Mana, unless restrained, keeps on growing. From this viewpoint one can immediately see how significant are the deviations from the normal procedure, which was for a chief to shed administrative and retain priestly functions. Thus the greatness of a chief's personal mana, his fertility in begetting power, and his self-imposed restriction of his sacerdotal functions were several aspects of the same thing.

Where the king engages himself too much in warlike enterprise, this marvellous balance is upset. He resigns the priestly functions rather than the military. A tug-of-war then develops between king and high priest, or rather between the two rival noble families. This happened, for instance, in Hawaii, where it led to the king's abolishing all religious institutions – the famous cancellation of all taboos by Kamehameha II – and later made the royal group, for quite ulterior reasons, protagonists of the European religion.

The priestly function was not only the indispensable core of the political one; it imposed its terms on the modes of coordination of the various political offices. This state of affairs had two aspects. First, the political hierarchy was a hierarchy of vetoes: the lower office was vetoed by the higher, and all by the king. The power to restrict was the yardstick by which power was measured; here was the social manifestation of power. Second, the exercise of this veto was in terms of taboo, that is, the actual sphere of any person's or office's power was delimited by the kind of taboos he could impose. Taboo thus provided the means of relating a person to his superiors and inferiors. One can imagine a Chancellor of the Exchequer declaring eight or nine shillings in every twenty taboo as a measure of the power conferred on him. It takes a stretch of the imagination to realise that in the Polynesian system this power could have been conferred on him only by somebody exercising an even more awful taboo, and that the Polynesian Chancellor would use the same term for his share in your pound and for the rights of his superiors, because these rights would concern him only as infringements of his own rights, just as taking away eight shillings is a restriction on your use of your twenty shillings.

The measure of a person's political authority is the taboos he can impose, and they can be rendered invalid and overruled only by the taboo of a higher official; this is the only possible limitation of function. Cook mentions the taboo of the Tongan food controller. It was his office to tell the people what not to eat. Once he had declared a kind of food taboo, it could not be eaten until the next harvest, and he could declare any kind of food taboo when it grew scarce (Cook 1784, III, i: 410-11). What caused the scarcity – lack of rain, ravages of war, excessive feasting – was irrelevant. In Polynesia, as in all other countries, positive commands were more common than prohibitions. Nevertheless, the structure dovetailed in terms of prohibition. Up to the last decade of the last century the supreme chief in Taumasanga, Samoa, had four messengers, or *tulafale*, who were members of another noble family. They had the power to taboo the killing of pigs and the use of coconut for feeding animals and poultry, though this taboo was never proclaimed. It was an attribute of these four, and their group was related to the chief in these terms. They themselves had *tulafale* from a third noble family of less exalted rank. These people could also impose taboos, but not such exacting ones as the four could.

The cases in which particular taboos roused revolt tell us much of the political nature of taboo. In 1850 chief Tavi of Tahiti issued an order for *rahui*, as the Tahitians called taxation by taboo, of preposterous dimensions: all the produce of one year – crops, animals, everything – should belong to his little boy. Moreover, he proclaimed this *rahui* without consulting his councillors. There followed a civil war in which he was defeated, and he had to leave the island. But this civil war was not fought over the issue of autocracy or the neglect of constitutional means, but over Tavi's right to impose this kind of taboo. To doubt his right to do so meant doubting his mana, and that, of course, involved his ancestors and his whole right to rule.

This graded power of prohibition had one source and mainspring, the paramount authority; and in the person of the paramount authority there was accumulated, as it were, the whole social tension of the society. Only thus can we understand the tremendous awe in which that person was held, for such a veneration of rank is something quite unusual among smaller populations. We must make a distinction between this awe and the taboos expressing it on the one hand, and the merely segregatory taboos on the other. These latter concerned not only the social distance between the ruler and the ruled, but also those between the ranks of society and the sexes. The mingling of these elements can be seen in the custom which dictated that the king should be carried by his slaves; since these were in any case his property, he could thus render them taboo without causing anyone any great inconvenience, whereas if he walked on the ground it became taboo to ordinary folk.

Against the background of this political taboo we can see that the same kind of taboo declared by private persons involves their mana in the same way. For example, it was a widespread custom for young men to declare their intended wives taboo. One is tempted to conjecture that this made infidelity an issue between the manas or rights of the men concerned without in any way involving the girls' families. It is on record that the sailors of a French ship, when ordered to sail, simply had their native sweethearts tabooed, and, when their ship returned, found things entirely to their satisfaction.[3]

NOTES

1. See Lehmann (1930: 54, 56-58) for details of such etymologies and for references.
2. I have space only to sketch in this background and I recommend the following books: Ellis's *Narrative of a Tour through Hawaii* (1826) and his *Polynesian Researches* (1831); Erskine's *Journal of a Cruise* (1853); de Freycinet's *Voyage autour du monde* (1839); the Martin-Mariner *Account of the Natives of Tonga* (1817); and Turner's *Samoa a Hundred Years Ago and Long Before* (1884).
3. For data touched upon in this section see: Gudgeon (1905: 130; 1906:38); Martin-Mariner (1817, I: 50; II: 79-90, 106, 141-45, 231-35); Cook (1784, III, i: 264 ff. and 359); von Kotzebue (1821, III: 211); Ellis (1826: 15, 72-98, 135, 391 ff.; Webster (1942: 366-69); Williams (1838: 60 f., 223); Williamson (1924, I: 184-86; III: 324); Tregear (1904: 95); Taylor (1870: 167-68); Stair (1897:121-28); von Langsdorff (1812, I: 132); Brown (1845: 35).

CHAPTER III

TABOO IN POLYNESIA (2)

I have outlined some Polynesian customs of taboo and indicated the relation existing between that concept and those of *mana* and *noa*. I have tried to show that the relation between *mana* and *tapu* is not one of opposites. In the languages in which the word 'noa' occurs it means 'aimless, vague, not tied up, not fixed to any purpose, free'. Taboo and noa are mutually exclusive. The abrogation of a taboo creates a state of noa regarding the tabooed object or the sphere or area in which the taboo has been in operation. It is a misunderstanding to apply Durkheim's notion of sacred and profane to taboo-noa contexts. Sacred-profane is a relation of tension and polarity: the profane threatens the sacred, the sacred has to be protected against the profane. These are concepts alien to the Polynesian taboo and noa, which are better understood by recourse to the simile of tying and untying.

In discussing the politico-ritual concept of mana I said that mana and taboo were often independent aspects of one thing. I described the ideal career of a man rising in power, gaining more and more mana, extending his power of imposing taboos, shedding functions and creating subsidiary powers, but retaining the priestly functions which were the mainspring of interdiction. I mentioned that in the Polynesian hierarchy ranks and offices were dovetailed in terms of interdiction, one restricting the other, and that this interdiction operated in the idiom of the priestly office, the basis of chiefly and royal authority. And I showed how the apparent exception, the abolition of taboos in Hawaii before the coming of missionaries, illustrated this thesis. I concluded by pointing out that the physical taboo of the chief's person is connected with this mainspring of his power.

Personal Taboos

I want now to show some of the contexts in which this personal taboo of a man of rank operates. It does so in a twofold manner. First, it restricts the actions of others and, one is tempted to say, those of the bearer or possessor of the tabooed body as well. Secondly, it makes it possible for a high personage to stake claims in terms of his respected body. This procedure was particularly common among the Maori, but we learn from various parts of Polynesia that a chief could claim a valuable object by saying that it was his head. It is this sort of anatomical taboo that is known as *tapa tabu* in Polynesia. The word *tapa* – Hawaiian *kapa*, Marquesan *tapatapa* – means 'to call, to name' (Tregear 1891:469). Lehmann insists that this word must not be used to explain the meaning of taboo; *tapu* is neither derived from *tapa* nor related to it etymologically (1930:303). The most interesting descriptions of the custom of *tapa tabu* are to be found in *Old New Zealand*. It is from this account that I take my first example – the confiscation of war booty through identification with parts of a tabooed body – as it occurred in a war between two Maori tribes, the Ngati Wakawe and the Ngapuhi.

Now the Ngati Wakawe retired with their canoes to a fortified island in the middle of an inland lake, thirty miles from the nearest point normally approachable by canoes, which were used only on the coast and were difficult to transport overland. But the pursuing Ngapuhi dragged a small flotilla overland and, in the course of their siege, brought up more and more canoes. The Ngati Wakawe, feeling secure, provoked their enemies in various ways, jeering at them across the water, cat-calling, challenging. The most foolish thing they did was to row to and fro in sight of shore in their great canoes. These men-of-war, capacious enough to hold fifty or sixty men, were made of costly hard wood and richly carved, and were easily the most valuable single objects among the Maori of old. Hence the display caused much agitation among the Ngapuhi on the lake shore, whose resolve to conquer grew apace. A long time before their attack, in order to make sure of the booty they coveted, each chief and noble warrior claimed a canoe as his property. These claims have become traditions. Chief Pomare shouted: 'That canoe is my backbone!' Chief Taheha: 'That canoe! My skull shall be the baler to bale it out!' – a very strong taboo indeed. Hongi Ika, called 'the eater of men', shouted – 'Those two canoes are my two thighs!' And so the whole flotilla was appropriated by the various chiefs, who thereby invalidated in advance any later claims based on conquest. A captor could claim the boat he seized only if it was not already *tapa tabu* (Maning 1884: 137-40). Land could also be claimed in this fashion. Shortland says that when a tribe occupied new territory a chief would claim a specially valuable piece of land by saying that it was his backbone (1854: 141).

If any object claimed by *tapa tabu* was also claimed by a commoner (by other means, of course), the taboo claim was the higher. The chief, however, compensated the commoner, giving him more than, perhaps even double, the value of the desired object. Failure to do so would create a conflict of rank or, in the Polynesian idiom, would 'damage his mana'. But if the rival claims were of the same order and ritual signif-icance, if the same object was under *tapa tabu* by two chiefs, the mat-ter became a straightforward conflict between their respective manas. One of the two would take possession and the other had either to accept his loss or resort to arms. Either issue determined the power of their respective manas, and in neither case was the prerogative of rank at stake. Indeed, nothing shows more clearly the meaning of mana and the tabooising power inherent in it. It is evident that the social control exercised by tabooising power and the conflicts arising from it are possible only if mana is – as, in fact, it was – carefully graded and part of the society's rank system. Rank dictated a man's degree of political power and organised sanction, and no sane person would claim a tabooising power that he did not possess in social fact. Com-moners contented themselves by making use of such power in a small way; they gave the names of important chiefs to their pet animals and thus prevented others from killing them.

We can advantageously set against the *tapa tabu* of the chief or man of high rank various customs allowing commoners to claim rights over things and persons. The Polynesian commoner did not taboo in terms of bodily parts, but by coupling the object with his name and thus declaring it taboo. In many other parts of the world the same effect is achieved by putting spells on things; an extreme example is from Dobu where, according to Fortune, every man commands at least one disease-bearing spell, known as *tabu* with which to protect his property (1932: 138-47). The confusing thing is that this use of spells is also known in Polynesia, alongside taboo by identification, and that it is, or was, called taboo there. To avoid this confusion we must distin-guish between the two sorts of taboo – by identification and by spell not according to the social function of the protective mechanism, but by relating that protective mechanism to other institutions of the same society. By this means, and not through the records of detailed obser-vation (which are in any case lacking), we may attain to some under-standing of the different sanctions involved. If the protection was a straight taboo by identification, injury challenged the mana of the owner and therefore provoked customary reactions to preserve his sta-tus. The spell technique, on the other hand, dissociated the protective mechanism from the owner's other rights and social activities. It was an historical accident – the predominance of the taboo idiom in Poly-nesia – that drew the spell technique into the orbit of taboo. I give an example from Samoa:

> But instead of appealing to the chiefs and calling for an oath [of innocence, after the alleged commission of a theft], many were contented with their

own individual schemes and imprecations to frighten thieves and prevent stealing. When a man went to his plantation and saw that some coconuts or a bunch of bananas had been stolen, he would stand and shout at the top of his voice two or three times: 'May fire blast the eyes of the person who has stolen my bananas! May fire burn his eyes and the eyes of his god, too!' This rang throughout the adjacent plantations, and made the thief tremble. They dreaded such uttered imprecations.... But there was another and more extensive class of curses which were feared and formed a powerful check on stealing, especially from plantations and fruit-trees, viz., the silent hieroglyphic taboo, or tapui (tapoe), as they call it. Of this there was a great variety. (Turner 1884: 184-85)

I shall quote three of Turner's eight examples. These are:

(a) The sea-pike taboo. If a man wished that a sea-pike might run into the body of the person who attempted to steal, say, his breadfruits, he would plait some coconut leaves in the form of sea-pikes and suspend them from one or more of the trees he wished to protect. Any ordinary thief would be terrified of touching a tree from which this was suspended. He would expect that after the next time he went to the tree a fish of the said description would dart up and mortally wound him.

(b) The ulcer taboo. This was made by burying in the ground some pieces of clam-shell and erecting at the spot three or four reeds, tied together at the top like the head of a man. This was to express the owner's wish and prayer that any thief might be laid low with ulcerous sores all over his body. If a thief transgressed and had any subsequent swellings or sores, he confessed and sent a present to the owner of the land, and he, in return, sent back some native herb as a medicine and pledge of forgiveness.

(c) The death taboo. This was made by pouring some oil into a small calabash and burying it near the tree. The spot was marked by a little hillock of white sand. The sight of one of these was also effectual in scaring away a thief. (1884: 185-87)

The main principles are readily observed: a display of dangerous charms which anybody can prepare, and the use of which is not tied up with a particular person or the ownership of the object which is to be protected. Its effect is restrictive, and as all restrictions in Polynesian society are described by the natives in one terminology, that terminology is, almost by definition, extended to this group of devices as well.

We must not forget, in speaking of personal taboos as they were used in *tapa tabu* that the restricting power of personal taboo acted independently of the will of the person owning a mana-charged body. To understand this better, we must realise that in Polynesian belief the parts of the body formed a fixed hierarchy which had some analogy with the rank system of society. Although it need not be stressed in a sociological context, it cannot be accident that the human skeleton was here made to play a peculiar part in this ascetic principle of mana-taboo. Now the backbone was the most important part of the body, and the limbs that could be regarded as continuations of the backbone derived importance from it. Above the body was, of course, the head, and it was the seat of mana. When we say this, we must realise that by 'mana' are meant both the soul-aspect, the life force, and a man's ritual status.

This grading of the limbs concerned people of all ranks and both sexes. It could, for example, be so important to avoid stepping over people's heads that the very architecture was involved: the arrangements of the sleeping-room show such an adaptation in the Marquesas. The commoner's back or head is thus not without its importance in certain contexts. But the real significance of this grading seems to have been in the possibilities it provided for cumulative effects in association with the rank system. The head of a chief was the most concentrated mana-object of Polynesian society, and was hedged around with the most terrifying taboos which operated when things were to enter the head or when the head was being diminished; in other words, when the chief ate or had his hair cut. Haircutting involved the same behaviour as actual killing, and the hands of a person who had cut a chief's hair were for some time useless for important activities, particularly for eating. Such a person had to be fed. This often happened to chiefs' wives or to chiefs themselves, and among the Maori these feeding difficulties were more than anything else indicative of exalted position. The hands of some great chiefs were so dangerous that they could not be put close to the head.[1]

Taboos of Impurity and Contagion

There is no point in describing or discussing the menstrual taboos of the Polynesians in any detail; they are in no way peculiar to the Polynesian taboo complex. One feature, however, ought to be mentioned, if only because it has not received the attention it deserves, and that is the extreme variation in the severity and also the objects of menstrual taboos, not only between one island and another but also between one tribe and another, as among the Maori. The taboos range from keeping the woman out of sight, through details of strict hygienic avoidance to her complete reintegration into daily life. Among the Marquesas a woman had to be kept out of sight for three days. Among most Maori tribes the woman moves about freely, works in the house, etc. Only the bodily secretions are tabooed. Among the Tuhoe tribe the taboo applied only to *kopa*, the cleansing material used by the women. Here the degree of precision and specialisation is remarkable; only one species of moss is to be used; only one spot in the forest, known only to the women of the village, is used for depositing the *kopa*. The humiliation experienced by a woman when a man sees her *kopa* is so great that it is regarded as sufficient cause for suicide.

Now whenever we find this kind of variation – where it is not due to separate development in long isolation – we assume that this differentiation has a positive function, that it is a diacritical symbol. This is very common in Africa. But menstrual taboos have no such function. Perhaps we may generalise on these lines: The individual forms of menstrual taboos have no social significance in their variation, but the general attitude towards taboos in Polynesia gives a great emphasis to any taboo that deals with an important situation. We find the same variation of restrictions in the circumstances surrounding childbirth. The strict taboos surrounding illness and death make care for the sick almost impossible. The reason for this behaviour is called *mate* or *matee*. Daniel Porte, in his *Journal of a Cruise, 1822*, says: '*Mate* expresses a degree of injury which could happen to a person or thing from the slightest hurt to the most cruel death. Thus a prick of a finger is *mate*. To have a pain in any part is *mate*; *mate* is to be sick, to be badly wounded is *mate*; and *mate* is to kill or to be killed, to be broken (when speaking of inanimate objects), to be injured in any way....'

Among most Polynesian peoples a house could no longer be used after a death. The death of a chief was the cause for extremely severe taboos. In Samoa his house could not be entered and traffic was diverted. The fishing lagoon was tabooed for some time; fishing was prohibited under the death penalty.[2]

Culture and Sanctions

Before I turn to sanctions I want to make two observations which may throw light on what can be called taboo-mindedness or taboo culture. The first concerns taboo as a means to an end. I have already discussed this to some extent in connection with *tapa tapu*, protective taboos of ownership (trees, crops, etc.), and the taboos of a food controller, as we called him. We can, then, say that in such a taboo culture many activities that are, in other cultures, carried out with other sanctions and described in other terminologies are in Polynesia drawn within the orbit of taboo. Secondly, we can learn much from the observations that the state of *noa* is sometimes achieved by causing two taboos to cross each other. For example, Maori women were forbidden to taste human flesh; if a Maori woman did so a great reverse would attend the men when they next went into battle. But the *wahine ariki*, the eldest woman of the eldest branch of the family from which the tribe traced its descent, had a main part to play when the warriors returned from battle. It was her duty to eat an ear of the first enemy killed by them. They were thus rendered *noa*.[3]

We know far too little for sociological purposes about the sanctions involved by breaking taboos in Polynesia. If we hear of sanctions, it is because somebody happened to see them used, but the older sources do not mention the absence of sanctions in a particular variety of taboos. But the severity, and what Frazer would call the 'reality', of sanctions in some instances should not be underrated. Ellis claims for Hawaii:

> The prohibitions and requisitions of the *tabu* were strictly enforced, and every breach of them punished with death, unless the delinquents had some very powerful friends who were either priests or chiefs. They were generally offered in sacrifice, strangled or despatched with a club or a stone within the precincts of the *heiou* or they were burnt.... An institution so universal in its influence and so inflexible in its demands contributed very materially to the bondage and oppression of the natives in general. The king, sacred chiefs, and priests appear to have been the only persons to whom its application was easy; the great mass of the people were at no period of their existence exempt from its influence, and no circumstance in life could excuse their obedience to its demands. (1826:367-68)

This is a very gloomy picture, redeemed from our standpoint only by the social discernment shown by the Rev. William Ellis. Usually we find the common people and the ruling families all lumped together. Although it is no argument against the truthfulness of the picture, it should be mentioned that Ellis concludes these lines in a polemical spirit against pagan institutions. There is a case against taboo, and Ellis, like many other missionaries, makes it. He ends by glorying in the state now (1823) reached, when the only taboo observed is that of what he calls the Sabbath.

NOTES

1. Brown (1845: 13); Taylor (1870: 164, 168 f.); Williamson (1924 and 1927, *passim*); Webster (1942: 349 and *passim*); Codrington (1891: 181); Firth (1939: 268-72); Maning (1884: 95-97); Martin-Mariner (1817, I, II, *passim*); Erskine (1853: 254).
2. Tregear (1890: 101; 1904: 41); Shortland (1854: 115, 292; 1851 and 1882 *passim*); Williams (1838: 211); Handy (1927: 47-48); Rollin (1929: 171); Best (1914 and 1925, *passim*); Marett (1921: 181-82); Malo (1903: 83 f.); Turner (1884: 146, 336-37); Taylor (1870: 170, 221).
3. This paragraph is constructed largely from Dr Steiner's notes. The Maori reference is to Shortland (1851: 68 ff.). (L.B.)

CHAPTER IV

A VICTORIAN PROBLEM: ROBERTSON SMITH

In the first chapter I remarked that the customs of taboo obtaining among the Polynesians were first described by a Protestant – a fact no doubt due to certain historical accidents, but yet not without some significance. We can thus call Polynesian taboo customs a Protestant discovery. With even more justice we can regard the *problem* of taboo as a Victorian invention. For in Western Europe preoccupation with the mechanisms and meaning of avoidances was unknown before the Victorian period and, as in the case of many other Victorian problems, psychoanalysis provides an epitaph which cannot be appreciated without some understanding of that era. Some remarks of a general nature are therefore necessary here, and all the more because we are inclined to take far too much for granted when we review a period which is not remote enough to have an existence separate from our times and experience.

The problem of taboo became extraordinarily prominent in the Victorian age for two reasons: the rationalist approach to religion and the place of taboo in Victorian society itself. The Victorian era was a rationalist age which differed from the previous Age of Reason in that it attributed importance not only to the various attempts at rational explanation, but also to the residual context which did not yield to the solvent of reason. This was particularly true of religion, which was then being adapted to the needs of an industrial society. Now the ground held by religion could be covered by various ethical theories, but there remained, unaccounted for, some very important human attitudes which were not susceptible to the same kind of treatment and which, indeed, seemed irrational under such examination. These attitudes and contexts, which had thus been divorced from their background and from institutional functions, became isolated to a degree which was new in human history. The more the links, props, and joints of the socio-religious thought structure were absorbed into theories of rational ethics, the more isolated became the little islands of prescribed ceremonial behaviour, the logical model of sacrifice, and the manifold 'don'ts' of religious prohibition. Consequently, these residual contexts – those which could not be dealt with in terms of ethical ratiocination and subjective theories of value – were put under the headings of magic and taboo, and were favoured with a certain type of objective approach which it became fashionable to call scientific. In this way magic and taboo – that is, the odd 'do's' and the odder 'don'ts' – emerged as the two main categories of religious *residua*. Then, once these complementary categories had been carefully invented by scholars, much ingenuity went into the scientific enterprise of proving the connection between them: the interdependence of magic and taboo.

There is yet another side to the Victorian interest in this problem, and one which cannot be overlooked. Victorian society itself was one of the most taboo-minded and taboo-ridden societies on record. It must not be forgotten that scholars like Frazer grew up among people who preferred, in certain circumstances, to say 'unmentionables' rather than 'trousers'.

We have no space to discuss the sociology of the Victorian period. A few hints must suffice. We are dealing with an expanding society in which new groups and classes could rise to comparative wealth; once arrived, they sought to arrange their lives to the pattern of a middle-class family, and they would go to any extreme to defend their new and hardly won privileges, suppressing even the memory of other ways of life. But we must realise that this was also the time in which the middle-class family fought its losing battle against other institutions of industrial society. This meant that attitudes were tied to well-defined and non-interchangeable contexts, which is tantamount with saying, to innumerable avoidances. Two related phenomena resulted: (1) a very sensitive awareness of avoidance customs as positive social factors, and (2) a very strictly departmentalised vocabulary.

It is well known that the most immediate insight into a society's concepts can be derived from the reading of the utopian fiction developed in that society. Therefore, in illustration of my first point, I shall refer to Butler's brilliant *Erewhon*, first published in 1872. Seldom has a book been so representative of its time. In this Utopia, which is at the same time an intentional parody of Victorian society, crimes are regarded as pathological and hence 'healed' by 'correctors' and divested of all social disapproval, whereas illnesses are regarded as crimes and provoke disapproval and isolation as punishment: the ill go to prison. To show how these concepts are socially active, Butler, with great ease, constructs a series of situations in which the mention of illnesses is tabooed. This technique comes so naturally to the writer that the reader is inclined to forget that for the first time in literary history invented customs are described by the use of this device.

I shall give only one example of what I mean by my second point: the contextual departmentalisation of words. At present the species *columba* is referred to by two English words: dove and pigeon. There are certain contexts, few enough, in which either word can be used. In other contexts only one of the two is permissible. To talk of pigeon in some Biblical contexts or in connection with Christian ritual may be very bad taste, in some cases almost sacrilegious. To talk of a dove pie instead of a pigeon pie would show a not altogether pleasant facetiousness. Such cases are quite exceptional in contemporary society, but they were not at all unusual in the society which developed the theories of taboo.

It is difficult for us to imagine the Victorian attitude in this matter, for today we live in a society which has gone to the other extreme. Nowadays concepts and attitudes are so rarely tied to contexts that they provide no contextual clue and consequently give rise to misunderstanding. I remember picking up a leaflet the other day which, by its format, suggested the religious. I quickly scanned the visible back page: 'You and his play. Satisfy his need to play, but see that he respects your property. Take an interest in his doings. Let him help you whenever possible. He can water the flowers. He can learn to pick off dead flowers and to recognise some weeds. Answer his questions truthfully, and if you don't know the answer say so.'

Even while I wondered which contemporary sect had chosen this particularly obnoxious, but quite impressive and consistent, way of talking about their God, I turned the pamphlet and saw: YOUR CHILD'S OUTDOOR PLAY. In the telling I have had to give a slow motion picture of a mistake which, for the brief second of its duration, was not as ridiculous as it sounds here. The point is that such a mistake was impossible in the period which provided the inducements for the forming of the main theories of taboo.

It is against this background that we must consider the work of two scholars, both Victorians, both Scotsmen, but a very unequal pair indeed: W. Robertson Smith and Sir James Frazer. Both were prodigies of learning, and both worked on a philological basis as interpreters of texts. But while Robertson Smith was a Semitic scholar, James Frazer was a classical one, and while the latter became one of the chief debunkers of religion in his period, religion, in the fullest meaning of the word, was the most dutiful concern of Robertson Smith throughout his life. The collaboration between these two men was close, and can be seen, perhaps more clearly than in other parts of his work, in Robertson Smith's theory of taboo. Indeed, it would be very difficult to decide who influenced whom at what point, even if all relevant manuscripts and all letters between the two men were published.

Evaluating Taboo and the Holy

Any discussion of Robertson Smith should begin with a few sentences which might well be taken as his motto. They occur in an early essay of his – it was written in 1869 – that bears the characteristic title 'Christianity and the Supernatural'. It is to be found in that one volume of collected *Lectures and Essays* which J.S. Black and George Chrystal published in 1912. In their preface the editors say that 'it has not been found possible within the compass of even a large volume to give more than a strictly limited selection from the manuscript material in the hands of the editors, and much that in their opinion is of considerable interest and value must be withheld, at any rate for the present'. This 'present' extends, to the dismay of all interested readers, to this day.

In 'Christianity and the Supernatural' in that volume the young Robertson Smith tries to define what he means by Christian apologetics:

> The word apologetical seems to point rather to a peculiar treatment than to a peculiar class of theological problems. Do we mean then that theology is ceasing to be constructive and must henceforth stand on the defensive only? If so, what are we called upon to defend: a theology already completely and scientifically constructed? Surely not: for when a scientific system is complete, it ceases to demand apologetic treatment. Or are we called on to admit that theological science has not attained, never can attain, constructive completeness? True, it will no longer be the results of theology that we are required to defend, but something prior to theology. What we shall have to defend is not our Christian knowledge but our Christian belief. (1912: 109-10)

In the same year, 1869, the Royal Society of Edinburgh received from the pen of this same young man a treatise: 'Theory of Geometrical Reasoning: Mr Mill's Theory of Geometrical Reasoning mathematically tested.' This essay, which was published in their *Proceedings*, is a belated effort to criticise and analyse some contemporary concepts in terms of eighteenth-century philosophy – Kantian philosophy in particular. It deserves our attention here only as a foil to Robertson Smith's essay on the supernatural. Now in the passage quoted from that essay, Robertson Smith exhorts himself to defend not the knowledge of but the belief in his religion. He calls this belief '*something prior to theology*'. Obviously, then, it cannot be described in terms of theology. In what terms, then? An earlier generation would have replied unhesitatingly, 'in the terms of natural religion', that is, of that reasonable edifice which stood over against revealed religion. Robertson Smith, however, did not take up his stand outside the body of religious tradition. His quest was to transform 'something prior to theology' into 'earlier religious attitudes', and it led him to an examination of primitive religion as it was contained in the common religious heritage of what Islam calls the Ahl al-kitâb, the peoples of the Book.

It is well known that Robertson Smith's researches in general, his article 'Bible' in the *Encyclopaedia Britannica* (1875) in particular, brought that devout clergyman into a tragic conflict with his coreligionists and resulted in the most celebrated heresy trial in the Free Protesting Church of Scotland in the nineteenth century (1912: chs.V-X). It would be wrong to assume that the break had been caused by Robertson Smith's preoccupation with the primitive or by any of his original theories; nobody minded those. The conflict arose over Robertson Smith's disregard for the assumed synoptic character of the Pentateuch. He had convinced himself that the Five Books of Moses were not written at the same time: this view was one of the basic tenets of that German movement called Higher Criticism.[1] The time was soon to come when, among earnest Protestants, it was to be regarded as slackness and cynical avoidance of the most profound and troubling problems of faith if a person dared not to be interested in that Criticism, which became the Higher the Lower the Church. Meanwhile the controversy raged, and Robertson Smith – its last great victim – was expelled from his Church. It was the last wrench. Henceforth the only scruples that uncompromising scholar felt were those of his 'scientific theology'.

Robertson Smith's theory of taboo – or rather his theory of the holy – is an essential part of a complex argument concerning animism among the Semites, the development of certain sacrificial rites and the relation between the ancient sacrificial feast and the Eucharist. Indeed Robertson Smith attached enough weight to his use of taboo in this argument to devote a special appendix to the subject in his *Religion of the Semites* (1889; 2nd edn. 1894).[2] That he did not regard Semitic rules of holiness, etc., as derived from primitive taboo concepts is evident from his precise description of their connection. 'Various parallels between savage taboos and Semitic rules of holiness and uncleanness', he wrote, 'will come before us from time to time; but it may be useful to bring together at this point some detailed evidence that the two are in their origin indistinguishable' (1894: 446). He is careful to say that an analysis of the Semitic rules of holiness yields elements which are as simple, and of the same nature as, rules of avoidance found elsewhere among peoples living in very simple societies and which, among such peoples, have *not* given rise to concepts dear to us.

In what does his analysis consist? In the usual examination of meaning Robertson Smith examines rules of conduct not very differently from the way we examine the implications of a statement heard in our daily life. An object is called by a certain name; do we know how people behave towards an object so named? If we do, their behaviour is the meaning of the name. It makes no difference to our method of explanation if the same source acquaints us with both the name and the behaviour. It is always the meaning that is explained and always the recorded behaviour that is used as explanation. This procedure derives from Robertson Smith's leading interest, which is theological. How ever much watered down, it is always the doctrine that demands explanation and not the ways of man. At the same time one notices a remarkably empirical element in his approach, which might easily mislead one into believing that he intended to explain human relations. Thus he says:

> Holy and unclean things have this in common, that in both cases certain restrictions lie on men's use of and contact with them, and that the breach of these restrictions involves supernatural dangers. The difference between the two appears, not in their relation to man's ordinary life, but in their relation to the gods. Holy things are not free to man, because they pertain to the gods; uncleanness is shunned, according to the view taken in the higher Semitic religions, because it is hateful to the god, and therefore not to be tolerated in his sanctuary, his worshippers or his land. But that this explanation is not primitive can hardly be doubted when we consider that the acts that cause uncleanness are exactly the same which among savage nations place a man under taboo, and that these acts are often involuntary, and often innocent, or even necessary in society.[3]

In this same quotation one can see how unquestioningly Robertson Smith assumes a relation between what we should nowadays call ritual purity or status on the one hand and voluntary actions on the other. This relation is not inherent – at least not with this overt function – in the religious doctrines which he is here examining. But because he has used these particular religious doctrines for obtaining guidance in his own life and has regulated it thereby, he cannot help projecting the same value scale into what is, to him, the account of the interactions of the supreme values of his religion. This can be done in all sincerity and simplicity, and doing it enables Robertson Smith to conduct his analysis without any rational evaluation of the Word of God, that is, without placing in himself the discriminating faculty which separates and classifies the various data, values, and rules found in the Bible. Robertson Smith continues:

> The savage, accordingly, imposes a taboo on a woman in childbed, or during her courses, and on the man who touches a corpse not out of any regard for the gods, but simply because birth and everything connected with the propagation of the species on the one hand, and disease and death on the other, seem to him to involve the action of superhuman agencies of a dangerous kind. If he attempts to explain, he does so by supposing that on these occasions spirits of deadly power are present; at all events the persons involved seem to him to be sources of mysterious danger, which has all the

character of an infection, and may extend to other people unless due precautions are observed. This is not scientific, but it is perfectly intelligible, and forms the basis of a consistent system of practice; whereas, when the rules of uncleanness are made to rest on the will of the gods, they appear altogether arbitrary and meaningless.

Now in olden times the coexistence in the Bible of supposedly rude and primitive notions with supposedly refined and advanced concepts was explained by the assumption that God himself had imposed these institutions, graded in value according to the subsequent stages of the community's spiritual attainment. These doctrines of the condescension of God and of progressive revelation held their ground for a long time. We see this viewpoint espoused by the Christian Neo-Platonists of the fourth and fifth centuries,[4] by medieval scholars such as Maimonides[5] and, neither last nor least, by the Anglican Dr John Spencer (1685), of whose book on Hebrew ritual Robertson Smith commented that 'it may justly be said to have laid the foundations of the science of comparative religion'. In the nineteenth century, however, Tylor's development of the concept of 'survivals'[6] offered itself as another approach. And it was of this concept that Robertson Smith availed himself to explain the presence of 'rules which are altogether arbitrary and meaningless' in the altogether superior value system of his cherished doctrine. One must assume two distinct value groups, one primitive, and known to be primitive, because it occurs elsewhere among the rude and untutored. One might, however, enquire into the possibility that, just as the refined and advanced harbour the primitive in their midst, so primitive systems may not be without some supposedly refined and advanced values. If this is so, what sense is left in the 'survival' explanation? And if there is none, what is the place of avoidance customs in a system which is neither advanced nor crude or, rather, is both?

It was, however, in terms of 'survivals' that Robertson Smith developed his argument:

> The affinity of such taboos with laws of uncleanness comes out most clearly when we observe that uncleanness is treated like a contagion, which has to be washed away or otherwise eliminated by physical means. Take the rules about the uncleanness produced by the carcases of vermin in Lev. xi. 32 *sqq.*; whatever they touch must be washed; the water itself is then unclean, and can propagate the contagion; nay, if the defilement affect an (unglazed) earthen pot, it is supposed to sink into the pores, and cannot be washed out, so that the pot must be broken. Rules like this have nothing in common with the spirit of Hebrew religion; they can only be remains of a primitive superstition, like that of the savage who shuns the blood of uncleanness, and such like things, as a supernatural and deadly virus.

It was in this context that Robertson Smith introduced the primitive taboo concept. We shall now examine the use he made of it.

NOTES

1. 'By the "higher criticism" is meant a critical inquiry into the nature, origin, and date of the documents with which we are dealing, as well as into the historical value and credibility of the statements which they contain.' Sayce (1895: 2). (L.B.)
2. Third edition, revised and enlarged, with additional notes and an introduction by Dr Stanley A. Cook, 1927.
3. This and succeeding quotations are from Smith (1894: 46-47).
4. St. Augustine (d. 430), Gregory Nazianzen (d.389) and others taught the denigration of paganism and the concomitant development of revealed religion from simpler and more childish elements to ever more perfect forms. For a general discussion of this and similar doctrines see Schmidt, 1931a. (L.B.)
5. Maimonides, or Rabbi Moses ben Maimon (1135-1204), was a Jewish philosopher, perhaps the greatest, of the Middle Ages. See Neumark, 1908, I, and Bréhier 1949: also Schmidt 1931a. (L.B.)
6. 'Among evidence aiding us to trace the course which the civilisation of the world has actually followed is that great class of facts to denote which I have found it convenient to introduce the terms "survivals". These are processes, customs, opinions, and so forth, which have been carried on by force of habit into a new state of society different from that which they had their original home, and they thus remain as proofs and examples of an older condition of culture out of which a newer has been evolved' (Tyler 1873, I: 16).

CHAPTER V

TABOO AND CONTAGION

I have tried to show how Robertson Smith's almost anthropological appreciation of primitive customs grew out of his main, and theological, interests. I say 'appreciation' advisedly, for he proceeds less by analysis than by appraisal of significance. In a set of laws, values, customs – that of the Hebrew Bible in general, of the Pentateuch in particular – a distinction is made between the purely spiritual and the less pure elements. The latter are found to be archaic, not relevant to present-day society, and in need of explanation. However, they have value in that, once explained, they throw light on the meaning of more highly prized passages. To adopt contemporary jargon, the notions which are irrelevant to Robertson Smith's religion are relegated to the background of Biblical society. This background is elucidated by reference to, and comparison with, contemporary simpler societies and, once understood, helps us to appreciate the development of those ideas that are allowed to remain in the foreground. We shall have occasion to see that this procedure is not without its dangers.

The people of the Pentateuch are described to us as living in a simple, all but tribal, society with a very vivid memory of its tribal past. It was therefore considered helpful to compare this ancient Hebrew society with certain well-documented stages of Arab tribal life or with contemporary Arab Bedouin society. In Robertson Smith's time such a procedure seemed a little more far-fetched than it does in ours, but we cannot give Robertson Smith full credit for ingenuity. A new attitude towards Arab civilisation in general and the Bedouin in particular had developed which, far from seeing the Muslim tribesmen as servants of the devil and Antichrist, revered them as survivals from the Biblical way of life. Of course, the Victorian painters who depicted the heroes of the New Testament in contemporary Bedouin dress had nothing to do with the learned Scot. Nevertheless, the spirit of the age need not be overlooked.

The initial reservation which a modern reader may find himself making – even if he agrees with this method of elucidating some concepts and laws of early Hebrew society – is concerned with the way in which the concepts to be explained are isolated. I said before that Robertson Smith explained in terms of survivals the coexistence of the primitive and non-spiritual with the (to him) spiritually relevant. Here again we ought to distinguish two things: first, the classification itself, and second, the author's inability to conceptualise a society in which both kinds of laws are equally indispensable. And, even while we disagree with Robertson Smith on both counts, we ought to realise that the first corresponds to a dominant attitude of his religion, and that the second could not have been otherwise unless he had anticipated some developments of twentieth-century anthropology.

'Lowest Form of Superstition'

The manner in which Robertson Smith states his problems makes it immediately evident to us how important a role a theory of taboo must play in his treatment. The Hebrew Bible presents a religion of taboos, and at the same time taboo stands for everything that Robertson Smith deprecates in the Hebrew Bible. For Robertson Smith these soulless, archaic 'don'ts' merely *survive* into contemporaneity with the lofty ideas of that Hebrew society; they are related to the usages of all primitive races; nevertheless, they throw some light on the possible development of notions of the holy. And the *holy* is the core of the problems of the Hebrew Bible, not only for the theologian but also for the sociologist who tries to see the precisely formulated theosophy of those documents in terms of the religious institutions they describe. For the Hebrew notion of holiness is the key to other basic concepts, such as life, death, creation, the obligations inherent in divine law, the meaning of revelation and the covenant. Of course, the Hebrew word rendered as 'holy', 'holiness' is much more precise than the word 'holy' in contemporary English usage, in which it may be employed as a synonym of 'saintly'. Such usage goes far beyond the meaning of the Hebrew word; but of this, later.

In accordance with these notions Robertson Smith proceeds to demonstrate Hebrew taboos as primitive survivals, first by pointing out that their antiquity is shown by the reappearance of many of them in Arabia, and secondly by an association with impurity, contagion and avoidance. For he regarded taboos operating on the assumption of contagion as 'the lowest form of superstition', though the highly complex Indian caste system and the sophisticated, highly consistent though manifold, attitudes corresponding to it have been maintained for at least forty centuries with the help of the concept of pollution. In any case assumption of the contagious nature of impurity is a condition of many taboo customs; the avoidance of certain impurities is only meaningful when the impurity can pollute.

For Robertson Smith taboo is the very vehicle of primitiveness; the mere presence of an element of contagion or transfer in a situation makes the whole situation one of taboo, that is, one to be discussed in terms of this 'lowest form of superstition'. And, as an example, he discusses an instance characterised by a transfer of impurity – the rather celebrated instance of the scapegoat. This is how the Pentateuch describes the institution of the custom:

> And Aaron shall lay both his hands upon the head of the live goat, and confess over him all the iniquities of the children of Israel and all their transgressions, even all their sins; and he shall put them upon the head of the goat, and shall send him away by the hand of an appointed man into the wilderness. And the goat shall bear upon him all the iniquities unto a land which is cut off; and he shall let go the goat in the wilderness. (Lev. xvi. 21-22)

Robertson Smith bases his interpretation on other instances which he considers analogous cases of the transfer of impurity:

> The carrying away of the people's guilt to an isolated and desert region has its nearest analogies, not in ordinary atoning sacrifices, but in those physical methods of getting rid of an infectious taboo which characterise the lowest forms of superstition. The same form of disinfection recurs in the Levitical legislation, where a live bird is made to fly away with the contagion of leprosy, and in an Arabian custom when a widow before remarriage makes a bird fly away with the uncleanness of her widowhood. (1894: 422)

Let us stop and consider. If we today were to find the scapegoat custom in the course of field research, how should we deal with it? First, we should distinguish this collective and public piacular occasion from those other and individual cases of 'disinfection' mentioned by Robertson Smith. Secondly, we should note that in the case of this collective ceremony not only does the transference and release mechanism operate, but also the purifying property of the desert is invoked, and invoked in this instance alone. And we should ask whether it was possible, whether it could ever have been possible, for a member of that society to participate in this ceremony without thinking of the collective exodus of his people into the desert, led 'by the hand of an appointed man', till the desert had absorbed their sins, till a new generation had been produced and had taken the place of the sinning generation, a new generation that could be led into the promised land, which was also 'the land cut off'? The main points here, the things that are significant for the participant, are the collective guilt, the cleansing desert. In the whole complex the vehicle is but one element, and not a very important one. That it is a goat has no implication beyond linking the release of the scapegoat animal with the sacrifices in which a goat also functions as a sin offering. 'And Aaron shall cast lots upon the two goats; one lot for the Lord and the other lot for the scapegoat. And Aaron shall bring the goat upon which the Lord's lot fell, and offer him for a sin offering. But the goat, on which the lot fell to be the scapegoat, shall be presented alive before the Lord, to make an atonement with him, and to let him go for a scapegoat into the wilderness' (Lev. xvi. 8-10).

Let us now ask ourselves what we have learned from this comparison between the scapegoat and the other instances cited by Robertson Smith, including the bird of the Arab widow. We can learn only two things: first, that there is a tendency among human beings to transmit undesirable properties, whereby the transmitting individual frees himself from them; and, second, that among the Semites there seems to have been a preference for using live creatures as instruments of transmission. Put crudely like this, we have gained very little, but I challenge anybody to say what more insight is to be gained here.

The Higher Transmission

At this point we might ask ourselves another question: Could not this meagre result have been achieved without reference to features which these instances have in common with avoidance behaviour? In other words, why taboo? We shall see that Robertson Smith, in order to maintain his distinction between the primitive and the valuable in the Bible, found it necessary to distinguish between *positive* and *negative* transmission. In the passage from which I have quoted he goes on to explain why the priest had to put his hands on the head of the goat: 'In ordinary burnt offerings and sin offerings the imposition of hands is not officially interpreted by the Law as a transference of sin to the victim, but rather has the same sense as in acts of blessing or consecration, where the idea no doubt is that the physical contact between the parties serves to identify them, but not specially to transfer guilt from one to the other.' Now what kind of transmission is involved in blessing? Indeed, what was a blessing to the ancient Hebrews? The action of *hitborah* – making a *braha*, a Hebrew word we translate as 'blessing' – has a much more powerful and general meaning than can be understood by reference to more recent usage of the non-Semitic word 'blessing'. And our word 'blessing' is mainly used in these Biblical contexts.

In the relation between God and man each can bless the other. When we scrutinise the instances in which the word is used by the ancient Hebrews, we find as its meaning the transmission of desirable properties or power in circumstances of ritual significance. The higher gives his *braha* to the lower as a matter of course for, being the higher, he also possesses the greater power and the more desirable properties. In these circumstances the recipient lowers himself, crouching or kneeling down, to imply his humble position in this *braha* transmission. But the lower may also *hitborah* the higher, man may *hitborah* God. In this case the action is usually translated 'bless' or 'praise'. Here we are within the logical mode of sacrifice: the recipient is not needy, but receives the gift as homage. In this instance it is the giver of *braha* who lowers himself, for here the posture is not an indication of the direction of transference but of the relationship existing between the parties concerned.

The same Semitic root is found in the Arab word *baraka* – a word which, in contemporary Arab Bedouin usage, means the coveted power of a person (Laoust 1939: 25, *n*. 1 and 49; Wellhausen 1887: *passim*; Westermarck 1926, I: chs I-III). Thus if a Bedu sees someone who is successful or skilful or shows the élan of great vitality, or a stranger who, it is polite to assume, is furnished with superior skill or gifts of God, etc., he will approach him and touch him with his hand to get what he calls his *baraka*. The Bedu in this case makes the same movement with his hand as the contemporary Jew when the Scroll of the Law is carried round the synagogue in procession and he touches it in reverence. Among the Bedouin *baraka* has another meaning as well, one which seems to recapture the ancient Babylonian use of the word: the kneeling position of the camel, in getting up or lowering itself (Wehr 1952: 47). The word may thus once have connoted both a particular kind of transmission and one of the postures appropriate to it.

The Hebrew Bible is so full of blessings, the implications of blessing are so important for any assessment of ancient Hebrew attitudes, that we cannot fail to see in it one of the basic concepts of their way of life. But however we look at it, contagion is the principle of the transfer in blessing no less than in Robertson Smith's 'primitive' pollution taboos. How, then, are we to say that the priest spreading his hands over the congregation, or the father touching the head of the child, is not indulging in one of 'the lowest forms of superstition'? Why are we to consider one and the same action as representing in the one case all that is unethical, pre-ethical, superstitious, and crudely non-spiritual, and in the other behaviour appropriate to the expression of the most sublime aspects of religion? Why should the one case be cruder or older than the other?

Robertson Smith applied avoidance behaviour as a distinctive criterion between the crude and the sublime. For, it will be observed, no avoidance behaviour is connected with cases of positive transmission such as blessing, and for Robertson Smith only the combination of avoidance behaviour *and* contagion constitutes the low and primitive form of transmission. It is the introduction of the category 'taboo' that makes possible a distinction that would otherwise be difficult to uphold.

Positive and Negative Transmission

We ourselves, however, can picture that old society by using as models simpler societies as we now know them, and we can see that positive and negative transmission are not merely contemporaneous by accident; they are interdependent. Any ritual or practice embodying belief in negative transmission strengthens attitudes toward positive transmission. What is remarkable about the two kinds of transmission, surely, is the way they combine to create a universe of properties, ordered only in so far as these properties are active, and they can be comprehended as active only in terms of transference and contagion. Only by conceiving these properties as active, human relationships can one conceive structured social life in terms of them. If we today had to study a living society of that type, our attention would be given to this interplay of active properties, and we should have to dismiss Robertson Smith's condemnation of the one kind for its connection with avoidance behaviour as relatively unimportant, if not as a red herring.

The way in which Robertson Smith uses the taboo concept in connection with the polluting qualities of impurity shows how discussion of customs in terms of origins and primary significance blurs their actual implication. Thus he writes:

> The impurity of menstruation was recognised by all the Semites, as in fact it is by all primitive and ancient peoples. Now among savages this impurity is distinctly connected with the idea that the blood of the *menses* is dangerous to man, and even the Romans held that.... Similar superstitions are current with the Arabs, a great variety of supernatural powers attaching themselves to a woman in this condition. Obviously, therefore, in this case the Semitic taboo is exactly like the savage one; it has nothing to do with respect for the gods but springs from mere terror of the supernatural influences associated with the woman's physical condition.

Once we have ascertained that avoidance mechanisms are characteristic of mankind in general, that dangerous situations are made the special object of avoidance customs, and, moreover, that in most societies menstruation is regarded as a source of uncleanness and danger, a catalogue of what actually does inspire the fear seems beside the point; we need to know what principles regulate that fear. In this connection a distinction between 'respect for gods' and 'mere terror' – a distinction worthy of much critical attention in a different context –

becomes quite irrelevant. In any case, in the framework of the life of the ancient Hebrews, terrors *not* connected or associated with the central religious experience are inconceivable, for there the moral universe of active properties, as I called it, is organised on monotheistic principles. The question of *how* this organisation came about – Robertson Smith's main question, I take it – cannot be solved by evaluating the objects with which the organisation is concerned.

To clarify what I mean by this organisation of active properties, I shall return to the two kinds of transmission – positive and negative – which we have been discussing, this time in connection with what, on Wellhausen's and Robertson Smith's own showing, was a common custom among heathen Arabs: the use of unclean things as amulets, because of their potency. 'Such amulets are called by the Arabs *tanjis, monajjassa*; and it is explained that the heathen Arabs used to tie unclean things, dead men's bones and menstruous rags, upon children, to avert the *jinn* and the evil eye' (Smith 1894: 448). Such a practice would be inconsistent with the Hebrew way of balancing positive and negative transmission. Furthermore, negative transmission proper is possible only in a society in which there is but one source of prohibition. That is, the absorption of prohibitory functions by the One God excludes, in the case of the Hebrews at least, the positive magical use of the unclean.

Robertson Smith, however, continues to illustrate the magical potency of the unclean among other peoples:

> As the elk clan of the Omahas believe that they cannot eat the elk without boils breaking out on their bodies, so the Syrians, with whom fish were sacred to Atargatis, thought that if they ate a sprat or an anchovy they were visited with ulcers, swellings and wasting disease. In both cases the punishment of the impious flows directly from the malignant influences resident in the forbidden thing, which, so to speak, avenges itself on the offender.... The more notable unclean animals possess magical powers; the swine, for example, which the Saracens as well as the Hebrews refused to eat (Solomon, vi. 38) supplies many charms and magical medicines.

But such association of the unclean and the magically potent yielded by the comparative method is inapplicable to the Hebrew Bible. Absorption of all taboos by the One God not only *indicates* His power: His power *consists* in this. The stipulation of all avoidance behaviour in terms of the law of the One God is therefore a far from primitive feature. Yet Robertson Smith concludes his case against uncleanness by saying that 'the irrationality of the laws of uncleanness, from the standpoint of spiritual religion or even of the higher heathenism, is so manifest that they must necessarily be looked on as having survived from an earlier form of faith and society. And this being so, I do not see how any historical student can refuse to class them with savage taboos.' Instancing irrationality as proof of primitiveness is such a strange procedure to the twentieth-century mind that I do not think it necessary to refute it.

I have already dealt with the notion that what, rightly or wrongly, is regarded as on two moral levels must necessarily be diachronic. I do not dispute the claim of the Semitic taboo concepts to great antiquity. Rather, I wish to point out that such antiquity does not exclude the possibility of taboos being created continuously up to recent times – and, indeed, up to the present day. Nor is the conclusion warranted that the One God, morally so much more perfect, is a newcomer to a society ruled by archaic and inherited notions very different from the beliefs connected with Him. In any case anthropologists from Andrew Lang to Father Schmidt[1] have tried to show that the concept of the One God is as old as anything else in human belief. And Robertson Smith himself broke down the barrier between the concepts attaching to the One God and the concepts of rude pre-history. In the next chapter I shall show how he did so.

NOTES

1. See Lang, 1898, especially chapters IX-XVII, and Schmidt 1931a.

CHAPTER VI

TABOO AND THE 'HOLY'

I have tried to show some of the reasons that prompted Robertson Smith to take such a great interest in taboo. I have also made a few critical remarks – very easily made after sixty years of research have gone by. These criticisms have so far concerned Robertson Smith's use and valuation of the notion of contagion.

I based my criticism on the evidence of the Pentateuch, which shows, at least in my opinion, the concept of a universe of values. Now two kinds of statement can be made about such a universe of values: (1) concerning the way in which it is related to the human society that conceives it, and (2) concerning the manner in which it is ordered. I pointed out that under the first heading, although some people would be inclined to do so under the second instead, it is profitable to discuss the principles which govern the interaction of these values and which make them into an active system that can be related to human activities and rules of conduct; the transmission of properties, including, of course, the notion of contagion, should be discussed in this context only. Under the second heading, that of order, certain aspects of monotheism can be analysed, if one wishes to do so. Finally, I pointed out that when we approach the subject in this manner, problems which can be resolved into questions as to the relative importance or priority of either group of principles are not very relevant or meaningful. It is worthwhile keeping all this in mind as we proceed.

'Holy' in Semitic Languages

Now the most important stimulus for Robertson Smith in his discussion of the holy was the Polynesian concept of taboo in which the notion of the forbidden merged with that of the ritually significant. It was from the viewpoint of taboo that he discussed *qadosh*. Let us first consider the words involved in Robertson Smith's discussion. They derive from two Semitic roots, *hrm* and *qds:* Hebrew *chérem* (ban), Arabic *harâm, harîm* and *ihâm;* and Hebrew *qadosh, qodesh* (spelt *kadesh* by Freud 1950: 41), *hitqadosh,* Arabic *qudis.* The meaning of the Arabic *harâm* corresponds to the Hebrew *qadosh* (Smith 1894: 149-50; Snaith 1944: ch. II).

It should be made clear from the outset that in the Pentateuch *qadosh* does not appear only with the specialised meaning which it has in the context of the Religion of the Book. It has many meanings outside that context. Among other things, it is the word all Semitic languages, including that of the neighbours of the Hebrews, used to denote cultic relevance. Consequently we find it used in reference to non-Jewish cults, indeed, to some cults which are extremely contrary to Jewish cultic life – for example, *qadisha,* temple prostitute and prostitute generally. All this is very confusing for the Old Testament scholar, but it need not concern us, for we are dealing not with a Hebrew word in all its uses, nor with a word found in a certain group of documents, but solely with the meaning that the word has in certain clearly defined cultic contexts.

We want to know the meaning of *qadosh* in Jewish cults within the Hebrew society described in the Pentateuch. Robertson Smith, in an attempt to elucidate this meaning, looked for comparisons to some of the meanings of the Polynesian *tapu.* He noticed a twofold similarity between *qadosh* and *tapu,* one referring to the appropriative-prohibitive aspect of the holy, to the identity of the ritually potent with the ritually unclean, and the other to the contagiousness of things *tapu* and *qadosh.* In his argument, which I shall present in some detail, these points are enumerated separately, but I do not see that separation matters, nor (as one might expect) is he able to maintain it from the nature of *tapu.* He begins by clearing away alternative explanations:

At present the most current view of the meaning of restrictions of man's free use of holy things is that holy things are the god's property, and I have therefore sought to show that the idea of property does not suffice to explain the facts of the case.... At first sight the holiness of the sanctuary may seem to be only the expression of the idea that the sanctuary belongs to the god, that the temple and its precincts are his homestead and his domain, reserved for his use and that of his ministers, as a man's house and estate are reserved for himself and his household. In Arabia, for example, where there were great tracts of sacred land, it was forbidden to cut fodder, fell trees or hunt game; all the natural products of the holy soil were exempt from human appropriation. But it would be rash to conclude that what cannot be the private property of men is therefore the private property of the gods, reserved for the exclusive use of them or their ministers. The positive exercise of legal rights of property on the part of the gods is only possible where they have human representatives to act for them, and no doubt

in later times the priests at the greater Semitic sanctuaries did treat the
holy reservations as their own domain.[1]

With the purely sociological approach that distinguishes him from his
predecessors, Robertson Smith goes on to stress the fact that no group of
people with such priestly privileges in property existed at the times
selected for investigation. He points out that 'in nomadic Arabia, sanctuaries are older than any doctrine of property that could possibly be
applied to a tract like the *harâm* at Mecca or the *himâ* of T'aif'. He insists
that the concept of property in grazing lands, watering places, etc., as
exercised in Semitic tribal society, could not provide the model for the
restrictions associated with sanctuaries; there was no connection at all:

There is no property in natural pastures. Every tribe indeed has its own
range of plains and valleys, and its own watering places, by which it habit-
ually encamps at certain seasons and from which it repels aliens by the
strong hand. But this does not constitute property, for the boundaries of the
tribal land are merely maintained by force against enemies, and not only
every tribesman but every covenanted ally has equal and unrestricted right
to pitch his tent and drive his cattle where he will. This is still the rule
among nomadic tribes, but where there are fixed villages the inhabitants
claim exclusive right to a certain circuit of pasture round the township.
Claims of this description are older than Islam, and are guaranteed by
Mohammed in several of his treaties with new converts in varying terms,
which evidently follow the variations of customary law in different parts of
the peninsula. In such cases we may legitimately speak of *communal* property in pasture-lands, but *private* property in such has never been known to
Arabian law. From this statement it is obvious that the Arabs might indeed
conceive the temple to be the personal property of the god, but could not
bring the rules affecting sacred pastures under the same category.

These tracts of sacred land, pasture land in particular, called *himâ* by
the Arabs, are known to us because, as one of the most important
pagan institutions, they were the subject of some of the earliest acts of
Islamic legislation. On *himâ* ground several tribal groups could meet
and graze their cattle peacefully without fear of conflict or disturbance.
The rules of behaviour show that visitors to the *himâ* were at the same
time protected by the local deity and restricted in their activities. Thus:

At the *himâ* of Wajj, attached to the sanctuary of al-Lāt at Tāif, the rules are
practically identical with those at Mecca; and when we observe that
Mohammed confirmed these rules, in the interest of the inhabitants, at the
same time that he destroyed al-Lāt and did away with the ancient sanctity
of the spot, it is natural to infer that in other cases also the *himâ* which he
allowed to subsist as a communal pasture-ground round a village or town
was originally a sacred tract, protected from encroachment by fear of the

god rather than by any civil authority. It is indeed plain that with such a property law as has been described, and in the absence of any inter-tribal authority, religion was the only power, other than the high hand, that could afford any security to a communal pasture, and we are not without evidence as to how this security was effected. The privileges of the *haram* at Mecca and Medina are still placed under a religious sanction; on those who violated the latter, Mohammed invoked the irrevocable curse of God and the angels and all men.

Semitic society is, however, not exclusively nomad. Robertson Smith continues:

> Hitherto we have been speaking of a type of sanctuary older than the institution of property in land. But even where the doctrine of property is fully developed, holy places and things, except where they have been appropriated to the use of kings and priests, fall under the head of public rather than of private estate. According to ancient conceptions, the interests of the god and his community are too closely identified to admit of a sharp distinction between sacred purposes and public purposes, and as a rule nothing is claimed for the god in which his worshippers have not a right to share. Even the holy dues presented at the sanctuary are not reserved for the private use of the deity, but are used to furnish forth sacrificial feasts in which all who are present partake. So too the sanctuaries of ancient cities served the purpose of public parks and public halls, and the treasures of the gods, accumulated within them, were a kind of state treasure, preserved by religious sanctions against peculation and individual encroachment, but available for public objects in time of need.

Having thus disposed of the notion of sanctuaries or deities as landowners, Robertson Smith turns to other instances of ownership by religious institutions:

> At certain Arabian sanctuaries the god gave shelter to all fugitives without distinction, and even stray or stolen cattle that reached the holy ground could not be reclaimed by their owners. What was done with these animals is not stated; possibly they enjoyed the same liberty as the consecrated camels which the Arabs, for various reasons, were accustomed to release from service and suffer to roam at large. These camels seem to be sometimes spoken of as the property of the deity, but they were not used for his service. Their consecration was simply a limitation of man's right to use them.

Having eliminated property and introduced the concept of consecration as a limitation on the rights of man, Robertson Smith finds his link to the concept of taboo. I shall quote almost in full the lengthy passage in which he makes this connection because it is also such an excellent illustration of Robertson Smith's lucid exposition of sociological and jural matters:

We have here another indication that the relations of holiness to the institution of property are mainly negative. Holy places and things are not so much reserved for the use of the god as surrounded by a network of restrictions and disabilities which forbid them to be used by men except in particular ways, and in certain cases forbid them to be used at all. As a rule the restrictions are such as to prevent the appropriation of holy things by men, and sometimes they cancel existing rights of property. From this point of view it would appear that common things are such as men have licence to use freely at their own good pleasure without fear of supernatural penalties, while holy things may be used only in prescribed ways and under definite restrictions, on pain of anger of the gods. That holiness is essentially a restriction on the licence of man in the free use of natural things, seems to be confirmed by the Semitic roots used to express the idea....

We have already found reason to think that in Arabia the holiness of places is older than the institution of property in land, and the view of holiness that has just been set forth enables us to understand why it should be so. We have found that from the earliest times of savagery certain spots were dreaded and shunned as the haunts of supernatural beings. These, however, are not holy places any more than an enemy's ground is holy; they are not hedged round by definite restrictions, but altogether avoided as full of indefinite dangers. But when men establish relations with the powers that haunt a spot, it is at once necessary that there should be rules of conduct towards them and their surroundings. These rules, moreover, have two aspects. On the one hand, the god and his worshippers form a single community – primarily, let us suppose, a community of kinship – and so all the social laws that regulate men's conduct towards a clansman are applicable to their relations to the god. But, on the other hand, the god has natural relations to certain physical things, and these must be respected also; he has himself a natural life and natural habits in which he must not be molested. Moreover, the mysterious superhuman powers of the god – the powers which we call supernatural – are manifested, according to primitive ideas, in and through his physical life, so that every place and thing which has natural associations with the god is regarded, if I may borrow a metaphor from electricity, as charged with divine energy and ready at any moment to discharge itself to the destruction of the man who presumes to approach it unduly. Hence in all their dealings with natural things men must be on their guard to respect the divine prerogative, and this they are able to do by knowing and observing the rules of holiness, which prescribe definite restrictions and limitations in their dealings with the god and all natural things that in any way pertain to the god.

From such a generalised description, it is impossible for Robertson Smith not to conclude:

Rules of holiness in the sense just explained, i.e., a system of restrictions on man's arbitrary use of natural things, enforced by the dread of supernatural penalties, are found among all primitive peoples. It is convenient to have a distinct name for this primitive institution, to mark it off from the later developments of the idea of holiness in advanced religions, and for this purpose the Polynesian term TABOO has been selected.

At this point Robertson Smith makes his distinction between taboos connected with religion proper on the one hand and other taboos on the other hand. Some classification must, of course, be made. The weakness of his is that the distinction does not arise as the result of an analysis of the way certain concepts are used in certain circumstances, and of the possible difference (in terms of behaviour and jural implication) of the contexts in which different terms are used. No. Robertson Smith's distinction is here based – I have already pointed out that we could not expect him to proceed in another fashion – on his knowledge of what religion proper is or, rather, ought to be:

> All taboos do not belong to religion proper, that is, they are not always rules of conduct for the regulation of man's contact with deities that, when taken in the right way, may be counted on as friendly, but rather appear in many cases to be precautions against the approach of malignant enemies – against contact with evil spirits and the like. Thus alongside of taboos that exactly correspond [!] to rules of holiness, protecting the inviolability of idols and sanctuaries, priests and chiefs, and generally of all persons and things pertaining to the gods and their worship, we find another kind of taboo which in the Semitic field has its parallel in rules of uncleanness. Women after childbirth, men who have touched a dead body and so forth, are temporarily taboo and separated from human society, just as the same persons are unclean in Semitic religion.

The Comparative Method

Here comes the delicate transition. So far Robertson Smith has been talking about Semitic religion in general, and in this quite general and comparative field he distinguishes two kinds of taboo. Now, turning to a much more special and restricted field, that of the Hebrew Bible, he reaches his conclusions by squaring the distinction drawn on general, comparative grounds with the very peculiar and carefully formalised terminology of one particular cult – we cannot even say, one particular people. In this process he finds that what he had put into a category in the course of his comparative approach (to the verification of his preconceptions) figures in the restricted field as a separate category: that of *qadosh* in the narrower sense. These were the advantages of what the last century called 'the comparative method'.

Let us follow Robertson Smith's argument closely, for I want you to observe how smoothly he continues, without the slightest indication that he has changed his ground:

In these cases the person under taboo is not regarded as holy, for he is separated from approach to the sanctuary as well as from contact with men; but his act or condition is somehow associated with supernatural dangers, arising, according to the common savage explanation, from the presence of formidable spirits which are shunned like an infectious disease. In most savage societies no sharp line seems to be drawn between the two kinds of taboo just indicated, and even in more advanced nations the notions of holiness and uncleanness often touch....

The fact that all the Semites have rules of uncleanness as well as rules of holiness, that the boundary between the two is often vague, and that the former as well as the latter present the most startling agreement in point of detail with savage *taboos*, leaves no reasonable doubt as to the origin and ultimate relations of the idea of holiness. On the other hand, the fact that the Semites – or at least the northern Semites – distinguish between the holy and the unclean, marks a real advance above savagery. All taboos are inspired by awe of the supernatural, but there is a great moral difference between precautions against the invasion of mysterious hostile powers and precautions founded on respect for the prerogative of a friendly god.

Now, quietly, the cat is let out of the bag:

The former belong to magical superstition – the barrenest of all aberrations of the savage imagination – which, being founded on fear, acts merely as a bar to progress and an impediment to the free use of nature by human energy and industry.

Observe the grand alliance: religion proper, taboos that imply holiness and have a moral aspect, progress, energy, industry. With their association we should have to leave ancient religion and take cognisance of other and more modern aspects of religion which have been adequately discussed by Tawney (1926) and Max Weber (1923: I and II). Let us return to our subject and observe how Robertson Smith's attempt to distinguish two kinds of taboo leads him into a circular argument. First, he clinches his points on property rights, taboo and holiness:

An owner is bound to respect other people's property while he preserves his own; but the principle of holiness, as appears in the law of asylum, can be used to override the privileges of human ownership. In this respect holiness exactly resembles taboo. The notion that certain things are taboo to a god or a chief means that only he, as the stronger person, and not only stronger but invested with supernatural power, and so very dangerous to offend, will not allow anyone else to meddle with them. To bring the taboo into force it is not necessary that there should be prior possession on the part of god or chief; other people's goods may become taboo, and be lost to their original owner, merely by contact with the sacred person or with sacred things. Even the ground on which a king of Tahiti trod became taboo, just as the place of a theophany was thenceforth holy among the Semites. Nor does it follow that because a thing is taboo from the use of man, it is therefore in any real sense appropriated to the use of a god or sacred person; the fundamental notion is merely that it is not safe for ordinary people to use it; it has, so to speak, been touched by the infection of holiness, and so becomes a new source of supernatural danger.

Then the contagion of the holy is contrasted with that of the impure: 'In this respect, again, the rules of Semitic holiness show clear marks of their origin in a system of taboo; the distinction that holy things are employed for the use of the gods, while unclean things are simply forbidden to man's use, is not consistently carried out....' We are not going into the question of whether such a distinction should be carried out or ever has been carried out, without an accompanying change in the attitude to holiness in 'religion proper'. We shall merely ask what, according to Robertson Smith, are the criteria for the consistency or inconsistency of the distinction between the two kinds of taboo, and we shall find that 'there remain many traces of the view that holiness is contagious, just as uncleanness is, and that things which are to be retained for ordinary use must be kept out of the way of the sacred infection'.

So there is the circle. The principle of contagion is low because it is part of 'the lowest form of superstition', but this 'lowest form' is composed not merely of the belief in contagion (which, of course, does not exist in isolation), but of a whole category of taboos as well. There is, nevertheless, no clear distinction between the idea of the holy and the lowest form of superstition because, different as they may otherwise be, they have in common the principle of contagion.

This kind of reasoning is not very satisfactory, either as an analysis of meaning or as an explanation of ritual and social contexts and situations. It is not even, if I may say so, a rewarding exercise in logic. As for its application to any given instance Robertson Smith, with great diligence and scholarship, accumulated from the records of various Semitic groups many instances illustrating that possessions, such as garments once associated with a given ritual occasion, cannot be reintroduced to profane functions. The notions behind this group of cases vary. In one context it is the belief that through contact the object became dedicated to that ritual purpose and could therefore never be used for any other purpose in the future. In other cases it is believed that the object – vestment, utensil, shoe, etc. – by virtue of that contact became so charged with the danger which accompanies a ritual, or with which a divine presence is fraught, that it itself became dangerous. Contagion, dedication, religion. Contagion, fear, superstition. Robertson Smith was not slow to realise that these are only two different ways of rationalising the same behaviour.

But we who are concerned with the interrelation of ritual concepts, that is, with rationalisations, must ask why the rationalisation turns one way in one case, and the other way in the second case. Robertson Smith did not ask these questions. If he had asked them, the answer would have been painfully easy: One of the two is the more primitive, hence the older, hence .... Well, we know the chain by now.

Moreover, Robertson Smith cited a number of cases where garments are discarded *before* the ritual occasion, as when Semites take off shoes or garments before a ritual, prayer, etc. He tried to explain this by saying that they wished in some cases to avoid the contamination of their garments, in other cases the contamination of the ritual. Yet can we take as an adequate reason for the frequent Biblical injunction (Exod. iii. 5; Josh. v. 15; etc.): Remove your shoes, for the ground on which you stand is *qadosh,* that the shoes could not otherwise be used afterwards?

I shall next deal with some criticisms of Robertson Smith by interested theologians before turning to his great contemporary, Sir James Frazer.

NOTES

1. Smith, 1894: 453. Quotations in this chapter are from pp. 145 ff. and 499 ff.

CHAPTER VII

THE HEBREW BIBLE: SNAITH AND FRAZER

Robertson Smith's treatment of the idea of *qadosh* and taboo has had a great influence on subsequent literature, not only sociological and ethnological, but also on theological commentaries on the Hebrew Bible in general and the Pentateuch in particular. Thanks to his efforts 'primitive religion' within – and, for better understanding, without – the Hebrew Bible, has become one of the main fields of theological interest. The literature resulting from such studies is vast and cannot be surveyed here.

I shall, however, discuss one book of this group: Snaith's *Distinctive Ideas of the Old Testament*. I have chosen it partly because it has impressed me more than the rest, partly because it is the most recent one in the field (1944). But before we go into Snaith's criticism of Robertson Smith and my criticism of Snaith we must, in order to avoid utter confusion, consider whether they were, after all, talking about the same thing. It is not enough to say that they were both concerned with the Old Testament. The statements we make about taboo and the idea of the holy in a text like the Pentateuch concern various levels of religious context which are themselves of varied content and meaning. These levels do not correspond to the various levels of abstraction of which we talk in sociology. They are inherent in the text; and we must not let the many so-called primitive features of the Pentateuch blind us to the fact that there are, in every instance we examine, three contexts and, correspondingly, three levels of meaning to be considered.

First, there are the implications of a given passage for a Semitic-speaking person of Asia Minor at the time at which cults such as the one under discussion developed. Such meaning derives from the general cultural idiom of the Semitic nomads, semi-nomads, and even of some urban populations. It cannot be fully investigated through the comparative study of religion. It can, of course, furnish a clue to the meaning of the two other levels, but it cannot yield their entire meaning.

Second, there is the meaning of the given passage for a person participating in the particular cult as one of its members.

Third, there is the meaning of the passage for the body of persons whose business it is to supervise the cult and to maintain the purity of the text. It is with some hesitation that I call this meaning 'esoteric', for I am not thinking of a sacred, priestly lore, but of the principles of consistency within a tradition – principles which must be discussed in terms of a certain logic and which thereby create this logic. This consistency is not something added from outside to the popular belief or to the 'pure text'. It is something which is always present but which is quite irrelevant to the particular role or general function of a given text in the actual cult. It is a property of the text relevant primarily to those who have a dual obligation towards text and ritual, and who not only participate in the ritual but make it their business to preserve it unchanged. Every perpetuated religious activity manifests such a doctrinal element, which is often conscious and which represents the principles of consistency of that religious tradition rather than particular tenets of belief.

The content of these three levels of meaning is not interchangeable. A statement concerning the first – the meaning of a passage within the framework of the idiom of an area – does not necessarily implicate the second – that is, the cultic realities of the participating society. Nor can an examination, logical or metaphysical, of the third – that is, of the properties of consistency of a custom or passage within the text – fail to reveal things which necessarily escaped the knowledge or attention of the ordinary participant (who is concerned with the second level). This distinction becomes very important if one believes that only the attitudes of the lay participants are structurally relevant. If we do believe this, we must admit that the cultic reality is different from the general idiom and from the doctrinal aspect of tradition, and cannot be deduced from documents, however complete. But if we do not impose such unreasonable limitations on ourselves, we are free to proceed with our examination.

Here, however, we must point out that Snaith and Robertson Smith were not concerned with the same levels of meaning. Indeed, Snaith is perhaps not entirely unconscious of this difference; so we must at least suspect from his criticism of Robertson Smith, who tried to see the Bible from the viewpoint of the ordinary Hebrew, making liberal use of general cultural idiom (our first level) to arrive at the second. Snaith, on the other hand, concerns himself, as one might expect of a contemporary theologian, mainly with the doctrinal element.

Snaith on the 'Holy'

Snaith's starting point is an undisguised reaction against two generations of teaching and research:

> Old Testament scholars have responded, equally with scholars in every branch of knowledge, to the stimulus of the New Scientific Method promoted in the first instance largely by Herbert Spencer's *Synthetic Philosophy*. They have made full use of such pioneering studies as Sir E.B. Tylor's *Primitive Culture* and Sir J.G. Frazer's two works, his many-volumed *The Golden Bough,* and his three-volumed *The Folklore of the Old Testament*. The result has been a tremendous gain in our understanding of Hebrew religion in its relation to other religions. Particularly, we have grown familiar with the common heritage of Hebrews and Gentiles in their awareness of the Supernatural. This has been a definite gain.
>
> Excellent, however, as this movement has been, there has been another and less satisfactory side to it. It is significant that for the last standard work in English on Old Testament Theology we have to go back to A.B. Davidson's *The Theology of the Old Testament,* which is dated 1901, and is therefore over forty years old. The modern tendency is seen in Oesterley and Robinson's *Hebrew Religion, Its Origin and Development* (2nd edn., 1937). Out of 417 pages of printed text, no less than 121 pages deal with such subjects as animism, *taboo,* and such-like items which necessarily occupy a large space in books on primitive religion. (1944: 11-12)

From which Snaith concludes:

> We are therefore of the firm opinion that it is high time for us to awake out of our semi-hypnosis, induced by the desire for comprehensiveness and broad-mindedness, and by the attractiveness of these studies in early comparative religion and native custom. Such studies of the ways and thoughts of primitive man have a strange fascination. This is partly due to the romanticism with which we colour a long-lost unmechanical and unsophisticated age, partly to a real interest in the doings of our brother-man of whatever period of the world's history, but partly also to the sense of superiority which they give us, whereby we can say, 'There but for the grace of centuries, go I'. However that may be, it is time for us now to be able to view the work of Tylor, Frazer, and their successors in its proper perspective. It has taken two generations for the Graf-Wellhausen theory of the literary structure of the Pentateuch to settle down to a moderately fluid mellowness. At last we have realised that there are limits beyond which literary analysis cannot be pressed without doing more harm than good....
>
> In a similar way, our preoccupation with origins and development has blurred our eyes from seeing whither the development was making, and equally has tied our tongues from asking why this way and no other way. Nay more, we can be accused, and with a considerable measure of justification, of being foolish enough to advance backwards, our faces always turned towards the point of departure.

In this respect Old Testament scholars have themselves largely to thank for the neglect of the Old Testament in these latter days. We have been lured by the attractiveness of a comprehensive outlook, possibly we have been afraid of being thought narrow and bigoted, and perhaps also we have been enticed, as Andrew Lang would say, by the fascinating devices of the naughty man. (1944: 13)

Now it so happens that Dr Snaith's attitude towards a valued text and the society it portrays coincides with that which mid-twentieth-century anthropology has developed towards every society. Anthropologists, too, revolted; we all have come to distrust the emphasis laid on common elements in any particular system – unless these common elements are presented either as human universals which have no exception or as logical models. The front, or part of it, has turned, and the sociologist is, willy-nilly, fighting on the side of the angels. We too are studying the distinctive features of every society.

Snaith's discussion of the various etymologies of *q-d-sh* goes over the old exercise grounds of Old Testament and Babylonian scholarship. After a long disquisition, he accepts, with some modification, Baudissin's explanation:

We are therefore driven back to Baudissin's suggestion that the root originally meant 'separation', inasmuch as it is clear that it deals with the things that belong to the gods as distinct from men. His statement, however, that the root *q-d-sh* signifies 'separation from, withdrawal' needs considerable qualification, especially when it is maintained that this is supported by Old Testament usage. It is true that the root stands for the difference between God and man, but it refers positively, and not negatively, to that 'wholly other' of whom Rudolf Otto writes. It refers positively to what is God's and not negatively to what is not man's. God is separate and distinct because He is God. He is not separated from this, that or the other because of any of His attributes or qualities or the like. A person or a thing may be separate, or may come to be separated, because he or it has come to belong to God. When we use the word 'separated' as a rendering of any form of the root *q-d-sh*, we should think of 'separated to' rather than of 'separated from'. The reference is not primarily to the act of separation, but rather to the fact that the object has now come into the category of the Separate. The verb in its causative form *hiqdish* means '*make* separate' rather than '*be* separate', but this is a derived form of the verb. We therefore insist, as of prime importance, that the root is positive rather than negative, that the emphasis is on the destination of the object and not on its initial character – all of which goes back to the fact that, in respect of the root *q-d-sh*, we must think of God first and of man and things second, and not vice versa. This is not to deny that the Hebrew *hiqdish* can ever mean 'to separate, withdraw from common (i.e., human) use', but it is to say that such meanings belong to the periphery of the word and not to its central core. When Baudissin gave 'separation' as the probable original significance of the root, he may well have been correct, but only in so far as he may have been thinking in terms of a positive 'Other'. As soon as he began to think of 'separation from' he was moving away from the central core. When he used the word 'withdrawal', he was at the outmost limits of the root. (1944: 29-30)

Hebrew *cherem*, according to Snaith, means something 'non-*qodesh* to one god because of its association with another god'. And, we may add, in a less polytheistic system it means the functional demarcation complementary to *qodesh*.

In his discussion of the word *chol*, which in very important respects corresponds to Polynesian *noa*, Snaith restates Robertson Smith's problem in a very remarkable way:

> *Chol* is non-*qodesh* because of its association with man. It can be translated either by 'profane' or by 'common'. It means 'profane' in so far as it is regarded as being the opposite of *qodesh*. It means 'common' in that it may be free to man, being untied by any *taboo*, whether *taboo* to man because it is *qodesh* to God and free to Him alone, or *taboo* to both God and man because it is unclean. *Qodesh is* always the opposite of *chol*, but that which is *chol* may or may not be free for man. It depends upon whether it is clean or unclean. The statement in Acts x. 14, 28 is confusing, for that which is common is not necessarily unclean. There was never any objection to a Jew eating that which is common, provided that it is not also unclean.
>
> The distinction between *qodesh* (holy) and *chol* (common) is clear in I Samuel xxi. 4. The priest answers David, 'There is no common bread here, but there is holy bread'. He asks if David's men have observed the sex-*taboo* of those who go forth to (sacred) war. David replies that although their journey was a common one (i.e., they are not going to war, but are on a peaceful errand; their mission is *chol* and not *qodesh*), yet actually the men have observed the sex-*taboo*, and have had no intercourse with women for the prescribed period. And their vessels will soon be holy when the holy food touches them. So the priest hands over the holy bread, actually having had no alternative before these hungry, desperate men, but having satisfied his own conscience that some sort of distinction had been made between the holy and the common.
>
> The distinction between *qodesh* and *chol* (profane, desecrate) is clear in Ezekiel xxii. 26, where Ezekiel's charge against the priests is that 'they have profaned (*chillel*) my holy things', and 'have put no difference between the holy and the common'. (Compare also Ezekiel xlii. 20, xliv. 23.)
>
> The root *ch-l-l* has cult associations from a very early date, in that wide sense of cult which would include taboo. It means 'untie', 'undo', and thence, as in Arabaic, 'become free, lawful', and in its derived forms 'make lawful', 'esteem lawful', whether rightly or wrongly. Hence it can mean both 'make legitimate' and 'profane'. The word is used of the illegitimate untying of a taboo in Leviticus xxi. 4, 9, xix. 29; Genesis xlix. 4 and its dependent I Chronicles v. Another case is Leviticus xxi. 15, but since this

concerns the High Priest, who belongs to Jehovah and is therefore *qodesh*, the meaning here may be that of making un-*qodesh*.

There is also a legitimate loosening of a *taboo* whereby *chol* means 'common' and not 'unclean', as in the previous paragraph. There are four such instances – namely Deuteronomy xx. 6 *(bis)*, xxviii. 30; Jeremiah xxxi. 5. All four deal with 'making *chol*' a vineyard when men begin to 'use' (so R.V. in the first three cases), 'enjoy' (R.V. at Jeremiah xxxi. 5), 'eat' (A.V. at Deuteronomy xx. 6 and Jeremiah xxxi. 5), or 'gather' (A.V. at Deuteronomy xxviii. 30) its fruit. The theory is that all the fruit belongs to Jehovah. It is therefore *qodesh*, and no man may eat any of it. This is acknowledged in the declaration made at the presentation of first-fruits, Deuteronomy xxvi. 5-1 I . When Jehovah has received these as a token acknowledgment, He allows the Hebrew to retain the rest of the vintage for his own use. The first-fruits never cease to be *qodesh*, since when they are picked they are handed over to Jehovah. The rest of the vintage ceases to be *qodesh*, and therefore becomes *chol*. It is that which has ceased to be *qodesh*, and in this case is free to man. The position is made quite clear in Deuteronomy xx. 6 (Douai Version), 'made it common, whereof men may eat'. (1944: 34)

Snaith then clarifies the connection between *qodesh* and prohibition:

From the general Semitic point of view *qodesh* and *cherem* are synonymous, both signifying that which is of the gods, the former in the centre and east, the latter in the west. But among the Hebrews and nearby peoples, *qodesh* stands for that which pertains to the native god, whilst *cherem* is its antithesis in that it pertains to any other god. On the other hand, *qodesh* and *cherem* are everywhere the antithesis of *chol*. This latter refers to that which definitely does not pertain to the gods. If it is 'clean' it is free to man. If it is 'unclean', it is prohibited to both gods and men. (1944: 36)

Snaith now makes some very pertinent observations on *qodesh* which contain a criticism of Robertson Smith, but which overshoot the mark. He says:

The word *qodesh*, then, comes in the first place among the Hebrews to refer to Jehovah alone. From this the step is easy to use it to refer to those manifested characteristics which belong to Jehovah uniquely. Here we find it necessary to emphasise the word 'manifested', especially because of the theory that the word 'holiness' describes a relation. We strongly dissent from the statement made by W. Robertson Smith that 'holiness is not so much a thing that characterises the gods and divine things in themselves, as the most general notion that governs their relations with humanity'. We are at least equally at variance with Skinner's statement that 'holiness in short expresses a *relation*, which consists negatively in separation from common use, and positively in dedication to the service of Jehovah'. The word 'relation' is correct in so far as it is the relation of a person or a thing to Jehovah which decides whether or not it is holy, but 'relation' is a dangerous word, for it hides the marked antithesis which is here. Holiness is of God, and not of man. A thing is holy only when it has passed over from one category to the other. (1944: 46-47)

Snaith thinks that *qodesh* refers to the manifested characteristics of the One God. We beg to differ. Relationship, not manifestation, is the *primary* implication of *qodesh*. So far Robertson Smith is quite right. However, Robertson Smith thinks that *qodesh* refers to a relation between God and man. Here again we differ, for nowhere in the Pentateuch can we find authority for the statement that a relation with humanity is meant. On the other hand, nowhere in the Bible, or in a similar document, do we find the notion that a supernatural power manifests itself without establishing a relationship, and it is this established relationship that is meant by *qodesh*.

Qodesh is, for the man of the Pentateuch, unthinkable without manifestation. Furthermore, it is a relation, and what is related to God becomes separated from other things, and separation implies taboo behaviour. According to taboo concepts, man must behave in a certain way once the relationship has been established, whether or not he is part of the *qodesh* relationship. For it does not follow from either the behavioural or the doctrinal element of *qodesh* that (1) in the establishment of the relationship the incipient part must be God, or that (2) man must be the other part.

The full relationship, including the ritual behaviour which it to some extent explains, is basically a triangular one, but two corners of the triangle may coincide. Thus the Pentateuch tells us of *qodesh*, holiness: (1) when God manifests Himself, then the spot is *qodesh* for it has been related to Him. Here the notion of contagion operates. (2) When some thing, animal, or human being has been dedicated to Him, then it is *qodesh* and hence taboo. Contagion, however, is in no way involved in this case. (3) The *baruch* relationship, the so-called blessing, also establishes holiness. God himself – this comes as a shock to most superficial Bible readers – is never called holy, *qodesh*, unless and in so far as He is related to something else. He is holy in His capacity as Lord of Hosts, though He is not here related to man. Very often the Bible says, The Holy One, blessed be He, or blessed be His name. The name is, in the framework of the doctrinal logic of the Pentateuch, always *qodesh* because it establishes a relationship; it has, so we primitives think, to be pronounced in order to exist.

Frazer's Essay on Taboo

Let us return from these comments on one of the shadows cast by Robertson Smith into this century to another famous Victorian scholar, Sir James Frazer, and to a great Victorian institution, the *Encyclopaedia Britannica*. Far too few sociologists are familiar with the very influential nineteenth-century editions of that great Scottish Encyclopaedia, which it then was. Though Scottish salesmanship was not slow in bestowing on it a name suitable for its spread south of the Tweed, it was for a long time published in Edinburgh, and its contributors, particularly in the last third of the nineteenth century, were chosen from among the most representative or promising members of the Scottish intelligentsia. A glance at the successive editions of the *Encyclopaedia Britannica* tells us much about the growth of interest in taboo during the nineteenth century. The seventh edition (1842) gives under the heading TABOO a few scant lines: 'A word used by the South Sea islanders, and nearly of the same import as prohibited or interdicted. It applies equally to persons and things, and is also expressive of anything sacred, devoted or eminent.' The importance attached to taboo could not have been very great. It was even less for the next edition, where we look for the word in vain. It has been swallowed up by that mysterious void, the encyclopaedic subconscious, and the city of Tabriz follows on the heels of Table Bay.

The next edition, however, the famous Ninth (1875) and the veritable monument of the second Scottish enlightenment, went in for science in a big way. In it Table Bay disappears into the void. In its place we find TABLES, MATHEMATICAL, an article of seventeen columns! After come the seven columns of the first essay on taboo ever published, Frazer's famous article 'Taboo'. It is to this article that I wish to devote the remainder of this chapter. It has exercised a great influence, for one thing. And then, too, it gives us something not easily found in *The Golden Bough*, a concise statement of Frazer's ideas on the subject.

Frazer opens the article with a definition of taboo. He says that taboo is 'the name given to a system of religious prohibitions which attained its fullest development in Polynesia, but of which under different names traces can be discovered in most parts of the world'. These are weighty words, but they do not imply what they would today, nor, I am afraid – despite evolution and progress – what they would have meant to some of the more lucid thinkers of the eighteenth century. The word 'system' has an attractive precision, but you will not find in this article, or in any other of Frazer's writings, an attempt to see that group of a society's customs and beliefs as a *system*, as interdependent units of a functioning whole. Nor will you find anything said about the sequel: that this system attained its fullest development in Polynesia. Frazer is not going to tell us how such systems develop. We shall be left to wonder what a full development of it really means, for we shall also be told that backwardness is the very essence of every taboo. Nor will Frazer ask why this happened in Polynesia, why the circumstances of Polynesian society were so conducive to the development of this system.

All these are really sociological questions, and failed to interest Frazer as they did Robertson Smith. Frazer, who had so much in common with Robertson Smith, including his background (he was a clergyman's son), was a classical scholar and an ethnologist. Sociology was quite alien to him. A sociologist might have hesitated to use such words and been aware that he could never live up to their implications. Frazer would not have noticed the implications of these impressive and well-balanced phrases. He was thus enabled to say the right words at the right time, sounding the clear ring of science, evolution, and wide learning.

Frazer then describes Polynesian *tabu*. First he gives the etymology we have already mentioned: *ta*, to mark; *pu*, adverb of intensity, hence *taboo*: something marked thoroughly. Indeed it is by this etymology that he can say that the 'vow of the Nazarite (Num. vi. 1-21) presents the closest resemblance to the Polynesian taboo', for it means 'one separated or consecrated' – precisely the meaning of taboo. Then he tries to elucidate the meaning of *tabu* by showing its relation to the concept of *noa*. Here he falls into the very common error, mentioned before, of regarding *noa* as 'profane', and thus as opposed to 'sacred' and 'taboo'. Next he goes on to the application of taboo:

> Although it was employed for civil as well as religious purposes, the taboo was essentially a religious observance. In Hawaii it could be imposed only by priests (I referred earlier to the special conditions of Hawaii), but elsewhere in Polynesia kings and chiefs, and even to a certain extent ordinary individuals, exercised the same power. The strictness with which the taboo was observed depended largely on the influence of the person who imposed it; if he was a great chief it would not be broken; but a powerful man often set at naught the taboo of an inferior.[1]

Frazer then proceeds by an obvious logical approach to sort the taboos he enumerates into general, particular, permanent, and temporary taboos:

> A general taboo applied, e.g., to a whole class of animals; a particular taboo was confined to one or more individuals of the class. Idols, temples, the persons and names of kings and of members of the royal family, the persons of chiefs and priests, and the property (canoes, houses, clothes, etc.) of all these classes of persons were always taboo or sacred. By a somewhat arbitrary extension of that principle a chief could render taboo to (i.e., in favour of) himself anything which took his fancy by merely calling it by the name of a part of his person.

Here follow examples of *tapa tapu* of which I have already spoken. In this passage and in later ones Frazer talks of things tabooed *to* persons and *for* persons. He does not, however, continue this line of thought by trying to establish two classes of taboos: those which make prohibitions both against some persons and in favour of others, and those which are only negative, and then correlating these two classes of taboos with kinds of sanctions. He merely says:

> Certain foods were permanently taboo to (i.e., in favour of or for the use of) gods and men, but were forbidden to women. Thus in Hawaii the flesh of hogs, fowls, turtle and several kinds of fish, cocoa-nuts, and nearly everything offered in sacrifice were reserved for gods and men, and could not, except in special cases, be consumed by women .... Sometimes certain fruit, animals and fish were taboo for months together from both men and women.

His discussion of duration similarly is but an illustration of the various possibilities:

> Seasons generally kept taboo were the approach of a great religious ceremony, the time of preparation for war, and the sickness of chiefs. The time during which they lasted varied from years to months or days. In Hawaii there was a tradition of one that lasted thirty years, during which men might not trim their beards, etc. A common period was forty days.

Frazer turns to general taboos invoked at mourning or on other ritual occasions. These he subdivides with playful if somewhat irrelevant precision into 'common' and 'strict' taboos:

> A taboo was either common or strict. During a common taboo the men were only required to abstain from their ordinary occupations and to attend morning and evening prayers. But during a strict taboo every fire and light on the island or in the district was extinguished; no canoe was launched, no person bathed, no one, except those who had to attend to the temple, was allowed to be seen out of doors; no dog might bark, no pig grunt, no cock crow. Hence at these seasons they tied up the mouths of dogs and pigs, and put fowls under a calabash or bandaged their eyes. The taboo was imposed either by proclamation or by fixing certain marks .... on the places or things tabooed.

Notice that Frazer – like Ellis, from whom the passage is quoted almost verbatim (Ellis 1826: 366-67) – describes the common taboo as more or less like the 'reasonable' observances clustered about similar events in his own society, but for the strict taboo he conjures up an appalling, yet slightly comic, picture of darkness, muzzled animals, etc. The result is certainly striking. His discussion then turns to sanctions:

> The penalty for the violation of a taboo was either religious or civil. The religious penalty inflicted by the offended *atuas* or spirits generally took the

form of a disease: the offender swelled up and died, the notion being that the *atua* or his emissary (often an infant spirit) had entered into him and devoured his vitals. Cases are on record in which persons who had unwittingly broken a taboo actually died of terror on discovering their fatal error. Chiefs and priests, however, could in the case of involuntary transgression perform certain mystical ceremonies which prevented the penalty from taking effect. The civil penalty for breaking a taboo varied in severity.

Frazer notes that in Hawaii police were appointed by the king to see that taboos were observed and offenders were killed, but that elsewhere punishment was milder. In Melanesian Fiji 'death was rarely inflicted, but the delinquent was robbed and his gardens despoiled. In New Zealand this judicial robbery was reduced to a system. No sooner was it known that a man had broken a taboo, than all his friends and acquaintances laid hands on him and carried off whatever they could lay hands on. Under this system (known as *muru*) property circulated with great rapidity. If, e.g., a child fell into the fire the father was robbed of nearly all he possessed'.

Here we can see in operation the two kinds of sanctions: the social and the religious (or 'ritual'). I am going to discuss this concept of religious penalties or ritual sanctions later, in connection with Radcliffe-Brown's theory of ritual values and sanctions.[2] In the present context I wish only to point out that Frazer is not, as one might suppose, speaking of one kind of sanction that is imposed by religious officials and another that is imposed by other officers representing the civil organs of the society. No. 'Civil' in Frazer's argument means 'real', while 'religious' refers to the unreal, imaginary or, to put it more euphemistically, to the actions of supernatural powers. This concept of religious penalties has vitiated his whole discussion of sanctions and has made it impossible to correlate kinds of transgressions with kinds of sanctions.

Frazer's approach, let me repeat, was not sociological. What it was, or at least how it is done, can be illustrated by reference to the last incident quoted: the child falling into the fire. The notion that small children are unclean, the new-born as taboo as the newly dead, has already been mentioned. Unclean things are not to be brought into contact with fire; we have noticed what complicated activities consequently ensue when it is necessary to dispose of unclean things, dangerous and polluting things, things of ritual impurity, e.g., menstrual garments and pads. Now Frazer tries to convey the idea of the ritual significance of fire in that system of values by making a list of all such instances; in such a list the separation of children from fire takes on special significance on account of all the other items listed. Further meaning may be attached to any such instance by citing, out of context, a superficially similar incident. Frazer gives us an 'explanatory' footnote:

The origin of this custom may perhaps be discerned in a custom of the Dieri tribe, Southern Australia. Among them, if a child meets with an accident, all its relations immediately get their heads broken with sticks and boomerangs till the blood flows down their faces, this surgical operation being suffered to ease the child's pain.

The Australian analogy does, to be sure, involve injured children, but it does not involve either a society of the slightest resemblance to a Polynesian society, or a taboo. The way in which this instance of magical healing is introduced foreshadows the many *non sequiturs* which abound in *The Golden Bough*. The next passage of the article demonstrates how mechanical a device Frazer's dichotomies often are. He continues: 'Besides the permanent and the artificially created taboos, there were others which arose spontaneously as a result of circumstances.' Under this heading he cites cases of persons dangerously ill being taken to sheds in the bush to die so that the house would not be defiled, for if they died in the house no one else could live there. How can we acquiesce in placing among activities that come about spontaneously as a result of circumstances the permanent fear of death evidenced in these customs, the separation made between the sphere of living things on the one hand, and the dead and their ritual on the other?

Frazer places in this same category, but as disconnected circumstances, the taboo on the mother after birth and the very strict taboo concerning the new-born infant. He does not see the completion of the cycle, the connection between birth and death, the mystery they have in common – not that this in itself would be a valid explanation of a social institution. But some connection there is, more than we find in Frazer's impressive catalogue of taboos, which is but a string of *à propos* held together by a few rhetorical devices. Of death he says:

> One of the strictest taboos was incurred by all persons who handled the body or bones of a dead person or assisted at his funeral. In Tonga a common person who touched a dead chief was tabooed for ten lunar months; a chief who touched a dead chief was tabooed for from three to five months according to the rank of the deceased. Burial grounds were taboo; and in New Zealand a canoe which had carried a corpse was never afterwards used, but was drawn on shore and painted red.

A propos 'red' he continues:

> Red was the taboo colour in New Zealand; in Hawaii, Tahiti, Tonga and Samoa it was white. In the Marquesas a man who had slain an enemy was taboo for ten days; he might have no intercourse with his wife and might not meddle with fire; he had to get someone else to cook for him.

How does he come to mention the Marquesas instance here? By a beautiful stylistic device. He had said, 'Red was the taboo colour in New Zealand; in Hawaii, Tahiti, Tonga and Samoa it was white.' Marquesas has not occurred in this recital, so he slips in a sentence that begins, 'In the Marquesas a man ....' And this man had to get some one else to cook for him. Cooking provides the next cue, and Frazer goes on: 'A woman engaged in the preparation of cocoa-nut oil was taboo for five days or more, during which she might have no intercourse with men.'

This is the rhetoric of association. The more clearly it stands out, the less trustworthy the scholarship of the author appears. But at the same time this technique of presentation increased the impressiveness of a recital that brought to the knowledge of the educated something widespread, confusedly interwoven, and very vital, the existence of which had not been suspected for the decline of general knowledge was already setting in, and the perusal of intelligent travel books was no longer a general habit.

Frazer, having constructed a picture of taboo in this peculiar manner, then tried to fit it into the general scheme of things, in a passage with the marginal title 'Use in Sociological Evolution':

> The original character of the taboo must be looked for not in its civil but in its religious element. It was not the creation of a legislator but the gradual outgrowth of animistic beliefs, to which the ambition and avarice of chiefs and priests afterwards gave an artificial extension. But in serving the cause of avarice and ambition it subserved the progress of civilisation, by fostering conceptions of the right of property and the sanctity of the marriage tie – conceptions which in time grew strong enough to stand by themselves and to fling away the crutch of superstition which in earlier days had been their sole support. For we shall scarcely err in believing that even in advanced societies the moral sentiments, in so far as they are merely sentiments and are not based on an induction from experience, derive much of their force from an original system of taboo. Thus on the taboo were grafted the golden fruits of law and morality, while the parent stem dwindled slowly into the sour crabs and empty husks of popular superstition on which the swine of modern society are still content to feed.

This is certainly a passage on which we would wish to congratulate the author for eloquence rather than good taste, Eloquence, indeed, and, if I may say so, not the agnostic eloquence of 'progress'. As the pitch of condemnation grows, it becomes more and more atavistic. Yet for whom was this written? He surely cannot be addressing himself to the swine of modern society, the swine that feed on empty husks of superstition. No: Frazer's voice is raised to reach those prodigals who feed with the swine, calling them to return to the paternal home of reason. What has he to offer the returned prodigal? But the eloquence of this peroration not only made an impression on so discerning a scholar as Robertson Smith, it also set in motion a train of thought which has given us, finally, Freud's *Totem and Taboo*.

What else does the great peroration yield? An ill-disguised anti-clerical bias which attacks, *faut de mieux*, the priests of bygone Polynesia; an exhibition of evolutionism at its slickest and least appetising; a justification, to a point, of what he regards as the most horrible superstitions, because they produced, according to his belief, a law of property and sexual propriety. All that fear and self-inflicted torture, all that pondering about life and death, all those proud and humble and desperate patterns of obedience in order to produce the *summum bonum* of the late nineteenth-century bourgeoisie.

NOTES

1. Frazer, 1875. Quotations from Frazer in this chapter are from pp.15-18.
2. See Radcliffe-Brown, 1933, and Chapter X below.

CHAPTER VIII

FRAZER AND HIS CRITIC, MARETT

I have shown (1) what, in terms of his catalogued examples, Frazer regarded as taboo, (2) what value judgements he allowed himself, and – which amounts to the same thing in this approach – (3) what function he attributed to taboo customs in the scheme of progress. But he did not, in his *Encyclopaedia Britannica* article, account for the existence of the customs he discussed.

What is the origin of taboo? What made man act so unreasonably? These were the explanations called for, and Frazer tried to give them in his *Lectures on the Early History of Kingship* (1905) and in the Taboo volume of *The Golden Bough* (1911). The solution he offered to these questions is an extreme case of what his chief critic Marett, followed by Evans-Pritchard, calls 'the intellectualist approach' (Marett 1914: 29-72; Evans-Pritchard 1933a), and I should like to say a few words about it before turning again to Frazer's treatment of taboo.

Frazer's approach may be indicated by two words: psychology and logic. All objects under his examination turn into things of the mind; customs, beliefs, rituals, and laws are all made of the same stuff. A thing cannot be *in* the mind without being *of* the mind and vice versa, and therefore Frazer dealt with it appropriately, with a particular double approach: psychology and logic. Here the classical scholar was indebted to a very remarkable historical accident. In the association psychology of the time Frazer found a method and a frame of reference almost predestined to lend an air of scientific inquiry to the discussion of sympathetic magic and the principles of contagion.

There is in Frazer an implicit belief that a relevant psychological statement can be made about every object of his interest, that is, about every element of culture, and that to give this statement wider relevance one needs a greater knowledge – not of psychology, but of that element of culture and others of similar form. It did not occur to Frazer that perhaps we ought to know more about the human mind than he did, that we have to widen our psychological knowledge in order to understand the customs and beliefs of mankind more fully. Many of us, to be sure, share his attitude, but we do so without sharing his belief that our particular psychological statements are relevant to the phenomena. Frazer not only thought psychological statements relevant, he implicitly believed that there is a relevant statement for every item of culture. He did not reject items as wrongly isolated, as too small and hence insignificant in terms of a general theory. No, each and all are made of the same stuff. However you subdivide them, they remain psychological matter. However you separate them, they remain significant. But once an item has been described and made meaningful in these terms, psychology becomes irrelevant and logic takes over.

It is the way in which Frazer combines psychology and logic which gives his approach its character, and in this combination logic plays the connecting role. If we liken the cultural element to a word we can describe Frazer's approach as follows: what compares with the word's sound structure is to be elicited by psychology; the syntax, in terms of which the word has purpose and meaning, is given by logic. For I do not intend here to dispute the propriety of calling by that name Frazer's notions about the proper relations between ends and means.

If a man beats a drum to get rain, the drum ritual is described in the one set of terms. Quite another set is used to say that drum beating is not the right means for producing rain. But there is yet another step; the instances in which the means do not fit the ends are anomalies which are to be explained in the first (psychological) set of terms. And how do we know which cases are anomalies of this sort? To know that, we must believe, as Frazer did, that the purpose of social action and the nature of the social context are self-evident. He knows which means would fit the ends in any situation, because he knows what *he* would do in the same situation and is thereby provided with a yardstick for measuring the efficacy of means. It is for this reason that the intellectualist approach has been called by a less kind name: the 'if-I-were-a-horse' school.

Those who discuss Frazer's intellectualism tend to overlook two points. The first is the interdependence of the two Frazerian beliefs, namely that you can make a relevant psychological statement about every element of culture and that purpose and context are self-evident. The one simplification is meaningless without the other. And second, that the assessment of ends and means on this grand scale creates a new notion of anomaly: a huge sector of human life, of the life of mankind, is branded as an anomaly which can be explained away in terms of normal thought. But, in order to be assimilated in such explanatory terms, this enormous sector of life has to be set aside. An ambivalent attitude, which foreshadows some later psychological notions, thus develops towards this anomaly.

The Association of Magic and Taboo

In this whole edifice of ill-adapted means of social action – this is perhaps the best definition of what Frazer calls magic – taboos, the magically conditioned avoidance customs, are but one corridor or storey (Frazer 1905: 52-59). Frazer was not the first to make this association. As Marett points out, it was Tylor who first remarked on taboo as part of magic.

So far back as when Dr Tylor published his epoch-making *Researches into the Early History of Mankind* (in 1865) we find the suggestion put forward of a certain community of principle between taboo and that 'confusion of objective with subjective connection' which 'may be applied to explain one branch after another of the arts of the sorcerer and diviner', till it almost seems as though we were coming near the end of his list, and might set down practices not based on this mental process as exceptions to a general rule. 'Many of the food prejudices of savage races', continues Dr Tylor:

> depend on the belief which belongs to this class of superstitions, that the qualities of the eaten pass into the eater. Thus, among the Dayaks, young men sometimes abstain from the flesh of deer, lest it should make them timid, and before a pig-hunt they avoid oil, lest the game should slip through their fingers, and in the same way the flesh of slow-going and cowardly animals is not to be eaten by the warriors of South America, but they love the meat of tigers, stags and boars, for courage and speed. (Marett 1914: 76-77)

And at that point Tylor stopped. In Frazer's psychological terminology, however, this relation between magic and taboo became more complicated. Looking back on his article in the *Encyclopaedia Britannica*, Frazer wrote in his preface to the third edition of the second part of *The Golden Bough*:

> When about the year 1886 my ever-lamented friend William Robertson Smith asked me to write an article on Taboo for the Ninth Edition of the *Encyclopaedia Britannica*,[1] I shared what I believe to have been at the time the current view of anthropologists, that the institution in question was confined to the brown and black races of the Pacific. But an attentive study of the accounts given of Taboo by observers who wrote while it still flourished in Polynesia soon led me to modify that view. The analogies which the system presents to the superstitions, not only of savages elsewhere, but of the civilised races of antiquity, were too numerous and too striking to be overlooked; and I came to the conclusion that Taboo is only one of a number of similar systems of superstition which among many, perhaps among all races of men have contributed in large measure, under many different names and with many variations of detail, to build up the complex fabric of

society in all the various sides or elements of it which we describe as religious, social, political, moral and economic. This conclusion I briefly indicated in my article. My general views on the subject were accepted by my friend Robertson Smith and applied by him in his celebrated *Lectures* to the elucidation of some aspects of Semitic religion. Since then the importance of Taboo and of systems like it in the evolution of religion and morality, of government and property, has been generally recognised and has indeed become a commonplace of anthropology. (1911, II: v-vi)

This interest led to the fuller treatment of the subject in *The Golden Bough* and to the expansion of one chapter in the first edition to a whole volume in the third, *Taboo and the Perils of the Soul*. To indicate the scope of this volume, I will quote the chapter headings. There are four main divisions: tabooed acts, persons, things and words. As tabooed acts we find: (1) taboos on intercourse with strangers, (2) on eating and drinking, (3) on showing the face, (4) on quitting the house, (5) on leaving food over. Next, tabooed persons: (1) chiefs and kings, (2) mourners, (3) women at menstruation and childbirth, (4) warriors, (5) manslayers, (6) hunters and fishers. Then, tabooed things: (1) iron, (2) sharp weapons, (3) blood, (4) head, (5) hair, (6) ceremonies of hair cutting, (7) disposal of cut hair and nails, (8) spittle, (9) foods, (10) knots and rings. Finally, tabooed words: (1) personal names, (2) names of relations, (3) names of the dead, (4) names of kings and other sacred persons, (5) names of gods, and (6) common words.

This table of contents gives us the impression of various groups of persons, widely differing among themselves, in situations and contexts that could not be more diverse. To say that Frazer was not aware of this or that he neglected such differences is to misstate his case: which is, that whereas *we* may make these distinctions the savage does not – that is the implication of being primitive. Frazer, to whom social contexts are self-evident, plainly discerned this lack of discernment in the primitive. Such an assumption is in fact inherent in an approach in which analysis is reserved for the meaning, in psychological terms, of the isolated items but no degree of analysis is necessary for distinguishing or evaluating social contexts. It is on this basis, rather than on an imputed ignorance of sociological matters, that any criticism of Frazerian methods must be made. Frazer's treatment is designed to render meaningful the things that belong to the meaningless, anomalous sector of human life; and their social contexts do not, to him, make such things meaningful. Conversely, the phenomena are considered the less primitive the more easily their meaning can be inferred from the social context.

Now none of this is ever said explicitly, for Frazer does not discuss his methods in abstract terms, but it can be deduced from passages such as the following, entitled 'The Meaning of Taboo' (The italics are mine.):

Thus in primitive society the rules of ceremonial purity observed by divine kings, chiefs, and priests agree in many respects with the rules observed by homicides, mourners, women in childbed, girls at puberty, hunters and fishermen, and so on. *To us* these various classes of persons appear to differ totally in character and condition; some of them we should call holy, others we might pronounce unclean and polluted. *But the savage makes no such moral distinction between them; the conceptions of holiness and pollution are not yet differentiated in his mind. To him the common feature of all these persons is that they are dangerous and in danger, and the danger in which they stand and to which they expose others is what we should call spiritual or ghostly, and therefore imaginary.* The danger, however, is not less real because it is imaginary; imagination acts upon man as really as does gravitation, and may kill him as certainly as a dose of prussic acid. To seclude these persons from the rest of the world so that the dreaded spiritual danger shall neither reach them, nor spread from them, is the object of the taboos which they have to observe. These taboos act, so to say, as electrical insulators to preserve the spiritual force with which these persons are charged from suffering or inflicting harm by contact with the outer world. (1911, II: 224)

So, you see, in Frazer's belief the lack of differentiation of contexts in savage society is not attributable to a social factor but to a psychological one: the lack of moral distinctions in the savage mind.

Now let us consider how Frazer relates taboos to magic, and what principles of elucidation he applies to both magic and taboo. We find a fair example of Frazer's correlation of magic and taboo in his discussion of attitudes and beliefs concerning the words *pig, swine,* etc., evinced by the inhabitants of rude Scottish fishing villages. The animal enters the beliefs of the villagers as the tabooed animal of the Bible, and is hence imagined to be a dangerous creature. The avoidance behaviour fitting this imaginary danger includes avoidance of the words *pig, swine,* etc., and if in disregard of the rule the words have been uttered, counter-magic is used to allay the imaginary danger. The counter-magic in this case is iron, which is touched while the appropriate formula stating that iron has been touched is murmured. This procedure becomes necessary even when the word is mentioned in church, as, for example, when the minister reads the passage from the Bible about the Gadarene swine. Frazer also notes that 'The fishermen think that if the word . . . be uttered while the lines are being baited, the line will certainly be lost' (1911, II: 233, n. 4).

There are two points to be noticed here. First, Frazer seems to think that the Scots fishermen have imbued the tabooed thing and its name with the magical properties complementary to taboo behaviour, and secondly, he thinks so even in an instance where the context clearly shows that ritual purity has given place to a notion of success and prosperity or luck.

This second point becomes clear when we turn to the case itself – Frazer's choice of which we find much less satisfactory than his generalisation on its basis – and compare the pig behaviour of the Scots fishermen with that of the Jews. Among the latter the abhorrence of the animal is, if anything, much stronger and more consistent than among the Scots group, yet we find no comparable magical concepts and practices complementary to the avoidance. Thousands of Jews who have had to choose between death and a meal of pork have chosen to die; nevertheless, the notion that mentioning the animal's name would impair their success in a gainful occupation is quite alien to them. We can see then that Frazer has not been describing or analysing the nature of pig taboos; he was dealing with the structure of luck concepts in a British fishing population. It is true, of course, that magical properties such as those in the Scots luck context could not attach to an animal which is not taboo in one way or another. This, I think, cannot be disputed, but it cannot affect the first point, which concerns the mingling of avoidance rationalisation with the rationalisation of protective mechanisms on the grounds that they are almost indistinguishable. That is why Frazer talks about positive and negative magic, meaning by the latter ritual avoidance behaviour or taboo (1905: 54). Here, too, the Scots case should make it clear that the concomitance of a certain magical belief or practice with certain avoidance behaviour has nothing to do with the degree of similarity between taboo and that kind of magic generally, nor with the degree of closeness to which the various kinds of ritual behaviour are blended in a given instance.

What, now, is the common element, according to Frazer, in taboo and magic? It is the misapplication of the association of ideas by similarity and contiguity (1905: 52-59). If I can make rain by producing thunder on a drum, this function of the drum gives rise to avoidance behaviour which may be the more marked the greater the ritual value associated with rain. But, you may object, in such cases the negative behaviour presupposes the existence in the same society of a positive magical behaviour, and not, as a rule, vice versa. Such objections are, however, superficial, being only one aspect of Frazer's assumption, that by examining two connected customs in a society one can make a relevant statement as to their interdependence in terms of a time sequence.

Marett's Criticism

A much more fundamental criticism is contained in Marett's 'Is Taboo a Negative Magic?', a valuable essay first published in 1907 and then reprinted in Marett's *Threshold of Religion* (1914). I believe that it is possible to discern two threads of argument running through the essay, the one constructive, the other a twofold criticism of Frazer. The positive argument, in which Marett tries to make out that taboo is negative *mana*, not negative magic, will be discussed in the next chapter. Of relevance here are (1) Marett's criticism of Frazer's misuse of association psychology, and (2) his introduction of the notion of sanction into the argument – the very notion Frazer so neglected.

Marett first, though not in the words we should choose today, makes several crucial points. I will discuss the lengthy passage in which he did so:

> First, to attack the theory that taboo is negative magic (in Frazer's sense of the term 'magic') on the side on which that theory is strongest, namely, where sympathy is most in evidence, I do not for one moment deny that in some taboos a sympathetic element is present and even prominent. Indeed, I see no harm in speaking, with MM. Hubert and Mauss, of sympathetic taboo, where 'sympathetic' stands for the differentia or leading character of a variety, and the genus 'taboo' is taken as already explained in independent terms. The presence of the sympathetic principle is, to my mind, amply and crucially proved in the case of those food restrictions mentioned in the passage quoted from Dr Tylor, the prohibition to eat deer lest one become timid, and so on. Another telling set of examples is provided by those remarkable taboos on the use of knots which, as Frazer has abundantly shown, are wont to be observed at critical seasons such as those of childbirth, marriage, and death. But even here, I suggest, the consequences tend to remain indefinite and vague, and that for more than one kind of reason.
>
> We can distinguish a sociological reason and a hierological or religious reason, though for the purposes of the historical study of religion, from the standpoint of which taboo is usually considered, the first may be treated as subordinate to the second. (1914: 80-84)

To this brilliant remark, which hits the nail on the head, we must add that the reverse is also true: if the purpose of our study is not historical, the hierological reason is to be treated as subservient to the sociological.

But what are 'sociological reasons'? Of course, the terminology is not very fortunate, and if by 'reason' we mean what Marett usually does mean, a causal nexus, I should be loath to say how a historical reason can act if it does not act through society, or what other cause a sociological phenomenon can have, or how, if it has some other cause, it can be described as a purely sociological phenomenon. But this is not the place to criticise Marett's terminology. Here we merely want to know what he means by it, and, when he talks about sociological reasons, he invariably means one of two things: conflicting interests or social sanctions.

To continue his argument:

> To begin with, these, no less than any other taboos, are customary observances, a portion of the unwritten law of society. To this fact, then, must be

ascribed part at least of the force that renders them effective. There are always penalties of a distinctively social kind to be feared by the taboo-breaker. In extreme cases death will be inflicted; in all cases there will be more or less of what the Australian natives call 'growling', and to bear up against public opinion is notoriously the last thing of which the savage is capable. Moreover, this social sanction is at the same time a religious sanction. To speak the language of a more advanced culture, State and Church being indivisibly one, to be outlawed is *ipso facto* to be excommunicate. Given the notion of mystic danger – of which more anon – social disapproval of all kinds will tend to borrow the tone and colour of religious aversion, the feeling that the offender is a source of spiritual peril to the community; whilst the sanctioning power remains social in the sense that society takes forcible means to remove the curse from its midst.

It may be argued that these social consequences of taboo-breaking are secondary, and thus scarcely bear on the question of the intrinsic nature of taboo. Such an objection, however, will not be admitted by anyone who has reflected at all deeply on the psychology of religion. On the broadest of theoretical grounds religion must be pronounced a product of the corporate life – a phenomenon of intercourse.

We are now in a discussion which is not innocent of Durkheim and Wundt. From here the argument leads directly to the distinction between communal and other taboos. Marett uses the term 'communal taboo' as a broad and helpful category. He does not imply by it the existence of a peculiar kind of sanction which, by its very nature, cannot apply to the breaking of any but communal taboos. He is out to slay a different dragon: sympathetic magic as a thought pattern, as the idiom of a group of taboos. This dragon he confronts with 'social reasons'. And this is how he sets about it in the succeeding passage:

Confirmation *a posteriori* is obtained by the examination of any particular taboos of which we have detailed information. Take, for example, the elaborate list of food-restrictions imposed amongst the Arunta on the *ulpmerka* or boy who has not yet been circumcised. (Here, by the way, in the systematic assignment of penalties to offences we seem to have a crucial disproof of the pure 'unconditionality' of taboo.) The sympathetic principle is probably not absent, though its action happens here not to be easily recognisable. When we learn, however, that eating parrots or cockatoos will produce a hollow on the top of the head and a hole in the chin, we may suspect that the penalty consists in becoming like a parrot or cockatoo. On the other hand, the same penalty, for instance premature old age, follows on so many different kinds of transgression that it looks here as if a tendency to dispense with particular connections and generalise the effects of mystic wrongdoing were at work. Meanwhile, in regard to all these taboos alike our authorities assure us that the underlying idea throughout is that of reserving the best kinds of food for the use of the elder men, and of thereby disciplining the novice and teaching him to 'know his place'. Here is social reason with a vengeance. Even if some suspect that our authorities overestimate the influence of conscious design upon tribal custom, they will hardly go the length of asserting that sympathy pure and simple has automatically generated a code so favourable to the elderly *gourmet*. A number of succulent meats to be reserved on the one hand, a number of diseases and malformations held in dread by the tribe on the other, and possibly a few sympathetic connections established by tradition between certain foods and certain diseases to serve them as a pattern – with this as their pre-existing material the Australian greybeards, from all we know about them, would be quite capable of constructing a taboo-system, the efficient cause of which is not so much mystic fear as statecraft. Even if the principle of sympathy lurk in the background, we may be sure that the elders are not applying it very consciously or very strictly; and again we may be sure that society in imposing its law on the *ulpmerka* is at much greater pains to make it clear that he must not eat such and such than why he must not – if only because there are so many excellent reasons of a social kind why the young should not ask questions, but simply do as they are bidden.

We can dismiss the picture of the Machiavellian Australian greybeards who construct laws for their own interest, and speak instead about the relation of food distribution to an age-set order, or about the necessary coordination of a political organisation and a system of ritual values – it does not matter which. Marett's contention can be modified in functional and structural terms. It still stands. It is a case of sociological horse-sense.

Now, the real attack!

But there is, I believe, another and a deeper reason why sympathy pure and simple cannot account for taboo. Taboo, I take it, is always something of a mystic affair. But I cannot see why there should be anything mystic about sympathy understood, as Dr Frazer understands it, simply as a misapplication of the laws of the association of ideas. After all, the association of ideas is at the back of all our thinking (though by itself it will not account for any of our thinking); and thinking as such does not fall within the sphere of the mystic. Or does the mystery follow from the fact that it is a 'misapplication' of the laws aforesaid? Dr Frazer writes [1905: 53], 'It is not a taboo to say, "Do not put your hand in the fire"; it is a rule of common sense, because the forbidden action entails a real, not an imaginary, evil.' It is not a taboo, but a rule of common prudence, for the savage. But not for the reason alleged. In his eyes there is nothing imaginary, but something terribly real, about the death or other disaster he observes to overtake the taboo-breaker. How, then, does he come to bring this kind of evil under a category of its own? Surely it ought to be the prime concern of Anthropology to tell us that. Then the savage must be aware that he is misapplying these laws; for taboo is for him a mystic affair. But if he knows he is indulging in error, why does he not mend his ways?

Clearly Dr Frazer cannot mean his explanation of magic or of taboo to be an explanation of what it is for the savage. Now, perhaps he is entitled to say that magic, in his sense, is not a savage concept or institution at all, but merely a counter for the use of the psychology that seeks to explain the primitive mind not from within but from without. He is, however, certainly not entitled to say that taboo is not a savage concept or institution. In Polynesia *tabu* is a well-recognised term that serves as perhaps the chief nucleus of embryonic reflection with regard to mystic matters of all kinds; in some of the islands the name stands for the whole system of religion. Moreover, from every quarter of the primitive world we get expressions that bear the closest analogy to this word. How then are we to be content with an explanation of taboo that does not pretend to render its sense as it has sense for those who both practise it and make it a rallying point for their thought on mystic matters? As well say that taboo is 'superstition' as that it is 'magic' in Dr Frazer's sense of the word. We ask to understand it, and we are merely bidden to despise it.

This seems to be a valid refutation of one of Frazer's arguments. How Marett himself answered the questions he raised is the subject of my next chapter.

NOTES

1. The Ninth Edition, though begun in 1875, was not completed until 1888.

CHAPTER IX

TABOO AS NEGATIVE *MANA*

So far I have described and explained the discovery of the Polynesian customs which provided the name for what was destined to become a major descriptive category of ethnography, namely taboo. I have also reviewed the main tenets of Frazer and Robertson Smith on the subject and in the last chapter started to evaluate Marett's criticism of Frazer. Since this criticism is the point of departure of Marett's positive contribution to the study of taboo, I should like to sum up briefly the position we have now reached.

Frazer tried to fit his notion of taboo and of the reasons for taboo into his theory of magic, which included a supposed analogy between magic and science. This analogy presupposes that a clear distinction can be made between magic and religion – a very doubtful supposition; it presupposes also a process of evolution in which like changes into like: intellectual magic into science. We have seen that Frazer deals with magic, religion, science, whichever happens to be his concern at the time, as means with self-evident ends, and that he discusses them to discover if, and to what degree, these means fit the ends.

Now I have been discussing Frazer more or less in his own terms, testing their consistency. This is not, strictly speaking, a sociologist's criticism, but rather an attempt by one who is convinced of the sociological irrelevance of Frazer's theories to stir them up a little in order to be stimulated by them. Sociological criticism, on the other hand, would be concerned with Frazer's basic tenets. For such criticism I refer the reader to Evans-Pritchard's essay, 'The Intellectualist (English) Interpretation of Magic', for I am not going to cover the same ground here. Since, however, Marett's criticism of Frazer is, superficially viewed, a sociological one, I shall quote as an example of sociological criticism Evans-Pritchard's most important objection to Frazer's analogy between magic and science:

> The apparent futility of Frazer's analogy between science and magic is due
> to the fact that he sees both as modes of thinking and not learnt modes of

technical behaviour with concomitant speech forms. If he had compared a magical rite in its entirety with a scientific performance in its entirety instead of comparing what he supposes to go on in the brain of a magician with what he supposes to go on in the brain of a scientist, he would have seen the essential difference between science and magic. (1933a: 27)

Marett came closer than most to this kind of criticism when, in his argument against those who regard the social consequences of taboo-breaking as secondary and therefore irrelevant to the intrinsic nature of taboo, he said:

> Such an objection ... will not be admitted by anyone who has reflected at all deeply on the psychology of religion. On the broadest of theoretical grounds religion must be pronounced a product of the corporate life – a phenomenon of intercourse. (1914: 81)

You may have been struck by the phrase 'reflected on the psychology of religion'. It is, oddly enough, this sort of reflection – not that on the nature of social relationships – that makes Marett's view of religion almost that of a sociologist. But there is also a faint similarity between such an outlook and that of the late Lévy-Bruhl, a point to which I shall return. Marett's bitter criticism of Frazer is based on this religious reflection, and his peroration on taboo, as fervid as any of Frazer's, ends with the exclamation, 'We ask to understand it, and we are merely bidden to despise it!' (1914: 84).

But what does Marett want to put in the place of the theory he criticises? Let us see how he arrives at the identification of taboo with negative *mana*. First, by rather disingenuous argument, he pretends not to know what magic is in Frazer's terms. Next, he identifies it with *mana*, or rather with what he here calls *mana*, for he has given the word a special meaning:

> Now, if 'magic' is to mean 'mana' (which, however, is not Dr Frazer's sense of 'magic', nor, indeed, mine, since I prefer to give it the uniformly bad meaning of *arungquiltha*, that is, of the antisocial variety of mana), then in describing taboo as negative magic we shall not, I believe, be far wide of the mark. Taboo I take to be a mystic affair. To break a taboo is to set in motion against oneself mystic wonder-working power in one form or another. It may be of the wholly bad variety. Thus it is taboo for the headman of the water totem in the Kaitish tribe to touch a pointing stick lest the 'evil magic' in it turn the water bad. On the other hand, many tabooed things, woman's blood or the king's touch, have power to cure no less than to kill; while an almost wholly beneficent power such as the clan totem or the personal *manitu* is nevertheless taboo. (Is Dr Frazer henceforth prepared to explain totemism on purely sympathetic principles? It would, on the other hand, be easy to show that the ideas of mana and of *manitu* and the like go very closely together.) (1914: 88-9)

We cannot let this pass without protest. Is Robertson Smith's life's labour to be wasted? To break a taboo sets in motion a mystic, wonder-working power! Very well. Let it stand for the moment while we turn our attention to the accuracy of Marett's following statements, one by one.

There are no wholly bad 'varieties' of anything. The assumption that taboo-breaking may release either good or bad power – to put it in a slightly more adult form of speech, destructive or protective power – is a flight of the imagination. Those tabooed things which have 'the power to cure no less than to kill' are not typical, they are rare. To say that the use of a tabooed thing for protection or cure means the release of good magic or mana through the breaking of a taboo is nonsense. The taboo is not broken! The beneficial power of the tabooed object is secured through special ritual behaviour which is in every case protective.

And the statement that a wholly beneficial power such as the clan totem or the personal *manitu* may be nevertheless taboo is quite wrong, is wrong in three ways. First, there are no wholly beneficial powers, not in religion, not in magic, not in 'real' life. The wholly beneficial power is an abstraction made by half-hearted rationalists from what they call higher religion, and has no place outside the world of abstractions. Secondly, anything tabooed is dangerous, for it hurts the breaker of the taboo; therefore, even if there were wholly beneficial things, nothing tabooed could ever be so. It is a contradiction in terms. Thirdly, perhaps most important, powers are not tabooed. They never are; it is their *manifestations* that may be tabooed, e.g., the altar of the god, a statue, etc. The totem spirit of the bear clan is not taboo. The Indians belonging to that clan must not kill bear. Asked why, they may reply: 'Because it is our totem.' Only by treating this linguistic usage as a logical proposition maintaining the identity of these bears romping in the forest with the totem animal can one cite this as a case of a tabooed, beneficial power.

Marett then praises the social utility of taboo:

> Indeed, it is inevitable that, whatever society prescribes a taboo in regard to some object in particular, that object should tend to assume a certain measure of respectability as an institution, a part of the social creed; and, as the law upholds it, so it will surely seem in the end to uphold the law by punishing its infraction. (1914: 89; see also 197-98)

In this common-sense argument the notion of respectability is entirely misplaced. The notion of something being dangerous and not tabooed (in a taboo-bestowing society), or of something dangerous which has not been tabooed but which, through being tabooed, becomes respectable, is quite preposterous.

Marett then applies the theory of sympathetic magic and taboo to three cases: tabooed woman, stranger, and chief – the classic examples of his opponents. He rightly concludes that what the three instances have in common cannot be sympathetic magic, and ends his essay in modest triumph:

> We have cast but a rapid glance over an immense subject. We have but dipped here and there almost at random amongst the endless facts bearing on our theme to see if the sympathetic principle – a perfectly genuine thing in its way – would take us to the bottom of the taboo feeling and idea. We conclude provisionally that it will not. Indefinite rather than definite consequences appear to be associated with the violation of a taboo, and that because what is dreaded is essentially a mysterious power, something arbitrary and unaccountable in its modes of action. Is, then, taboo a negative *mana*? Yes – if *mana* be somewhat liberally interpreted. Is it a negative magic, understanding by magic sympathetic action? With all my respect and admiration for the great authority who has propounded the hypothesis, I must venture to answer – No. (1914: 97-98)

The more we read this, the less we tend to be impressed. There is, first, the concept of mana which, with all its pervasive magical radiance, illuminates so little. All Marett had to say about mana could be put in the form of adjectives accompanying the magnificent words of fluid power, the *élan vital sociologique*. If we knew all about mana, we should then get colour and life for our perception from Marett. Marett himself, however, tells us only of its powerful radiation and omnipresence. Its working he discusses in tautologies about power. The more power some savage has, the more mana; but we move in a circle, for there seems to be no power without mana in savage life (1914: 99-121; 1932 and 1935).

Everything that Marett says about mana can be put very briefly and simply. In primitive life and society three sorts of power are conceived in the same terms: (1) the socially active power of persons; (2) the magical, that is, supposedly supernatural powers of people who have specialised in that direction; and (3) the power of supernatural beings, gods, etc., themselves. In my opinion this is neither a theory nor an approach to one. Frazer's, for all its faults, managed to give to those who cared to adopt it some insight into the working of magic: its homeopathic principles. There is a definite pattern of thought in what Frazer regards as magic, and the statement about something being negative magic, whether right or wrong, is a significant one. But I cannot see anything meaningful or significant in negative mana, unless we talk about mana in the restricted Polynesian sense as I did at the beginning of this book. There, within that culture and structural type, we find a very intricate relationship between 'mana' and 'tabu', referring to the relationship between the political and religious functions and powers of a chief, between creation and restraint, between life and death. In Polynesia 'mana' and 'tabu' are the bases of a terminology in which the

Polynesian could refer to the most important facts of delegation of authority as exercised by interdiction. In Polynesia power is veto power. Here is real *negative* mana – for anyone who would like to confuse the issue. But where is it outside this culture and outside this social type?

Marett belongs to those thinkers on society and religion who are responsible for the creation or maintenance of two compartments, the one containing the member of an advanced society who reasons on scientific lines with an adult and well-adapted mind, the other containing the savage, the child, the insane or unbalanced. Frazer did a good deal of work on the foundations of this dichotomy. Marett simplified it and confirmed it critically. Lévy-Bruhl, in his notion of a prelogical mode of existence, gave the last turn to the screw. Freud, building on the same foundations, destroyed them.

Lévy-Bruhl and the Function of Taboo Concepts

I cannot give an introduction to Lévy-Bruhl's main theories here. I have not space for even an outline. I must refer you to Lévy-Bruhl's Herbert Spencer Lecture (1931a) for a concise summary of his views on primitive thought and to Evans-Pritchard's essay (1933b) for a critical appreciation. Nor shall I go into what Lévy-Bruhl means by taboo or point out how easily he fits the primitive notion of taboo into the pattern of non-rational behaviour. To do so would take us again over ground we have already covered, approached from but a slightly different angle. Consequently, I shall limit myself to explaining the function of taboo concepts in Lévy-Bruhl's theory of transgression. This part of Lévy-Bruhl's work was written after his two important books (1910 and 1922), and at a time when the author scarcely had an axe to grind or any basic facts to explain. In *Primitives and the Supernatural* (1931b) we see a Lévy-Bruhl who takes primitives and their taboos for granted and tries to describe how these things work.

In this book Lévy-Bruhl treats taboos in groups of contexts, and it is with these contexts rather than with taboos that he is primarily concerned. The two main sets of taboo contexts are defilement-purity and transgression. This sort of treatment, for all its psychological bias, seems to me sociologically sounder than anything we have discussed so far, but then it is a very late book, written after all those I have mentioned here, after Freud, and after continuous discussion of Durkheim's principles. I hope I am not overstressing a Lévy-Bruhl side issue when I say that a very important social function of taboo is brought to our notice: that is, taboo concepts as instrumental in classifying and identifying kinds of transgression. These processes of classification and identification are indispensable in social learning. We can thus claim the sociology of learning as one vantage point, independent of others, from which to survey taboos.

One of the contexts of transgression discussed by Lévy-Bruhl in this connection is very familiar: the cutting in twain of an exogamous group:

> So too, among the Kikuyu, 'it sometimes happens that a young man unwittingly marries a cousin; for instance, if a part of the family moves away to another locality a man might become acquainted with a girl and marry her before he discovered the relationship. In such a case the *thahu* (result of the violation of the taboo) is removable. The elders take a sheep and place it on the woman's shoulders, and it is then killed, the intestines are taken out, and the elders solemnly sever them with a sharp splinter of wood ... and they announce that they are cutting the clan, by which they mean that they are severing the bond of blood relationship (of the clan) which exists between the pair. A medicine man then comes and purifies the couple.' In so much as there was clan relationship between them, their union was incestuous, but when this relationship is ended, the incest disappears. The marriage being 'regularised', no fatal consequences are to be feared. (1931b: 220)

The removal of the taboo is made to coincide with the formation of the two exogamous kin groups; and the latter process is regularised in terms of taboo, and *not the other way round*. If we keep this in mind, we can get a far clearer picture of one of the social functions of taboo. This classification of transgression is not compatible with our concepts of punishment. Here again, Lévy-Bruhl is right. But what conclusions does he draw from this difference? Let me quote:

> In a 'crime' like incest, like the infringement of an 'avoidance', we cannot help seeing, above all, the violation of an actual law, and regarding reparation of the misdemeanour as essential; we see in it nothing that is outside the world of ordinary experience, unless the actual law be regarded as emanating expressly and directly from the Divine wisdom and will. The attitude of primitives, whose mentality is intensely mystical, is quite different. When a 'crime' of this sort is committed, they ask first of all: 'How can this unheard-of event have occurred? Is an unseen, malevolent force about to exert its evil influence on us? What disasters does this transgression portend, and how shall we parry the blow?' The act itself and its doers are of secondary importance. They do not trouble about them more than is necessary to find a satisfactory answer to these questions.
>
> We are thus naturally led to the second point. The terms 'crime' and 'punishment', like the term 'transgression', run the risk of misleading us. To us a transgression signifies the violation of a rule, the infringement of a material or a moral law. To primitives, it is an abnormality, something unusual and unheard of – a sinister omen, the manifestation of a malign and unseen power. So too, when we are told that sorcerers, incestuous persons, violators of certain taboos, etc., are 'punished' with death or some other penalty, we see in this (and it is thus that most observers have under-

stood it) the 'chastisement' of their crime. We are introducing here the concepts that are current among us; our point of view is juridical and ethical; that of the primitives is above all mystic. (1931b: 224)

In this passage we find both the advantages and disadvantages of Lévy-Bruhl's approach. At first it looks as though we are to gain greater sociological insight, but in the end we are thrown back into the abyss of mystique. But we need not retain Lévy-Bruhl's independent category 'primitive punishment' as opposed to the *rational* concept of punishment – as if, since the beginning of the world, there had ever been a rational punishment! We can instead rephrase the extremely suggestive comparisons of this passage and talk about correlations of certain modes of social learning and classification of transgressions with certain types of punishment.

Now, briefly, to Lévy-Bruhl's other contribution to the theory of taboo: its defilement-purity context:

> The words 'clean, unclean, defiled' have many meanings for the primitive's mind; they have a figurative sense, a derivative (moral) sense, and yet others. The original meaning [of unclean], according to the foregoing instances, seems to be: 'exposed to an evil influence, under the threat of misfortune'. 'Purified' means 'placed out of reach of such an influence, fortified against such a threat'. As a direct consequence, 'unclean and sullied or defiled' also signifies 'that of which the vicinity or the touch is dangerous'. We have already noted the spontaneous, ever-present tendency of primitives to shun what is unfortunate, and to connect themselves with what is successful. Proximity, and even more, contact, are causes of participation. (1931b: 234-35)

Lévy-Bruhl argues further that as the individual is never really separate from other members of a primitive community but, like the organs and tissues in the human body, united with them by a sort of 'organic solidarity', not only he himself is endangered by uncleanness or defilement, even unwittingly contracted, but also, almost always, many others as well. Whatever affects the individual strikes at the rest of his circle. If he is defiled, defilement spreads to those who are organically one with him:

> What we term *infection* is thus implicitly contained in this solidarity. From the primitive's point of view, it is a direct consequence of it, but not always a necessary one. ... We are dealing with one of those material representations of immaterial qualities, or immaterial representations of material things familiar to the primitive mind, which we do not succeed in grasping easily, and which it is still more difficult to explain. Seen from one aspect, to be 'unclean' is a kind of essentially mystic quality, which makes a person find himself in the power of an evil influence and in imminent danger of

disaster. From another aspect, it is a material defilement, a blemish that adheres physically to the unclean person or object, which can be transferred, or communicated through contact, or removed by cleansing, etc. The primitive mind does not choose between these two representations, nor does it make one the symbol of the other. It has never disjoined them, but neither can one say that it confounds them. (1931b: 242-43)

These two statements must, I believe, be taken in conjunction: 'purified' means 'put out of reach'; one who is defiled is never alone in his danger. We can make this latter statement simpler and more general by saying: the endangered is always dangerous. These observations deserve comment. They show that we need not distinguish two kinds of protective mechanisms. Moreover, since the endangered is dangerous, the purified safe, we see how the principle of contagion allows – indeed, brings about – a kind of socialisation of danger. Through contagion there is social participation in danger, and social relations are describable in terms of danger. These concepts can be discussed from the point of view of social integration, without reference to classes of transgression, just as we do not need the notion of contagion to clarify the function of transgression-classifications in processes of social learning. We are dealing with two separate social functions; but as no society can afford to keep them separate, we find them expressed in the same terms.

CHAPTER X

VAN GENNEP AND RADCLIFFE-BROWN

In 1909 Van Gennep published his classic *Rites de Passage*, some parts of which are a general rendering of an earlier work, *Tabou et Totémisme à Madagascar* (1904), considering taboos in their various social contexts. *Rites de Passage* is even today a work which must be seriously studied by any one interested in the functions of ritual and ritual concepts; we have still a great deal to learn from it. Neither book is directly concerned with propounding a theory of taboo – something to be thankful for – but both enhance our psychological knowledge of taboo. Every student of ritual abstention is struck by the almost incredible uniformity of taboos the world over. Van Gennep, especially in his *Rites de Passage*, shows them to us as parts of customs and institutions which are more complex but which exhibit the same degree of uniformity.

He concerns himself with ritual behaviour occasioned by passing from one social status to another and from one age or relationship to another. He shows us the eternal pattern of transformation, of becoming, in which the stage *before* transformation and the one *after* are socially recognised, safeguarded, and protected. The passage over the border itself, however, is unrelated to such safeguards and lies in a sphere of danger. In passing through, and even in enacting, these dangers various ritual abstentions are observed, and in this context one suddenly discovers that the greater number of taboos are indeed concerned with the various delimitations of our spheres and boundaries, our time spans and our experiences. Taboos are concerned with the passings of things into the body and out of it; they guard the body's orifices. Taboos control such changes as the passage to a strange or alien setting from a more familiar one. One aspect of taboo undoubtedly consists in providing an idiom for the description of everything that matters in terms, quite literally, of transgression; of passing, that is, from inside-outside the individual's rights or competence.

Any one who reads these two books, and nobody interested in the subject should fail to do so, will immediately notice their obvious influence on some of our most valuable field monographs, such as Junod's (1927). Indeed, any one who writes on any aspect of taboo whatsoever should take his instances from Van Gennep rather than from Frazer.

Radcliffe-Brown and Social Values

My main concern in this chapter is with the contribution made to the subject by my teacher, Radcliffe-Brown. I shall refer to his well known *Andaman Islanders* of 1922 and to his Frazer Lecture for 1939 on 'Taboo'. His contribution consists mainly in discussion and definition of what he calls social values and/or ritual values, discussion of some relevant customs in these terms, and an attempt to relate these values and value concepts to a very elusive thing, 'social structure'. The concepts he uses are an outgrowth from the French school of sociology (or perhaps more precisely, a result of a confrontation of the main ideas of the French school with other ideas which are present in the earlier views of Rivers [1914, 1926]). Their application in the contexts which concern us here is, of course, quite original, and, for all its persuasive air of certainty, tentative.

The Andaman Islanders introduces this concept of social value in a context peculiarly interesting to our subject, for it occurs in a discussion of protective powers, a topic obviously related to the sociology of danger. Let me quote (the italics are mine):

> It would seem that the function of the belief in the protective power of such things as fire and the materials from which weapons are made is to maintain in the *mind of the individual the feeling* of his dependence upon the society; but viewed from another aspect the beliefs in question may be regarded as expressing the social value of the things to which they relate. This term – social value – will be used repeatedly, and it is therefore necessary to give an exact definition. By the social value of anything I mean the way in which that thing affects, or is capable of affecting, the social life. Value may be either positive or negative, positive value being possessed by anything that contributes to the wellbeing of the society, negative value by anything that can adversely affect that wellbeing.
>
> The social value of a thing (such as fire) is a matter of immediate experience to every member of the society, but the individual does not of necessity consciously and directly realise that value. He is made to realise it indirectly through the belief, impressed upon him by tradition, that the thing in question affords protection against danger. A belief or sentiment which finds regular outlet in action is a very different thing from a belief which rarely or never influences conduct. ([1922] 1948: 264)

Two different functions of such beliefs are mentioned: (1) a belief maintains a feeling in the mind of an individual. (We do not arrive at this supposed function by means of observation, but by rationalist introspection at its most naïve); (2) a belief *expresses* a social value. And since a social value is the way a thing affects, or is capable of affecting, social life, the belief in the protective power of a thing expresses the way it affects or is capable of affecting social life. Thus we are given a thing, social life, and belief relating to the thing; and we are told that there is a relation between a person's belief in the thing and the thing's effect on social life. This relation is characterised as one of 'expression', as though the way a thing is capable of affecting social life could be discerned or discussed apart from its presentation in this expression. This kind of thinking is just as fallacious as saying that words express thought, and then speaking of thought as though it were something that could be discussed in a non-expressed state.

In this, and in many a similar context, Radcliffe-Brown is saying that there are individual minds or processes of thinking and that there is also the entity called social life. Social life does not stand in a whole-and-parts relation to individual minds: they are different realities. But because those things which occur in individual minds – those thoughts – are also effective in social life, we need a kind of middle term referring to them. 'Social value' is the middle term for these things. And we can talk about a thing having social value without referring to either social life or individual minds. The whole proposition is narrowed down in the following manner: '(1) Any object that contributes to the wellbeing of the society is believed to afford protection against evil; (2) the degree of protective power it is believed to possess depends on the importance of the services it actually renders to the society; (3) the kind of special protection it is supposed to afford is often related to the kind of special service that it does actually render' ([1922] 1948: 264-65).

We must realise that although the first principle is presented as a kind of logico-sociological axiom, it is nothing of the kind. It is a general statement about certain psychological processes, and as such it is either a right or a wrong statement. Verification must proceed on a completely empirical basis. If we find a single instance in which an object contributing to wellbeing is *not* believed to give protection, or where a thing, though believed to do so, does *not* contribute to wellbeing, the statement as made is wrong. So are the other two generalisations which are derived from it. We must not be misled by phraseology which imitates the general propositions of science.

Ritual Values and Taboo

By a further narrowing down, which to me seems very arbitrary, Radcliffe-Brown distinguishes a special type of social value which he calls 'ritual value'. (He uses also the term 'ritual status' in his discussion of taboo):

> I propose to refer to the customs we are considering as 'ritual avoidances' or 'ritual prohibitions' and to define them by reference to two fundamental concepts for which I have been in the habit of using the terms 'ritual status' and 'ritual value'. I am not suggesting that these are the best terms to be found; they are merely the best that I have been able to find up to the present. In such a science as ours, words are the instruments of analysis and we should always be prepared to discard inferior tools for superior when opportunity arises.
>
> A ritual prohibition is a rule of behaviour which is associated with a belief that an infraction will result in an undesirable change in the ritual status of the person who fails to keep the rule. This change of ritual status is conceived in many different ways in different societies, but everywhere there is the idea that it involves the likelihood of some minor or major misfortune which will befall the person concerned. ([1939] 1952: 134-35)

Is this an adequate definition of ritual prohibition? What, then, are the dietary restrictions placed on pregnant women in so many societies? Radcliffe-Brown is narrowing down the range of prohibitions to those which can be explained in terms of ritual status:

> We have already considered one example. The Polynesian who touches a corpse has, according to Polynesian belief, undergone what I am calling an undesirable change of ritual status. The misfortune of which he is considered to be in danger is illness, and he therefore takes precautions and goes through a ritual in order that he may escape the danger and be restored to his former ritual status.
>
> Let us consider two examples of different kinds from contemporary England. There are some people who think that one should avoid spilling salt. The person who spills salt will have bad luck. But he can avoid this by throwing a pinch of the spilled salt over his shoulder. Putting this in my terminology, it can be said that spilling salt produces an undesirable change in the ritual status of the person who does so, and that he is restored to his normal or previous ritual status by the positive rite of throwing salt over his shoulder. ([1939] 1952: 135)

This description of infraction and restoration of ritual status need not detain us. But can the fact that avoidance customs are used to resolve situations fraught with danger be explained in terms of ritual values, even in Radcliffe-Brown's terms of positive and negative values?

> If Jack loves Jill, then Jill has the value of a loved object for Jack, and Jack has a recognisable interest in Jill. When I am hungry I have an interest in food, and a good meal has an immediate value for me that it does not have at other times. My toothache has a value to me as something that I am interested in getting rid of as quickly as possible. ([1939] 1952: 140)

This polarity, it will be noticed, is not, according to Radcliffe-Brown, peculiar to what he calls ritual value. But what is this chief concept, ritual value itself? Radcliffe-Brown writes:

Another distinction which we make in our own society within the field of ritual avoidances is between the holy and the unclean. Certain things must be treated with respect because they are holy, others because they are unclean. But, as Robertson Smith and Sir James Frazer have shown, there are many societies in which this distinction is entirely unrecognised. The Polynesian, for example, does not think of a chief or a temple as holy and a corpse as unclean. He thinks of them all as things dangerous. An example from Hawaii will illustrate this fundamental identity of holiness and uncleanness. There, in former times, if a commoner committed incest with his sister he became *kapu* (the Hawaiian form of *tabu*). His presence was dangerous in the extreme for the whole community, and since he could not be purified he was put to death. But if a chief of high rank, who, by reason of his rank was, of course, sacred (*kapu*), married his sister he became still more so. An extreme sanctity or untouchability attached to a chief born of a brother and sister who were themselves the children of a brother and sister. The sanctity of such a chief and the uncleanness of the person put to death for incest have the same source and are the same thing. ([1939] 1952: 139)

And why? Because 'they are both denoted by saying that the person is *kapu*'.

In studying the simpler societies it is essential that we should carefully avoid thinking of their behaviour and ideas in terms of our own ideas of holiness and uncleanness. Since most people find this difficult it is desirable to have terms which we can use that do not convey this connotation. Durkheim and others have used the word 'sacred' as an inclusive term for the holy and the unclean together. This is easier to do in French than in English, and has some justification in the fact that the Latin *sacer* did apply to holy things such as the gods and also to accursed things such as persons guilty of certain crimes. But there is certainly a tendency in English to identify sacred with holy. I think that it will greatly aid clear thinking if we adopt some wide inclusive term which does not have any undesirable connotation. I venture to propose the term 'ritual value'. ([1939] 1952: 139)

At this stage of the argument 'ritual value' is a translation of *sacer*. *Sacer* is the 'taboo' term of one of the many religions, not a term from an objective, scientific vocabulary. It can be put to some descriptive use, but it is certainly not an analytical concept. *Sacer* has an unsuitable connotation in English; therefore Radcliffe-Brown translates it as 'ritual value'. We must realise that this is merely translation, that the argument for it is put forward like the argument for any other translation, and that when Radcliffe-Brown says that 'we adopt' this term, we adopt it in the place of another term which is unsuitable: that means translation. A term arrived at in this ingenious way cannot be used as an explanation. The only explanation that could be given by it is of this sort: 'Why is that mountain big?' 'Because it is *magnus*.' Radcliffe-Brown continues:

> Anything – a person, a material thing, a place, a word or name, an occasion or event, a day of the week or a period of the year – which is the object of a ritual avoidance or taboo can be said to have ritual value. Thus in Polynesia chiefs, corpses and newly-born babies have ritual value. For some people in England salt has ritual value. For Christians all Sundays and Good Friday have ritual value, and for Jews all Saturdays and the Day of Atonement. The ritual value is exhibited in the behaviour adopted towards the object or occasion in question. Ritual values are exhibited not only in negative ritual but also in positive ritual, being possessed by the objects towards which positive rites are directed and also by objects, words or places used in the rites. A large class of positive rites, those of consecration or sacralisation, have for their purpose to endow objects with ritual value. It may be noted that in general anything that has value in positive ritual is also the object of some sort of ritual avoidance or at the very least of ritual respect. ([1939] 1952: 139)

Observe how ritual value by degrees becomes a thing. We first knew it as a translation of *sacer*. Now we are told that it is something people exhibit in ritual: 'the ritual value is exhibited in the behaviour'. Exhibited! Another 'wide inclusive term' has taken the place of the word 'express'. Ordinary values, in *The Andaman Islanders*, were 'expressed'. Now 'ritual values' are 'exhibited'.

There is something else ritual and social value have in common: polarity. Toothache has a value because we don't like to have it: this is a negative value. We try to rid ourselves of it. In the same way we have negative ritual values exhibited in negative ritual or ritual avoidance. The ritual value is exhibited in ritual behaviour, quite unlike *sacer* of which ritual value purports to be a translation. What happens to it when it is not exhibited? This is the child's famous question: what does the wind do when it does not blow? Anyhow, when these ritual values are exhibited, they are positive and negative. But where is the polarity of this concept, the logic of which caused some misgivings even during its conceptualisation? It is not the polarity of unclean and holy, as things can be tabooed as dangerous without being unclean. Is it perhaps the polarity of dangerous and holy? But the holy is dangerous in most societies we have studied and, where it is not dangerous, it has little or no social significance. (In the Christian cult, for example, the concept has been split, and the Devil has the danger functions.) I fail to see the usefulness of these ratiocinations on positive and negative ritual values.

Radcliffe-Brown then establishes the connection between general social values and ritual values:

Amongst the members of a society we find a certain measure of agreement as to the ritual value they attribute to objects of different kinds. We also find that most of these ritual values are social values as defined above. Thus for a local totemic clan in Australia the totem-centres, the natural species associated with them, i.e., the totems, and the myths and rites that relate thereto, have a specific social value for the clan; the common interest in them binds the individuals together into a firm and lasting association.

Ritual values exist in every known society, and show an immense diversity as we pass from one society to another. The problem of a natural science of society (and it is as such that I regard social anthropology) is to discover the deeper, not immediately perceptible, uniformities beneath the superficial differences .... The ultimate aim should be, I think, to find some relatively adequate answer to the question – *What is the relation of ritual and ritual values to the essential constitution of human society?* ([1939] 1952: 141-42)

But the study of ritual behaviour resolves into a study of symbols and meaning:

So far as ritual avoidances are concerned the reasons for them may vary from a very vague idea that some sort of misfortune or ill-luck, not defined as to its kind, is likely to befall anyone who fails to observe the taboo, to a belief that non-observance will produce some quite specific and undesirable result. Thus an Australian aborigine told me that if he spoke to any woman who stood in the relation of mother-in-law to him his hair would turn grey.

The very common tendency to look for the explanation of ritual actions in their purpose is the result of a false assimilation of them to what may be called technical acts. In any technical activity an adequate statement of the purpose of any particular act or series of acts constitutes by itself a sufficient explanation. But ritual acts differ from technical acts in having in all instances some expressive or symbolic element in them.

A second approach to the study of ritual is therefore by a consideration not of their purpose or reason but of their meaning. I am here using the words symbol and meaning as coincident. Whatever has a meaning is a symbol and the meaning is whatever is expressed by the symbol. ([1939] 1952: 142-43)

But in a society in which a corpse is regarded as dangerous, a distinction between the actual corpse and the symbolic meaning of the corpse, if made at all, is not made in the same way as the distinction drawn by an Englishman between the scattered white mineral upon his table and the symbolic meaning of spilled salt.

What is explained when we say that the meaning of a corpse is death? Or what is the meaning of menstrual secretions in a given taboo society? If I were to say that this secretion is regarded as the negative, and hence dangerous, concomitant of fertility, which thus draws upon itself all the negative aspects of fertility and by this association with other negations of fertility becomes associated with death, what have I said? What more than a long-winded and lamentable prose poem appropriate to a textbook of contemporary drawing room psychology? How can we verify statements of this kind? I think it far better not to make them.

In any case, why explain taboos in terms of symbol and meaning? What lies at the root of the confusion? Simply this: that Radcliffe-Brown is trying to express danger in terms of values. But we talk about values on a different level of abstraction from that on which we talk about danger. The value level is more abstract, lends itself more readily to theorising, and for this very reason we all tend, as Radcliffe-Brown does, to describe danger behaviour in terms of value. Once we have embarked on this course clarification becomes impossible, for we have hold of the wrong end of the stick. Instead of explaining danger behaviour in terms of negative values, we may – and should – explain value behaviour in terms of positive danger (to remain within the same verbal convention): an approach very close to Robertson Smith's. This, however, is a subject on which I will touch in my last chapter.

Lastly, I should like to show the way the relation between sanctions and taboos appears as an afterthought in this chain of reasoning. Radcliffe-Brown says:

> For every rule that *ought* to be observed there must be some sort of sanction or reason. For acts that patently affect other persons the moral and legal sanctions provide a generally sufficient controlling force upon the individual. For ritual obligations conformity and rationalisation are provided by the ritual sanctions. The simplest form of ritual sanction is an accepted belief that if rules of ritual are not observed some undefined misfortune is likely to occur. In many societies the expected danger is somewhat more definitely conceived as a danger of sickness or, in extreme cases, death. In the more specialised forms of ritual sanction the good results to be hoped for or the bad results to be feared are more specifically defined in reference to the occasion or meaning of the ritual. ([1939] 1952: 150)

These sanctions thus apply to rites without reference to their positive or negative character, that is, whether or not they are taboos. In the class of phenomena related to one kind of sanctions we can never isolate taboos.

Further: what does Radcliffe-Brown mean by ritual sanctions? It is a misleading term for nonhuman agencies, but are nonhuman agencies not concomitant with some sort of social pressure? Does not the identification by society of certain ill effects with the result of the infraction of expected behaviour act as a kind of social pressure? This, too, needs some further discussion.

What have we learned from Radcliffe-Brown's *Taboo* essay? At least two things: (1) that it is impossible to describe danger behaviour in terms of value, and (2) that one cannot describe supposedly nonhuman sanctions without some reference to social pressure. This result is wholly negative, but it is, I believe, rather salutary.

CHAPTER XI

WUNDT AND FREUD

Wundt, the German counterpart of the English mid-Victorians, contributed during his long career to a wide range of disciplines. He started in 1857 with experimental physiology and ended, with philosophy, only at his death in 1920. Before considering his specific statements about taboo I should like to say a few words about his 'folk psychology'. He first lectured on this subject in 1874, but the ten volumes of his *Völkerpsychologie* (1927) did not begin to appear until a quarter of a century later, in 1900 when Wundt was sixty-seven. We are thus dealing with a mature work, and one which embraces a very wide field.

Wundt broke with the intellectualist approach of the classical evolutionists. He insisted, on the one hand, that the primitive reaction of man's mind to nature is a direct intuitive response, a 'mythological apperception', and, on the other hand, that the psychological life of the individual is constantly determined by and interwoven with his social setting. The one cannot be understood without the other. It is from this approach that the wide range of folk psychology derives. 'Its problem relates to those mental products which are created by a community of human life and are therefore inexplicable in terms merely of individual consciousness, since they presuppose the reciprocal action of many' (1916: 3).

'Folk' Psychology

This, then, is what Wundt means by 'folk' as opposed to 'individual' psychology. But to what sort of a collectivity does *Volk* refer? For it is more than 'the many'. In general German usage *Volk* refers to a community (*Gemeinschaft*) of racially related people held together by ties of language, history and culture. Confusion can arise; the word can also designate groups of men such as troops or a ship's company, or classes, especially peasants and proletariat. This is muddling enough, and it is partly, as he explains, to avoid similar or worse confusion that Wundt rejects two terms suggested as synonyms for folk psychology. (1) Social psychology (*Sozialpsychologie*) will not do because it 'at once reminds us of modern sociology which, even in its psychological phases, usually deals exclusively with questions of modern cultural life' (1916: 4). In this context, on the other hand, *Volk* has the same overtones as the English word 'folk' in 'folk song'. (2) The term 'community psychology' (*Gemeinschaftspsychologie*) is also rejected as being too narrow in its implications. Wundt is concerned not only with such associations as family, tribe and local community, but also with 'the union and reciprocal activity of a number of peoples ... so that, in this case, folk psychology really becomes a psychology of mankind'.

Wundt's special treatment of taboo is also conditioned by his schematic representation of the history of culture in terms of (1) the period of primitive man, (2) the period of totemism, (3) the period of gods and heroes, and (4) the period of humanity. A good example of the role of taboo in this scheme is furnished by Wundt's discussion of the totemic age and Polynesia's two notable advances during that era: first, by the development of a celestial mythology, which need not concern us here, and secondly, by the development of taboo.[1] Wundt wrote:

> There is, moreover, one further custom, taboo, which has grown up under totemic influence and has received its richest development, with manifold transformations and ramifications, within this very transitional culture of Polynesia. The earliest form of taboo, which consists in the prohibition of eating the flesh of the totem animal, has, it is true, disappeared. But the idea of taboo has been transferred to a great number of other things, to sacred places, to objects and names, to the person and property of individuals, particularly of chiefs and priests. The tremendous influence of these phenomena, whose origin is closely intertwined with totemism, clearly shows that this entire culture belongs essentially to the totemic age. (1916: 131-32)

One can scarcely imagine a more spurious connection between taboo and totemism. Wundt completely misunderstood Robertson Smith and Frazer. After condemning Frazer's derivation of all forms of totemism from conception-totemism as an ultimately individualist view, Wundt turns to taboo. He comments that as a thing tabooed is a thing to be avoided on account of either its sanctity or its impurity, the whole concept clearly arises from an undifferentiated fear:

> If, now, we associate the term 'taboo' in a general way with an object that arouses fear, the earliest object of taboo seems to have been the totem animal. One of the most elemental of totemic ideas and customs consists in the fact that the members of a totem group are prohibited from eating the flesh of the totem, and sometimes also from hunting the totem animal. This pro-

hibition, of course, can have originated only in a general feeling of fear, as a result of which the members of a totemic group are restrained from eating or killing the totem animal. In many regions where the culture, although already totemic, is nevertheless primitive, the totem animal appears to be the only object of taboo. This fact alone makes it probable that totemism lies at the basis of taboo ideas. The protective animal of the individual long survived the tribal totem and sometimes spread to far wider regions. Similarly, the taboo, though closely related to tribal organisation in origin, underwent further developments which continued after the totemic ideas from which it sprang had either entirely disappeared or had, at any rate, vanished with the exception of meagre traces. This accounts for the fact that it is not in Australia, the original home of the totem, that we find the chief centre of taboo customs, nor in Melanesian territory, where the totem is still fairly common, nor in North America, but in Polynesia. (1916: 194)

Proceeding with the idea that the sphere of taboo widens as totemic ideas proper recede, Wundt traces a gradual shift of taboo from the totem animal to man himself, as chief or priest, and from man to his possessions. For serious criticism of Wundt, and for a very original approach to the subject of taboo, we must turn to Freud.

Freud's 'Totem and Taboo'

Even if Freud were not the most influential psychologist of our century, it would be impertinence for a non-psychologist to criticise his work on psychological grounds. I want to discuss his theories only in as far as they are believed or assumed to have some bearing on sociological generalisations. Yet even a humble student of Freud does not readily impose this limitation upon himself, for Freud had a flair for popular writing and expounded his most important ideas to the public for whom popularisations are meant. To this public, which some people call 'general' and others 'educated', he persuasively reveals his reasoning step by step, and the ignorant outsider whose assent is wooed and obtained before each new step is taken may well feel that his dissent would be just as legitimate as his agreement. Legitimate, it may be, but not relevant. For, as Freud's readers soon discover, the plausibility of the theories may be ideologically important, but it is not relevant proof, and no one who does not actually experience the praxis of psycho-analysis has access to this relevant proof.

One of Freud's celebrated works, *Totem and Taboo*, is composed of the following essays: (1) The Horror of Incest; (2) Taboo and Emotional Ambivalence; (3) Animism, Magic and the Omnipotence of Thought; (4) The Return of Totemism in Childhood. It is with the second of these essays that I want to deal, though it will readily be seen that the subject matter of the first and third is not unrelated to our problem.

'The meaning of "taboo", as we see it,' writes Freud, 'diverges in two contrary directions. To us it means, on the one hand, "sacred", "consecrated", and on the other, "uncanny", "dangerous", "forbidden", "unclean"' (Freud 1950: 18). We note here that 'sacredness' and 'forbidden' are different branches of *meaning*. We are not discussing here the phenomena of religious emotion or abstentive behaviour; we are merely talking about meanings. We do not expect to find repeated by the master of depth psychology what we found rather peculiar in the make-up of the superficial thinkers of the nineteenth century. However, there it is: 'sacredness' is different from 'forbidden'. And what *is* 'sacredness'? In what terms of language or experience can anyone explain what sacredness is without involving principles of interdiction? Surely nobody means by sacredness a degree of beatitude or a means of beatification, or a species of value though Radcliffe-Brown does seem to mean almost that. Is Freud going to do what the rest did – pretend that there is sacredness apart from interdiction? Is he going to reiterate the claim that interdiction is older and more primitive than this fabulous, non-interdictory sacredness, and conclude therefore that the latter derived from the former through the alchemy of evolution?

Well, even if Freud is not going to repeat precisely what the others have tried to convey, he certainly starts by summing up very sympathetically what they have said: 'The converse of "taboo" in Polynesian is "noa", which means "common" or "generally accessible". Thus taboo has about it a sense of something unapproachable, and it is principally expressed in prohibitions and restrictions' (1950: 18). What does taboo do when it does *not* express itself in prohibitions and restrictions?

Using a German idiom, Freud writes: 'Our collocation "holy dread" would often coincide in meaning with "taboo".' And he continues: 'Taboo restrictions are distinct from religious or moral prohibitions. They are not based upon any divine ordinance, but may be said to impose themselves on their own account. They differ from moral prohibitions in that they fall into no system that declares quite generally that certain abstinences must be observed and gives reasons for that necessity.'

Prohibition without sacredness, in fact. 'Taboo prohibitions have no grounds and are of unknown origin.' But does their attribution to divine command – and some taboos are so attributed – mean that reasons are given for them or that their origin is known? 'Though they are unintelligible to us,' Freud writes, 'to those who are dominated by them they are taken as a matter of course.'

So far Freud has given us a very lucid resumé of the views of Robertson Smith and Frazer. I have gone through all this in previous chapters and have tried, in the proper context, to refute the notions (1) that taboos are only ancient and are not continuously created, and (2) that where taboos coexist with monotheism they are necessarily older than monotheism or relate to another sphere of religious experience. When, in conclusion, Freud states very bluntly that 'it is generally supposed that taboo is older than gods and dates back to a period before any kind of religion existed', a flat contradiction – a denial that any society had a pre-religious age – would be quite beside the point. The assumption of such an age is part of Freud's reconstruction of human history, which includes also the assumption of a primaeval horde which slew its father and originated religion (1950: 125-26). Moreover, these crude assumptions are at the same time a way of discussing the structure of human drives and, in that capacity, concomitants of certain methods of healing neuroses. There is consequently no point in discussing in sociological terms theories so differently contrived. If, however, Freudian teaching comes to follow the attitude of the younger disciples, it is difficult to see why the hypothesis of a pre-religious age should be maintained. For most of these younger disciples have discarded the myth of our murdered *Urvater*, and the ensuing bad conscience of mankind, as a construct unnecessary for the analysis of drive structures – a point on which we, of course, cannot venture an opinion. And if this nineteenth-century dogma becomes unnecessary, there can be no reason to exempt statements concerning the interdependence of certain forms of taboo and monotheism from the probings of sociological research.

After his introductory remarks Freud gives an extract from Northcote Thomas's article in the Eleventh Edition of the *Encyclopaedia Britannica* (1911). This article is an elaboration of the older one by Frazer in the Ninth Edition (1875) and gives a mass of those rather confusing data that I have so often referred to. After going through the catalogue of these outlandish customs, Freud concludes:

> If I judge my readers' feelings aright, I think it safe to say that in spite of all they have now heard about taboo they still have very little idea of the meaning of the term or of what place to give it in their thoughts. This is no doubt due to the insufficiency of the information I have given them and to my having omitted to discuss the relation between taboo and superstition, the belief in spirits, and religion. On the other hand, I am afraid a more detailed account of what is known about taboo would have been even more confusing, and I can assure them that in fact the whole subject is highly obscure.
>
> What we are concerned with, then, is a number of prohibitions to which these primitive races are subjected. Every sort of thing is forbidden; but they have no idea why, and it does not occur to them to raise the question. On the contrary, they submit to the prohibitions as though they were a matter of course, and feel convinced that any violation of them will be automatically met by the direst punishment. We have trustworthy stories of how any unwitting violation of one of these prohibitions is in fact automatically punished. An innocent wrongdoer, who may, for instance, have eaten a forbidden animal, falls into a deep depression, anticipates

death, and then dies in bitter earnest. These prohibitions are mainly directed against liberty of enjoyment and against freedom of movement and communication. In some cases they have an intelligible meaning and are clearly aimed at abstinences and renunciations. But in other cases their subject matter is quite incomprehensible; they are concerned with trivial details and seem to be of a purely ceremonial nature.

Behind all these prohibitions there seems to be something in the nature of a theory that they are necessary because certain persons and things are charged with a dangerous power which can be transferred through contact with them, almost like an infection. (1950: 21)

Freud, discussing Wundt's comment that taboo is 'an expression and derivative of the belief of primitive peoples in "demonic" power', points out that fear and demons are themselves creations of the human mind, 'made by something and out of something' (1950: 24). He then turns to Wundt's teaching of a primitive lack of differentiation between awe and aversion:

> Wundt has important views on the double significance of taboo, though these are not very clearly expressed. According to him the distinction between 'sacred' and 'unclean' did not exist in the primitive beginnings of taboo. For that very reason those concepts were at that stage without the peculiar significance which they could only acquire when they became opposed to each other. Animals, human beings or localities on which a taboo was imposed were 'demonic', not 'sacred', nor, therefore, in the sense which was later acquired, 'unclean'. It is precisely this neutral and intermediate meaning – 'demonic' or 'what may not be touched' – that is appropriately expressed by the word 'taboo', since it stresses a characteristic which remains common for all time both to what is sacred and to what is unclean: the dread of contact with it. The persistence, however, of this important common characteristic is at the same time evidence that the ground covered by the two was originally one, and that it was only as a result of further influences that it became differentiated and eventually developed into opposites.
>
> According to Wundt, this original characteristic of taboo – the belief in a 'demonic' power which lies hidden in an object and which, if the object is touched or used unlawfully, takes its vengeance by casting a spell over the wrongdoer – is still wholly and solely 'objectified fear'. That fear has not yet split up into the two forms into which it later develops: veneration and horror.
>
> But how did this split take place? Through the transplanting, so Wundt tells us, of the taboo ordinances from the sphere of demons into the sphere of belief in gods. The contrast between 'sacred' and 'unclean' coincides with a succession of two stages of mythology. The earlier of these stages did not completely disappear when the second one was reached but persisted in what was regarded as an inferior and eventually a contemptible form. It is, he says, a general law of mythology that a stage which has been passed, for the very reason that it has been overcome and driven under by a superior

stage, persists in an inferior form alongside the later one, so that the objects of its veneration turn into objects of horror. (1950: 24, 25)

Taboo Customs and Obsessional Neurosis

In his entire discussion of the ethnographic material Freud has really stressed two, and only two, points: the difference between, and distinctiveness of, sacredness and horror, and the automatic nature of the taboo sanction. There is a certain arbitrariness in this narrowing down of the rather complex problems and institutions involved. Nevertheless, in so doing, Freud remains in the best tradition of the Victorian intellectualists.

He then goes on to forge the link between social custom and diseased mind:

Anyone approaching the problem of taboo from the angle of psychoanalysis, that is to say, of the investigation of the unconscious portion of the individual mind, will recognise, after a moment's reflection, that these phenomena are far from unfamiliar to him. He has come across people who have created for themselves individual taboo prohibitions of this very kind and who obey them just as strictly as savages obey the communal taboos of their tribe or society. If he were not already accustomed to describing such people as 'obsessional' patients, he would find 'taboo sickness' a most appropriate name for their condition. Having learnt so much, however, about this obsessional sickness from psychoanalytical examination – its clinical aetiology and the essence of its psychical mechanism – he can scarcely refrain from applying the knowledge he has thus acquired to the parallel sociological phenomenon. (1950: 26)

After a brief warning – too soon and too easily dismissed – that the similarity between taboo and obsessional disease may be purely superficial, Freud comments that the first resemblance between the two lies in the fact that their 'prohibitions are equally lacking in motive and equally puzzling in their origin'. He finds other resemblances:

As in the case of taboo, the principal prohibition, the nucleus of the neurosis, is against touching; and thence it is sometimes known as 'touching phobia' or '*délire du toucher*'. The prohibition does not merely apply to immediate physical contact but has an extent as wide as the metaphorical use of the phrase 'to come in contact with'. Anything that directs the patient's thoughts to the forbidden object, anything that brings him into intellectual contact with it, is just as much prohibited as direct physical contact. The same extension also occurs in the case of taboo.

The purpose of some of the prohibitions is immediately obvious. Others, on the contrary, strike us as incomprehensible, senseless and silly, and prohibitions of this latter sort are described as 'ceremonial'. This distinction, too, is found in the observances of taboo.

Obsessional prohibitions are extremely liable to displacement. They extend from one object to another along whatever paths the context may provide, and this new object then becomes, to use the apt expression of one of my women patients, 'impossible' – till at last the whole world lies under an embargo of 'impossibility'. Obsessional patients behave as though the 'impossible' persons and things were carriers of a dangerous infection liable to be spread by contact on to everything in their neighbourhood. I have already drawn attention to the same characteristic capacity for contagion and transference in my description of taboo. We know, too, that anyone who violates a taboo by coming into contact with something that is taboo becomes taboo himself and that then no one may come into contact with *him*.

I will now put side by side two instances of the transference (or, as it is better to say, the *displacement*) of a prohibition. One of these is taken from the life of the Maoris and the other from an observation of my own on a female obsessional patient.

(i) A Maori chief would not blow a fire with his mouth; for his sacred breath would communicate its sanctity to the fire, which would pass it on to the pot on the fire, which would pass it on to the meat in the pot, which would pass it on to the man who ate the meat, which was in the pot, which stood on the fire, which was breathed on by the chief; so that the eater, infected by the chief's breath conveyed through these intermediaries, would surely die (Frazer, 1911b: 136).

(ii) My patient's husband purchased a household article of some kind and brought it home with him. She insisted that it should be removed or it would make the room she lived in 'impossible'. For she had heard that the article had been bought in a shop situated in, let us say, 'Smith' Street. ['*Hirschengasse*' and '*Hirsch*' in the original.] 'Smith', however, was the married name of a woman friend of hers who lived in a distant town and whom she had known in her youth under her maiden name. This friend of hers was at the moment 'impossible' or taboo. Consequently the article that had been purchased here in Vienna was as taboo as the friend herself with whom she must not come into contact.

Obsessional prohibitions involve just as extensive renunciations and restrictions in the lives of those who are subject to them as do taboo prohibitions; but some of them can be lifted if certain actions are performed. Thereafter, these actions *must* be performed; they become compulsive or obsessive acts, and there can be no doubt that they are in the nature of expiation, penance, defensive measures and purification. The commonest of these obsessive acts is washing in water ('washing mania'). Some taboo prohibitions can be replaced in just the same way; or rather their violation can be made good by a similar 'ceremonial'; and here again lustration with water is the preferred method. (1950: 27-28)

Freud finds four points in common between taboo customs and the symptoms of obsessional neurosis: ' (1) the fact that the prohibitions lack any assignable motive; (2) the fact that they are maintained by an internal necessity; (3) the fact that they are easily displaceable and that there is a risk of infection from the prohibited object; and (4) the fact that they give rise to injunctions for the performance of ceremonial acts' (1950: 28). The sociologist cannot refrain from a few remarks on these four points:

1. *Lack of assignable motive for prohibitions.* As a rule prohibitions are never assignably motivated unless they form a topic of discussion or explanation between those who issue the prohibition and those who have to obey. This is an elementary observation, which no theory of drives can invalidate. If it were otherwise, if the absence of offered motivation really were the criterion Freud maintains it is, the bylaws of a railway company would be closer to taboo than parental orders.
2. *Maintenance through an internal necessity.* Is the inner need really operative in a case like that of the Maori chief in the same way as it is in the case of the patient? Freud apparently thinks it is. But he gives no reason for such a belief, and no argument is advanced which could shatter our conventional assumption of social determinism for the actions of a chief who is, at every moment of his activities, motivated by the sum total of tribal customs relating to chiefship. These customs, as far as they can be said to be real, are present in his motivations and in those of the tribesmen who respond to him.
4. *Injunctions for the performance of ceremonial acts arising from the prohibitions.* Again, this is begging the question. Sometimes it is the other way round. What do we mean when we describe a patient's actions as ceremonial? My misgivings here are twofold. First, in social life ceremonies are distinguished from other activities which are not ceremonies. In the case of the patient, however, this is not so. *All* activities of the patient are rigid, circumscribed, and the fact that many types of morbid behaviour resemble ceremonial behaviour rather than other social behaviour is a fact which has nothing to do with taboo. Secondly, even if what are called ceremonies performed by the patient differ from his other activities, and this difference allows us to compare successfully his ceremonies with a ceremonial behaviour established by a society, even then we could never be justified in talking of ceremonies as being (a) private and morbid, (b) public, social, and what have you. To say that is like saying that an observation of a schizophrenic patient uttering words and responding to them with different voices is relevant to the clarification of the nature and operation of discussion; and that discussion is an exchange of opinions which takes place (a) between people holding different opinions, and (b) in the soliloquy of a patient of a certain kind. Such a classification serves as a description of a symptom, i.e., it may help you to distinguish a normal from an abnormal person, but it is not going to enhance your knowledge of discussions. In fact, you know you are dealing with a case of illness when the various opinions held by a person become

mental isolates, so that the unfortunate person, in being aware of them, behaves as though he were several persons. In the same way a person strictly observing self-imposed ceremonies is ill. And the stricter the observance, the more independent and isolated the source of it, the greater the degree of morbidity.

3. Freud's third notion, of *morbid contagion concepts*, is paralleled or extended by another which he calls 'omnipotence of thought' (1950: 85-90). This omnipotence is an active principle, to be found in magic, dream life, child psychology and mental aberration. This active principle corresponds closely to the passive one of contagion, and both principles together make for what we may call the transcience of socio-psychological space. In cases where rational activities are impaired, this combination of omnipotence of thought with fear of contagion survives as the sole cohesive principle and serves to bring about those processes whereby relationships are made to appear material or spiritual. The degree of 'spirituality' is a function of the time element: the greater the distance in time between cause and effect, in blessing or in curse, the more the non-material aspect – that of the omnipotence of thought – seems to matter. And vice versa: the smaller the time margin between the cause and effect, the more the aspect of mere material contagion seems to dominate. Thus the principles of matter, passiveness, low magic seem to form one alliance; those of thought, activity, higher magic, religion and spirituality another. But in them we recognise two different sets of abstractions rather than two different groups of things. And reading through Freud's material confirms in psychological terms our former assertion that in their institutionalised form crude taboos and the lofty things of the spirit necessarily coexist.

Unfortunately, Freud, in order to apply his concept of ambivalence fully, narrows down still further the range of taboo phenomena which are of interest to him:

The clinical history of a typical case of 'touching phobia' is as follows: Quite at the beginning, in very early childhood, the patient shows a strong *desire* to touch, the aim of which is of a far more specialised kind than one would have been inclined to expect. This desire is promptly met by an *external* prohibition against carrying out that particular kind of touching. [Both the desire and the prohibition relate to the child's touching his own genitals.] The prohibition is accepted, since it finds support from powerful *internal* forces [that is, from the child's loving relation to the authors of the prohibition], and proves stronger than the instinct which is seeking to express itself in the touching. In consequence, however, of the child's primitive psychical constitution, the prohibition does not succeed in *abolishing* the instinct. Its only result is to *repress* the instinct (the desire to touch) and banish it into the unconscious. Both the prohibition and the instinct persist: the instinct because it has only been repressed and not abolished, and the prohibition because, if it ceased, the instinct would force its way through into consciousness and into actual operation. A situation is created which remains undealt with – a psychical fixation – and everything else follows from the continuing conflict between the prohibition and the instinct.

The principle characteristic of the psychological constellation which becomes fixed in this way is what might be described as the subject's *ambivalent* [to borrow the apt term coined by Bleuler] attitude towards a single object, or rather towards one act in connection with that object. He is constantly wishing to perform this act (the touching), and looks on it as his supreme enjoyment, but he must not perform it and detests it as well. The conflict between these two currents cannot be promptly settled because – there is no other way of putting it – they are localised in the subject's mind in such a manner that they cannot come up against each other. The prohibition is noisily conscious, while the persistent desire to touch is unconscious and the subject knows nothing of it. If it were not for this psychological factor, an ambivalence like this could neither last so long nor lead to such consequences. (1950: 29-30)[2]

Here is the core of the matter, and the limitation. Freud himself – a sound psychologist with an astounding knowledge of the human mind – Freud himself would never have tried to explain (a) institutionalised menstruation taboos, (b) the actual psychological experience of a girl during her first menses in a society which has no menstrual taboos, in terms of these ambivalent emotions.[3] No delight is occasioned by the menstrual emission. The psychoanalyst would be the last to claim that, for he has found feelings of fear and guilt in far greater prominence during this experience than we who are not psychologists would expect. And neither the fear the girl feels nor the fear her state inspires in others can be related to a contrary feeling of delight which is kept in balance. But since the menstrual taboos stand for a whole class of taboos, we can thus see the severe limitation imposed by this principle of ambivalence.

Finally, Freud asks:

In our analytical examination of the problems of taboo we have hitherto allowed ourselves to be led by the points of agreement that we have been able to show between it and obsessional neurosis. But after all taboo is not a neurosis but a social institution. We are therefore faced with the task of explaining what difference there is in principle between a neurosis and a cultural creation such as taboo.

Once again I will take a single fact as my starting point. It is feared among primitive peoples that the violation of a taboo will be followed by a punishment, as a rule by some serious illness or by death. The punishment threatens to fall on whoever was responsible for violating the taboo. In obsessional neuroses the case is different. What the patient fears if he performs some forbidden action is that a punishment will fall not on himself but on someone else. This person's identity is as a rule left unstated, but can usually be shown without difficulty by analysis to be one of those closest and most dear to the patient. Here, then, the neurotic seems to be behaving altruistically and the primitive man egoistically. Only if the violation of a taboo is not automatically avenged upon the wrongdoer does a collective feeling arise among savages that they are all threatened by the outrage; and they thereupon hasten to carry out the omitted punishment themselves. There is no difficulty in explaining the mechanism of this solidarity. What is in question is fear of an infectious example, of the temptation to imitate – that is, of the contagious character of taboo. If one person succeeds in gratifying the repressed desire, the same desire is bound to be kindled in all the other members of the community. In order to keep the temptation down, the envied transgressor must be deprived of the fruit of his enterprise; and the punishment will not infrequently give those who carry it out an opportunity of committing the same outrage under colour of an act of expiation. This is indeed one of the foundations of the human penal system and it is based, no doubt correctly, on the assumption that the prohibited impulses are present alike in the criminal and in the avenging community. (1950: 71-72)

Too many of these statements are demonstrably wrong. I have space only to pick out the central point. There is never a situation in social life, primitive or otherwise, where this alternative obtains between what Radcliffe-Brown calls 'ritual' sanctions and I prefer to call 'psychological' ones on the one hand and, on the other, organised punitive activities in which men do what taboo failed to do, watch to see whether taboo works or not, etc. No such situation exists. None has been recorded by Freud. Moreover, knowing our primitive man, we should expect to find some features of the psychological sanctions imitated in the punitive actions. But we do not hear of savages adorning their taboo-breakers with spots to imitate a deadly rash before they stone or club them to death. How irrelevant these remarks are when compared, for example, with the concluding sentences on the nature of human punishment! We did not expect a sound sociological theory from Freud. To expect too much is the most vulgar form of ingratitude, and, surely, we have been given very much.

NOTES

1. These paragraphes on Wundt are based on notes left by Steiner and follow the outline from which he delivered this part of his lecture. (L.B.)
2. Passages in square brackets are from footnotes.
3. 'The countless taboo regulations to which the women in savage communities are subject during menstruation are said to be due to a superstitious horror of blood, and this is no doubt in fact one of their determinants. But it would be wrong to overlook the possibility that in this case the horror of blood also serves aesthetic and hygienic purposes, which are obliged in every case to cloak themselves behind magical motives' (1950: 98).

CHAPTER XII

THE PROBLEM OF TABOO

In this final chapter I intend to sum up what has seemed of profit in our discussion of the various implications of taboo. I regret very much that I have been unable to exhaust the more relevant literature and to touch on all the problems which seem to matter. It was not possible to do so in twelve lectures. I regret even more that I have been unable to discuss Barton's *Ifugao Law* (1919) as an instance of a description of both the rights and the prohibitions of a society in terms of taboo; or to attempt an appreciation of Junod's classification of taboos in his *Life of a South African Tribe* (1927); or, finally, to discuss Radcliffe-Brown's articles on joking relationships and avoidance (1940b, 1949), and the bearing of his analysis of that kind of behaviour on our problem.[1]

I maintained at the outset that the customs we call taboo neither represent one kind of institution nor pose one kind of sociological problem. I have been interested, rather, in separating from one another the various problems which have been lumped together under this heading. I hope, therefore, that it will cause no surprise if I end by doing precisely the same thing – though in a more general manner – instead of posing the question: After having reviewed all these questions – all of which contained something wrong and something useful – what do we decide upon as a definition of taboo?

Now, I have devoted the better part of three chapters to a description of Polynesian taboo customs, in order to show the relevance of these classical instances to the much wider group of phenomena which bear the same name. I pointed out that Polynesian taboo is atypical: differ as they might among themselves, the various Polynesian societies had the taboo idiom in common. This idiom was derived from certain avoidance customs in which one could describe widely different things – a man's rights over an object, a royal minister's power to select the crop the subject was to farm, and the supreme chief's relation to petty dignitaries – in terms of delegated interdiction rather than delegated authority. This unique feature explains why it was in Polynesia rather than some other part of the globe that the oddness of avoidance customs and the people's protestations of fear impressed themselves on the European as particularly remarkable. That it should be so is understandable, but unfortunate. It put the nineteenth-century student in the position of an art critic who knows nothing of the world's sculpture except the highly specialised and perfected art of Periclean Athens, and who, therefore, on the discovery of the universe of plastic art, discusses the idols of the Congo and the images of Easter Island in Praxitelean terms. Little can be thus clarified.

Dr Mead – and I shall base my concluding criticisms on her article 'Tabu' in the *Encyclopaedia of the Social Sciences* (1937: 502-505),[2] which is the most able summing-up of the position published in recent years – takes up an extreme position among those who are impatient of these Polynesian *imponderabilia*. She makes 'special Polynesian usages' (we will not criticise her terminology at this point) a term almost of castigation. Thus: 'Special Polynesian usages have coloured the interpretation of the institution. If the term is to be employed successfully in comparative discussions, it must be stripped of these accidents of interpretation ....'

Dr Mead regards Polynesia as different on three counts:

1. She thinks that, contrary to the impression created, the notions of sacredness and uncleanness are much more clearly separated in the Polynesian taboo concept than in some other regions, e.g., Australia. Thus the great riddle of how something can be holy and unclean at the same time is, according to her, not a Polynesian riddle at all. I am not going to deal with this part of her argument: it is not well documented and is rather too assertive.

2. In Polynesia she finds 'a great contrast between the Maori attitude according to which a commoner would die if he had accidentally eaten the sacred food of a chief, and the Hawaiian attitude whereby the taboos had so lost emotional content that they had to be enforced by policing and capital punishment'. The Maori and the Hawaiians are, indeed, two extremes. Their difference lies, as I have tried to explain, in their political organisation. Among the Maori supreme power was at the same time political and sacerdotal; the chief was thus the mainspring of fear and prohibition. In Hawaii kingship and priesthood were separated; the taboo power was a bone of contention between the two sets of ruling families lined up behind king and high priest respectively. It is useless to talk about cultural variations in a culture area unless we assume the possibility, and investigate the occurrence, of a variation in political organisation.

3. Dr Mead sums up Polynesian taboo as follows:

   The 'Polynesian idea' ... contains the following elements: (a) any prohibitions enforced automatically, that is the punishment followed inevitably without external mediation; (b) or the edicts of chiefs and priests, which are supported either by the superior mana of these individuals or by the temporal or spiritual forces which they have under their control; (c) prohibitions against theft or trespass for which the sanctions are specific magic formulae; (d) religious prohibitions which are referred in native theology to the decree of some deity or spirit; (e) any prohibitions which carry no penalties beyond the anxiety and embarrassment arising from a breach of strongly entrenched custom.

She comes out strongly on the side of Frazer and Freud by saying that only the first point should be regarded as taboo in the strict sense. The term must be restricted, she remarks, 'to describe prohibition against participation in any situation of such inherent danger that the very act of participation will recoil upon the violator of the taboo'. She excludes from the meaning of taboo all those attitudes according to which a supernatural power, manifesting itself apart from the dreaded object, imposes the restriction and punishes the transgression by other means as well. I shall come back to this point later. For the moment, I want to remark only that, even in so narrow a field, Margaret Mead's taboo constitutes a quite useless category. As proof I shall quote from Herskovits' *Trinidad Village*:

> The dichotomy between the guard as protective magic and the trick as an aggressive and ill-intentioned force is not clearly sustained, for there is much overlapping between the two. At times the worker of magic achieves a blend of a guard and a trick. When this is done as protection against thieves, the charm, whether hung above a doorway or buried under a doorstep, or in the centre of a field to protect a harvest, or placed on top of a buried money jar, is intended primarily to frustrate the ability of the thief to act.... But if, because of a trick the thief holds, he succeeds in stealing despite the power of the guard, then the trick or punishing element that is associated with the guard will either expose him, or exact whatever penalty the maker of the combined guard and trick has set.
>
> If a man is the owner of an ordinary guard, one of a generalised type to be obtained as preventative against all forms of envy or malice or evil design, then towards the close of the year 'if you have a little trouble', or even if there was no trouble at all, 'you look back to the man who gave it, and have him strengthen it'. Since all guards and tricks must be removed during intercourse, and many of these bear in addition individual taboos – such as prohibitions on given foods while wearing them, or taboos against touching the ground – it is not difficult to see that there is need to be assured that nothing had been done during the year to render them ineffective. To reactivate a guard or trick involves bathing the consultant with special herbs to ward off ills that might be about, and those of the future; and, of course, a present to the practitioner in appreciation of his services ....
>
> An important trick, provided for a man to give him advantages in his work or his trading enterprises or his fishing, will require a visit from the

practitioner to the house of his client. For the renewal of the power of the trick, or guard, if of importance in keeping a man at employment that is coveted by others ... the work [of the lookman, connected with renewal and purification] is done by night. (1947: 242-45)

Very well, here is a taboo imposed to guard property against thieves. When the thief touches the property, the taboo recoils on him without any additional or outside supernatural promptings: it is a taboo in Dr Mead's sense. This taboo may be dangerous to the owner himself, and it would fall within Dr Mead's definition if he were to protect himself by taboo behaviour (abstentions of various kinds) against this powerful weapon. But this is not quite the case: he observes rites and abstentions in order to reload the guard and to prevent its becoming ineffectual. The owner's unrestrained sexual behaviour may blunt the taboo.

Surely the main interest of these by no means unique attitudes lies in the possibility that they can be seen in terms of one logical model, part of which is the restrictive behaviour which makes or keeps the charm powerful, and another part the restrictions which the charm is intended to impose on others in the interest of preserving the owner's property. Surely it is quite unscientific to discuss the second part in terms of taboo and then claim that the first part does not fall into the same category. We ought rather to try to simplify as far as possible the logical models by the help of which we assimilate the facts confronting us; in so doing, it may sometimes be found advisable to put a few logical models in place of one for sake of simpler arrangement. But I do not see that Dr Mead's procedure is motivated by any such notions. In this case a field of observation and comparison is restricted solely to allow the undisturbed application of a particular psychological terminology.

I should like to revert to a former point: the restriction of the taboo mechanism to automaticity and mechanical independence. I shall quote Margaret Mead herself, when she says of Polynesian taboos:

Furthermore, among true taboo prohibitions, those whose breach is followed by automatic punishment, there are in Polynesia two main classes: taboos associated with the inherent sanctity of gods, chiefs and priests, and taboos associated with the inherent uncleanness of certain occurrences, such as menstruation, childbirth, bloodshed and death.

There is no need to repeat what I have said at such length about the merits of this dichotomy. Here I want to remark on the notion of autonomous, mechanical punishment without supposed outside interference and the statement that such punishment may be associated with the inherent sanctity of gods, priests, etc. Unless Dr Mead means the sanctity inherent in an idol – and she does not say so – what does she (or anybody else) mean by behaviour towards an object regulated by sanctions thought to proceed automatically from that object, but yet associated with the sacredness inherent in a god? What is the nature of this association? If it is in the nature of a relation between cause and effect, we are not told so. If not, what?

I think a misunderstanding is at work here, one due to a limitation which Dr Mead would no doubt call cultural, but which to my mind is a limitation in the field of religious experience. Such lack of experience does not, of course, completely invalidate the statements of the inexperienced. Nevertheless one is inclined to make reservations of the kind one would make when asked to read a treatise on sexual psychology composed by a eunuch, though, of course, sexual phenomena can be observed by all, and the observations can be analysed by the intelligent.

Another point of interest is made by Dr Mead when she says:

> The description of a novice or a sacred king as taboo is too loose; it should be said that certain acts are taboo to them because their committing such acts has been culturally defined as producing a dangerous situation. For example, an adolescent girl on the Northwest Coast of America may drink water, but she must drink it through a drinking tube; if her lips came directly in contact with water, this contact would result automatically in disaster.

Here it might be said that all situations of danger, not merely those created by taboo-breaking, are socially or culturally defined, and that it is precisely this relation between the defined danger and the restrictive pattern which we should study in each case. For until taboos are involved, a danger is not defined and cannot be coped with by institutionalised behaviour. To speak of danger is not equivalent to speaking of the possibility of defeat or annihilation; danger is not a quantitative concept, though we sometimes think of it thus today when we say that a high temperature is dangerous from a certain point onward, or that an illness becomes dangerous, takes a dangerous turn. To face danger is to face another power. Indeed, the older meaning of the English word danger is 'power', 'jurisdiction', 'dominion', 'the power to dispose of or to harm'.

Danger is narrowed down by taboo. A situation is regarded as dangerous: very well, but the danger may be a socially unformulated threat. Taboo gives notice that danger lies not in the whole situation, but only in certain specified actions concerning it. These actions, these danger spots, are more challenging and deadly than the danger of the situations as a whole, for the whole situation can be rendered free from danger by dealing with or, rather, avoiding the specified danger spots completely. Dr Mead is looking at the relation the other way round when she says that 'a taboo takes its meaning from the definition of any experience or of those who experience it as inherently dangerous. The situation may be childbirth, handling the dead, retreat from a vision, being the eldest born or blowing a sacred flute.'

The narrowing down and localisation of danger is the function of taboo of which we are now speaking. The dangerous situation is then defined in terms of such localisation, which in its turn is meaningless without abstentive behaviour. It is the job of the psychologist to study the emotions of fear in terms of the human mind, to conjecture the situations in which these fears are allayed, and to relate these situations to the conditioning of the individuals concerned. But to study how danger is localised in social institutions, and what social pressure is needed in order to regulate abstentions so that the danger can remain localised, is to approach the problem sociologically .

I began my discussion with the suggestion that taboo is an element of all those situations in which attitudes to values are expressed in terms of danger behaviour, and with the warning that all the things discussed under the heading of taboo cannot be seen in terms of a single problem – for it is a major fact of human existence that we are not able, and never were able, to express our relation to values in other terms than those of danger behaviour. Social relations are describable in terms of danger; through contagion there is social participation in danger. And we find expressed in the same term, those of taboo, two quite separate social functions: (1) the classification and identification of transgressions (which is associated with, though it can be studied apart from, processes of social learning), and (2) the institutional localisation of danger, both by the specification of the dangerous and by the protection of society from endangered, and hence dangerous, persons.

NOTES

1. Dr Steiner left no notes to indicate what shape these discussions of Barton, Junod or Radcliffe-Brown might have taken. (L.B.)
2. In this chapter all quotations from Mead are from this article.

BIBLIOGRAPHY

Barton, R. F., 1919 'Ifugao Law', *University of California Publications in American Archaeology and Ethnology*, vol. 15: 1-127.

Best, E., 1914 'Ceremonial Performances Pertaining to Birth, as Performed by the Maori of New Zealand in Past Times', *Journal of the Royal Anthropological Institute*.

———, 1924 *Maori Religion and Mythology*. New Zealand Dominion Museum Bulletin, no. 10.

———, 1925 *Tuhoe, The Children of the Mist*. New Plymouth, New Zealand: Avery.

Black, J. S. and Chrystal, G.,1912 *The Life of William Robertson Smith*. London: Black.

Bougainville, Baron de, 1837 *Journal de la navigation autour du globe de la frégate La Thétis et de la corvette L'Espérance pendant les années 1824, 1825 et 1826*. 2 vols, Paris: Arthus Bertrand.

Bréhier, E.,1949 *La philosophie du Moyen Age*. Second edn Paris: Albin Michel.

Brown, W., 1845 *New Zealand and Its Aborigines*. London: Smith Elder and Co..

Butler, S., 1872 *Erewhon*. London: Trubner and Co. (London: Cape, 1949).

Codrington, R. H., 1891 *The Melanesians*. Oxford: Clarendon.

Cook, Capt. J., 1784 *A Voyage to the Pacific Ocean . . . in His Majesty's Ships the Resolution and Discovery, in the Years 1776, 1777, 1778, 1779 and 1780*. 3 vols (I and II by Capt. James Cook, F.R.S., III by Capt. James King, LL.D., Dublin), London: printed for G. Nicoll and T. Cadell.

———, 1893 *Captain Cook's Journal during his First Voyage round the World made in H.M. Bark 'Endeavour', 1768-71*. (A literal transcription of the original MSS. ed. Capt. W. J. Z. Wharton, R.N., F.R.S.) London: Stock.

da Thiene, P. G., 1939 *Dizinario della lingua Galla*. Harar, s.n.

de Freycinet, L.,1839 *Voyage autour du monde, enterpris par ordre du roi, exécuté sur les corvettes de S.M. l'Oranie et la Physicienne, pendant les années 1817, 1818, 1819 et 1820*. 2 vols, Paris: Imprimerie Royale.

Durkheim, E., 1925 *Les formes élémentaires de la vie religieuse: le système totèmique en Australie*. 2nd edn Paris: Alcan.

Ellis, W., 1826 'Narrative of a Tour Through Hawaii, or Owhyhee; with Remarks on the History, Traditions, Manner, Customs and Language of the Inhabitants of the Sandwich Islands', extr. *Quarterly Review*, vol. 25.

————, 1832-4 *Polynesian Researches*. 2nd edn London: Fisher, Son and Jackson.

Encyclopaedia Britannica, 1842, 7th edn 1842; 8th edn 1860; 9th edn 1875; 11th edn 1911.

Erskine, J. Elphinstone (Capt. R.N.), 1853 *Journal of a Cruise among the Islands of the Western Pacific, including the Feejees and others inhabited by the Polynesian Negro races, in Her Majesty's ship 'Havannah'*. London: Murray.

Evans-Pritchard, E. E., 1933a 'The Intellectualist (English) Interpretation of Magic'. Cairo, extr. *Bulletin of the Faculty of Arts*, vol. 1, pt. 2.

————, 1933b 'Lévy-Bruhl's Theory of Primitive Mentality', Cairo, extr. *Bulletin of the Faculty of Arts*, vol. 2, pt. 1.

Firth, R., 1939 *Primitive Polynesian Economy*. London: Routledge and Kegan Paul.

Fortes, M. and Evans-Pritchard, E.E., 1940 eds, *African Political Systems*. Oxford: O.U.P.

Fortune, R. F., 1932 *Sorcerers of Dobu*. London: Routledge.

Frazer, Sir J., 1875 'Taboo', *Encyclopaedia Britannica*, 9th edn.

————, 1905 *Lectures on the Early History of Kingship*. London: Macmillan.

————, 1911 *The Golden Bough*, part 2: *Taboo and the Perils of the Soul*. London: Macmillan.

Freud, S., 1950 *Totem and Taboo*. London: Routledge and Kegan Paul.

Gudgeon, W. E., 1905 'Maori Religion', *Journal of the Polynesian Society*, vol. 14: 107-30.

————, 1906 'Tipua-Kura, and other Manifestations of the Spirit World', *Journal of the Polynesian Society*, vol. 15: 27-57.

Handy, E. S. Craighill, 1927 *Polynesian Religion*. Berenice Pauahi Bishop Museum Bulletin, no. 34, Honolulu.

Herskovits, M. J. and F. S., 1936 *Suriname Folk-Lore*. New York: Columbia University Press.

————, 1947 *Trinidad Village*. New York: Knopf.

Junod, H., 1927 *The Life of a South African Tribe*. 2nd edn 2 vols London: Macmillan.

Kern, H., 1886 *De Fidjitaal vergeleken met hare verwanten in Indonesië en Polynesië*. Amsterdam: Müller.

Krusenstern, A.J. von, 1812 *Reise um die Welt in den Jahren 1803, 1804, 1805 and 1806 auf Befehl S. Kais. Maj. Alexanders. Auf den Schiffen Nadesha u. Neva*. Berlin: Haube.

La Pérouse, J. F. de Galaup, Comte de, 1797 *Voyage autour du monde*. Paris: Milet-Mureau.

Lang, A., 1898 *The Making of Religion*. London: Longman.

Laoust, H., 1939 *Essai sur les doctrines sociales et politiques de Takī-d-dīn Ahmed b. Taimīya*. Cairo: L'Institut Français d'Archeologie Orientale.

Lehmann, Fr. R., 1930 *Die Polynesischen Tabusitten*. Leipzig: Voigtländer.

Lévy-Bruhl, L., 1931a *La mentalité primitive*. Herbert Spencer Lecture, Oxford.

————, 1931b *Le surnaturel et la nature dans la mentalité primitive*. Paris: Alcan, (1936 *Primitives and the Supernatural*, trans. Lilian A. Clare, London: Allen and Unwin).

————, 1947 *La mentalité primitive*. Originally 1922, 4th edn Paris: Alcan (1923 *Primitive Mentality*, trans. Lilian A. Clare, London: Allen and Unwin).

————, 1951 *Les fonctions mentales dans les sociétés inférieures.* Originally 1910, 9th edn Paris: Alcan (*How Natives Think*, trans. Lilian A. Clare, London: Allen and Unwin, 1926).

Lisiansky, U., 1814 *A Voyage round the World in the years 1803, 1804, 1805 and 1806; performed by order of His Imperial Majesty Alexander the First, Emperor of Russia, on the Ship Neva.* London: Longman.

Malinowski, B., 1948 'The Problem of Meaning in Primitive Language', in C.K. Ogden and I.A. Richards *The Meaning of Meaning*, London, International Library of Psychology, Philosophy and Scientific Method, 1923; reprinted in Malinowski, B., *Magic, Science and Religion.* Glencoe, Ill.: Beacon Press, 228-76.

Malo, D., 1903 *Hawaiian Antiquities.* Honolulu: Hawaiian Gazette Co.

Maning, F. E., 1884 [pseud. 'a Pakeha Maori'] *Old New Zealand: a Tale of the Good Old Times.* London: Richard Bentley and Son.

Marett, R. R., 1914 *The Threshold of Religion.* 2nd edn London: Methuen.

————, 1921 'Tabu', *Encyclopaedia of Religion and Ethics.* London: Clark, vol. 2, 181-5.

————, 1932 *Faith, Hope and Charity in Primitive Religion.* Oxford: Clarendon.

————, 1935 *Head, Heart and Hands in Human Evolution.* London: Hutchinson.

Martin, J. and Mariner, W., 1817 *An account of the Natives of the Tonga Islands in the South Pacific Ocean with an Original Grammar and Vocabulary of Their Language, compiled and arranged from the extensive communications of Mr William Mariner.* 2 vols, London: Murray.

Mead, M., 1937 'Tabu', *Encyclopaedia of the Social Sciences.* London: Macmillan, vol. 7, 502-5.

Mitford, Mary Russell 1893 *Our Village. Rural Character and Scenery 1824-1832.* London: Macmillan.

Moore, R. J. B., 1940 'Bwanga among the Bemba', *Africa* (International African Institute), vol. 13, no. 3, 211-34.

Neumark, D., 1908 *Geschichte der jüdischen Philosophie des Mittelalters.* 2 vols, Berlin: Reimer.

Pedersen, J., 1926 *Israel.* 2 vols, Oxford: O.U.P.

Radcliffe-Brown, A. R., 1931 'The Present Position of Anthropological Studies', British Association for the Advancement of Science, Centenary Meeting, Section H. – Anthropology.

————, 1933 'Social Sanctions', *Encyclopaedia of the Social Sciences.* New York: Macmillan, vol. 13, 531-4.

————, 1939 'Taboo' (Frazer Lecture) reprinted in 1952.

————, 1940a 'On Social Structure', *Journal of the Royal Anthropological Institute* 70, reprinted in 1952.

————, 1940b 'On Joking Relationships', *Africa* XIII(3): 195-210, reprinted in 1952.

————, 1945 'Religion and Society' (Myers Lecture) reprinted in 1952.

————, 1948 *The Andaman Islanders.* Originally 1922, Cambridge: C.U.P.

————, 1949 'A Further Note on Joking Relationships', *Africa* XIX: 133-40.

————, 1952 *Structure and Function in Primitive Society.* London: Cohen and West.

Rashi, 1887 *Der Rashi-Kommentar zu den fünf Büchern Moses vollständig ins Deutsche übersetzt mit beigedrucktem Bibel-Texte in einem Bande, v. Julius Dessauer.* Budapest, s.n.

Rivers, W. H. R., (1914) *Kinship and Social Organisation.* London: London School of Economics Studies in Economics and Political Science, no. 36.

———, 1926 *Social Organisation.* London: Kegan Paul.

Rollin, L., 1929 *Les Iles Marquises.* Paris: Société d'éditions géographiques, maritimes et coloniales.

Sayce, A. H., 1895 *The 'Higher Criticism' and the Verdict of the Monuments.* London: Young.

Schmidt, P. W., 1931a *The Origin and Growth of Religion: Facts and Theories.* trans. H. J. Rose, London: Methuen.

———, 1931b *Ursprung der Gottesidee.* 12 vols, Münster: Aschendorff, 1926-55, vol. 3.

Shortland, E., 1851 *The Southern Districts of New Zealand.* London: Longman.

———, 1854 *Traditions and Superstitions of the New Zealanders.* London: Longman.

———, 1882 *Maori Religion and Mythology.* London: Longman.

Smith, W. Robertson, 1869 'Theory of geometrical reasoning. Mr Mill's theory of Geometrical Reasoning mathematically tested', *Proceedings of the Royal Society of Edinburgh,* vol. 6: 477-83.

———, 1875 'Bible' *Encyclopaedia Britannica,* 9th edn., vol. 3.

———, [1889] 1894 'Lectures on the Religion of the Semites: First Series, The Fundamental Institutions', 2nd, revised edn. London: A. and C. Black. 1927, 3rd edn, with an Introduction and Notes by Stanley Cook. London: A. and C. Black.

———, 1912 *Lectures and Essays of William Robertson Smith* (including 'Christianity and the Supernatural', 109 *sqq* [1869]), eds. J. S. Black and George Chrystal, London: Black.

Snaith, N. H., 1944 *Distinctive Ideas of the Old Testament.* London: Epworth Press.

Spencer, J., 1685 *De legibus Hebraeorum ritualibus et earum rationibus.* Cantab.: Cornelius Crownfield.

Stair, J. B., 1897 *Old Samoa.* London: The Religious Tract Society.

Tawney, R. H., 1926 *Religion and the Rise of Capitalism.* London, Murray.

Taylor, R., 1870 *Te Ika A Maui.* 2nd edn London: Macintosh.

Thomas, Northcote, 1911 'Taboo', *Encyclopaedia Britannica,* 11th edn.

Tregear, Edward, (1890) 'The Maoris of New Zealand', *Journal of the Anthropological Society,* vol. 19: 97-124.

———, 1891 *The Maori-Polynesian Comparative Dictionary.* Wellington, New Zealand: Lyon and Blair.

———, 1904 *The Maori Race.* Wanganui, New Zealand: Willis.

Turner, G., 1884 *Samoa A Hundred Years Ago and Long Before.* London: Macmillan.

Tutschek, C., 1845 *A Grammar of the Galla Language.* ed. L. Tutschek, M.D., 2 vols, Munich: Franz Wild, vol. 2.

Tylor, E. B., 1873 *Primitive Culture.* 2 vols, London: Murray.

Vancouver, Capt. G., 1798 *A Voyage of Discovery to the North Pacific Ocean and Round the World, in the years 1790-95.* 3 vols, London: printed for G.G. and J. Robinson.

Van Gennep, A., 1904 *Tabou et Totémisme à Madagascar*. Paris: Leroux.

———, 1909 *Les Rites de Passage*. Paris: Nourry.

von Kotzebue, O., 1821 *A Voyage of Discovery into the South Sea and Bering's Straits for the purpose of exploring a North-East Passage, undertaken in the years 1815-1818, at the expense of his Highness the Chancellor of the Empire, Count Romanzoff, in the Ship Rurick, under the command of the Lt. in the Russian Imperial Navy, Otto Von Kotzebue*, trans. H. E. Lloyd, 3 vols, London: Longman.

von Langsdorff, G. H., 1812 *Bemerkungen auf einer Reise um die Welt in den Jahren 1803 bis 1807*. 2 vols, Frankfurt: Wilmanns.

Weber, M., 1923 *Gesammelte Aufsätze zur Religionssoziologie*. 3 vols, Tübingen: Mohr.

Webster, H., 1942 *Taboo, A Sociological Study*. Stanford: Stanford University Press.

Wehr, H., 1952 *Arabisches Wörterbuch für die Schriftsprache der Gegenwart*. Leipzig: Harrasowitz.

Wellhausen, J., 1883 *Prolegomena zur Geschichte Israels*. 2nd edn, Berlin: Reimer.

———, 1887 *Reste arabischen Heidentums*. Berlin: Reimer.

Westermarck, E., 1926 *Ritual and Belief in Morocco*. 2 vols, London: Macmillan.

Wilkes, C., 1845 *Narrative of the United States Exploring Expedition, During the Years 1838,1839, 1840,1841,1842*. 5 vols, Philadelphia: Putman.

Williams, J., 1838 *A Narrative of Missionary Enterprises in the South Sea Islands*. London: Snow.

Williamson, R. W., 1924 *The Social and Political Systems of Central Polynesia*. 3 vols, Cambridge: C.U.P.

———, 1937 *Religion and Social Organisation in Central Polynesia*. Cambridge: C.U.P.

Wullschlägel, H. R., 1856 *Deutsch-Negerenglische Wörterbuch, nebst einem Anhang Negerenglische Sprüchworter enthaltend*. Löbaw, s.n.

Wundt W., 1916 *The Elements of Folk Psychology*. trans. E. L. Schaub, London: Allen and Unwin.

———, 1927 *Völkerpsychologie*, 4th edn, 10 vols, Leipzig: Kröner.

REVIEWS OF *TABOO*

Anon, 1956 *The Listener* 23 August: 281.

Anon, 1957 *Times Literary Supplement* 18 January: 18.

S.G.F. Branden, 1958 *British Journal of Sociology* 9(1) March: 104.

W. Cohn, 1957 *American Sociological Review* 22(1) January: 132.

C. Dubois, 1957 *American Anthropologist* 59(2) April: 357-58.

V. Lanternari, 1957 *Studi e Materiali di Storia delle Religioni* 28(1): 137-38.

Lord Raglan, 1957 *Man* 57 February: 27.

PART III: RELIGIOUS TRUTH

HOW TO DEFINE SUPERSTITION?[1]

Introduction: Derivation and Usage

Superstition derives from a Latin root. Speakers of Latin used the word *superstitio* to give the impression that something was too much of a good thing – something above and beyond the regular. In Latin literature, *superstitio* might be qualified by adjectives (like *turpis, inanis, insana*) which makes it appear likely that *superstitio* as such was not regarded as stupid or ignoble, but needed these adjectives to express such a notion. Most instances of Cicero's use of the word seem to indicate that by *superstitio* he was thinking of credulity as opposed to the pursuit of solid knowledge. The Roman Catholic attitude is best expressed in the words of the Tridentine Council (1545-63): *superstitio* is *verae pietatis falsa imitatrix* (a false imitator of true piety). Homer calls things 'superstition' when they are, either abhorred, or observed with a zealous or fearful, but erroneous relation to God.

As to the possible use of the word in modern philosophy, I should like to refer to Wittgenstein who calls superstition a firm reliance on causality: whenever A happens, B has to happen too, regardless of the relation of an element C to the second part of that equation. Such a belief in causality is superstitious.[2]

Thus we see how, through the ages, the word has been employed with two meanings which are closely connected: that of mock knowledge, and that of mock belief, or a belief masquerading as knowledge (in the pragmatic sense).

Both the early travelling priests who gave such admirable accounts of tribal and exotic life, and those laymen who described these things during the age of reason and afterwards, used superstition to denote pagan rituals, or traditions, or religious attitudes. In their terminology superstitious and pagan were interchangeable. Something was called superstitious because of its relation to the *observer's own* system *and not* because of its doubtful place in the *observed* system.

In the anthropological literature of the last twenty years the word is rarely used; if it is, it does not occur as a specific part of a descriptive terminology. Rather, it is a stylistic device to now and then use words with loose meaning – especially words with a long tradition, the haphazard use of which may give an impression of amiable quaintness or even sophistication.

It seems that only outside anthropology is the word used to a purpose. In anthropological discussions, one is apt to say that conscious or unconscious evaluations resulting in differentiations of creeds are unscientific. (But it may happen to the anthropologist or comparative sociologist that he is asked by someone not fully acquainted with that science how superstition should be defined. It was possibly this kind of question which made me think about the subject and led me to repeat my considerations in your presence.)

How to Define Superstition?

When a person who pursues formal sociology sets out to define anything it is only fair to warn those concerned about the limitations of his scope. Thus, I have to say that an investigation of anything means to me (in the described capacity) to investigate how, and how far, this thing can be expressed in terms of social relationships. Primarily I am not concerned with religions: I study religious institutions. Primarily I am not concerned with legal concepts: I study legal institutions, etc. The units of my observation are social groups and not individuals. It may sound superficial but it is the case that I take no more interest in the psychology of the individual than a crystallographer takes in chemistry. No admonition – such as that crystals after all are chemical compounds – can make him realise the uselessness of crystallography.

Two more considerations should be given at the outset. The first concerns the ambiguous use of the (non-sociological) term 'belief', the second the danger of confusing our problem with the age-old discussion of the difference between religion and magic.

Belief and Superstition

Belief, and its equivalents in other European languages, has come to mean all possible positive attitudes towards the so-called religious phenomena. That is to say, belief in this loose way of speaking means the acceptance of the validity of myth, or the rationalisation of society's readiness to repeat at certain intervals a certain ritual, or the quality of an individual's trusting faith which he sets in a deity acceptable to his society, etc. However, belief or faith also has a very special meaning developed within the Christian religion and paralleled perhaps in late Buddhism. In such a context the word implies that acceptance of a *structure* which is regarded as a total definition of reality different from the reality of common experience. By means of a peculiar relation to this total reality the individual transforms the reality of common experience. This peculiar relationship is called a belief or faith and to it corresponds: either the opposition of the two realities, or a hierarchy of the levels of experience, or the declaration that the reality of common experience is a delusion. 'Belief', in this sense, differs widely from the first instance, and it has to be stressed that a word with this implication does not occur e.g., in the Hebrew Bible. We find there words translated by faith which mean an intensive trust not differing in its kind from the trust we may have in our father, general and king.

Religious organisation being manifold, let us first consider whether it is not uncertainty about the determining feature of some religious organisations which leads us to set aside these attitudes and actions as superstitions. Two examples will suffice.

Take the case of a small Catholic Alpine village (and you can find parallels in many other Catholic country districts of Europe). In this village the people are accustomed, if an illness has befallen any member or organ of their body, to make of wax or metal a model of that stricken part (be it a hand or foot, the kidneys or the uterus), to take this model to church and put it in front of the image of a certain saint, in most cases preferring the healing power of the Virgin Mary. It is obvious that the Catholic faith as such does not necessitate these offerings. If we regard Catholicism abstractly as a compound of doctrines and institutions, series of books of different degrees of holiness, and sets of statements made by those in leading positions in the Catholic Church, we can easily see that the custom described 'does not fit in'. Though it may not be contrary to any conception of the Church, we regard it as not being part and parcel of that system of beliefs, in fact we may call it a 'superstition' in the early Latin sense of the word. If, however, we make the village our unit of observation and consider the Catholic faith only insofar as it helps to explain certain attitudes in the village which would otherwise be difficult to understand, we immediately adopt a different point of view. Taking the local church as the local cultic centre, and the attitudes towards illness, healing (and implicitly death) displayed in the ritual idiom of the collectivity – no matter who else shares that idiom – we are forced to conceive this custom as part of the social fabric of that society. Possibly we find more than one person concerned in the production of these models, in which case two different scales of values are necessary to manipulate the transaction, and the coordination of these two kinds of value is a complex social affair. Furthermore, we are dealing not with a mere individual attitude but with a standardised behaviour that concerns elements which cannot be isolated: the illness is part of a whole circle of phenomena called 'human life'; while the desired healing partakes of another circle which is described in terms of grace, individual prosperity and prosperity of the community as a whole. The model laid down at the Virgin's feet is one of many such objects the removal of which would alter the meaning of the statue. Thus, we could continue to show both that the custom cannot be isolated, and that it is completely woven into the fabric of social relationships. If we were to sever this custom from its setting by futile dissections, we could do the same for the role of the parish priest at the harvest, his relationship to the sacredness of harvest tools, and the gifts of agricultural produce given to the priest, etc. By cutting out all these things we would receive a picture of the religious life of an agricultural community to which nothing in reality corresponds. We may then muse about the circumstances under which such a community could be real; and, in the end, we would have to adopt for it a different social, economic, perhaps even geographical setting. What has led us to the mistake we made is the diversity of social organisation in complex and compound societies. The Catholic Church is one body, the huge organised community of all believers of that country another, the small Catholic village a third organism.

Take the second case. Jews belonging to a certain 'esoteric' sect, called Hasidism, which until recently prevailed in Eastern Europe, have certain surprising customs. Thus, they may write on little scraps of paper prayers and wishes concerning their business affairs, their health, the marriage of their daughters, the redemption of the Holy Land or the Coming of the Messiah and put these papers under stones lying on and around the grave of a great Hasidic Rabbi. Being removed from this plane of life, he will, when conversing with the Lord of Hosts, press the wishes of the believers with much more vigour, and he will achieve much more than they could, given their human life contained in their human figures which suffer so much from the interference of the ever-present Will to Evil. Old-fashioned Jewish orthodoxy may shudder and describe this custom as an obnoxious superstition; and it is curious indeed, how it goes against any tendencies and motions of the Jewish faith. Apart from certain esoteric movements, Jewish religious organisation in the diaspora differs from some others in this: it is not what Max Weber calls charismatic, or rather organised round a personal charismatic centre. Since the breaking-up of the ancient priestly caste and the remnants of theocracy, the Jews have formed communities of which the leaders were learned men, and the heads of which were Rabbis able to interpret the Law. Their theological erudition, combined with that kind of social responsibility that goes with it, made them leading figures; but it did not happen that their saintliness was taken as a proof of their belonging to a different category of beings, and that the justification of the religious community lay in its relationship to this saintly and powerful being in its midst. In such an organisation we find the merits and the religious achievements of the members expressed in terms of the degrees of their nearness, or the kinds of personal services they provided, to the charismatic personality. The beginnings of such attitudes are discernible in Judaism now and then in esoteric circles; the main bulk of the people, however, especially when in non-Jewish surroundings, tended always towards an organisation which agrees more or less with Weber's classic definition of a sect: an organisation of religious experts. It was only at the end of the eighteenth century that this particular esoteric movement began to gain hold of the Jewish masses in Eastern Europe and to transform their religious organisation. The discrepancy between customs grown up in relation to charismatic rabbis on the one hand, and the orthodox and traditional belief on the other, is due to our comparing two different historical strata. It is not useful to describe such difference in terms like 'deviation' or 'superstition'.

In these two cases I hope to have summed up most of the possible situations regarding which I should desist from employing the term superstition. I shall now proceed to give some examples of what truly can be called superstition, trying to classify these examples. Before I do that a few words are necessary about the range of phenomena of which we think when we use the word religion.

Religion and Superstition

It may be fussy to insist that the term 'religious' is not a sociological term. But it is precisely on this ground that the sociologist should refuse to define religion. We can, however, describe the working of religion in a scientific way. All human societies are characterised by a peculiar relation between certain sets of values and rituals. By ritual is meant a social action which directly links up only with social actions of the same kind, and which consists in the enactment of social relationships (relations between two groups, between a group and its deity, etc.) in the most general way of which the society is capable. Through every ritual values are created (which the Oxford School of Social Anthropology calls ritual values). These values cannot exist without the perpetual reenactment of the ritual. It is of secondary interest which of these rituals the respective society includes in what it calls its religious sphere.

The range of religious possibilities can best be described by reference to extreme types. The ritual values that derive from rituals spread through all the spheres of human life. At one extreme, this idiom exists in order to refer to the institutions of the society and, in the same terms, to all the forces outside society. (Every description of primitive religion has to begin with a statement of this kind.) At the other extreme, an idiom can derive from ritual and ritual values which refers to the integration of society and the integration of the soul in the same terms.

On the moral level a member of the society of the first type may reflect, 'If this society behaves well it will fit well into the whole arrangement of the institutions of the universe'; while the second may say, 'When all people are really good society is perfect'. In the first case, no reference to the goodness and aims of society is possible except by referring at the same time to other natural entities moving on the same plane. In the second case, no description of what is a really good man can be given unless it describes at the same time his integration into society.

On the noetic level things may be expressed slightly differently. The first man may say: 'Chieftainship, the constellation of Orion, woman, and the rivers were created together by the same force. The monthly cycle of the female and certain astral events are "the same thing".' The second may say: 'The soul of man comes from God. Man has to rebuild himself on the ground of this recognition. When all people are thus united in themselves this society cannot but serve its main purpose: the glorification of the Lord.' I could extend these two series of imaginary statements considerably, but here I will remark only on two significant differences. Human society, as seen by the second type, has much in common with the universe, as seen by the first type. In the first case, the dangers to man lurk outside society, the operating unit is society, the perfected aim is a well-balanced universe. In the second case, the dangers live inside society, the operating unit is the human soul, the achievement is the annihilation of evil in society. If, in the first types of society, individuals take great pains either to avert the attack of the extra social forces, or to find agreement with them – pains which should be due only to the forces which are manifest within society – such behaviour will be found inconsistent with the ritual values of society. In the second case, a person may be able to describe with astounding material exactitude the nature and the working of social institutions, but he will be vague and incoherent about his so-called soul; and the more this soul matters to him, and the more the integration of the soul and society appear to be one and the same thing, the less need there is to speak of the 'soul' with the same definiteness that is used in speaking about means of transport, or the education of children. I do not mean to suggest that there are two entirely different types of religion. These are just the extremes, and you will find many intermediate types.[3]

NOTES

1. Steiner was invited to deliver this lecture to the Oxford University Graduate Society in 1943. The typewritten text, corrected in Steiner's hand, is preserved among Steiner's papers at the Deutsches Literaturarchiv, Marbach am Neckar, and is dated 1944. We have expanded the cryptic opening into a consecutive text, and reproduce Steiner's concluding notes in a footnote. The lecture is published here for the first time.
2. Steiner's reference is presumably to: 'There is no possible way of making an inference from the existence of one situation to the existence of another, entirely different situation. There is no causal nexus to justify such an inference. We *cannot* infer the events of the future from those of the present. Superstition is nothing but belief in the causal nexus' (Wittgenstein 1974: 5,135-5,1361). [Eds]
3. Steiner's lecture breaks off with further notes and examples. Initially he states that, 'Objections to the validity of this morphology can be based on reports about the so-called "Shamanism" of the Siberian aborigines.' The morphology in question is presumably Steiner's twofold distinction in religious orientation: one in which the universal context of a society is the preeminent value, and the other in which the social context of the individual's soul predominates. His text then enumerates four 'examples', with little further detail; these must be the 'examples of what truly can be called superstition' of which he earlier promised a typology. The first three are 'Wild huntsmen', 'Metempsychosis in Judaism', and the Russian 'Cradle pole'. In different ways he seems to have considered these not to have belonged to the main morality cults of the societies in question. Steiner's fourth example brings his discussion back to Britain: 'Luck and bad luck ... Lucky-unlucky polarity has no implications like sinful-good'. His instances of this last type (black cats, spilled salt, broken mirrors) suggest he concluded with a series of domestic, British, superstitions, or evil omens – black cats crossing one's path, spilled salt being thrown over the shoulder (also an example in *Taboo* drawing upon Radcliffe-Brown's 1939 article, see p. 192 above), broken mirrors as harbingers of seven years of bad luck – with no bearing on moral issues. [Eds]

BIBLIOGRAPHY

Wittgenstein, Ludwig (1921) 1974 *Tractatus Logico-Philosophicus*, trans. D.F. Pears and B.F. McGuiness, London: Routledge.

ENSLAVEMENT AND THE EARLY HEBREW LINEAGE SYSTEM: AN EXPLANATION OF GENESIS 47:29-31, 48: 1-16

In his recent *Studies in Biblical Law*, Dr Daube has analysed the story of Joseph in order to find the concomitant legal conceptions of the early Hebrews; his main reference was to the first part of the story (1947: 3-15). Here I want to examine what I regard as the climax of the Biblical narrative.

If, as is often done, we consider the story of Joseph simply as a tale, the consummate artistry with which the narrative is unfolded imposes as the climax the meeting of Joseph and his brothers in Egypt. If, however, we consider the Joseph story basically as a description of a man whose kinship bonds were severed by his sale into slavery and of his later relations to his kinship group, the climax is revealed in the passages which I want to examine here. Some years' study of servile institutions and their structural ramifications in simpler societies (see Steiner 1949) has enabled me to elucidate certain features of the Biblical narrative which before seemed difficult.

Among the relevant verses (Gen., 47:29-31, 48:1-16), the following are the ones of chief interest:

> Gen., 47.29. And the time drew nigh that Israel must die: and he called his son Joseph, and said unto him, If now I have found grace in thy sight, put, I pray thee, thy hand under my thigh, and deal kindly and truly with me; bury me not, I pray thee, in Egypt.
>
> 47.31. And he said, Swear unto me. And he sware unto him. And Israel bowed himself upon the bed's head.
>
> 48.5. And now thy two sons, Ephraim and Manasseh, which were born unto thee in the land of Egypt before I came unto thee into Egypt, *are* mine; as Reuben and Simeon, they shall be mine.

48.6.   And thy issue, which thou begettest after them, shall be thine, *and shall be called after the name of their brethren in their inheritance.*

In the first place, it is surprising to find Jacob addressing his son in this deferential manner. Interpretations which account for this by Joseph's exalted position in Egypt do not take cognisance of the father-son relationship in the patriarchal society of the Hebrews.

The second difficulty is the oath. To 'put the hand under the thigh' has been interpreted by the leading commentators (e.g., Rashi, 1887: 57f., 121) as touching the genitals, and this act is quite inconsistent with the fundamental family taboo of the Hebrews. The only other instance of putting one's hand under a person's thigh while making a vow does not refer to such a contact between near kinsmen, let alone between a son and his progenitor; it is the description of the oath of Abraham's servant Eliezer (Gen., 24.2).

The notion that, as Delitzsch puts it, 'Jacob desires Joseph to put his hand under his thigh, and thus to assure him on the ground of the covenant of circumcision made with Abraham, the actual proof of faithful love ...' (1888, vol. 2: 355) had to be discarded after Pedersen's study of the oath among the Semites. Pedersen compares the Biblical procedure with similar customs found among the Arabs who, however, swear by their own, not by the other person's, genitals. According to Pedersen, in the Arab formula, the male genitals signify the children, and, what is more, the whole kin. Among the Arabs it is thus 'an oath by that kin from which (the person who swears) will be severed if he violates his vow' (1914: 150). This Arab procedure would be nonsensical if it were used in an agreement between persons deeply interested in the wellbeing of the identical group of people. To this must be added the inconsistency we have already mentioned: the severe Hebrew family taboo (Gen., 9:21-25, Lev., 18:6-18).

There seems to be only one answer: that Joseph, because of his sale into slavery, is legally no longer Jacob's son. This selling is a renunciation of family solidarity with and responsibility for Joseph, and although the sale took place without the father's knowledge, it must affect the father as it does all other kinsmen. This would explain Jacob's deferential address: as this is a formal occasion and binding promises are to be given, the words exchanged between the two persons must, in a formal manner, exactly correspond to their actual social relationship.

This explanation also throws some light on the third point: the sons of Joseph are to be received as future progenitors and *patres* of the 'tribes' into what Professors Evans-Pritchard and M. Fortes call the 'maximal lineage' (1940). No such attention is given to the other grandchildren of Jacob. There are no grounds for regarding this as a mark of deference to or as an indemnification of Joseph; Joseph expresses no gratitude for having been preferred to his brothers.

Holzinger is one of the many who have dealt with the passage according to the rules of 'Higher Criticism'. He distinguishes two different narratives which have been combined: in the one narrative Joseph's sons are blessed, but not Joseph himself; in the other narrative, Jacob, after going through a rite of adoption by having the lads sit on his knees, returns them to Joseph, blessing him, 'but his words shift to the children very quickly' (1888: 253).

It is not within the power of Joseph's former kinship group to take him back. He has become a freeman in Egypt, but this does not make him a member of his family again. On the contrary, having been freed in Egypt he then became attached to the court of the king, and in that capacity he is part of the Egyptian social structure.

In most societies a slave's manumission makes him a member or an affiliated member (client) of the former master's family. In fact, in ancient Mesopotamia, adoption seems to have been one of the chief forms of enfranchisement. Adoption or clientage does not reinstate the former slave into his previous kinship structure (Mendelsohn 1949: 1-33; Simcox 1894: *passim*). Much depends on the mode of enslavement. We know of most simpler societies that aliens who had been enslaved against the will of their smallest solidarity group, e.g., as prisoners of war, tend to run away; a man sold by his family rarely does so.

Perhaps quite a different case in an entirely different social setting may help to explain further the nature of this kinship obligation in the enslavement complex.

In her description of the institutions of the North-West American Tsimshian, Viola E. Garfield mentions a case of enslavement. A chief wanted 'to humble a rich and powerful lineage in his tribe, a lineage of which he was jealous.' He asked for one of their women in marriage, and sold her after the wedding to a neighbouring chief. Her relatives bought her free, but could not refuse the influential chief when he asked for her again. Once more she was sold and redeemed, and yet a third time was asked in marriage by the same chief. By then the family had been considerably impoverished, and, when they gave the woman away, they made public in the appropriate manner, that they were not going to ransom her any more. 'So far as they were concerned she was dead.' Her name was no more mentioned by her people, and she died a slave (1939: 272).

This declaration as dead means the formal renunciation of all kinship obligations and this is implied in every sale into slavery by a person's kinship group – in cases where slavery is institutionalised, and if the 'sale' is not merely a selling into debtor slavery. The latter is a very common institution of African and Malaysian societies. There, the fact that the party selling retains the right to redeem the person who is sold, means that kinship obligations are acknowledged.

The sociological and historical significance of this part of the Joseph story is twofold. The legal conceptions underlying it are different from the slave law of Exodus, Deuteronomy and Leviticus, which correspond to the slave laws of the Mesopotamian cultures. Both kinds of societies, differ as they may amongst themselves, are no longer tribal societies in the strict sense. Both kinds of societies distinguish between two categories of slaves: nationals and enslaved aliens. The later Biblical law conceives of the enslaved male nationals as temporary slaves. The point of interest is not so much the possibility of automatic release after the fixed number of years (Exod., 21.2), but the unbroken kinship ties with and obligations towards the enslaved which make them 'nationals'. In this lies the chief difference between alien and national slaves, not in the participation in the activities of the ritual community. In this latter respect, as Isaac Mendelsohn has recently pointed out, the two groups are hardly distinguishable (1949: 34-74).

I suggest that the Joseph story goes a long way in explaining the evolution which led to the later legal customs.

Moreover, these passages describe to us minutely a lineage system working in a way we would not expect among the Semites. The reason is that we have tended to investigate the kinship organisation of the Semites more in terms of family units than in terms of lineages. The splitting-off and the reabsorption of the minimal lineage remind us of phases in the growth of African kinship groups, as described by Professors Evans-Pritchard and Fortes.

NOTES

1. This paper was first read at the International Congress of Anthropological and Ethnological Sciences, Brussels, 1948. Steiner's typescript survives in his *Nachlaß* at the Deutsches Literaturarchiv, Marbach am Neckar. The text was edited by Laura Bohannan, who made minor editorial amendments, and added the bibliographical references. We have followed Laura Bohannan's version, which appeared in 1954 in *Man* 54 no. 102: 73-75.

BIBLIOGRAPHY

Daube, D., 1947 *Studies in Biblical Law*, Cambridge: C.U.P.
Delitzsch, F., 1888 *A New Commentary on Genesis*, trans. S. Taylor 2 vols, Edinburgh: T. and T. Clark.
Fortes, M. and Evans-Pritchard, E.E., 1940 eds, *African Political Systems*, Oxford: O.U.P.

Garfield, V. E., 1939 *Tsimshian Clan and Society*, Seattle: University of Washington Publications in Anthropology, vol. 7, no. 3: 167-340.

Holzinger, H., 1888 'Genesis', *Kurzer Hand-Commentar zum Alten Testament*, (20 vols), vol I, Leipzig: Mohr.

Mendelsohn, I., 1949 *Slavery in the Ancient Near East*. New York: O.U.P.

Pedersen, J.,1914 *Der Eid bei den Semiten*, Studien zur Geschichte und Kultur des Islamischen Orients, no. 3, Strassbourg: Trübner.

Rashi, 1887 *Der Rashi-Kommentar zu den fünf Büchern Moses vollständig ins Deutsche übersetzt mit beigedrucktem Bibel-Texte in einem Bande, v. Julius Dessauer,* Budapest: s.n.

Simcox, E. J., 1894 *Primitive Civilisations*, London: Swan Sonnenschein and Co.

Steiner, F., 1949 'A Comparative Study of the Forms of Slavery', Oxford: Unpublished D. Phil. Thesis, Magdalen College.

CHAGGA LAW AND CHAGGA TRUTH[1]

On Gutmann's *Das Recht der Dschagga*

When Dr Gluckman, before the last vacation, suggested to me that I should read a paper on a monograph of my own choice, I suggested the book I am going to discuss.[2] Dr Gluckman then said that, as I knew, the programme of this term's seminar should be somewhat different from the previous one, as we were going to discuss either monographs that had been written in the attempt to elucidate a sociological problem, or with the intention to isolate for detailed scrutiny one aspect of the social life of a people.

Considering this, I said that my choice still held, and that I regarded Gutmann's book a very interesting specimen in such a series. Later on some doubts assailed me as to the reasonableness of the repetition of my choice. I had to take some time to reconvince myself. I should like now, before dealing with the Chagga people and the author, to repeat to you some of the arguments I used to convince myself.

This book is the only major contribution in German to descriptive social anthropology, as we understand it, in its classical stage. By this I mean a stage when a sound and solid knowledge of a people could not fail to produce a book which, even when outdated, would set standards for knowledge, research and its presentation. Such a claim cannot be made for Prof. Thurnwald or any other German student to whose works we go for data, and for data only. But Gutmann's *Das Recht der Dschagga* is, in this sense, a classic. However, as this argues only for the book's inclusion in the series to which attention was given last year, it need not concern us here.

Another point is this: Gutmann's books in general and this book in particular are based on a rational approach and examination of the social phenomena. During the last half century and more, this approach has been alien to all those Germans who are truly representative of the intelligentsia of their nation, with its peculiar ambitions and frustrations. It can be said that in that period state and social order were the central mystery of German life, particularly for all those who live with mysteries. A rational, scientific approach (which by its nature is not limited to natural science) was suspected of being superficial. Sociology was written, as we know. It had several starting points, none of which was a contribution on another society.

One starting point was philosophy, an examination of the applicability of philosophical thought and categories to social and historical phenomena. This approach was of course never suspected of superficiality. We owe to it important contributions to our science, such as the works of Simmel and von Wiese. But it also produced a flood of literature which is far from being helpful.

Another approach was more typical of the German situation. In this chaos of mysterious society which, however, seems to have had a clearly defined history, there were nuclei and clusters of consistent behaviour. These could be singled out for analysis and explained in terms of those religious movements of the past which had formed them. It was very fortunate that the genius of Max Weber discovered this possibility. But the actual structure of his own society remained mysterious for the German intellectual. When he was confronted with another society which was strikingly different from his own, he did not arrange his experiences in a translation pattern, with reference to his own structure. He could not do this because his awareness of his own society lacked important rational elements. Nothing can be explained by reference to mysteries. Almost invariably he found an honourable escape by most busily and skilfully collecting those observable items which seemed to need least contextual reference. The challenge to sociology of the historical school of ethnology was legitimate, and as such not harmful. But these theories were harmful by providing people whose urgency concerning the unravelling of universal history was unbelievable with an ever-ready excuse for their escapist collecting. Standards of relevance and significance were destroyed; anything could become valuable in the all-embracing jigsaw puzzle which would be completed by somebody else. Thus the fiction was preserved that people who had the whole equipment of modern thought and science at their beck and call, were facing the multiform social universe with all the active interest that befits civilised man. This I feel to be a moral issue and I wish it to be regarded as something apart from the scholarly merits and faults of diffusionist schools.

Gutmann does not only belong to the few Germans who were the exceptions. He towers above them. Perhaps the fact that he was a missionary is decisive. Concerning Smith and Junod we may wonder how these men, working as missionaries among their tribes, could find enough additional energy and zest to do for us what they did, and to muster the necessary knowledge. With Gutmann it is different. In his case we must be grateful that he had been brought up and trained to be a German missionary and not a German ethnologist.

The third point, and this is more relevant here than what I mentioned so far, is that this book, quite apart from Gutmann's other writings, has a very important place among field monographs on legal systems because of its scope and approach. These monographs differ because they treat various aspects of legal systems. The subject matter is more or less the same: the types of jural relationships prevalent in a society, the society's sanctions and acts of arbitrations, the notions relating to the principles involved in general and to the justification of procedure in particular, and the social forces conditioning the distribution and the working of the respective offices.

In Rattray's *Ashanti Law and Constitution* (1929), 'constitution' is the operative word. It indicates Rattray's chief interest. He sets out to describe as much as possible of what is called here a social structure in terms of a constitution, probing deeper and deeper into a network of laws and jural obligations, the ultimate consistency of which he assumes – as the sociologist ought to assume that the society under investigation is integrated. Schapera's work (1938), another high mark of sociological jurisprudence, is chiefly concerned with giving a complete list of vested rights and titles in Tswana society. Llewellyn and Hoebel's *The Cheyenne Way* (1941) is based directly on case studies. From the analysis of conflicts and their arbitration they come to conclusions as to the nature of the conflict and the rules governing sanction and arbitration.

Gutmann does not give a single case, A versus B. He gives typical cases, which may be only ideal cases or telescoped ones, in explanation of laws of which he has a knowledge beyond proof. He does so as a man would describe the laws of his own society to a foreigner. Gutmann's chief interest is to show the stratification of jural provinces in law – individual and clan, clan and clan, chief and clan – and to relate the institutions to what he calls throughout the book the individual soul. He fails in this, but achieves other things. By confusing the history of clanship and chiefship with the actual meaning in jural relations of these institutions, he defeats his own ends. The emphasis of the book is on procedure. Gutmann does not ask to what a man is entitled when something happens to him, but what are the social mechanisms which he is *forced* to set into motion. But Gutmann covers a much larger field than that, and his book should be called: social action in Chagga society.

Gutmann's book has 733 pages. It was published in 1926, in a series dealing with developmental psychology. In this series the book is supposed to take its place as a treatise on the developmental psychol-

ogy of law seen through the instance of an incipient legal system. For-
tunately, Pastor Gutmann failed to furnish anything as absurd as this.
One has to put up with a lot of things to place a book.

The huge tome has no index. Still worse, instead of an index, it has
an epilogue, an essay by a professor of psychology. He starts by giving
a few data abut the author, which I felt obliged to read, and sums up
the importance of the book by saying that it is a book written by a German man chiefly for the German people in that nation's hour of dear-
est [*sic*] stress (1926)!

This book is the result of twenty years life spent with an African
people. Gutmann worked among the Chagga as a Lutheran missionary
and was greatly appreciated both by the native population and the
German administrators, to whom, it seems, he often had to say unkind
things. The first German war interrupted his stay in Chagga land. He
was the first German, whom, in 1926, the Lutheran mission sent back
to East Africa. The British government, having made enquiries about
his work, welcomed him.

Gutmann has published many articles and books on the Chagga.
One book deals with their folklore, another with their religion; another
gives a general account for the general reader. As a result there was a
saying among German ethnologists that the Chagga were now the
best-known primitive people; they ought to be left to Gutmann, and he
should not publish any more.

In 1924, Charles Dundas published a book on the Chagga, *The Kilimanjaro and its People*. It is a minor work, compared with Gutmann's
efforts. But it is interesting because Dundas gives an account of a different time. Gutmann is not interested in the culture change caused by
the Europeans, which for him is a moral issue but not the proper field
of ethnology and sociology. He preserved in his book many institutions
which he may have seen functioning only at the beginning of this century. So there ought to be an up-to-date account, which Dundas's book
is not. His very sketchy book cannot attempt to fill any of the gaps Gutmann could not help leaving. The 'best-known primitive tribe' can do
with many more investigators.

Germans tend to complain that this is a very difficult book. This is
partly due to the fact that Germans are not accustomed to think while
reading books on savages. If the book is found difficult on these grounds
by a reader, he should be warned not to study any book of either the
functional or the structural school. Some difficulties are due to the language. It seems that Gutmann has acquainted himself thoroughly with
S. Kierkegaard's writings and with some of the outpourings connected
with the Kierkegaard revival in Germany after the first war. His use of
words like fear and loneliness testify to this. His Chagga is not the superstitious, fearful creature fighting against an overpowering and incom-

prehensible world, like the savages of earlier writers; it is a man afraid of the nothingness of his isolation, man fighting against isolation. All this does not harm his picture of primitive society, and his quaint language nowhere degenerates into existentialist verbiage. But he coins words as he goes along, and more irritating still are his native words. He translates every native word which has a ritual significance and calls the thing by this name only. The Chagga chief, for example, gives judgement standing on a piece of grass outside the assembly house, which is used for this purpose only. This is the 'lawn of verdict'. When two people quarrel and afterwards make up their differences, they squat on a piece of skin. This is the 'skin of allegiance'. There are about twenty more such terms which occur singly and in groups at regular intervals, epithets in a Homeric epic, only more so. There are many trite statements in the book which ill accord with such a specialised vocabulary. Gutmann does not seem to agree with feminism, and he has many odd things to say about the best use women can make of their lives. He uses words which certainly do not come from Kierkegaard, like 'motherly bliss', 'womanly fulfilment', 'radiance of female existence' – which phrases do not occur where babies are concerned but in the most unexpected places.

The Chagga, the agricultural Bantu-speaking population of the Kilimanjaro slopes, number, according to Gutmann's estimate, fewer than a hundred thousand, and, according to Dundas (two years earlier), 120,000. There are thirty-one recognised chiefdoms, the largest of which has 17,000 souls, while there are twenty chiefdoms with fewer than 1,000 each.

There are approximately 400 'sibs' in Chagga land. Gutmann is not very consistent in the use of the word. It is always an exogamous, patrilineal kinship group – sometimes a major lineage, sometimes the local branch which combine with branches of other lineages in forming the territorial unit. These I will call clans. The owners of the land were an age group which associated itself with the chief in the chiefdom's jurisdiction. The age group cuts across lineages. The chief was the warleader; he had many charismatic functions. There are individually held lands, clan lands, lands for which the responsibility rests with the ruling age group. But the village does not seem to matter as a unit, unless it coincides with a chiefdom.

This is how Gutmann divides up his matter:

1. Norms of blood and clanship;
2. Norms of territorial allegiance;
3. Norms of arbitration;
4. Crimes against norms;
5. Legal procedure;
6. The 'lawn of verdict' and the individual soul.

This last chapter, in which the author tries to relate the various spheres to the individual, is subdivided:

Feeling of justice
The oath and the native
The lie
The conscience

It is, of course, quite impossible to do more than give an idea of Gutmann's general approach and to select a chapter or rather parts of a chapter for detailed review. As the last chapter is the most unusual one in books dealing with legal systems, I will mention some of its striking features.

Gutmann assumes three changes to have taken place in Chagga society prior to European intrusion. First, he assumes that once upon a time the Chagga were matrilineal, or, in his terms, matriarchic; second, that the clan had in the past a different kind of cohesion, which was being loosened while the individual household achieved more and more independence; third, the emergence of chiefship which infringed the political rights of the clans. The recurrent explanation of behaviour patterns in terms of these three changes would be confusing even if we were led, somehow, to place them in time and space, even if these changes were well documented, even if we were told how they affected each other. But far from this, these three changes have not even the same degree of probability.

The second change is plausible enough. Many traditions can be quoted – and are quoted by authors other than Gutmann – about the coming of chiefly clans from other parts. They brought cattle with them, subdued the agriculturists among whom they settled. Similar events have taken place all over East and Central Africa. But it is another matter to make the foreign intrusion solely responsible for the change of a kinship regime to territorial units. The scattered major lineages, of which the clans are only parts, tell their tale. It cannot be claimed that they were scattered by the chiefs; some territorial organisation must have existed which welded clans of different lineages together, and this means a mutual adaptation. In his hypothesis Gutmann assumes no such body politic; for him it is something alien to kinship bonds, and therefore, imposed by a culture change. Moreover, in Gutmann's time, we could see the clans as political organisations only in reference to certain political offices. The holders of these offices represent the clan in its dealings with the chief. The political rights of the clans are vested in offices, and these offices and the present centre of territorial organisation are interdependent. It is neither here nor there to argue that these offices are defence mechanisms necessitated by the growth of chiefship, and that at some earlier date the clan would have been more powerful because there were no chiefs. No data from the present structure can explain in what, exactly, this power would have consisted. Gutmann, much more painstakingly than Dundas, follows the stories of the chiefs of old, reconstructing genealogies and calculating their time depth. Some of the great events of this history seem to have taken place in the eighteenth century at the latest. We may wonder, then, when this great age of the untrammelled clans has been.

Perhaps it is unfair, but I cannot help feeling that part of the confusion and a good deal of the hankering after the golden age of pure clanship is caused by that dichotomy into 'artificial' society and harmonious, non-contractual community. Such a dichotomy, painfully realised in times when 'artificial' society is chaotic and ill-understood, seems to have coloured Gutmann's vision of Chagga life. If so, it is a pity that he had ever read Tönnies.

As to the third change, the loosening of the larger kinship group in favour of the small household unit, some of the data produced in illustration of this are unconvincing, others argue for the opposite. Gutmann wishes us to believe that once upon a time the clan was a self-subsisting economic unit, not, as today, the homestead. At the same time he insists that the so-called women's market, a barter market (1926: 425 *sqq*) run under the auspices of clan officials and outside the chief's sphere, designed, primarily, for the interchange of the produce of the clan's homesteads, and a very archaic institution, antedates chiefship (which may be the case), the very chiefship which he holds partly responsible for the jural and economic independence of homesteads. Nothing of this fits, even without application to field data.

The point of the historical argument which invites detailed criticism is a very interesting one. Chagga age groups cut across clans. The groups are formed of people who were circumcised and initiated together. The place of this ritual is the chief's yard, and there should be one son of the chief undergoing the ceremony together with the commoners. He is the leader of the age group to be. This leadership is very important in the political life of the Chagga and goes a long way to explain their attitude to chiefship and loyalty. Now Gutmann tells us, and why should we doubt this, that in the old times initiation was a clan affair, taking place on clan grounds. Then the change must have been a profound religious change, which cannot be accounted for by the intrusion of foreign cattle-owning groups. I think that the largest group of even assumed facts is missing in this theory of Chagga history.

And as to the first change, that of mother right into father right, it is regrettable that Gutmann has followed this old trend which has led astray the acute observer, causing errors and omissions. The errors are easily remedied; they are quite common mistakes, e.g., claiming as matrilineal feature the fact that we find female ancestors as founding ancestors of clans. This is very common where patrilineages and polygyny go together, and one group of a man's sons who have a mother in common branch off, making this woman the point of fission. This is not only common in Negro Africa; it seems to occur among the Somali, and Prof. Hoernle mentions it from the Hottentots.

Far more damaging are the omissions. Gutmann tells the stories of some female chiefs of old. This is tangible matriarchy for him (though we fail to see why, even if all these assertions about female chiefs were true, peculiarities of the intruding chief clans could reflect on the original structure of the other clans). It becomes clear, however, that these female chiefs are widows of chiefs and that they rule while their sons are under age. The sons are under the tutelage of a male relative of the dead chief, a man deputises for her as judge, another as war leader. If Gutmann had not taken for granted that these women were full fledged chiefs, he might have investigated the constitutional features which made necessary these instances of nominal chiefship. He describes how these women wielded personal power, how they tried to stay in power by playing off one son against another. This is one of the unexpected places where Gutmann offers his praise of motherly bliss and womanly fulfilment (*Wie weit die Mutterinstinkte wirken können, so weit geht Glück und Herrschaft des Weibes*, 1926: 506).

He also tells the story of the one childless woman chief. She came to a very grievous end. She was a chief's young widow, surviving his grandsons and ruling before his great-grandsons came of age. Gutmann tells that according to tradition, she married several women, having the right over the children born in this wedlock (1926: 515). She was the *pater* of the children, while the *genitor*, a man selected by her for that purpose, had no rights over the children. One descendant of this female pater group actually became chief two generations later. As further details were of no interest to the matriarchy issue, Gutmann has not investigated them. This is a pity, because here we have a custom resembling Nuer ghost marriage and, more closely still, a Dahomean marriage type. This latter institution has been described in Herskovits' (1938) book on Dahomey, but I saw its significance only after Mrs Bohannan showed me a paper in which she analyses, among other types of Dahomean marriage, this one.[3] There she uses, by analogy with the distinction between *pater* and *genitor*, the analytic concepts of *jus in uxorem* and *jus in genetricem*, thus elucidating this pattern. Whether the isolated Chagga instance conformed to this pattern, or whether it was a case of raising seed to the dead chief, we shall never know. One cannot help blaming this on the author's pseudo-historical preoccupations.

Gutmann's preoccupation with mother right makes him overlook another very interesting social feature. The Chagga are patrilineal and have a dual unilateral descent. That means that an individual's other clan, the kin on the left as the Chagga call it, the mother's people, are the people of the clan into which she was born. Here the nearest relatives are the mother's brother, his son, mother's parents, mother's father's parents and so on. These persons matter in ritual and their clan is the individual's second home. Here he takes refuge when his own clan cannot protect him or if he has quarrelled with his own people. The mother's clan is important as far as jural relationships and solidarity are concerned. Quite different from the mother's people is the woman's line, in Dr Fortes's words, a submerged lineage. This peculiar line, which loops in and out of the clans – mother, mother's mother, mother's mother's mother, etc. – seems to be a recognised tie. It is often referred to, and when a woman dies without leaving a daughter, it is said that this woman's line has died out.

But Gutmann cannot give any data about the functions of this line, not because he is unobservant, but because he lumps together again and again these two things: mother's people and woman's line, in order to show the importance of other people than those of one's patrilineage.

I am stressing these defects to show two things: how even a thorough knowledge of a people is not protection enough against distortions caused by a historical interest of a certain kind, and how far below the level of conjectural history of badly documented periods of Asiatic and European civilisation these constructions do fall, if we base our comparison only on the consistency and the plausibility of the assumptions.

Gutmann's descriptive accuracy and brilliance is seen at its best when he deals with long stretches of interlocking social activities. Not only does he pay attention to circumstances which are usually neglected by the ethnographer, he marshals the facts in such an imposing and convincing way that generalisations are almost unnecessary. When the time comes for a comprehensive tribal economic history of African to be written, extracts from this book will belong among its purple passages and will set standards. The account of socage work for the chief is astoundingly accurate. He goes into every detail of division of labour among the sexes. Socage work is done in three groups (1926: 367 *sqq.*); men, women and boys work in three different columns, each of them having tasks set which no other column could be asked to perform. (The boys are young men before their initiation – eighteen to twenty year olds, including very strong youngsters.) It is only because Gutmann gives these facts that we realise what in Chagga terms may be the mark of servility and why this work seems to exist on a contractual basis. Penal labour also existed; it was a punishment for socage slackers and recalcitrant groups in newly conquered districts. This shameful, humbling work differed from socage labour in only one respect: the absence of any division of labour. So it seems that at this one point come together various principles as fundamental as the meaning of sex, human dignity and labour organisation. I think that to have drawn attention to this is no mean performance.

I am rather critical concerning Gutmann's very valuable analysis of Chagga concepts of truth, veracity, lying and feeling guilt. This is one of the most stimulating chapters of the book, and I am convinced that any critic who does justice to it will do so from a point of view very much influenced by Gutmann's interesting data and surmises.

Chagga Truth

Before turning to a critical appreciation of this Chagga material,[4] I should like to outline, as briefly as possible, my own viewpoint. First, I must insist that any concept of truth to which observable behaviour relates and which can thereby be made the object of sociological study, is something very different from a logician's concept of truth. I do *not* mean by this that the Westerner, holding the logician's concept of truth, finds among the Chagga another and incompatible sort of concept.

Secondly, truth has many meanings in any society. If we, for instance, were to ask a neo-positivist logician about truth, we should be told that truth is a substantive which ought to be avoided: this substantive is abstracted from statements about properties of verified statements; it is sense to talk about true statements; it is nonsense to talk about the truth; furthermore, there is an emotional residue in 'truth' which has nothing to do with verification. Agreed. But this 'emotional residue' *is* of interest to the sociologist. It is a social reality, while logical properties of statements are not. As anthropologists we are interested in the social reality of 'truth' rather than in its logical connection with verification. The logician may restrict himself, but the anthropologist is concerned with all the applications of 'truth' in a given society, and in simpler societies – the Chagga are a case in point – he finds it connected with the institution of the oath and he finds oath, vow, and swearing concerned in the formation of jural relationships and in legal procedure.

Here again there are significant variations in emphasis. The Greek word ἀλήθεια in itself means non-forgetting, and it refers to the exact rendition of a past event. The Hebrew oath as mentioned in the Bible refers in most cases to the future: the person committing himself to the formality declares that he will do something and, when he has actually done it, the word is true; but there is neither truth nor falsehood in words when they are uttered.

Witnessing is another context of truth. While today – I do not want to go into the procedure of Roman law – the witness is the eyewitness, an instrument of verification, in other societies he is nothing of the sort: he helps to establish 'truth' because no 'verification' is possible. This latter attitude to witnessing prevails to some extent even in our approach to verification. No statement of one of the parties is evidence, while the statements of witnesses are evidence, although from a logical, and not a contextual viewpoint, they need verification and are different from objects which judge and court can directly examine and 'witness' themselves.

In many types of legal procedure the place of the verifying witness is taken by persons who, under oath, declare their solidarity with one of the parties and his statements. Thereby the character of their assertion is changed, and it must call forth a different reaction. This change lies in social reality and not in the logical properties of the statement. We know witnessing of this type from Teutonic and Celtic Europe and also from African societies, for example, the Bogos of Eritrea (Vinogradoff 1920: 318 and 350; Grönbech 1931: vols 1 and 2, *passim*; Munzinger 1859).

Witnessing and the oath are interdependent in a very significant way. The oath invokes as witness (usually not as an eyewitness) a person, a great power, or a powerful being: with some Africans, it is the chief or the king; with others it is a divine power; with some Siberian tribes it was the dangerous bear in the forest. This power would then become hostile to the oath-taker if his claims to the power's solidarity were unwarranted. Functionally, such an oath is an abridged ordeal.

We can thus see that truth and verification are not the same. We can also see that there are at least two groups of truth concepts: the one relating to a change in the social reality of a statement, the other to the degree of applicability of a myth to one or more situations of life. The difference between the two is plainly visible when one considers how they have been fused together in the Pentateuch (Exod. xxv, xxx, xxxi) to create absolute truth. There the centre of religious life is what the text calls *ohel mo'ed*, which is usually translated as 'tabernacle'. *Ohel* means tent and nothing more. *Mo'ed* occurs in this context alone and is therefore much discussed. Rosenzweig – the philosopher and collaborator in the Buber translation of the Hebrew Bible – has written an interesting essay on the translatability of a group of terms including this phrase. *Mo'ed* is apparently derived from the same root as *'od*, 'still', 'yet', *'ad*, 'till', and *'ed*, 'witness'. Other derivatives of the word occur in statements about what happens inside the Holy of Holies: the shrine of *'edut*, 'witness?'; and about the perpetuated *hiwwa'ed*, action of God, i.e., 'his making himself present as a witness'. It means that in the tent of witness the God bears witness to himself for man, with the help of the shrine of witness which contains the law, the paramount social reality (Buber and Rosenzweig 1936: 126). The manifestation of the God of the People is thus explained in terms of jural truth, and thereby jural truth and mythical truth become one.

Through the identification of the Greek truth of the past and the Hebrew truth of the future, European truth achieved a timeless quality. The acceptance of Absolute Truth in turn made possible mystical truth, which is identified with life and with the way to the absolute, all three being one and accepted as the incarnate God. Then, with the secularisation of religion in the West, truth as absolute was misapplied to scientific statements and theories, which seek verification only in order to lead to further veritable statements and theories. After this had been accomplished, the completely perverted question was asked, whether this absolute truth – now attributed to science – could be found in religion as well.

A full understanding of the nature of truth, in the sense in which I use the word, will be attained only after studies by many people who are experts both in comparative religion and comparative jurisprudence. Here I have outlined merely what I think the necessary equipment for an investigation into the truth concepts of a simple society.

To describe Chagga concepts of truth and lie, Gutmann deals first with these words and indicates the contexts in which they are used. This method was rare enough when he wrote, and we can only wish he had devoted more than a few paragraphs to it. Unfortunately, he is most concerned with eliciting meaning from common derivation, and some error consequently creeps into the investigation. It is one thing to enumerate the various contexts in which a word is used at any one time and to derive the meaning of the word from the sum total of its associations. It is quite another thing to relate words in terms of their common derivation as I have just done with some words in the Pentateuch. Once a word has been separated from its associates, its separate existence and usage are a significant part of the current mode of thought and expression. An investigation of current concepts may then be obscured by the philological approach. For example, an historical study of the word 'litter' would give us little relevant information on the connection, if any, between British attitudes to birth control and the Anti-Litter League concerned with keeping Britain tidy.

The Chagga call a completely reliable statement *lohi* or *loi. Ki lohi:* this is true. *Kja lohi:* to speak true. The related verb *iloha* refers to actions of magic designed to damage another person. Gutmann therefore assumes that the original meaning of the *lohi* group is 'to utter incantations'. One can, however, avoid the derivational approach and say, from Gutmann's data, that the *lohi* group implies incantation and response to it: the binding and the bound word. Gutmann does, however, qualify his statement by saying that the 'oath character' of *lohi* is still felt. He tells us: 'For this reason members of the Moshi District who had become Christians, several times said they would like to have not only the chiefs' oath formula, *so mangi*, together with its associated variations, but also the word *lohi* banned from Christian speech usage' (1926: 703).

There are three words that can be used for 'report, message, statement': *mboni* from *iwona*, to see, to say what one has seen; *sumu* from *isuma*, to dig out. The phrase *isuma mboni* means 'to transmit a detailed account of a fully grasped group of circumstances'. The third word, *oloho*, is a rarer form from the *lohi* family of words.

All these words seem, to us, to imply veracity of statement; consequently, one interesting feature of their usage is that only *lohi* words are felt as opposites to something that is not true. *Sumu*, the seen, for example, does not stand as antonym to some other word. Still more interesting, *lohi* seems to have two alternatives. One, connected with the Swahili *uwongo*, lie, has a curious field of meaning: *yongwo*, to make public; *mhambo*, mere rumour. The chief meaning of *wongo*, according to Gutmann, is 'mere talk' (*Gerede*) (1926: 702); perhaps he means informal talk. But the opposite of *ki loha*, 'this is true', is *ki wongo*. One wonders whether Gutmann is justified in translating it, as he does, by 'It's a lie' (1926: 702). The other word, or rather usage, is a composition of *wongo*, talk, and *wuowu*, fear: to talk out of fear; an intentional lie. Talk influenced by fear and the statement of jural relevance are thus opposites. Again Gutmann gauges the field of meaning of *wuowu*, fear, with the help of related words meaning to escape, extricate oneself; one word is used of reptiles throwing off their skins (1926: 709 ff.).

The survey of Chagga truth concepts would not be complete without a mention of certain signals or signs – I hesitate to call them symbols, as they seem to me part of the language and in no way more symbolic than other parts of speech behaviour, though resisting verbal conceptualisation both in Chagga and in our languages. I refer to certain ejaculations and to the use of the Dracaena leaf.

From the way in which this leaf is used we may deduce that it implies impersonal identification, serving as a mark of ownership without reference to individuals. I will select three of its uses to illustrate this point.

The clan copses where the ancestor shrines are to be found are clan property. Clan members may do things there which other people may not; they may even cut wood. But when people bearing arms cross their own clan copse, they must attach Dracaena leaves to their weapons. Apparently no awe was felt during this procedure, which was not explained as a protective measure: it was the link between the clan's arms and the clan's ancestors. Every clan used the same leaves (1926: 308-309).

When a man had been aggressive to another and had persuaded himself, or had been persuaded by others, that he was in the wrong, he would take an animal – goat, calf, or even cow – arrange a wreath of

Dracaena leaves around the animal's neck, and take it as a present to the man he had wronged. This procedure made explanations unnecessary; it revealed the guilt and resolved it at the same time (1926: 605 ff.).

When a man had a grudge against another and wanted to harm him, he would, when his enemy had become intoxicated at a feast, follow him to his hut and crouch outside to eavesdrop, in the hope that in his drunken state his enemy might grumble against or even curse the chief. If he did so, the eavesdropper plucked a Dracaena leaf, stuck it into the thatch of the hut and ran for another witness who had to join in his listening. When the case against the enemy is made fool-proof by the extra witness, the future accuser makes some nasty jeering noises. The enemy then leaves his hut, sees the Dracaena leaves and realises his position. But even if the second witness had heard nothing, he would still swear to the words of the first witness, saying: 'I had been called for such and such a purpose; I saw the Dracaena leaf, but they had stopped speaking' (1926: 618 ff). I suggest, therefore, that the use of this leaf is complementary to the *lohi* words and that one cannot be discussed without the other.

A witness in court merely agrees to the words of the party under oath. He speaks *lohi.* In addition an eyewitness identifies the man with ejaculations which do not identify individuals and do not include names. Such ejaculations are: 'You, I am holding you!', or 'I have seen you are caught!' These ejaculations are regarded as important, but they do not belong to the words sworn to. They refer to a reality of a different relevance and establish a relation between the accused and the witness, not between the witness and the court (1926: 615-17).

Gutmann devoted many pages to the defence of his Chagga against European statements that they are constantly lying. He does so on psychological grounds, speaking of bullying officials and the defence mechanisms of the individual soul. But clearly the Dracaena leaf and *lohi* obtain apart from the culture contact situations to which Gutmann's defence is relevant, and it is also clear that Chagga concepts of truth apply to contexts covered by the European concept of lying. For example, Gutmann describes the talks preceding law cases, when the clan members assemble and decide to stick to the version of their fellow clansman. All this is just talk, but the story to which they finally bind themselves is *lohi* (1926: 706).

Gutmann thus leads us a long way towards an analysis of truth concepts and their relation to structural situations. He stops at the threshold. I have actually overelaborated some of his remarks, for I am convinced that they open a new approach to important problems.

Gutmann also contrasts the feeling of justice, which he very concisely describes, with the love of fairness. He recognises these as two different principles, and again moves towards a structural arrangement of these matters and again stops short. His material shows that fairness concepts predominate in the jural relationships between chief and clans and that they have no place in clan law, the harshness of which he rather deplores (1926: 689-96 and *passim*).

His very human analysis of what could be called Chagga conscience shows that here too there are two different spheres. One is that of clan conscience. When a man has wronged or murdered, without being found out, a member of another clan, he makes a dying confession to his kin so that they may compose the matter. But he does so as a concession to clan interests, not through his fear of death (1926: 716 f). Individual conscience, which acts upon a man who has not the backing of his clan, is quite another matter. Here too Gutmann, although he does not go very far in his comparison of conscience types and structural situations, shows what could be done by relating a people's institutions to the individual.

I wish to conclude with Gutmann's analysis of a crucial phrase which for him sums up the Chagga householder's feeling of frustration brought on by his own misbehaviour: 'The posts of my house are hitting me' (1926: 730 ff.). A similar phrase was used in olden times of Chagga life and strife. When raiding parties had overrun a district and the inhabitants had in advance taken their cattle and valuables into safety, leaving only houses for the raiders to burn, the strange and lonely countryside made the raiders feel awkward. To describe this sensation, one said: 'The banana plants are beginning to hit them.' When a speaker came up to the war-leader to persuade him to return, he said simply: 'The banana plants are hitting the men.' After this announcement retreat was usually ordered. The enemy was defeated not by armed strength but by the emptiness of a man-made landscape. The banana plants implied agriculture and an ordered life; but they were seen in a frustrating and alien emptiness.

When the householder himself had gone astray in his ways, overreached himself, or quarrelled with kinsfolk it was not the alien land which turned against him, but the very texture of his most familiar retreat proved alien land. His house, everywhere the symbol of a man's safety and independence, is not after all his own; it is built with the consent, help, and blessing of his kinsmen, and important housebuilding ceremonies testify to this interdependence. If a man alienates himself from the source of solidarity, he feels lonely where he was suffered to be independent.

When I read these passages in Gutmann's book, I felt that very few of us can aspire to so profound a knowledge of another people's thought. In this as in many other chapters, I felt that more important – as human achievement – than the author's analytical work was this vast formulated knowledge and insight.

NOTES

1. This text derives from a paper that Steiner entitled: 'On Gutmann's *Das Recht der Dschagga*, Seminar Paper, Oxford, Feb. 1949'. Laura Bohannan edited a little less than its second half which was published under the title 'Chagga Truth. A note on Gutmann's account of the Chagga concept of truth in *Das Recht der Dschagga*' in October 1954 *Africa* 24(4): 364-69. Apart from a brief introductory paragraph, we reprint this article as the section here entitled 'Chagga Truth'. A typed fair copy of Steiner's original paper, apparently made for the Bohannans' editorial use, survives in the bound volume *Franz Baermann Steiner, Lectures and Papers Oxford 1949-52* in the library of the Institute of Social and Cultural Anthropology of the University of Oxford. We have edited the remainder of Steiner's original paper from this source; it constitutes the first half of the present essay. The section called 'Chagga Truth' is reprinted by permission of the editor of *Africa* (the Journal of the International Africa Institute).

2. The seminar in question was the class on 'Fieldwork in social anthropology'. According to the *University Gazette*, Gluckman presided over this during Michaelmas term and would do so again in Trinity term. However, when Steiner delivered his paper in February 1949 (during Hilary term), the class is advertised as run by Evans-Pritchard and Fortes. [Eds]

3. Laura Bohannan's paper was published in the year that Steiner delivered this seminar (see Bohannan 1949). [Eds]

4. Most of the data to which Dr Steiner refers occur in Part VI: *Der Spruchrasen und die Einzelseele* (689-735), and particularly in the section *Die Lüge* (702-25), Gutmann, 1926. [L.B.]

BIBLIOGRAPHY

Bohannan, Laura, 1949 'Dahomean marriage: a revaluation' *Africa* 19(4): 273-87.

Buber, Martin and and Rosenzweig, Franz, 1936 *Die Schrift und ihre Verdeutschung*, Berlin: Schocken Verlag.

Dundas, Charles, 1924 *The Kilimanjaro and its People: a History of the Wachagga*, London: H.F. and G. Witherby.

Grönbech, V., 1931 *The Culture of the Teutons*. trans. W. Worster, 3 vols, London: Jespersen og Pios Forlag.

Gutmann, B., 1926 *Das Recht der Chagga*, Munich: Beck.

Herskovits, Melville J., 1938 *Dahomey. An Ancient West African Kingdom*, 2 vols, New York: J.J. Augustin.

Llewellyn, K.N. and E. Adamson Hoebel, 1941 *The Cheyenne Way: Conflict and Case Law in Primitive Jurisprudence*, Norman: University of Oklahoma Press.

Munzinger, W., 1859 *Über die Sitten und das Recht der Bogos*, Winterthur: Wurster.

Rattray, R.S., 1929 *Ashanti Law and Constitution*, Oxford: Clarendon.

Schapera, Isaac, 1938 *A Handbook of Tswana Law and Custom*, London: International African Institute.

Vinogradoff, P., 1920 *Outlines of Historical Jurisprudence*. (2 vols), Vol. I, Oxford: O.U.P.

BIBLIOGRAPHY AND REFERENCES TO VOLUMES I AND II

Note

A bibliography of F.B.S.'s published writings to 1993 will be found in 'Special Bibliography: The Writings of Franz Baermann Steiner (1909-1952)', *Comparative Criticism*, 16 (1994): 281-92. A selection is listed here. In the absence of a catalogue of F.B.S.'s unpublished writings in his *Nachlaß*, they are here listed selectively in descriptive form. Our bibliography includes Ms drafts and all completed anthropological writings by F.B.S. and a check-list of the typescripts of his aphorisms, as well as selected letters by and to F.B.S., listed – according to the state of his papers – either individually by date, or globally as datable correspondences. The listings do not include notebooks, folders, excerpts, and notes, which can be identified by their description in our Introductions or by box numbers (S29, etc.). References in the main text preceded by 'Ms' and a date are to section I of the bibliography (unpublished sources), all others are to section II (published works).

Abbreviations

H.G.A. = H.G. Adler. F.B.S. = Franz Baermann Steiner. Ms = manuscript. PC = Personal Communication.
* = reprinted in this edition.

I. Manuscript Sources

*i. F.B.S.'s Unpublished Writings in the Schiller Nationalmuseum,
Deutsches Literaturarchiv, Marbach am Neckar*

1934	'Studien zur arabischen Wurzelgeschichte'. Typescript. 1 + 33 pp.
1936	Diary I. Quarto exercise book. Blue cover. 56pp.
1936-37	Diary II. English quarto exercise book. Grey-green cover. 48pp.
1937a	'Einführung in die Kunstgeschichte der Naturvölker' (Introduction to the History of Art of Primitive Peoples). Three lectures. Delivered in Prague. Typescript. 30 pp.
?1937b	'Völkerkunde für Jugendliche' (Ethnology for Young People). Draft for a book. Typescript. 21 pp.
1937-38	Diary III. Quarto exercise book. Without cover. 48pp.
1938	('Hundeopfer und Wehengeständnis, ihre Beziehungen zum Nordeurasischen Wiedergeburtsglauben' [Dog sacrifice and parturition confession, their relations to North-Eurasian beliefs in reincarnation]). Paper delivered to the Congrès International des Sciences Anthropologiques et Ethnologiques, Deuxième Session, Copenhagen 1938. Typescript. 4 pp.
1939a	Diary IV. English quarto exercise book. Red cover. 48pp.
1939b	'Curriculum vitae'. Prepared by F.B.S. Typescript. 5 pp.
?1942	'Wir, die in der Oxforder Ortsgruppe der "Association of Jewish Refugees" ...'. (We, the Oxford Group of the 'Association of Jewish Refugees'...). Undated memoir. 2pp.
*1943	'Brief an Georg Rapp' (Letter to Georg Rapp). October. Typescript by H.G.A. 13 pp.
*1944a	'How to Define Superstition? Draft of a Lecture.' Being an Address to the Oxford Graduate Society. Typescript. 7 pp.
?1944b	'Der Mensch und das Leid' (Man and Suffering). Typescript. Prepared by H.G.A. 2 pp.
*1946	'A letter to Mr Gandhi'. Typescript. 25 pp.
1947a	'Allerlei Feststellungen und Versuche. 1944-47' (Sundry Essays and Discoveries. 1944-47). 3 vols. Typescript edited under F.B.S's direction by Esther Frank.
*1947b	'Malinowski und Conrad'. Oxford. April. In 1947a.
?1947c	'Erinnerung an einen Wendepunkt' (Memory of a Turning Point). Cycle of aphorisms, preceded by title aphorism, based on 1947a. Pasted Typescript. Ed. F.B.S. pp. 8.
?1947d	'Feststellungen und Versuche'. Cycle of aphorisms, arranged in 20 sections, mostly titled, based on 1947a. Pasted Typescript. Ed. F.B.S. 143 pp. Includes 3: *'An dem Rand der Gesellschaftswissenschaften' (On the Margins of the Social Sciences). 1 + 10pp.
1947e	Letter to Paul Bruell. 13 April. Typescript. Prepared by Paul Bruell.
*?1947f	'Memorandum'. Typescript. 7pp.
*?1948a	'Language, Society, and Social Anthropology'. Typescript. 5 pp.

?1948b   Curriculum vitae. Prepared by F.B.S. Request for stipend to study social structure of Jewish villages in the Atlas mountains. 1p.

1948c   'Feststellungen und Versuche'. January-June. A Selection. Ed. H.G.A. Typescript. 26 pp. Contains * 'All the possibilities', 'More human effort ...', 'The body is the time ...'.

1948d   'Feststellungen und Versuche'. July-October. A Selection. Ed. H.G.A. 12 pp. Contains * 'Art and science ...', 'A lie can slough off the truth ...', 'The concept of history ...'. 'In ideal terms ...', 'The chief sociological principle...', 'The relation between chronological and morphological series', 'The so-called "culture element"...'.

1948e   'Feststellungen und Versuche'. November-December. A Selection. Ed. H.G.A. 15 pp. Contains * 'Tacitus is the first...', 'It is strange that Simmel ...', 'A society no more consists ...'.

1949a   'A Comparative Study of the Forms of Slavery', D.Phil. Thesis, Magdalen College, University of Oxford. Typescript. 379pp.

*1949b   'On Gutmann's *Das Recht der Dschagga*. Seminar paper'. Oxford. February. Typescript. 1 + 23 pp.

1949c   'Some Remarks on Slavery. Notes for a Lecture'. Seminar. Oxford. 9 March. Typescript. 1 + 6 pp.

1949d   'Caste outside India. Notes [for] a Lecture'. Dr Srinivas's Seminar. Oxford. 6 June 1949. Typescript. 1 + 4 pp.

1950a   'Feststellungen und Versuche'. January-February. A Selection. Ed. H.G.A. Typescript. 14 pp. Contains *'Time is power ...'.

1950b   'Feststellungen und Versuche'. March-April. A Selection. Ed. H.G.A. Typescript. 29 pp. Contains *'Aristotle ...', 'The words "structure" and "system" ...', 'It is misleading to treat herds ...', 'For the French ...', 'Descriptive sociology', 'Social structure...', 'A category ...', 'The formation of spatial concepts ...', 'Someone asked the spider ...', 'When Rasmussen ...', 'People have two ...', 'The secret of biology ...', 'The foundations of sociology ...'.

1950c   'Feststellungen und Versuche'. June. A Selection. Ed. H.G.A. Typescript. 34 pp. Contains * 'The sociology of children ...'.

1950d   'Feststellungen und Versuche'. June (1). A Selection. Ed. H.G.A. Typescript. 10 pp.

1950e   'Feststellungen und Versuche'. June (2). A Selection. Ed. H.G.A. Typescript. 10 pp.

1950-52a   'Tabu'. Typescript. 12 Lectures. 1 + 44 + 1 pp.

*1950-52b   'Aristotle's Sociology'. A Lecture at Oxford University. Typescript. 2 + 1 pp.

?1951a   Theory of Classification. Fragmentary Chapter headed 'Introduction to the Problem and the Terminology used'. Typescript and handwritten notes. 10 + 11pp.

1951b   'Lectures on the Division and Organisation of Labour'. Oxford. Hilary. Lectures A-F + 1949a pp. 88-104 with handwritten annotations. Lecture G. Typescript. 38 pp.

*1951-52   'Two lectures on Kinship'. Delivered at the Institute of Social Anthropology, Oxford University. Typescript. 3 pp.

1952a   Diary V. Bound quarto volume.
*1952b   'Some problems in Simmel'. Three Lectures delivered at the
            Institute of Social Anthropology, Oxford University. Typescript.
            12 pp.
?1953   Anon. 'Book List. Franz Steiner'. Systematic catalogue of
            Steiner's books on Anthropology, Archaeology, Psychology,
            Social Theory, Sociology, etc. Over 600 items. Typescript. 38 pp.
1957   A *Prolegomena to a Comparative Study of the Forms of Slavery.*
            Prepared for publication by Paul Bohannan. Edited version of
            1949a. Typescript. 198pp.

ii. Unpublished Letters to and about F.B.S. and Memoirs Concerning him at the Schiller Nationalmuseum, Deutsches Literaturarchiv, Marbach am Neckar

Adler, H.G. 1953 'Brief an Dr [Chaim] Rabin'. (Letter to Dr [Chaim] Rabin).
    21 March. 18 double-sided pp.
Bergman, Shmuel Hugo 1952 Letters to F.B.S. 22 February and 4 June.
Bohannan, Laura and Paul 1949-51 Four letters from the field to F.B.S.
Bruell, Paul Letters to H.G.A 11 November, 28 December 1955; 28 March, 4
    April 1958. With Transcripts of F.B.S's letters to Bruell 3 February, 9
    August, 9 November 1936; 22 December 1937.
*Buchanan, Diana 1953 Letter to H.G.A. 20 June.
Canetti, Elias 26 Letters to F.B.S. 18 February 1939-5 July 1952.
Canetti, Veza 23 Letters to F.B.S. ca. 14 August 1939- ca. 14 March 1952.
Douglas [Tew], Mary Five letters to F.B.S., ca.1950-51.
Frank, Esther 1964 'Erinnerungen an F.B. Steiner'. (Memories of F.B.
    Steiner). Typescript. Prepared by H.G.A. 4-8 May. 9 pp.
Forde, Daryll, Seven Letters to F.B.S. written between 25 June 1947 and 15
    May 1950.
Marcus, Joseph, Four letters to F.B.S., 28 January 1942, 29 June 1942, 26
    December 1945, 29 March 1946.
Radcliffe-Brown, A.R. 1942 Testimonial for F.B.S. to the Czechoslovak Min-
    istry of the Interior. 6 January.

iii. F.B.S.'s Unpublished Writings and Other Sources in the Institute for Social and Cultural Anthropology, University of Oxford

Faculty of Anthropology and Geography *Lecture Lists: 1943-4 to 1952-3.*
    Oxford University Gazette.
Franz Baermann Steiner 'Lectures and Papers. Oxford 1949-1952'. Bound
    Volume. Typescript. Contains 'Lectures on Tabu' (229pp.), 'Division and
    Organisation of Labour' (102pp.), 'On Gutmann's *Das Recht der Dschagga*'
    (40pp.), 'Notes on Comparative Economics' (20pp.). Typescript prepared
    for publication by Laura and Paul Bohannan.

iv. F.B.S.'s Letters to Veza and Elias Canetti. Private Collection, Zürich

Ca. 115 letters written between ca. 11 July 1940 and ca. 14 August 1952.

v. F.B.S.'s Letters to Isabella von Miller-Aichholz.
Private Collection, Vienna
20 letters written between 11 February 1951 and 2 June 1952. Manuscripts and typescripts.

vi. Letters and Other Written Communications to the Editors

The names of all sources who provided personal communications to us verbally and by fax, e-mail or letter are given in our acknowledgements. We here list additional writings, memoirs etc. in our possession.

Chandavarkar, Anand 1996 'Remembering Franz Steiner. Some random notes.' Typescript. 3pp.

Douglas, Mary 1994 Conversation. 14 January. Typescript. 4pp.

Murdoch, Iris 1952-3 References to F.B.S. in Journals. Edited and transcribed by Peter Conradi. 1997 Typescript. 5pp.

Pitt-Rivers, Julian 1997 Memoirs. Typescript. Extract. 4 pp. Numbered 36-40.

Wright, David 1993 Letter to the editors of 10 July. With copies of three undated letters from F.B.S.

Ziegler, Nicolas 1994 'Die Versenkung des Flüchtlingstransporters Struma' (On the Sinking of the Refugee Vessel *Struma*). Typescript with chart. 8pp.

———, 1996 'Zu Federbaum *iberis semperflorens*' (On the feathered tree *iberis semperflorens*). Typescript with drawing and xerox. 3pp.

II. Published Sources

i. A Selection of F.B.S.'s Published Writings

1935   Lešehrad, Emanuel *Die Planeten*, translated from the Czech by Franz B. Steiner, Prague: Orbis.

*1936   'Orientpolitik', *Selbstwehr. Jüdisches Volksblatt*, 30, 41, Prague, 1 October: 6-7.

*1938   'The Gypsies in Carpathian Russia', *Central European Observer*, 16, 5, Prague, 4 March: 70-71.

1939a   'Skinboats and the Yakut "xayik"', *Ethnos* 4(3-4): 177-83.

1939b   'Hundeopfer und Wehengeständnis, ihre Beziehungen zum Nordeurasischen Wiedergeburtsglauben' (Dog sacrifice and parturition confession, their relations to North-Eurasian beliefs in reincarnation). Abstract of a paper delivered to the Congrès International des Sciences Anthropologiques et Ethnologiques, Deuxième Session, Copenhagen 1938.

1941   'Some Parallel Developments of the Semilunar Knife', *Man* 41, January/February, Article No. 3: 10-13.

1950a   'Amharic Language', *Chamber's Encyclopaedia*, London, I, 371.

1950b   'Danakil' *Chamber's Encyclopaedia*, London, IV, 359.

1950c   'Galla' *Chamber's Encyclopaedia*, London, VI, 371.

1950d   'Somalis' *Chamber's Encyclopaedia*, London, XII, 705.

1951   Review of J.P. Murdock *Social Structure*, *British Journal of Sociology* 2(4): 366-68.

1952   Review of Sylvia Pankhurst *Ex-Italian Somaliland, British Journal of Sociology* 3(3): 280-81.

*1954a   'Enslavement and the Early Hebrew Lineage System: an Explanation of Genesis 47: 29-31, 48: 1-16', *Man* 54, No. 102: 73-75.

*1954b   'Notes on Comparative Economics', *British Journal of Sociology* 5(2): 118-29.

*1954c   'Chagga Truth. A Note on Gutmann's Account of the Chagga Concept of Truth in *Das Recht der Dschagga'*, *Africa* 24(4): 364-69.

1954d   *Unruhe ohne Uhr. Ausgewählte Gedichte*, (ed.) H.G. Adler, Veröffentlichungen der Deutschen Akademie für Sprache und Dichtung 3, Darmstadt: Lambert Schneider.

*1956a   *Taboo*, with a Preface by E.E. Evans-Pritchard, London: Cohen and West.

1956b   'Sätze und Fragen' (a selection of aphorisms), *Neue Deutsche Hefte* 29, September, pp. 356-58.

*1957   'Towards a Classification of Labour', *Sociologus* NS 7(2): 112-30.

1964   *Eroberungen. Ein lyrischer Zyklus*, (ed.) H.G. Adler, Veröffentlichungen der Deutschen Akademie für Sprache und Dichtung 33, Darmstadt: Lambert Schneider.

1967   *Taboo*, with a Preface by E.E. Evans-Pritchard, Harmondsworth: Pelican.

1983   'Notiz zur vergleichenden Ökonomie', translation of 1954b by Peter Bumke, in Kramer, Fritz and Sigrist, Christian (eds) *Gesellschaft ohne Staat. Gleichheit und Gegenseitigkeit*, Frankfurt am Main: Syndikat, pp.85-100.

1988   *Fluchtvergnüglichkeit.Feststellungen und Versuche* (ed.) Marion Hermann, Frankfurt: Flugasche.

1992   *Modern Poetry in Translation: Franz Baermann Steiner*, New Series No.2, with translations and an introduction by Michael Hamburger, London: King's College.

1995   'Feststellungen und Versuche. Aufzeichnungen über Gesellschaft, Macht, Geschichte und verwandte Themen' (ed.) Jeremy Adler, *Akzente* 42(3): 213-27. Includes 'Über den Prozess der Zivilisierung' (On the Process of Civilisation).

2000   *Gesammelte Gedichte*, (ed.) Jeremy Adler, Deutsche Akademie für Sprache und Dichtung, Darmstadt; Göttingen: Wallstein Verlag.

ii) Published Sources Cited in the Introductions to Volume I and Volume II

Adler, H.G., 1960 *Theresienstadt 1941-1945. Das Antlitz einer Zwangsgemeinschaft*, 2nd edn, Tübingen: J.C.B. Mohr (Paul Siebeck).

————, 1976 'Die Dichtung der Prager Schule', in *Im Brennpunkt ein Österreich*, Manfred Wagner (ed.), Beiträge zur österreichischen Kultur- und Geistesgeschichte Volume 1, Vienna: Europaverlag, pp. 67-98.

————, 1998 *Der Wahrheit verpflichtet. Interviews. Gedichte. Essays* (ed.) Jeremy Adler, Gerlingen: Bleicher Verlag.

Adler, Jeremy, 1992 'The Poet as Anthropologist: on the Aphorisms of Franz Baermann Steiner', in E. Timms and R. Robertson (eds) *Austrian Studies III: Psychoanalysis in its Cultural Context*, Edinburgh: Edinburgh University Press, pp.145-57.

————, 1994a '"The step swings away" and other poems by Franz Baermann Steiner' (translated and introduced), *Comparative Criticism* 16: 139-68.

————, 1994b 'Special bibliography: the writings of Franz Baermann Steiner (1909-52)', *Comparative Criticism* 16: 281-92.

————, 1994c 'An Oriental in the West: the originality of Franz Steiner as poet and anthropologist', *Times Literary Supplement* 7 October, pp. 16-17.

————, 1995a 'Die Freundschaft zwischen Elias Canetti und Franz Steiner', *Akzente* 42 (3): 213-27.

————, 1995b 'Erich Fried, F.B.Steiner and an Unknown Group of Exile Poets in London', in *Literatur und Kultur des Exils in Großbritanien*, Zwischenwelt 4 (ed.) Siglinde Bolbecher *et al.*, Vienna: Theodor Kramer Gesellschaft, pp.163-92.

————, 1996 'Franz Baermann Steiner: A Prague Poet in England', in *'England? Aber wo liegt es?' Deutsche und österreichische Emigranten in Großbritannien 1933-1945*, Charmian Brinson *et al.* (eds) Munich: iudicium, pp. 125-40.

————, 1998 'H.G.Adler is Deported to Theresienstadt ...', in *Yale Companion to Jewish Writing and Thought in German Culture, 1096-1996* (ed.) Sander L.Gilman and Jack Zipes, New Haven and London: Yale University Press, pp. 599-605.

Adorno, Theodor and Horkheimer, Max, (1944) 1988 *Dialektik der Aufklärung. Philosophische Fragmente*, Frankfurt am Main: Fischer Taschenbuch.

————, (1972) 1979 *Dialectic of Enlightenment*, trans. John Cumming, London: Verso.

Adorno, Theodor W., 1992 'Um Benjamins Werk. Briefe an Gershom Scholem 1930-1955', *Frankfurter Adorno Blätter* V: 143-84.

Anderson, Perry, 1968 'Components of the National Culture', *New Left Review*, July-August 50: 3-57.

Anon, 1956 Review of *Taboo*, *The Listener* 23 August: 281.

Anon, 1957 Review of *Taboo*, *Times Supplement* 18 January: 18.

Anon (Rodney Needham), 1967 'Dirt is disorder', Review of Mary Douglas 1966 *Purity and Danger*, *Times Literary Supplement*, 16 February, p. 131.

Anon, 'The Oldest System-Program of German Idealism', in Pfau, Thomas 1988 *Friedrich Hölderlin: Essays and Letters on Theory*, trans. and ed. Thomas Pfau, Albany: State University of New York Press, pp. 154-56.

Atze, Marcel, 1998 *Ortlose Botschaft. H.G. Adler, Elias Canetti, Franz Baermann Steiner. Ein Freundeskreis im englischen Exil*, Marbach: *Marbacher Magazin* 84.

Banse, Ewald, 1929 *Frauenbilder des Morgenlands*, Schaubücher 5, Zürich und Leipzig: Orell Füssli Verlag.

Barnouw, Dagmar, 1979 *Elias Canetti*, Sammlung Metzler 180, Stuttgart: Metzler.

Bartolf, Christian 1998 (ed.), *Wir wollen die Gewalt nicht. Die Buber-Gandhi-Kontroverse*, Berlin: Gandhi-Informations-Zentrum

Baur, John I. H., 1961 *Bernard Reder*, New York: Whitney Museum and Frederick A. Praeger.

Bayley, John, 1998 *Iris. A Memoir of Iris Murdoch*, London: Gerald Duckworth and Co.

Beattie, John, 1964 *Other Cultures*, London: Cohen and West.

Beidelman, T.O., 1966 Review of Mary Douglas 1966 *Purity and Danger*, *Anthropos* 61(3-6): 907-8.

Bell, Matthew, 1994 *Goethe's Naturalistic Anthropology. Man and Other Plants*, Oxford: Clarendon Press.

Benn, Gottfried, 1966 *Gedichte. Gesammelte Werke*, Vol. 3, Wiesbaden: Limes.

Berghahn, Marion, (1984) 1988 *German-Jewish Refugees from Nazi Germany*, Oxford and New York: Berg.

Bergman, Shmuel Hugo, 1950 'A Great Task', in Manka Spiegel (ed.), *The Hebrew University of Jerusalem. April 1950. Semi-Jubilee Volume*, Jerusalem: Goldberg's Press.

————, 1961 *Faith and Reason. An Introduction to Modern Jewish Thought*, trans. and ed. by Alfred Jospe, New York: Schocken Books.

————, 1969 'Erinnerungen an Franz Kafka', in *Exhibition. Franz Kafka*, ed. Reuben Klingsberg, Catalogue of an Exhibition at the Jewish National and University Library, Jerusalem: Daf Chen, pp. 2-12.

————, 1985 *Tagebücher und Briefe*, 2 vols, I: *1901-1948*, II: *1948-1975*, (ed.) Miriam Sambursky, Königstein/Taunus: Jüdischer Verlag bei Atheneum.

Bohannan, Laura, 1949 'Dahomean Marriage: a Revaluation', *Africa* 19(4): 273-87.

Bohannan, Paul, 1963 *Social Anthropology*, New York and London: Holt, Rhinehart and Winston.

von Bormann, Alexander, (1983) 'Romantik', in Walter Hinderer, ed., *Geschichte der deutschen Lyrik vom Mittelalter bis zur Gegenwart* (1983) Stuttgart: Reclam.

Branden, S.G.F.,1958 Review of *Taboo*, *British Journal of Sociology* 9(1) March: 104.

Brod, Max, 1966 *Der Prager Kreis*. Stuttgart and Berlin: Kohlhammer.

Brown, Judith M., 1989 *Gandhi: Prisoner of Hope*, New Haven and London: Yale University Press.

Bryant, Clifton D., (ed.), 1972 'Introduction', *The Social Dimension of Work*, Englewood Cliffs, New Jersey: Prentice Hall.

Bumke, Peter, 1983 'Vorbemerkung', 'Tausch und Wert in Stammesgesellschaften', in Kramer, Fritz and Sigrist, Christian (eds) *Gesellschaft ohne Staat. Gleichheit und Gegenseitigkeit*, Frankfurt am Main: Syndikat, pp. 47-51.

Bunzl, Matti, 1996 'Franz Boas and the Humboldtian Tradition. From *Volksgeist* and *Nationalcharakter* to an Anthropological Concept of Culture', in George W. Stocking Jr. (ed.) *Volksgeist as Method and Ethic. Essays on Boasian Ethnography and the German Anthropological Tradition*, History of Anthropology 8, Madison: University of Wisconsin Press, pp. 17-78.

Burton, John W., 1992 *An Introduction to Evans-Pritchard*, Fribourg: University Press, Studia Instituti Anthropos vol. 45.

Buschan, Georg 1922-26 *Illustrierte Völkerkunde*, 3 vols, Stuttgart: Strecker und Schröder.

Canetti, Elias, 1960 *Masse und Macht*, Hamburg: Claassen.

————, 1962 *Crowds and Power*, transl. Carol Stewart, London: Gollancz.

————, 1966 *Aufzeichnungen 1942-1948*, Munich: Hanser.

————, 1978 *Das Gewissen der Worte. Essays*, Munich: Deutscher Taschenbuch Verlag.

————, (1979) 1987 *The Conscience of the Words* and *Earwitness* trans. Joachim Neugroschel, London: Picador.

————, 1985 *Das Augenspiel. Lebensgeschichte 1931-1937*, Munich: Hanser.

————, 1995 'Franz Steiner', in 'Aufzeichnungen 1992', *Akzente* 3 June 1995: 204-209; reprinted in 1996 *Aufzeichnungen 1992-1993*, Munich: Hanser, pp.17-24.

Chadha, Yogesh, 1997 *Rediscovering Gandhi*, London: Century.

Chandavarkar, Anand, 1994 'Franz Steiner', Letter to the Editor, *The Times Literary Supplement*, 25 November: 25.

Clifford, James, 1988 'On Ethnographic Self-Fashioning: Conrad and Malinowski', in James Clifford, *The Predicament of Culture. Twentieth-Century Ethnography, Literature, and Art*, Cambridge, MA, and London: Harvard University Press.

Cohn, W., 1957 Review of *Taboo*, *American Sociological Review* 22 (1) January: 132.

Collini, Stefan, 1996 'Outsiders and the "Reformer's Science"', *The Times Literary Supplement* 28 June: 4-5.

Conradi, Peter J., 1989 *Iris Murdoch: the Saint and the Artist*, 2nd edn, Basingstoke and London: Macmillan Studies in Twentieth-Century Literature.

————, 1997 'Preface', to Iris Murdoch *Existentialists and Mystics: Writings on Philosophy and Literature*, London: Chatto and Windus.

Cranstone, B.A.L. and Steven Seidenberg (eds), 1984 *The General's Gift: A Celebration of the Pitt Rivers Museum Centenary 1884-1984, Journal of the Anthropological Society of Oxford Occasional Papers*, No 3.

Dalton, Dennis, 1993 *Mahatma Gandhi: Nonviolent Power in Action*, New York: Columbia University Press.

Defoe, Daniel, (1719) 1994 *Robinson Crusoe*, Harmondsworth: Penguin Popular Classics.

Demetz, Peter, (ed.), 1982 *Alt-Prager Geschichten*, Frankfurt: Insel.

————, 1997 *Prague in Black and Gold. The History of a City*, London: Allen Lane. The Penguin Press.

Douglas, Mary, 1964 'Taboo', *New Society*, 12 March: 24-5.

————, (1966) 1984 *Purity and Danger: An Analysis of the Concepts of Pollution and Taboo*, London: Routledge and Kegan Paul.

————, 1975 *Implicit Meanings. Essays in Anthropology*, London and New York: Routledge.

————, 1980 *Evans-Pritchard*, Glasgow: Fontana Modern Masters.

Drehscheibe Prag. Deutsche Emigranten. Staging Point Prague. German Exiles 1933-1939 1989 Exhibition Catalogue (ed.) Peter Becher, Munich: Adalbert Stifter Verein.

Dubois, C., 1957 Review of *Taboo, American Anthropologist* 59 (2) April: 357-8.

Dumont, Louis, 1966 *Homo hierarchicus: le système des castes et ses implications*, Paris: Editions Gallimard.

Eichner, Hans, 1970 *Friedrich Schlegel*, New York: Twayne.

Evans-Pritchard, E.E., 1951a 'The Institute of Social Anthropology', *The Oxford Magazine*, 26 April: 354-60.

————, 1951b *Social Anthropology*, London: Cohen and West.

————, 1951c 'Some Features of Nuer Religion', R.A.I. Presidential Address, *Journal of the Royal Anthropological Institute* 81: 1-12.

————, 1952 'Obituary Franz Baermann Steiner: 1908-1952' [1909-1952], *Man* 52, No 264: 161.

————, 1956a *Nuer Religion*, Oxford: O.U.P.

————, 1956b 'Preface' to Franz Steiner, *Taboo*, London: Cohen and West, pp. 11-13.

————, 1959 'The Teaching of Social Anthropology at Oxford', *Man* 59, July, No. 180: 121-24.

————, 1962a 'Social Anthropology: Past and Present' (The Marrett Lecture, 1950), in E.-P., *Essays in Social Anthropology*, London: Faber and Faber, pp. 13-28.

————, 1962b 'Religion and the Anthropologists' (The Aquinas Lecture, 1960), in E.-P. *Essays in Social Anthropology*, London: Faber and Faber, pp. 29-45.

————, 1962c 'Anthropology and History' (Simon Lecture, University of Manchester, 1961), in E.-P. *Essays in Social Anthropology*, London: Faber and Faber, pp. 46-65.

————, 1965a 'The Comparative Method in Social Anthropology' (L.T. Hobhouse Memorial Trust Lecture, 1963), in E.-P. *The Position of Women in Primitive Societies and Other Essays in Social Anthropology*, London: Faber and Faber, pp. 13-36.

————, 1965b *Theories of Primitive Religion* (Sir D. Owen Evans Lectures at the University College of Wales, Aberystwyth, 1962), London: Oxford University Press.

————, 1970 'Social Anthropology at Oxford', *Journal of the Anthropological Society of Oxford* 1(3): 103-9.

————, 1973 'Genesis of a Social Anthropologist', *The New Diffusionist* 3: 17-23.

————, 1981 *A History of Anthropological Thought*, ed. André Singer, London: Faber and Faber.

Fardon, Richard, 1990 'Malinowski's Precedent: The Imagination of Equality', *Man* NS 25 (4): 569-87.

————, 1999 *Mary Douglas: An Intellectual Biography*, London and New York: Routledge.

Fárová, Anna, 1986 *František Drtikol. Photograph des Art Deco*, (ed.) Manfred Heiting, Munich: Schirmer Mosel.

Firth, Raymond, 1975 'An appraisal of Modern Social Anthropology', *Annual Review of Anthropology* 4: 1-25.

Fleischli, Alfons, 1970 *Franz Baermann Steiner. Leben und Werk*, Dissertation, University of Freiburg (Switzerland), Hochdorf: Buchdruckerei Hochdorf AG.

Fortes, Meyer, 1978 'An Anthropologist's Apprenticeship', *Annual Review of Anthropology* 7: 1-30.

Freud, Sigmund, 1930 *Das Unbehagen in der Kultur*, Vienna: Internationaler Psychoanalytischer Verlag.

Friedmann, Maurice, 1988 *Martin Buber's Life and Work. The Early Years 1878-1923*, London and Tunbridge Wells: Search Press.

Gandhi, M.K., 1946 'Jews and Palestine', *Harijan: a Journal of Applied Gandhism*, 21 July: 229. Excerpted in *The Jewish Chronicle*, 26 July (27 Tammuz 5706).

Gellner, David, 1997 'Preface' to Ernest Gellner *Nationalism*, London: Weidenfeld and Nicholson.

Gellner, Ernest, 1998 *Language and Solitude: Wittgenstein, Malinowski and the Habsburg Dilemma*, Cambridge: Cambridge University Press.

Gilbert, Martin, 1998 *Israel: A History*, London, Moorebank NSW and Auckland: Doubleday.

Gillies, A., 1945 *Herder*, Oxford: Blackwell.

Godwin, Joscelyn, 1979 *Robert Fludd. Hermetic Philosopher and Surveyor of Two Worlds*, London: Thames and Hudson.

Goldberg, David J., 1996 *To the Promised Land: A History of Zionist Political Thought from its Origins to the Modern State of Israel*, Harmondsworth: Penguin.

Goody, Jack, 1995 *The Expansive Moment*, Cambridge: Cambridge University Press.

Gopal, Sarvepalli, 1975 *Jawaharlal Nehru: A Biography, Vol I 1889-1947*, London: Jonathan Cape.

Graebner, F., 1911 *Die Methode der Ethnologie*, Heidelberg: Winter.

Green, Bryan S., 1988 *Literary Methods and Sociological Theory. Case Studies of Simmel and Weber*, Chicago and London: University of Chicago Press.

Habermas, Jürgen, 1985 *The Philosophical Discourse of Modernity*, translated by Frederick Lawrence, Cambridge: Polity Press.

Haddon, Alfred C., 1934 *History of Anthropology*, The Thinker's Library, No. 42, London: Watts and Co.

Hamburger, Michael, 1992 'Introduction', in *Modern Poetry in Translation. Franz Baermann Steiner. With Translations by Michael Hamburger*, New Series, No. 2, 5-21.

Hamburger, Michael and Middleton, Christopher, 1962 *Modern German Poetry 1910-1962. An Anthology with Verse Translations*, London: MacGibbon and Kee.

Hamilton, Ian, 1996 'Life and Letters; An Oxford Union', *New Yorker*, 19 February: 70-74.

Harris, Marvin, 1968 *The Rise of Anthropological Theory. A History of Theories of Culture*, London: Routledge and Kegan Paul.

Hatto, Arthur T. 1995 'Ethnopoetik: Traum oder Möglichkeit?' *Nordrhein-Westfälische Akademie der Wissenschaften*, Abhandlungen 95, *Formen mündlicher Tradition*: 11-25.

Haumann, Heiko, 1990 *Geschichte der Ostjuden*, Munich: Deutscher Taschenbuch Verlag.

Heine-Geldern, Robert, 1964 'One Hundred Years of Ethnological Theory in the German-Speaking Countries: Some Milestones', *Current Anthropology* 5(5): 407-18.

Hermann-Röttgen, Marion, 1988 'Nachwort' in Marion Hermann-Röttgen (ed.) Franz Baermann Steiner, *Fluchtvergnüglichkeit. Feststellungen und Versuche*, Stuttgart: Flugasche, 129-38.

Hirschfeld, Gerhard, 1996 'Durchgangsland England? Die britische 'Academic Community' und die wissenschaftliche Emigration aus Deutschland', in *'England? Aber wo liegt es?' Deutsche und österreichische Emigranten in Großbritannien 1933-1945*, Charmian Brinson et al. (eds) Munich: iudicium., pp. 59-70.

Hoensch, J.K., 1987 *Geschichte Böhmens*, Munich: Beck.

Hoffmann, Dierk O., 1982 *Paul Leppin. Eine Skizze mit einer ersten Bibliographie der Werke und Briefe*, Bonn: Bouvier.

————, 1997 'Czech Nationalists Occupy the German Landestheater / Ständetheater in Prague' in *Yale Companion to Jewish Writing and Thought in German Culture, 1096-1996* Sander L.Gilman and Jack Zipes (eds), New Haven and London: Yale University Press, pp. 390-394.

von Humboldt, Wilhelm, (1836) 1848 *Über die Verschiedenheit des menschlichen Sprachbaues und ihren Einfluß auf die geistige Entwicklung des Menschengeschlechts*, in Wilhelm von Humboldt, *Gesammelte Werke* Vol. VI, Berlin: Reimer, pp. 1-425.

Huntingford, G.W.B., 1955 *The Galla of Ethiopia. The Kingdoms of Kafa and Janjero*, Part II, *North-Eastern Africa, Ethnographic Survey of Africa* (ed.) Daryll Forde, London: International African Institute.

'Institute of Social Anthropology. Annual Report 1948-9', 1949 *Oxford University Gazette* 79, 4 August: 1186-87.

'Institute of Social Anthropology. Annual Report 1949-50', 1950 *Oxford University Gazette* 80, 3 August: 1136.

'Institute of Social Anthropology. Annual Report 1950-1', 1951 *Oxford University Gazette* 81, 26 July: 1199-1200.

'Institute of Social Anthropology. Annual Report 1951-2', *Oxford University Gazette* 82, 31 July: 1207-8.

'Institute of Social Anthropology. Annual Report 1952-3', 1953 *Oxford University Gazette* 83, 30 July: 1182-83.

Jamme, Christoph and Schneider, Helmut, 1984 eds. *Mythologie der Vernunft. Hegels 'ältestes Systemprogramm' des deutschen Idealismus*, Frankfurt: Suhrkamp.

Janik, Allan and Toulmin, Stephen, 1973 *Wittgenstein's Vienna*, New York: Simon and Schuster.

Kafka, Franz, 1958 *Briefe 1902-1924*, Frankfurt: Fischer.

Kaiser, Gerhard, 1996 *Geschichte der deutschen Lyrik von Goethe bis zur Gegenwart*, Vol. I, *Von Goethe bis Heine*, Frankfurt: Suhrkamp.

Kapitza, Peter, 1968 *Die frühromantische Theorie der Mischung. Über den Zusammenhang von romantischer Dichtungstheorie und zeitgenössischer Chemie*, Münchener Germanistische Beiträge 4, Munich: Hueber.

Kieval, Hill J., 1988 *The Making of Czech Jewry. National Conflict and Jewish Society in Bohemia, 1970-1918*, New York and Oxford: Oxford University Press.

Kluback, William, 1988 'The "Believing Humanism" of Shmuel Hugo Bergman', *Review of the Society for the History of Jews from Czechoslovakia*, 89: 129-39.

Kolmar, Gertrud, 1970 *Briefe an die SchwesterHilde (1938-1943)*, Munich: Kösel.

Krejčí, Jaroslav and Machonin, Pavel, 1996 *Czechoslovakia, 1918-92. A Laboratory for Social Change*, London and New York: Macmillan Press Ltd.

Kuper, Adam, (1973) 1996 *Anthropology and Anthropologists: the Modern British School*, 3rd edn, London: Routledge.

————, 1977 (ed.) *The Social Anthropology of Radcliffe-Brown*, London: Routledge and Kegan Paul.

Kuper, Hilda, 1984 'Function, history, biography: reflections on fifty years in the British anthropological tradition', in George W. Stocking Jnr. (ed.) *Functionalism Historicized: Essays in British Social Anthropology, History of Anthropology* Vol. 2, Madison: University of Wisconsin Press, pp. 192-213.

Lang, Bernhard, 1984 'Spione im gelobten Land: Ethnologen als Leser des Alten Testaments', *Ethnologie als Sozialwissenschaft*, Sonderheft 26: 158-77.

Lanternari, V., 1957 Review of *Taboo, Studi e Materiali di Storia delle Religioni* 28 (1): 137-38.

Leach, Edmund R., 1984 'Glimpses of the unmentionable in the history of British anthropology', *Annual Review of Anthropology* 13: 1-23.

Leppin, Paul, 1905 *Daniel Jesus. Ein Roman*. Berlin [Magazin Verlag] and Leipzig: F. Rothbarth.

Lessing, G.E. (1756) 1973 *Briefwechsel über das Trauerspiel*, in *Werke*, (ed.) H.G. Göpfert, Vol. IV, *Dramaturgische Schriften*, Munich: Hanser, pp.153-227.

Lévi-Strauss, Claude, 1962 *Le totémisme aujourd'hui*, Paris: Presses Universitaires de Paris.

Lewis, Ioan, 1955 *Peoples of the Horn of Africa: Somali, Afar and Saho*, Part I, North-Eastern Africa, Ethnographic survey of Africa (ed.) Daryll Forde, London: International African Institute.

Lichtenberg, Georg, 1968-92 *Schriften und Briefe* (ed.) Wolfgang Promies, 6 vols, Munich: Hanser.

Liebersohn, Harry, 1988 *Fate and Utopia in German Sociology, 1870-1923*, Cambridge, MA and London: MIT Press.

Lienhardt, Godfrey, 1961 *Divinity and Experience: the Religion of the Dinka*, Oxford: Clarendon Press.

————, 1964 *Social Anthropology*, Oxford: Oxford University Press.

————, 1974 'E-P: A Personal View. Sir Edward Evans-Pritchard, 1902-1973', *Man NS* 9: 299-304.

Lindenberger, Herbert, 1971, *Georg Trakl*, New York: Twayne.

Lips, Julius, n.d. *Einleitung in die vergleichende Völkerkunde*, Leipzig: Weimann.

Lowie, Robert H., 1937 *The History of Ethnological Theory*, New York: Rinehart and Company.

Mach, Ernst, 1900 *Die Analyse der Empfindungen*, 2nd, rev. edn, Jena: Gustav Fischer.

Malinowski, Bronislaw, 1923 'The Problem of Meaning in Primitive Language', supplement 1 in Ogden, C.K. and Richards, I.A. *The Meaning of Meaning. A Study of the Influence of Language upon Thought and the Science of Symbolism*, London: Routledge and Kegan Paul, 296-336.

––––––, 1967 *A Diary in the Strict Sense of the Term*, London: Routledge and Kegan Paul.

Mayer, Reinhold, 1963 (ed.), *Der babylonische Talmud*, Munich: Goldmann.

Melville, Hermann, (1851) 1938 *Moby Dick or The Whale*, with an introduction by Viola Meynell, The World's Classics, London: Humphrey Milford.

Meyrink, Gustav, 1915 *Der Golem. Ein Roman*, Leipzig: Kurt Wolff.

Milbank, John, 1990 *Theology and Social Theory: Beyond Secular Reason*, Oxford: Basil Blackwell.

Murdoch, Iris, 1956 *The Flight from the Enchanter*, London: Chatto and Windus.

––––––, 1989 *The Message to the Planet*, London: Chatto and Windus.

––––––, 1997 *Existentialists and Mystics: Writings on Philosophy and Literature*, London: Chatto and Windus.

Neubauer, John, 1978 *Symbolismus und symbolische Logik. Die Idee der ars combinatoria in der Entwicklung der modernen Dichtung*, Humanistische Bibliothek 28, Munich: Fink.

––––––, 1980 *Novalis*, Boston: Twayne.

Nietzsche, Friedrich, 1954 *Die Geburt der Tragödie*, in *Werke* (ed.) K.Schlechta, Vol. I, Munich: Hanser, pp. 7-134.

O'Brien, William Arctander, 1995 *Novalis: Sign of Revolution*, Durham: Duke University Press.

Orwell, George, 1970 *Collected Essays, Journalism and Letters*, Vol. 1, Harmondsworth: Penguin.

Perckhammer, Heinz, 1930 *Von China und Chinesen*, Schaubücher 28, Zürich und Leipzig: Orell Füssli Verlag.

Pitt-Rivers, Julian, (1954) 1971 *The People of the Sierra* 2nd edn, Chicago and London: University of Chicago Press.

Plichta, Dalibor, 1961 *Mary Durasová*, Prague: Nakladatestvi Československých Výtvarných Ulemělců.

Polišenský, J.V., 1991 (1947) *History of Czechoslovakia in Outline*, Prague: Bohemia International.

Primus, Zdeněk, 1990 *Tschechische Avantgarde 1922-1940. Reflexe europäischer Kunst und Fotografie in der Buchgestaltung*, exhibition catalogue, Münster-Schwarzach: Vier-Türme-Verlag.

Radcliffe-Brown, A.R., 1933 'Social Sanctions', *Encyclopaedia of the Social Sciences*, Vol. XIII, New York: Macmillan, pp. 531-34.

––––––, 1940 'On Social Structure', *Journal of the Royal Anthropological Institute* 70, reprinted in Radcliffe-Brown 1952, pp.188-204.

––––––, 1951a 'Review' of E.E. Evans-Pritchard 1951 *Social Anthropology*, *British Journal of Sociology* 2: 365-66.

————, 1951b 'The Comparative Method in Social Anthropology', The Huxley Memorial Lecture for 1951, *Journal of the Royal Anthropological Institute* 81: 15-22, reprinted in Adam Kuper (ed.) 1977 *The Social Anthropology of Radcliffe-Brown*, London, Henley and Boston: Routledge and Kegan Paul, pp. 53-69.

————, 1952 *Structure and Function in Primitive Society: Essays and Addresses*, London: Cohen and West.

Raglan, Lord, 1957 Review of *Taboo, Man* 57 Feb: 27.

Ratzel, Friedrich 1885, 1885, 1888 *Völkerkunde* 3 vols, Leipzig: Bibliographisches Institut.

Richards, I.A., 1925 *Principles of Literary Criticism*, London and New York: Kegan Paul and Harcourt Brace.

Rilke, Rainer Maria, 1955 *Duineser Elegien*, in *Sämtliche Werke*, (ed.) Ernst Zinn, Vol. I. Frankfurt am Main: Insel, pp. 683-726.

Ripellino, Angelo Maria 1994 *Magic Prague*, translated by D. N. Marinelli, London: Macmillan.

Ritchie J.M., 1998 *German Exiles. British Perspectives*, Exile Studies 6, New York etc.: Lang.

Rothenberg, Jerome, (ed.) (1968) 1985 *Technicians of the Sacred. A Range of Poetries from Africa, America, Asia, Europe & Oceana*, 2nd edn, Berkeley: University of California Press.

Rothenberg, Jerome and Rothenberg, Diane, 1983 *Symposium of the Whole. A Range of Discourse Toward an Ethnopoetics*, Berkeley: University of California Press.

Rybár, Ctibor, 1991a *Židoská Praha*, Prague: TV Spektrum and Akropolis.

————, 1991b *Das jüdische Prag*, Prague: TV Spektrum and Akropolis.

Ryding, James N., 1975 'Alternatives in nineteenth-century German Ethnology: a case study in the Sociology of Science', *Sociologus* 25: 1-28.

Sayer, Derek, 1998 *The Coasts of Bohemia. A Czech History*, New Jersey: Princeton University Press.

Schapera, Isaac, 1955 'The Sin of Cain', *Journal of the Royal Anthropological Institute* 85: 33-43.

Schiffer, Reinhold, 1979 'Ethnopoetics: Some aspects of American Avant-Garde Primitivism', *Dutch Quarterly Review of Anglo-American Letters* 9:1, 39-51.

Schmidt, Gilya Gerda, 1991 *Martin Buber's Formative Years*, Tuscaloosa: University of Alabama Press.

Scholem, Gershom, 1941 *Major Trends in Jewish Mysticism*, Jerusalem: Schocken.

————, 1956 'Seelenwanderung und Sympathie der Seelen in der jüdischen Mystik', *Eranos Jahrbuch* XXIV: 55-118.

————, 1963 *Judaica 1*, Frankfurt: Suhrkamp.

Serke, Jürgen, 1987 *Böhmische Dörfer. Wanderung durch eine verlassene literarische Landschaft*, Vienna and Hamburg: Zsolnay.

Sharp, Francis Michael, 1981 *The Poet's Madness. A Reading of Georg Trakl*, Ithaca and London: Cornell University Press.

Sheppard, Richard, 1994 *Ernst Stadler (1883-1914). A German Expressionist Poet at Oxford*. Magdalen College Occasional Paper 2, Oxford: Magdalen College.

Shimoni, Gideon, 1977 *Gandhi, Satyagraha and the Jews: a Formative Factor in India's Policy towards Israel*, Jersusalem Peace Papers, Jerusalem: Leonard Davis Institute for International Relations at the Hebrew University of Jerusalem and the Jerusalem Post.

Simmel, Georg, 1923 *Soziologie. Untersuchungen über die Formen der Vergesellschaftung*, 3rd edn, Munich and Leipzig: Duncker und Humblot.

———, (1900) 1920 *Philosophie des Geldes*, 3rd edn, Munich and Leipzig: Duncker und Humblot.

Sombart, Werner, 1902, *Der moderne Kapitalismus*, 2 vols. Leipzig: Duncker und Humblot.

———, 1911, *Die Juden und das Wirtschaftsleben*, Leipzig: Duncker und Humblot.

Spender, Stephen, 'Amateurs of Poetry: *Poetry London No. Ten: New Poets Number*, *The Sunday Times*, 4 March 1944.

Spiegel, Manka (ed.), 1950 *The Hebrew University of Jerusalem: 1925-50*, Semi Jubilee Volume, Jerusalem: Goldberg's Press Ltd.

Srinivas, M.N., 1952 *Religion and Society among the Coorgs of South India*, Oxford: Clarendon.

———, 1973 'Itineraries of an Indian Social Anthropologist', *International Social Science Journal* 25: 129-48.

Stocking, George W. Jnr, (1968) 1982 *Race, Culture, and Evolution: Essays in the History of Anthropology*, Chicago: University of Chicago Press.

———, (1995) 1996 *After Tylor: British Social Anthropology 1888-1951*, London: Athlone.

———, (ed.) 1984a 'Dr Durkheim and Mr Brown: Comparative Sociology at Cambridge in 1910', in George W. Stocking Jnr (ed.) *Functionalism Historicized: Essays in British Social Anthropology*, History of Anthropology Vol. 2, Madison: University of Wisconsin Press, pp. 106-30.

———, (ed.) 1984b *Functionalism Historicized: Essays in British Social Anthropology*, History of Anthropology Vol. 2, Madison: University of Wisconsin Press.

Summers, Sue, 1988 'The Lost Loves of Iris Murdoch', *Mail on Sunday*, *You*, 5 June, pp. 16-22.

Thornton, Robert with Skalník, Peter, 1993 'Introduction: Malinowski's Reading, Writing, in 1904-1914', in Thornton, Robert and Skalník, Peter (eds) *The Early Writings of Bronislaw Malinowski*, trans. Ludwig Kryżanowski, Cambridge: Cambridge University Press.

Tönnies, Ferdinand, 1963 *Community and Society*, trans. Charles P. Loomis, New York: Harper and Row.

Troeltsch, Ernst (1912) 1931, *The Social Teaching of the Christian Churches*, trans. Olive Wyon, 2 vols, New York: Macmillan.

Tully, Carol, 1997 *Creating a National Identity. A Comparative Study of German and Spanish Romanticism with Particular Reference to the Märchen of Ludwig Tieck, the Brothers Grimm, and Clemens Brentano, and the costumbrismo of Blanco White, Estébanez Calderón, and López Soler*, Stuttgarter Arbeiten zur Germanistik 347, Stuttgart: Heinz.

Unger, Erich, 1930 *Wirklichkeit. Mythos. Erkenntnis*. Munich and Berlin: Verlag R. Oldenbourg.

————, (1928) 1992 'Mythos und Wirklichkeit' in *Vom Expressionismus zum Mythos des Hebräertums. Schriften 1909 bis 1931* (ed.) Manfred Voigts, Würzburg: Königshausen und Neumann, pp. 88-92.

Voigts, Manfred, 1989 'Nachwort', in Unger, Erich 1989 *Politik und Metaphysik* (ed.) Manfred Voigts, Würzburg: Königshausen und Neumann.

Wagenbach, Klaus, 1958 *Franz Kafka. Eine Biographie*, Frankfurt am Main: Fischer.

Wasserstein, Bernard, 1994 'Their own Fault. Attempts to shift the blame for the Holocaust', *The Times Literary Supplement*, 7 January 1994: 4-5.

Weber, Max, 1919 'Wissenschaft als Beruf', in 1951, *Gesammelte Aufsätze zur Wissenschaftslehre*, Tübingen: J.C.B. Mohr.

Whitman, James, 1984 'From Philology to Anthropology in mid-nineteenth Century Germany', in George W. Stocking Jnr (ed.) *Functionalism Historicized: Essays in British Social Anthropology*, History of Anthropology Vol. 2, Madison: University of Wisconsin Press, pp. 214-29.

Wiemann, Dirk, 1998 *Exilliteratur in Großbritannien 1933-1945*, Wiesbaden: Westdeutscher Verlag.

Wiener, Oskar, 1919 (ed.), *Deutsche Dichter aus Prag. Ein Sammelbuch*, Wien and Leipzig: Strache.

Winter, J.C., 1979 *Bruno Gutmann 1876-1966: A German Approach to Social Anthropology*, Oxford: Clarendon Press.

Wittgenstein, Ludwig, 1960 *Schriften. Tractatus logico-philosophilus, Tagebücher 1914-1916, Philosophische Untersuchungen*, Frankfurt am Main: Suhrkamp.

————, 1967 'Bemerkungen über Frazers *The Golden Bough*', *Synthese* 17: 233-53.

————, (1958) 1969 *Preliminary Studies for the 'Philosophical Investigations'. Generally known as The Blue and the Brown Books*, Oxford: Blackwell.

Wolff, Kurt, 1950 (ed.) *The Sociology of Georg Simmel*, London and New York: Macmillan.

Wright, David, 1990 *Elegies*, Emscote Lawn, Warwick: Greville Press.

Yates, Frances A., 1982 *Lull and Bruno. Collected Essays*, Vol. I, London, Boston and Henley: Routledge and Kegan Paul.

NAME INDEX TO VOLUME I

SUBJECT INDEX TO VOLUME I

Note: Franz Baermann Steiner is referred to throughout the index as F.B.S.